Asian American Matters
A New York Anthology

Russell C. Leong | Editor

Asian American and Asian Research Institute
The City University of New York

Asian American Matters

A New York Anthology

THE CITY UNIVERSITY OF NEW YORK

www.aaari.info/cunyforum

Facebook: cunyforum   Twitter: cunyforum

Asian American Matters: A New York Anthology is a commemorative compilation of new, revised, and selected work from CUNY FORUM, a journal established in 2013 by Russell C. Leong for the Asian American and Asian Research Institute, of The City University of New York.

CUNY FORUM is an annual print and on-line commons for scholars, writers, practitioners and activists to promote Asian American/Asian topics within the context of both the Americas and Asia. Access to selected FORUM materials, AAARI videos, books, educational materials, and conferences can be found online.

◆

The Asian American and Asian Research Institute (AAARI), of The City University of New York (CUNY), is a university-wide organization that works across the twenty-four CUNY colleges to facilitate, foster, educate, and conduct original research and programming on issues that concern Asian America and Asia. AAARI seeks to support international and domestic faculty, scholars, students, community, and leaders by providing them with various platforms such as the CUNY FORUM, lecture series, conferences, seminars, film festivals and other activities for the dissemination of information on Asian American and Asian trends, research, history, current events, culture, and arts across many disciplines.

Asian American and Asian Research Institute
The City University of New York
25 West 43rd St., Suite 1000, New York, NY 10036

Phone: 212-869-0182 / 0187   E-mail: info@aaari.info
Fax: 212-869-0181   URL: www.aaari.info

Facebook: aaaricuny
Twitter: aaaricuny
YouTube: aaaricuny
iTunes: aaari

ISBN-13: 978-0-962-94978-8

For Peter Kwong (1941-2017)
Hunter College, The City University of New York

*"When I was a kid I read too many martial arts novels
—it's always about fighting against injustice, fighting against
government, fighting against the rich, the nasty merchants, and
against the greedy landlords. It's always about standing up
for the little guy. This is what kung fu movies are all about."*

EDITOR
RUSSELL C. LEONG

PUBLISHER
JOYCE O. MOY   *Executive Director, Asian American and Asian Research Institute - CUNY*

ASSISTANT PUBLISHER
ANTONY WONG   *Program Coordinator, Asian American and Asian Research Institute - CUNY*

STAFF
Journal Design:	**WILLIAM TAM & ANTONY WONG**
Information Technology:	**ZHU-HUI WU**
Editorial Intern:	**TIANA CHENG-WILSON**
Proofreader:	**J. MAYOR**

ACKNOWLEDGMENTS

The editor is indebted to his mentors and colleagues in Asian American Studies who inspired and often provided advice for this book, and for earlier issues of *CUNY FORUM*. These include: Bayoumi Moustafa, K.W. Lee, Franklin Ng, Meena Alexander, Shirley Hune, Peter Kiang, Phil Tajitsu Nash, Glenn Omatsu, Tomie Arai, Vinit Parmar, Vijay Prashad, Prema Kurien, Tarry Hum, Vinay Lal, Mary Uyematsu Kao, Robert Lee, Jack Tchen, Luis H. Francia, John J. Chin, Ming Xia, Kenneth J. Guest, Vivian Louie, Betty Lee Sung, Kyoo Lee, Jennifer Hayashida, and Peter Kwong. The dozens of scholars, writers, activists, and artists who contributed to *Asian American Matters* and to *CUNY FORUM* during the past five years constitute the backbone of this endeavor, and to each of them we are grateful.

Through being the CUNY Thomas Tam Visiting Professor for two years (2011-13) at Hunter College, I had the opportunity to work with Joyce O. Moy, Executive Director of the Asian American and Asian Research Institute (AAARI), of The City University of New York, and her staff. I would like to make special mention of the day-to-day editorial help provided by Antony Wong, above and beyond his duties as Assistant Publisher and Program Coordinator for AAARI. Antony, as my de facto associate editor, also helped coordinate efforts of the production and design staff which includes William Tam, Zhu-Hui Wu, our editorial intern Tiana Cheng-Wilson, and office interns Claire Chun and Jia Ying "Jessica" Mei.

Finally, with the impetus of Peter Kwong's untimely passing, we were spurred to finish and expand the book and to dedicate its collective pages to advance activist scholarship for new generations of students, scholars, and activists. Thus, these pages reflect a spectrum of issues from U.S./China relations, to old and new immigrant Asian communities, to cultural activism and LGBT concerns, to matters of faith and institutional justice within and outside of the university.

—Russell C. Leong
Editor

ASIAN AMERICAN MATTERS

3 WRITING ACROSS, AGAINST AND BEYOND BORDERS 99

4 ACTIVISM, ART & MEDIA 143

Collage

Clockwise starting from the left:

Asian American DREAMer rally across from Trump Tower, New York (October, 5, 2017)
Photo by Antony Wong

Mosque in Penang, Malaysia
Photo by Ming Xia

Separation Wall in Bethlehem, Palestine
Photo courtesy of Meena Alexander

Yuri Kochiyama at 125th Street subway station in New York City
Photo courtesy of the Kochiyama Family

"Jai Maa Durga," Acrylic on Canvas, 48" x 60"
By Rahul Mehra

Meeena Alexander with two students on the Al-Quds campus in Palestine
Photo courtesy of Meena Alexander

"Ground Zero Flag," 60' x 30' exact replica of the flag displayed at Ground Zero at the time of 9/11 terrorist attacks. Flag has been on display annually at 116 Mott Street in Manhattan Chinatown since September 2002 in honor of those lost during 9/11.
Photo by Antony Wong

CREATE FORUMS FOR CHANGE

Another America

September 11, 2001 / September 11, 2017

Today, it's another city, they say.
Another New York. Another L.A.
Another America, changed forever.
Newscasters, generals, and presidents say.

Today, it's another city, they say.
Bring Third World terrorists to justice.
Look for someone slightly darker
(than even me),
Maybe a guy not so slant-eyed, taller,
Who speaks Arabic,
Not Chinese or English or Spanish.

Today, it's another city, they say.
He, or she, or they, may be praying or plotting
In a mosque. In a temple. In a church.
In a truck, car, or plane.

Today, it's another city, they say.
Nah. Mexicans don't qualify as the enemy.
They just cross borders, every day, they say.
Not even Chinese, or Russians are enemies.
That's another place, another time.

Today, it's another city, they say.
But what if the enemy lurks within?

Within the alley of the aorta.
Within the barrio of the brain.
Within the gutter below the skin.
Within the bullet of the eye.
Within the twist of the blade
Within your back?

Dead or alive, I'm a different person
Than who I was yesterday.
Look me in the eye, I say.
For it's another America, today.

—Russell C. Leong

Originally published in Asian Americans on
War & Peace (UCLA Asian American Studies
Center, 2002), and revised for this edition.

Sidewalk on the corner of Centre & Hester Streets, Manhattan Chinatown
Photo courtesy of Antony Wong

Why Do Asian American Matters, Matter?

RUSSELL C. LEONG, EDITOR

Asian America breathes, works, loves, fights, and challenges our notions of what is American and what is Asian today. The two words together do not form a hyphenated identity. Instead, they configure a whole entity, call for a new reality, and lead the way to social action. We contend that—Asian American matters—do matter.

From Manila, to New Spain, to New York

WE BEGIN WITH THE WORLD THAT WE KNOW, as we unblind the past and open the future to thinking about Asian Americans in new ways. In the introduction to her illuminating book, *The Making of Asian America* (2015), historian Erika Lee charts the passage of the first Asians brought to the Americas by the Spanish, beginning in the 16th century. "New Spain" encompassed the regions that Spain colonized and from whence it drew workers and slaves, including Mexico and Central America, and what is today the southwestern United States. Within Spain's Pacific orbit was also the Philippines, Guam, and the Mariana Islands. Though Asians constituted a much smaller pool of labor than the earlier transport of enslaved Africans to the New World, the conditions of their servitude were similar.

As Lee states, some "40,000 to 100,000 Asians from China, Japan, the Philippines, and South and Southeast Asia crossed the Pacific from Manila and landed in Acapulco during the 250-year history of the galleon

"Panalangin No. 7" (Prayer No. 7)
2013, 2017 © Copyright by Artist: Jun-Jun Sta. Ana

trade." From this beginning rooted in Spanish colonization and the slave trade, Asians in the Americas during the 19th, 20th, and 21st centuries subsequently encountered various kinds of legal exclusion, racism, and discrimination that limited their choices and opportunities to work, to marry, to settle, and to worship. "Asian Americans," Lee states, "continue to confront both American racism and global inequalities through their transnational lives, activities, and identities that are simultaneously effecting change in the United States and across the Pacific Ocean." Thus, for three centuries, Asians have always "mattered" to the Americas and to Asia, and still matter, in quite different ways, today.[1]

Post-9/11 Thought, Activism & Culture

This transnational optic of history provided by Erika Lee, together with contemporary responses by writers within this volume, provide the fulcrum and reason for publishing *Asian American Matters: A New York Anthology*. This book provides a national forum for over 40 writers, activists, artists, and academics that have chosen, in various ways, to identify themselves as either Asian American, or who visualize, historicize, and interpret the Americas through an Asian lens. Such an optic is multi-dimensional, simultaneously localized and transnational in word, form, and practice.

Asian American Matters is the first edited collection of its kind to emphasize mostly writers and writing from the East Coast who bring forth fresh ideas and practices originating in the past two decades post-September 11, 2001, to what we now call "Asian American Studies" (AAS). Many of the scholars featured in this dialogue are associated with the nation's two largest public university systems, The City University of New York (CUNY), and the University of California. Students within such public universities have historically been at the vanguard of organizing for Asian American Studies, Ethnic Studies, Women's and LGBT Studies at their various campuses, from the late 1960s to the present.

For this anthology, we sought to include here an array of not only post-9/11 themes and topics, but also of genre and form ranging from social science research to poetry, from memoir to cultural manifesto. Because the writers included in this anthology often are transnational subjects themselves, the following locales, in addition to the U.S., are engaged or alluded to in their analyses or creative works: Bangladesh, China, India, Tibet, Pakistan, Jordan, Malaysia, Singapore, Mexico, Egypt, Cuba, Peru, Palestine, Israel, Vietnam, Korea, the Philippines, Japan, and Germany, etc.

Finding Race, Creating Place

Asian American Studies, a movement and a comparative field of study established at universities and schools across the nation, is fast-reaching its half-century of existence. AAS was born in the late 1960s with the birth of Civil Rights, Black Power, and the movement for Ethnic Studies by African-American, Native-American, Chicano, and Asian American students and community activists. Its original participants included scholars, activists, artists, and others who also identified themselves with emerging Third World and national liberation movements in Asia, Africa, and Latin America. With a mission to "serve the people" of our communities within the U.S., Asian American Studies took its theoretical positions and political insights from thinkers across the globe. Frantz Fanon. Lu Xun. Chinua Achebe. Paulo Freire. Angela Davis. Albert Memmi. W.E.B. Dubois. Martin Luther King, Jr. José Rizal. Malcolm X. Mahatma Gandhi. Saul Alinsky. C.L.R. James.

The consequences of U.S. race relations inevitably led to the ideological and cultural construction of "place" among America's peoples of color. As author/filmmaker Karen L. Ishizuka states, "In the late 1960s, pushed by a racist war against people who looked like us and pulled by the promise of a Third World that called for self-determination instead of assimilation, Asians throughout the United States came together to create a home we never had. We called it Asian America."[2] The idea of "Asian America" is more necessary than ever as Asians, once again, have become invisible in the post-Charlottesville dialogue on U.S. black-white race relations. (As artist Tomie Arai's powerful cover image attests, all races and ethnicities do matter—all shades, orientations, and issues of color.)

In the five decades since the Vietnam War, Asian America has grown. To clarify though, Asian America is not a state, a nation, or a territory. Asian Americans have staked no claims for territorial or national sovereignty, unlike some Pacific Islander peoples who are struggling for their national sovereignty in Hawai'i and elsewhere in the Pacific. Yet, Asian America may in the broadest geo-demographic sense, encompass a loosely-knit grouping of communities from San Francisco to New Orleans, from Minneapolis to Maine, that range from earlier 19th and 20th century Chinese, Japanese, Korean, and Filipinos first brought to Hawai'i, to later communities that encompass Vietnamese, Cambodian, Indian, Pakistani, Burmese, Indonesian, Bangladeshi, Hmong, Laotians, etc. and now which may also include newer groups from the Middle East. Today, Asian Americans roughly number 20.4 million, or 6.4% of the U.S. population. In New York City alone, Asian Americans—including Chinese, Indian, Pakistani, Bangladeshi, Nepali, Filipino, and Korean—represent 1.3 million, or 15.3% of the city's population, and can be found clustered in Manhattan's Chinatown, Western and Eastern Queens, and Brooklyn.[3]

Five Dimensions of Asian American Studies	
Recognition of AA communities	as part of the broader societal, political, philosophical and cultural matrix of the U.S. during the 250+ years of continuous migration of Asians to the Americas.
Academic field of intellectual and activist inquiry	which, nearing its 50th year, has developed into what we know as Asian American Studies, within the comparative context of Pacific Islander Studies, Ethnic Studies, and Latin American, Asian, African, Islamic, and Diasporic Studies.
Continuous intellectual, technological, economic, philosophical, and literary interface	among the Americas, the Pacific, and Asia, which produces new thinking and practices.
Environmental and ecological community	concerns in Asian American communities, including but not limited to industrial pollution in ethnic or indigenous communities, urban gentrification and displacement, and how global Asian capital affects the local quality of life.
Liberatory education	that challenges the status quo and calls for the inclusion of diverse faiths, genders, races, ethnicities, and classes in both curriculum and research.

Beyond demographics or geography, Asian America, and by extension Asian American Studies, is a political term with five intersecting dimensions. Each of the articles in this anthology addresses one or more of these five dimensions.

A Critique of America's National and Transnational Identity

The prior experience and current expression of Asians in the Americas (as reflected in this anthology) provide a counterpoint to, and a missing critique of, the parochial, legal, and cultural interpretations of the relation of Asians, and Asia, to the Americas. Without such a corrective, critical arenas including American education and curriculum, federal and state immigration policies, and mass media portrayals will remain entrenched in racial myths and embroiled in narrow misconceptions that limit the humanity, the cultures, and the transnational work of Asian Americans.

During the 20th and first decades of the 21st century, for example, U.S. imperialist wars, including the dropping of nuclear weapons, were waged against the peoples of Japan, Korea, Vietnam, Cambodia, Laos, Iran, Iraq, Afghanistan, Yemen and Syria, resulting in death, devastated societies, displaced individuals, and the migration of war and economic refugees to the U.S.

Yet, some believe the September 11, 2001 terrorist attacks were a form of "blowback" for American-waged wars against the Middle East. As activist scholar Vijay Prashad puts it: "Some say that the U.S. has only now lost its "virginity," that it remained unsullied from the Old World dilemmas in the New

World Dreams... 9/11, an event against the Geneva Convention, brought the war stateside, a war that has been ongoing for some time, at least for five decades."[4] Within my own poem, "Another America," written the day-after the 9/11 attacks, I ask of myself, "But what if the enemy lurks within?" This and other hard questions we must face as Asian Americans who pay our taxes to support the U.S. military-industrial complex, and the continuing global "War on Terror."

In our current post-9/11 world, issues of immigration, incarceration, and human rights and justice can be better understood in comparative terms across political, racial, ethnic, economic and cultural divides. Here in the U.S., the "War on Terror" has led to the surveillance and terrorization of its own immigrants, refugees, residents and aliens alike. Muslims and South Asians, in particular, have become the targets, and being undocumented has become criminalized.

Yet, after 9/11, Asian Americans were actually one of the first groups to initiate a dialogue with Muslim Americans. Japanese and Muslim Americans especially felt a shared history in relation to the way the law has been used to demonize and incarcerate members of their communities. This includes cases from World War II, such as *Korematsu* v. *United States*, which challenged the government's internment of Japanese Americans. In law classes throughout the nation, *Korematsu* is examined as a central case of constitutional law. It is one example that demonstrates how utilizing an Asian American lens can call attention to, and redress, the discriminatory and unconstitutional patterns of law perpetuated against East Asians then, and today, against Muslims, Arabs, and South Asians across the U.S.

Since 9/11, Arabs, Middle Easterners, and South Asians have often found themselves the victims of racial violence. And the violence persists. Just recently on June 18, 2017, a seventeen-year-old Muslim girl, Nabra Hassanen, was abducted and killed after attending Ramadan prayers at a mosque in Fairfax, Virginia. A few months prior, on February 22, 2017, a white American man shot two South Asian men, who he had mistaken for Iranians, at a restaurant in Olathe, Kansas. Srinivas Kuchibhotla was killed, while Alok Madasani was injured and survived. Even as of this writing, there are calls by some for "Muslim internment camps," creating the necessity for Asian American groups to unite and to resist this recurring abomination.

Asian America and Asian Americans were born out of the strife and instability of migration, labor, and war. At the same time, individual Asian American activist/scholars including Yuri Kochiyama, Grace Lee Boggs, K.W. Lee, Urvashi Vaid, James Yamazaki, Helen Zia, and Peter Kwong, have fought for, and written about, human rights in various arenas, be it against the exclusion laws of the 19th and 20th centuries, the internment of Japanese Americans during World War II, the global proliferation of nuclear power, or the Vietnam War.[5]

Many Asian Americans have also supported the Civil Rights and Black Power movements, freedom of the press, issues around gender equality for LGBT peoples, labor rights for Asian and Latino service workers, Muslim Americans, and most recently, in support of the Black Lives Matter movement. Yet, beyond the well-known individuals cited above, there are thousands of "unsung heroes" and "untold stories" of ordinary Asian Americans organizing, writing, and fighting against injustice at home, in neighborhoods, at the workplace, in schools, and in government and the military.[6]

Can Asian American Studies Spur a Revolution of Values?

Fifty years ago, on April 4, 1967, Rev. Martin Luther King, Jr. delivered his "Beyond Vietnam" speech at Harlem's Riverside Church, questioning the U.S. involvement in Vietnam, and the consequences of U.S. military actions in Asia.

According to Rev. King, "A true revolution of values will soon look uneasily on the glaring contrast of poverty and wealth. With righteous indignation, it will look across the seas and see individual capitalists of the West investing huge sums of money in Asia, Africa, and South America, only to take the profits out with no concern for the social betterment of the countries and say, 'This is not just.'"

Rev. King's words were not only prescient, but even more accurate today, at this moment in time when the U.S. government, rather than alleviating the "contrast of poverty and wealth" (and I add here too, the climate and environment), instead promulgates the building of billion-dollar border walls (and instituting travel bans) to keep out immigrants and refugees, withdraws from the global Paris Climate Accord, and maintains the militarized neo-colonial status of its Pacific territories, including Guam, American Samoa, and the Northern Mariana Islands. These are simply not satisfactory answers to Rev. King's challenge if we are at all serious about creating more just, humane and environmentally sustainable societies across nations, East and West, North and South.

Institutionally and internationally, I believe that we must use Asian American Studies to help build a new revolution of values. We can help build a change in values through a number of concrete platforms, in coalition with students, faculty, and others involved in: Ethnic, Women's, Gender and LGBT Studies; Comparative Global and Diasporic Studies; Arab, Islamic, and South Asian Studies; Pacific Islander and Indigenous Studies; Asian, Latin American and Africana Studies; and, Religious Studies, Comparative Literature, and American Studies.

Such collaborative institutional, programmatic, and academic platforms may include, but are not limited to:

- *Creating intellectual and activist forums* which challenge and critique current research
- *Utilizing technology* to democratize and disseminate education
- *Providing mentorship and leadership* at the school, community, national, and transnational level
- *Envisioning and supporting art, culture, literature, and gender diversity* as tools for change
- *Fostering community-based teaching, innovative curricula, and institutions* which lead to liberatory education.

Each of the contributors to this volume speaks to the intersection of new thinking, community-based research, and social activism. See the separate chapter introductions which highlight each author's essay.

I. Taking on a Post-9/11 World with Asian American Studies

II. Fifty Years of Pasts & Futures

III. Writing Across, Against and Beyond Borders

IV. Activism, Art & Media

V. Community Research and Online Methodologies

VI. Passages: Peter Kwong

*   *   *

Eyeing the future, *Asian American Matters: A New York Anthology* helps to extend the meaning of "what matters" in today's Asian America, for all Americans.

Author

Russell C. Leong, educated in the U.S. and Taiwan in film and comparative literature, is a consulting senior editor for International Projects at UCLA and the founding editor of CUNY FORUM, for The City University of New York's Asian American and Asian Research Institute.

GRAPHIC TOOLKIT

With a graphic eye to the future of Asian America, scholars and writers, activists and artists alike must dare to create new platforms for translating and transmitting the lessons of 50 years of Asian American Studies—its activism, art, and scholarship—to the broader public. This includes materials that can be read and enjoyed at the K-12 level, and which can be easily translated into multiple Asian languages that reach new and older immigrant communities. *Asian American Matters* proposes the following "graphic toolkit":

Children of the Atomic Bomb: A UCLA Physician's Eyewitness Report and Call to Save the World's Children, is a research website project developed by Dr. James N. Yamazaki, UCLA professor emeritus of pediatrics, together with the UCLA Asian American Studies Center.

URL: www.aasc.ucla.edu/cab/

1. History Retold as Graphic Story

Utilizing the graphic comic and graphic novel as a way to retell and reconfigure traditional scholarly materials including: archival historical studies of individuals, institutions, communities, and movements.

Sample topics might include, but are not limited to:

- 250-year migration of Asians to the Americas
- Contemporary Asians in Cuba, Peru, Jamaica, Trinidad, Mexico, Brazil, and Guyana
- 20th century Asian LGBT Movement
- Asian Women's Movement from the 1960s onward
- Asian faith and religious communities
- Stories of individuals including Grace Lee Boggs, Yuri Kochiyama, James Yamazaki, et al.

This method requires pairing artists, writers and scholars to create a coherent and colorful narrative based on scholarly materials.

The Best We Could Do: An Illustrated Memoir, by Thi Bui (Abrams, 2017)

2. Biography and Family as Community History

Working with local historical societies, temples, churches, ethnic papers, and other institutions to teach individuals and families ways to create and chart their own histories of migration and settlement.

Workshops on how to utilize archival, census, and other materials; how to collect, preserve, and utilize family photos, videos, and online sources; and working with local educational institutions to create electronic repositories.

Community institutions can also create their own "community histories" from their own perspectives and teach families (two and single parent, same-sex couples, non-traditional) ways to create and chart their own individual, family and multi-generational histories of migration and settlement.

Untold Civil Rights Stories: Asian Americans Speak Out for Justice, by Asian Americans Advancing Justice & UCLA Asian American Studies Center (book, 2009 & online module, 2017)

3. Developing Liberatory Education

Developing new classroom materials for K-12, based on Asian American themes, ideas, and issues around social justice, gender and immigrant equality, and interethnic coalition-building.

Building websites, timelines, and open-access materials for American teachers to incorporate such materials into "the arts of necessity and cultures of liberatory education" in the classroom. Not only recognized leaders and heroes, but more important, the ordinary unsung women and men of our communities.

Untold Civil Rights Stories was first published as a book, and subsequently developed into open-access curriculum modules for K-12 teachers.

"Martyrs of Humanity," a cartoon by D. R. Fitzpatrick in The St. Louis Post-Dispatch (February 12, 1948)

4. Lal Salaam: A Blog by Vinay Lal

On the occasion of the anniversary of the death of Mohandas K. Gandhi (January 30, 2013)

"There is but no question that Mohandas Gandhi remains, more than six decades after his assassination, the most iconic figure of modern India. He was one of the most widely photographed men of his time; an entire industry of nationalist prints extolled his life; and statues of his abound throughout India and, increasingly, the rest of the world. Gandhi has been a blessing to cartoonists, ever since he signaled his arrival on the political scene in South Africa; and most Indian artists of consequence over the course of the last half-century, from M. F. Husain and Ramkinkar Baij to Ghulam Muhammad Sheikh and Atul Dodiya, have engaged with Gandhi in their work."

–Vinay Lal

See Blog: "Reflections on the Culture of Politics & the Politics of Culture," by Vinay Lal (History, UCLA), utilizing multiple platforms of scholarship and communication-books, webcasts, and teaching-across nations.

URL: https://vinaylal.wordpress.com/

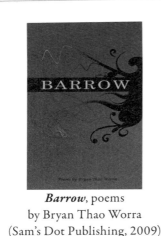

5. On the Other Side of the Eye

"I know how much a difference even a single word, a single sentence can make in a life." –Bryan Thao Worra

See Blog: "Poetry, science fiction, fantasy, community and culture from a Lao American Perspective," by award-winning Laotian writer Bryan Thao Worra.

URL: thaoworra.blogspot.com

Barrow, poems
by Bryan Thao Worra
(Sam's Dot Publishing, 2009)

---

* Kenneth J. Guest's *Cultural Anthropology: A Toolkit for a Global Age* (New York: W. W. Norton & Company, 2013) provided the idea of learning strategies as a "toolkit."

Notes

1 Erika Lee, *The Making of Asian America: A History* (New York: Simon & Schuster, 2015): 1–56.

2 Karen L. Ishizuka, *Serve the People: Making Asian America in the Long Sixties* (New York: Verso Press, 2016); See, also: Steve Louie and Glenn Omatsu, *Asian Americans: The Movement and the Moment* (Los Angeles: UCLA Asian American Studies Center, 2014).

3 Asian American Federation – Note Native Hawaiian and Pacific Islanders (NHPIs) are now reported separately by the U.S. Census Bureau. There is a lot of overlap with Asians because large numbers of Native Hawaiian individuals identify as Asian or other PI as well. In the U.S., NHPI number 1.3 million (0.4% of U.S. population). There are only 15,915 NHPIs in New York City (0.2% of NYC's population).

4 Jerry Kang, "Thinking through Internment 12/7 and 9/11," in Russell C. Leong and Don T. Nakanishi, eds., *Asian Americans on War & Peace* (Los Angeles: UCLA Asian American Studies Center Press, 2002): 55–62; Vijay Prashad, "War Against the Planet," in Russell C. Leong and Don T. Nakanishi, eds., *Asian Americans on War & Peace* (Los Angeles: UCLA Asian American Studies Center Press, 2002): 29–38; Alfred W. McCoy, *In the Shadows of the American Century: The Rise and Decline of US Global Power* (Chicago: Haymarket Books, 2017).

5 The following authors have multiple books, reviews of their work, and some biographies written about them; here, I've cited an example from each author as follows: Yuri Kochiyama, *Passing It On: A Memoir* (Los Angeles: UCLA Asian American Studies Center Press, 2004); Grace Lee Boggs, *Living for Change: An Autobiography* (Minneapolis: University of Minnesota Press, 1998); K.W. Lee (author), Edward T. Chang (translator), *Lonesome Journey: The Korean American Century* (Seoul: Korea University Press, 2016), and selected excerpts in *CUNY FORUM* 2:1 (AAARI-CUNY, 2014); Urvashi Vaid, *Irresistible Revolution: Confronting Race, Class, and the Assumptions of LGBT Politics* (New York: Riverdale/Magnus Books, 2012); James Yamazaki, *Children of the Atomic Bomb: An American Physician's Memoir of Nagasaki, Hiroshima, and the Marshall Islands* (Durham: Duke University Press, 1995) and website, www.aasc.ucla.edu/cab/index.html; Helen Zia, *Asian American Dreams: The Emergence of an American People* (New York: Farrar Strauss Giroux, 2000); Peter Kwong, *Forbidden Workers: Illegal Chinese Immigrants and American Labor* (New York: The New Press, 1998).

6 Stewart Kwoh and Russell C. Leong, co-editors, *Untold Civil Rights Stories: Asian Americans Speak Out for Justice* (Los Angeles: The Asian Pacific American Legal Center and the UCLA Asian American Studies Center, 2009).

1

TAKING ON A POST-9/11 WORLD WITH ASIAN AMERICAN STUDIES

· WE THE PEOPLE ·

"We have been telling and selling the story of 'good groups' and 'bad groups' for over a century."
—Vivian Louie
CUNY FORUM 2:1 (2014)

Thousands of protesters fill the streets of Midtown Manhattan in massive rally on the eve of the presidential inauguration (January 19, 2017)
Photo by Alice Chung

AT THIS VERY MOMENT of writing, the virulent anti-Asian rhetoric, and anti-Muslim violence within the U.S. demands a "call to respond" from those working within and outside of the university. Yet, such American racialization is in fact nothing new, going back centuries as Moustafa Bayoumi points out in his lead essay: "Asian American Studies, the War on Terror, and the Changing University." As a call to respond, we've gathered here scholars and writers to discuss the relationship of Asian American Studies to Muslim, Islamic, or Arab Studies, in light of today's calls for exclusion, and to respond broadly to Bayoumi's essay.

Responders include: Prema Kurien, Rajini Srikanth, Sylvia Chan-Malik, Erik Love, Eric Tang, Mariam Durrani, & Raymond Fong.

For useful reading on South Asian and Muslim American activism, Islamic histories, and contemporary interpretations, see:

- Moustafa Bayoumi, *How Does It Feel to Be a Problem?: Being Young and Arab in America* (New York: Penguin Books, 2008)
- Sunaina Maira, *The 9/11 Generation: Youth, Rights, and Solidarity in the War on Terror* (New York: NYU Press, 2016)
- Deepa Iyer, *We Too Sing America: South Asian, Arab, Muslim, and Sikh Immigrants Shape our Multiracial Future* (New York: The New Press, 2017)
- Christopher de Bellaigue, *The Islamic Enlightenment: The Struggle Between Faith and Reason, 1798 to Modern Times* (New York: W.W. Norton, 2017)
- Vijay Prashad, *Uncle Swami: South Asians in America Today* (New York: The New Press, 2012)
- Mohsin Hamid, *Exit West: A Novel* (New York: Riverhead Books, 2017)

Asian American Studies, the War on Terror, and the Changing University
A Call to Respond

MOUSTAFA BAYOUMI

Moustafa Bayoumi

Who Gets Included—and Who Doesn't?

I BELIEVE IT'S CRUCIAL WE DEBATE what the nature of Asian American Studies itself actually is and reflect on the changing nature not only of Asian American Studies, but also of the university, particularly during the age of the War on Terror. In fact, I would like us to consider those three things—Asian American Studies, the War on Terror, and the changing nature of the university—all together, and in so doing perhaps enlarge the purview of this discussion. I think this could lead us to reconsider the nature of Asian American Studies itself. How should we think of Asian American Studies? At bottom, is Asian American Studies driven by the pursuit of creating a more diverse and accurate vision of our country, or is there another reason why different Asian American subgroups will come together under the umbrella of Asian America? Is the motivation, unity, and force behind the concept of Asian American Studies largely due to the Asian geography of our different national origins, or is Asian American Studies more fundamentally about the organization and structure of power within the United States? To answer this question, we can begin with another, namely "who gets included—and who doesn't get included—within Asian American Studies?"

Muslim Americans and Arab Americans

Let's consider two different, yet overlapping groups, Muslim Americans and Arab Americans, in this question, and examine what their relationship is and should be to Asian American Studies. As somebody who has worked in Asian American Studies and who has also researched Muslim Americans and Arab Americans for a very long time now, I can confidently report to you that since the post-9/11 era the very idea of Muslim American has been, by now, almost naturalized into an ethnicity. But it's not an ethnicity, of course. To be a Muslim is to belong to a faith tradition, but the terms and the ideas behind Muslims today are used very often, if not the vast majority of the time, in an almost racial way. We shouldn't lose sight of how a faith tradition populated by people from many different countries of the world is, in our contemporary United States, talked about in primarily ethnic and racial terms. There is a politics behind this shifting category phenomenon, but let us in Asian American Studies be vigilantly aware that Muslim American is not another ethnicity to add to the pan-ethnic and pan-national origin pot that makes up Asian-American identity.

Before 9/11: Another American Reality

We must also be vigilant in remembering that Muslim Americans are not solely a post-2001 population in the United States. In fact, the history of Islam in this country is completely fascinating, little known, and profound. But if we only talk about Muslim American life after 2001, we run the risk of forgetting or not even knowing about this past. Islam has existed in this country since the colonial era. In fact, large

Transcribed by Antony Wong & Zhu-Hui Wu

numbers of people from Africa who were themselves Muslim in practice and belief were brought as slaves to this country. And so, if we only start to think about Islam as originally connected to parts of Asia, and to a post-9/11 reality, we're doing a disservice to the important idea that there are always multiple ways of being American. Put another way, there's a real danger when we start putting Muslim Americans on Asian American syllabi only through a post-9/11 framing. We have to consider how we talk about Islam and Muslims carefully so as not to assume Muslim Americans are considered another Asian ethnicity, and especially not as a kind of recently arrived Asian ethnicity to boot.

That being said, there is, of course, a large segment of the Muslim-American population with origins from different parts of Asia. In the United States, Muslim Americans hail from at least seventy-seven different countries of origin, according to the Pew Research Center, and many of those are Asian nations.[1] As a world religion, Islam has a rich and complex history, and so it should be no surprise that Muslim Americans reflect a rich and complex history as well. The complexity of the Muslim American experience is something that Asian American Studies has never really grappled well with, I believe. The same can be said about religion in general. Then it gets perhaps even more complicated when considering Arab Americans. Of course, not all Arab Americans are Muslims. In fact, two-thirds of the Arab-population is Christian, and yet still, many Americans confuse Arab Americans for Muslim Americans, and I wonder how equipped our students are, say by the end of an Asian American survey course that includes Arab or Muslim Americans, to intelligently discuss the differences and overlaps between these two groups.

What is Middle Eastern American?

We have been brought together here today to consider how South Asian Americans, Southeast Asian Americans, and Middle Eastern Americans fit within Asian American Studies. And yet, what is a "Middle Eastern American" to begin with? Where is the "Middle East," and to which East is it in the middle of? Of course, the phrase itself is a completely colonial construction (we don't talk about Far East Americans, rightly choosing to use the term Asian Americans instead). My family roots are from Egypt, which as we all know is in the northeast corner of Africa. Does that make me African American? Many people who are from the Arab region do sometimes refer to themselves as Middle Eastern and, increasingly, as coming from MENA (Middle East North Africa). A sign of how this complexity is being tackled, the federal government has just proposed adding MENA to the U.S. Census, which would be the first change to the racial categories of the Census since 1997.[2]

Has Asian American Studies thought about the ways that Arab Americans and Muslim Americans fit within the purview of Asian American Studies? If we think about Asian American Studies as being a place where you get recognition of your national-origin roots, as a place where the geography of origins is paramount, then shouldn't Asian American Studies at least include those Arab Americans who hail from West Asia and those Muslim Americans who hail from Asia generally? If we did so, however, we would also end up dividing the MENA region that way. You can see the problem.

The Problem with the Geography of Origins

This conundrum arises, I believe, because it assumes that the fundamental way of organizing Asian American Studies is around the geography of origins. I think that's wrong. Asian American Studies is not about the geography of Asia, really, but about the ways in which people are interpellated and organized and come together within the United States as different types of "Asians." In fact, there's every reason to include Muslim Americans, Arab Americans, and others under the umbrella of Asian American Studies. Such inclusion need not be exclusive, needless to say. We should also be developing Muslim American Studies on its own and connecting it to African American Studies, too, as one example. But what we need to underscore is that Muslim Americans and Arab Americans ought to be part of Asian American Studies, and that the acknowledgment of this inclusion will also illustrate that the prime motivator of Asian American Studies is the politics of the United States and not the accident of maps and borders in Asia.

Let me give you two very brief examples that unfortunately we're all too painfully aware of. Both revolve around the candidacy of Donald Trump for president. As we all know, Trump proposed excluding Muslims from entering the United States "until we find out what the hell is going on," and he promised, at one point at least, to fulfill this pledge within his first one hundred days in office. This ought to sound familiar to us. The United States has in its history excluded large numbers of people from entering the country based on completely racist assumptions. I'm referring of course to the various Chinese and Asian exclusion acts. Furthermore, in recent months we have much discussion over the Syrian refugee crisis. Earlier in the campaign for the Republican nominee for president, we witnessed a hysteria around Syrian refugees entering this country. That panic then led to a mayor in Roanoke, Virginia citing the sordid past of Japanese internment as a positive example of what we should do because of the Syrian refugee crisis, which was erroneously connected to allowing ISIS terrorists into the U.S. "I'm reminded that President Franklin D. Roosevelt felt compelled to sequester Japanese foreign nationals after the bombing of Pearl Harbor," Mayor David Bowers, a Democrat even, wrote in a statement to his constituents, "and it appears that the threat of harm to America from ISIS now is just as real and serious as that from our enemies then."[3]

The Repetition of Racialization

The repetition of this sort of racialization within the U.S. is every reason why Muslim Americans and Arab Americans could be, and I think should be, included under the umbrella of Asian American Studies. This inclusion stems not from some coincidence of geography, but primarily because what's happening today reflects a logic, an internalized racial logic, within the United States that ought to unite us in order for us to work toward changing this unacceptable state of affairs. Furthermore, we have to understand the structural challenges to this situation. Consider, for example, how in the United States today, there is plenty of government funding doled out in the name of so-called National Security Studies. Tens of millions of dollars are going into universities around the country for studying "national security" through a variety of lenses. One of these is the development of Critical Language institutes, which often include studying various Asian languages and cultures (and this includes diaspora communities in the United States, too). Within National Security Studies, we can see how the U.S. government is already establishing an infrastructure to study Muslims and Muslim Americans, and I don't want to be studied solely by the government. The study of Asian Americans, Muslim Americans, and Arab Americans must be critical work that is decoupled from an exclusive National Security lens and which ought to be performed primarily by people who have connections to the grassroots and with also a social justice agenda attached.

Asian American Studies: Origin-based, or Based on a Politics of Transformation?

Ultimately, the question is whether we want Asian American Studies to be a scholarly practice that offers opportunity and recognition for people based on the geography of their national origins, or if we want Asian American Studies to be a critical practice that is driven not primarily by a desire for recognition and inclusion but by a fundamental politics of transformation that seeks to create a more just and equitable society for everyone. What's at stake is not just getting our share of resources at the university's table, but understanding the historical and contemporary legacies of racial formation, their intersectional realities, the ways that domestic racism and international adventurism are connected, and much more. Asian American Studies is perfectly positioned to engage in this kind of work, and this is also the primary reason why we should include Muslim American Studies and Arab American Studies within Asian American Studies today.

Thank you to the Asian American and Asian Research Institute (AAARI) and to Russell Leong for inviting me to come and talk at the CUNY Conference on Resurgent Realities: East Coast Asian American Studies, on May 13, 2016, about this important question concerning the state of Asian American Studies today. I look forward to responses and divergent views from my colleagues in Asian American Studies, Middle Eastern Studies, Arab Studies, American Studies, and Ethnic Studies.

Notes

1   "Muslim Americans: No Signs Of Growth In Alienation Or Support For Extremism," *Pew Research Center* (August 30, 2011), http://www.people-press.org/2011/08/30/section-1-a-demographic-portrait-of-muslim-americans/

2   Gregory Korte, "White House Wants to Add New Racial Category for Middle Eastern People," *USA Today* (October 2, 2016), http://www.usatoday.com/story/news/politics/2016/09/30/white-house-wants-add-new-racial-category-middle-eastern-people/91322064/

3   Natalie DiBlasio, "Mayor: Japanese Internment Camps Justify Rejecting Refugees," *USA Today* (November 19, 2015), http://www.usatoday.com/story/news/2015/11/18/roanoke-mayor-syrian-refugees/76016936/

The Church of St. Francis Xavier, New York (April 2, 2017)
Photo by Russell C. Leong

Who are Asian Americans?

Prema Kurien

Picking up on Moustafa Bayoumi's call urging Asian American Studies scholars to rethink who gets included and who gets excluded within Asian America, and the purpose of Asian American Studies, I could not agree more that these issues need to be examined, particularly in light of recent developments.[1] However, I come at this from a slightly different perspective than Bayoumi does.

Having worked in Asian American Studies (focusing on research on Indian Americans) for a long time, both on the East and West Coasts, I have noticed a tendency within Asian American programs on both coasts, to primarily, and sometimes exclusively, focus on East Asian Americans. I have frequently come across scholars in this field describing Asian Americans as a racial ('yellow') group with cultural commonalities based on Confucianism, whose families have an obsessive focus on their children attending elite colleges to obtain professional degrees. However, this framing masks the racial, cultural, religious, and economic diversity within Asian America, and even within the East Asian American community itself.

East Asians are actually a minority of Asian Americans, comprising less than 40 percent of the Asian American population.[2] Asian Americans (both documented and undocumented) are the fastest growing group in the United States, and are expected to surpass Hispanics as the largest immigrant group in the United States by around the middle of the century. However, the groups that are responsible for the recent growth of the Asian American population are not East Asian, they are South Asian.[3] Consequently, we are faced with this strange dilemma/phenomenon of many Asian American programs across the country excluding a majority of Asian Americans from the definition of Asian America, and from their curriculum!

In this essay, I will focus on how the meaning and content of Asian American Studies changes when South Asian Americans are included in the curriculum. I also encourage readers to please watch the passionate presentation by Kelvin Ng, a Columbia University undergraduate student, during the Asian American and Asian Research Institute's 2016 annual conference, Resurgent Realities: East Coast Asian American Studies, on the importance of including the diversity of South East Asian Americans within Asian American Studies as well.[4]

South Asians actually played a key role in the development of the Asian American category and identity in the United States. Asian exclusionists in California first created the umbrella term "Asiatic" when they wanted to include immigrants from British India (comprising present day India, Pakistan, and Bangladesh) among the groups that they opposed. Chinese immigration to the United States had been greatly curtailed by the Chinese Exclusion Act of 1882. In 1905, the Japanese and Korean Exclusion League formed in San Francisco. In 1907, the League renamed itself the "Asiatic Exclusion League" to include Indians among the groups that it opposed. Indian immigrants from the subcontinent began to be viewed as a bigger threat than other Asian groups. In 1910, a Senate Immigration Commission declared that Indians (then called "Hindus") were "universally regarded as the least desirable race of immigrants thus far admitted to the United States."[5]

Between 1913 and 1914, Congress attempted to come up with a way to exclude Indians from the United States without specifically using race, ethnicity, or national origin, for fear that overt discrimination would cause unrest in British India. By this time, Australia, Canada, and other British colonies had already started excluding Indian immigrants using indirect criteria. In a letter to the Speaker of the House, Secretary of Labor William Wilson asked, "Can we, who are not connected by governmental ties or obligations with the Hindus, afford to do less for our people and country than those who are bound by a common citizenship under the Imperial [British] government?"[6] A series of Congressional hearings on

"Hindu Immigration" were held in 1914, and Denver S. Church, a congressman from California, suggested a bill defining Asia based on geography rather than race.[7]

The Asiatic Barred Zone Act of 1917 (Immigration Act of 1917) developed out of this bill, excluding laborers from a wide area from Turkey and the Arabian Peninsula in the east, to some of the Pacific Islands in the west, from entering the United States. Since there was little migration from other parts of the region except for India (Chinese and Japanese were already excluded under separate laws and agreements), the law mainly targeted British Indians. In other words, South Asians were central to the development of the concept of the "Asiatic Barred Zone" in the United States, a profoundly significant event in Asian American history.

In 1970 however, the U.S. Census reclassified people "having origins in the Indian subcontinent" as white. By this time, the civil rights laws had come into effect and census data was used to measure and track discrimination against groups. A 1975 report by the Ad Hoc Committee on Racial and Ethnic Definitions of the U.S. Federal Interagency Committee on Education, describes how people from the Indian subcontinent presented a problem to the committee as it deliberated on how to classify groups for the 1970 Census. The committee had to decide whether or not Indians were a "discriminated minority." The full summary of their discussion is as follows:

> The question at issue was whether to include them in the minority category "Asian" because they came from Asia and some are victims of discrimination in this country, or to include them in this category [Caucasian/White] because they are Caucasians, though frequently of darker skin than other Caucasians. The final decision favored the latter. While evidence of discrimination against Asian Indians exists, it appears to be concentrated in specific geographical and occupational areas. Such persons can be identified in these areas through the use of a subcategory for their ethnic subgroup.[8]

In other words, it appears that Indians were the earliest Asian group to be considered a successful ethnic group, foreshadowing the later designation of a wider group of Asian Americans as "model minorities." Upon learning of this decision, however, the Association of Indians in America (AIA), formed in 1967, mobilized to make the argument that Indians in the United States did experience discrimination, and should be included under the category of "Asian" as they had been in the 1917 Asiatic Barred Zone Exclusion Act.[9] Through its efforts, AIA helped to introduce a new census category, "Asian Indian," for the 1980 Census, and obtain minority status for Indian Americans as "Asians."

* * *

There are often two common explanations for the exclusion of South Asian Americans within Asian American Studies. The first is that Asian American Studies was formed by the mobilization of Japanese, Chinese, and Filipino activists, and should therefore focus on these three groups. However, it would seem strange to have an academic field that is static and is not informed by changes in the Asian American community today!

Another more common justification is that many students who self-identify as "Asian American," and who take Asian American Studies courses to learn about their histories and communities, tend to be East Asian. However, this is because South and South East Asian Americans have also internalized this common American view that "Asian" means East Asian—one of the shibboleths that Asian American Studies should demolish, rather than reinforce.

An important justification for Asian American Studies (and other types of Ethnic Studies programs) is the need to focus on the histories, and contributions of groups, that have been ignored or marginalized by American society. Surely it is very problematic if Asian American Studies perpetuates the problem by ignoring a majority of groups that comprise Asian America.

In this post-9/11 period, brown-skinned individuals including South Asian Americans from a variety of religious and ethnic backgrounds, Arabs, and Muslims have often been bracketed together, becoming hyper-visible targets of religio-racial profiling and harassment, which has greatly escalated over the past few months. While some Asian American leaders and organizations such as South Asian Americans Leading Together (SAALT) view this as a central issue of concern for Asian American groups to deal with, others do not consider this to be an "Asian" problem, or view it as a distraction from addressing concerns that affect larger groups of Asian Americans. Consequently, the cleavage between South and East Asians has only widened in the recent period.

It is unfortunate that many faculty and students in Asian American Studies do not consider religion to be an issue that should be included in the curriculum, and also do not view Islam as an Asian religion (even though 62.7 percent of the world's Muslims are in Asia, and Muslims comprise 24 percent of the Asian population).[10] The Pew Research Center's 2012 study of Asian American religions indicates that a surprisingly small minority of Asian Americans, only four percent, are of Muslim background.[11] This is probably one of the reasons that Muslim Americans are viewed as being of Arab background, even though most Arab Americans are Christian.

While Arab Americans do comprise the largest single category, they only make up 26 percent of Muslim Americans. The South Asian region is the second largest source of immigrant Muslims in the United States, and South Asian American Muslims comprise 16 percent of Muslim Americans.[12] Consequently, including the experiences of South Asian Americans within the curriculum can provide a window through which larger Muslim American and Muslim Asian issues can be examined.

As defined by the "Asiatic Barred Zone," a large part of the region that we now consider as the "Middle East" was considered as being part of Asia ("West Asia"). Since then though, economic, political, and social political developments in the region, as well as self-recognized solidarities on the part of Americans of Middle Eastern and North African (MENA) descent, have led to the creation of Middle Eastern Studies programs in universities around the country. There has also been a demand for a MENA category, which may be included in the 2020 Census.

Even if Arab Americans are able to obtain recognition as a separate group, Asian Americans should unite with them to protest racial and religious profiling and other issues. As I have previously discussed in *CUNY FORUM, Volume 3:1*, it is important for Asian American Studies to make it possible for Asian Americans to perceive the commonalities they have with other racial and ethnic groups, and forge solidarities, instead of forming an insular silo.[13] Rather than rejecting geography as the basis for group formation, I prefer to embrace it, and recognize that consequently, Asian Americans cannot be defined on the basis of race, religion, language, or culture but have instead been shaped by historical developments driven by labor needs like many other groups in the United States.

Asian Americans are not just yellow—they are also black, brown, white and everything in between. All the major religions of the world are found in Asia, and among Asian Americans. Asian Americans hail from very different linguistic, cultural, and economic backgrounds—meaning that Asian Americans have a stake in the varied social justice mobilizations that have been developing in this country, particularly recently. If Asian American Studies programs can display the full range of groups comprising Asian America, students and faculty in Asian American Studies will realize that they are uniquely positioned to be at the forefront of the "fundamental politics of transformation that seeks to create a more just and equitable society for everyone" that Bayoumi calls for.[14]

Notes

1 Moustafa Bayoumi, "Asian American Studies, the War on Terror, and the Changing University: A Call to Respond" *Asian American Matters: A New York Anthology* (AAARI-CUNY, 2017): 21-24.

2 "American Community Survey (ACS)," *United States Census Bureau* (2015), https://www.census.gov/programs-surveys/acs/news/data-releases/2015/release.html

3 "A Demographic Snapshot of South Asians in the United States," *South Asian Americans Leading Together* (2015), http://saalt.org/wp-content/uploads/2016/01/Demographic-Snapshot-updated_Dec-2015.pdf

4 AAARI-CUNY, "South Asia, South East Asia, the Middle East and More: A Part or Apart of the AA Syllabus?," *CUNY Conference on Resurgent Realities: East Coast Asian American Studies* (May 13, 2016), https://is.gd/E9BY24

5 Joan M. Jensen, *Passage from India: Asian Indian Immigrants in North America* (New Haven: Yale University Press, 1988): 141.

6 *Ibid.*: 154.

7 *Ibid.*: 152.

8 Virginia Y. Trotter and Bernard Michael, *Report of the Ad Hoc Committee on Racial and Ethnic Definitions of the Federal Interagency Committee on Education* (Washington, D.C.: Federal Interagency Committee on Education, 1975).

9 Manoranjan Dutta, "Statement of Manoranjan Dutta, On Behalf of the Association of Indians in America, Inc.,"(1976): 33–37 in *1980 Census: Hearings Before the Subcommittee on Census and Population of the Committee on Post Office and Civil Service, House of Representatives, Ninety-fourth Congress*, Second Session, June 1 and 2, 1976. No. 94-80. Some other Indian organizations at the time did not support this effort and wanted Indians to remain in the "White" category.

10 "World's Muslim Population More Widespread Than You Might Think," *Pew Research Center* (January 31, 2017), http://www.pewresearch.org/fact-tank/2017/01/31/worlds-muslim-population-more-widespread-than-you-might-think/

11 "Asian Americans: A Mosaic of Faiths," *Pew Research Center* (July 19, 2012), http://www.pewforum.org/2012/07/19/asian-americans-a-mosaic-of-faiths-overview/

12 "A Demographic Portrait of Muslim Americans," *Pew Research Center* (August 20, 2011), http://www.people-press.org/2011/08/30/section-1-a-demographic-portrait-of-muslim-americans/

13 Russell C. Leong, "Prema Ann Kurien: An Interview with CUNY FORUM," *CUNY FORUM* 3:1 (2015): 91.

14 Bayoumi, *Asian American Matters*: 23.

Commentary

Seize the Moment: A Time for Asian American Activism
Rajini Srikanth

In two waves of resignations—one before and one after the inauguration of Donald Trump and the pronouncement of his executive orders—sixteen (of the twenty) members of the President's Advisory Commission on Asian Americans and Pacific Islanders stepped down from their positions. Dr. Paul Watanabe (University of Massachusetts Boston), among those who resigned before the inauguration, said that he had heard enough from Trump during the presidential campaign and the post-election transition period for him to decide that it would be "untenable for me to serve as his advisor."[1] Those who resigned post-inauguration, wrote in their letter to President Trump, dated February 15, 2017:

> [W]e object to your portrayal of immigrants, refugees, people of color and people of various faiths as untrustworthy, threatening, and a drain on our nation. The fact is that Native Peoples, immigrants from all parts of the world, and people of color have built this country. Among the commissioners there are immigrants, refugees, and descendants of those who have experienced systematic discrimination. We, and the communities that we represent, have worked diligently to make America great and have fought to keep it free. We have and will always strive to ensure that America, our America, will never go back to the days of exclusion, segregation, and internment.[2]

The commissioners, even though representing Asian American and Pacific Islander (AAPI) communities, underscored their commitment to uphold the principles of justice for all Americans—specifically, "protecting the civil rights of all Americans" and "access to health care and economic and educational opportunities for all."[3] This emphasis on the intersections between AAPI priorities and those of other vulnerable communities is an evocation of the founding principles of the Asian American Movement of the late 1960s—a movement that drew its inspiration from the Civil Rights Movement within the United States and the anti-imperial and decolonization movements in Asia and Africa.

There was a period within Asian American Studies (primarily in the 1980s and early 1990s) when the revolutionary and defiant stance of the early years morphed into a narrow focus on identity and gaining visibility within the United States. These were not urgencies to be denied or trivialized, but for those who saw in the Asian American Movement's early years a commitment to social justice, anti-imperialism, and the capacity to critique the United States' militaristic ventures, this focus on how to gain a foothold in the U.S. body politic was perceived as performing a compliant citizenship. The yearning to belong, to be considered a bona fide member of the U.S. political and social landscape, required one to be the "good" citizen—the high-performing immigrant or descendant of immigrants, the meritorious member of the United States, the non-troublemaker. Asian Americans embraced a commodified multiculturalism, taking pleasure in foregrounding ethnic identity and paying attention to the myriad sub-ethnicities subsumed within the label "Asian American."

Moustafa Bayoumi's challenge to Asian American Studies reminds us not to eclipse key facets of the Asian American Movement's impulses and driving force: anti-racism, anti-imperialism, decolonization, and social justice.[4] Of course, an integral part of the Movement's pioneers' resistance to, and defiance against, oppressive structures was the demand to value the Asian American identity and the contribution of Asian Americans to the United States. These activists were claiming space, claiming voice, and claiming a meaningful role in the U.S. body politic and U.S. sociocultural fabric. Their demands for these inclusions were loud, even while they were compatible with the wider global dimensions of what the Asian American Movement embraced. As to whether the Movement ever intended to limit itself to the narrow confines of East Asian and Filipino/a communities (the primary players in the early years of the Asian American Movement), one cannot say with certainty. However, the academic field that grew out of the Movement did, for a short while, become a narrow quest for identity. People's understanding of what constitutes "Asian America" replicated U.S. colonial and imperial imaginings of "Asia" (from which South Asia and West Asia were excluded).

Bayoumi points out that even if the field is going to establish its boundaries on the basis of connection to a geopolitical mass, then "Asia" includes West Asia, South Asia, East Asia, and Southeast Asia. So, even at a technical geographical level, the "Asia" of Asian America is capacious, vast, and complex. By acknowledging the multi-facetedness of the term "Asian" in Asian American—such that U.S. residents of Afghani, Iranian, Indian Trinidadian, Chinese Panamanian, or Ugandan Asian descent can also be subsumed under it—we recognize the complicated histories that have given rise to Asian communities across the world.

The vastness, the messiness, of Asian America forces us to question all labels that operate within narrow confines. "Asian American" is a category that illuminates the inapplicability of categories and draws attention to the tenuous nature of constructed domains. And while the category "Asian American" is crucial to draw attention to and make visible the rich lives of over 21 million Americans, one cannot become too attached to the box into which one is placed. Yes, for census purposes it is important to be counted so that people of Asian descent can be seen officially to warrant the attention of the government for economic, health care, and educational programs. But, it is also absolutely crucial to be counted in ways that do not render the experiences of Americans of Asian descent trivial.

Bayoumi cautions against looking to September 11, 2001 as the moment at which Asian American Studies jettisoned its preoccupation with identity and became increasingly politicized and outward looking—forging solidarity with targeted communities that became constructed as the enemy. Long before 9/11, Bayoumi in 1994 had already posed the question, "Is there an 'A' for Arab in Asian American Studies?"[5] But the nationalistic atmosphere and aggressive militarism that went into overdrive after 2001—exemplified by "retaliatory" shootings and fatal killings of South Asian men (who in the vigilante imagination served as proxy for the 9/11 hijackers); the setting up of the Guantanamo Bay prison facility housing over 700 Muslim men picked up in Afghanistan; the surveillance of Arab, Muslim, and South

Asian communities; the late night raids of homes, detentions, and deportations of Arab, Muslim, South Asian, and Cambodian Americans—underscored for Asian Americans that much more was at stake than a recognition of one's identity. What was under attack was life itself, and the survival and freedom of Asian American communities. What 9/11 prompted was a re-awakening of the activist stance of Asian American Studies and, more generally, a visible demonstration of solidarity with Arab Americans and Muslim Americans. The National Council of Asian Pacific Americans (which includes thirty-five member organizations) issued vigorous statements against anti-Muslim rhetoric, "bigotry, and xenophobia."[6]

Perhaps the boldest and most defiant stance taken by one segment of Asian Americans—those who belong to the national academic organization, the Association for Asian American Studies (AAAS)—was an April 2013 resolution supporting the academic boycott of Israel. For many Asian Americans, and non-Asian Americans alike, this open articulation of support for Palestinian rights and self-determination, in response to the call by Palestinian civil society for support in their fight against Israeli oppression and occupation, came as a surprise. However, Asian Americans—particularly Filipino Americans, with their intimate knowledge of U.S. imperialism—have long been resistant to unconditional U.S. support of Israel and U.S. complicity in the violation of Palestinian rights. Bayoumi himself has written about the initial opposition in 1947 by the Philippine delegation to the United Nations' Partition Plan, which called for the creation of the state of Israel. Though the Philippine delegation was morally opposed to the Partition Plan, it was pressured by the United States to vote in favor of it, Bayoumi writes.[7] Palestine and West Asia are not foreign to the consciousness of Asian Americans, and so the 2013 vote by AAAS in favor of the academic boycott of Israel could be construed as the field's return to its own revolutionary roots.

The Third World Liberation Front (of which the Asian American Movement was a part) was born in the 1960s as a powerful oppositional, anti-racist, and anti-colonial movement, with dual national and global focus. Today, in 2017, Asian American Studies must return to the defiant energy of that foundational moment, and stand in solidarity with immigrants, refugees, Muslims, people of color, and all vulnerable populations in the United States. Asian American Studies must seize the moment and refuse to be silent when manufactured fears about national security, and false promises of economic rejuvenation, become the justifications for ugly nativism.

Notes

1 Walbert Castillo, "16 Quit Commission for Asian Americans, Pacific Islanders since Trump's Election," *USA Today* (February 20, 2017), http://www.usatoday.com/story/news/politics/2017/02/20/asian-americans-pacific-islanders/98137484/ (accessed March 6, 2017).

2 https://www.scribd.com/document/339498786/Letter-to-President-Trump-from-10-Members-of-the-President-s-Advisory-Commission-on-Asian-Americans-and-Pacific-Islanders (accessed March 6, 2017).

3 *Ibid.*

4 Moustafa Bayoumi, "Asian American Studies, the War on Terror, and the Changing University,: A Call to Respond" *Asian American Matters: A New York Anthology* (AAARI-CUNY, 2017): 21-24.

5 Confirmed by Moustafa Bayoumi in an e-mail correspondence to the author.

6 "PRESS RELEASE: Asian American Leaders Call for Action Against Anti-Muslim Hate, Xenophobia, and Bigotry," *The National Council of Asian Pacific Americans* (December 17, 201), http://www.ncapaonline.org/asian_american_leaders_call_for_action_against_anti_muslim_hate_xenophobia_and_bigotry (accessed March 6, 2017).

7 Moustafa Bayoumi, "Staying Put: Aboriginal Rights, the Question of Palestine, and Asian American Studies," *Amerasia Journal* 29:2 (UCLA Asian American Studies Center, 2003): 221–228.

'Why Do You Study Islam?': Religion, Blackness, and the Limits of Asian American Studies

Sylvia Chan-Malik

In many of my professional encounters, I am asked the question: *Why do you study Islam?* For a long time, I fumbled with the response. I've always understood the query's impetus. How does the asker situate me—a cisgender (East) Asian American woman who does not cover her hair or look "Muslim"—within common-sense paradigms around race, gender, class, and religion? As such, the question feels overly personal, and an answer is, and has always been, hard. The reasons we study what we study are at once intensely intimate and wildly alienating: driven by what we know everything yet nothing about; shaped by what draws, confounds, and terrifies us. Perhaps that is particularly applicable to those of us in Ethnic Studies fields—how we are fueled by desires to track how race makes, delimits, and forecloses humanity, how we are to live in the face of distortion and violence.

Over the years, I've arrived at a standard answer—an "elevator pitch," if you will—that generally succeeds in transitioning the focus away from me and onto the work. It goes something like: *I started* in the *Ph.D. program in Ethnic Studies at UC Berkeley the week before 9/11. I was interested in Black-Asian cultural intersections and political coalitions. I got involved in activism between Japanese Americans and Muslim Americans. I became interested in Islam as a religion. I noticed tensions between Black, South Asian, and Arab American Muslims. I met my future husband, a second-generation African American Muslim. There was little existing scholarship on the intersections of race, gender, and Islam in the United States. So I decided to study them.*

It occurs to me now that my answer leaves out mention of my scholarly and political investments in the field of Asian American Studies (AAS). That would require more engagement from me in that conversation than I'm generally inclined to offer. However, on the occasion of this roundtable to consider Asian American Studies, the War on Terror, and the changing nature of the university for *Asian American Matters*, I am grateful for the opportunity to add this: I study race, gender, religion, and Islam in the U.S. because of, through, and against the capaciousness and limits of Asian American Studies. To rephrase this in terms of how AAS should incorporate and consider the scholarly and political exigencies of the War on Terror, I want to suggest that while the field must certainly enlarge its purview and highlight the critical continuities between historical legacies of Asian immigration, exclusion, and U.S. orientalism and contemporary logics of anti-Muslim racism and terror, it is also imperative that its practitioners acknowledge and articulate the field's limitations, and in particular, as I will discuss in a moment, its abilities—and inabilities—to address religion and Blackness.

Though I am receptive to many of Moustafa Bayoumi's suggestions in his call for this roundtable, namely that Asian American Studies "include Muslim American Studies and Arab American Studies," I want to urge caution about how this sentiment may be advanced as praxis.[1] While I believe AAS is an ideal institutional and ideological locale to take up initial questions of who is "Middle Eastern American" and the racialization of Muslims in the U.S., I am unsure of whether AAS should "include" these issues and topics, as much as position itself as a *juncture*, or even a *transfer point* in their formation, one which fosters exchange between multiple sites, i.e., Ethnic Studies, Religious Studies, American Studies, Islamic Studies, Women's and Gender Studies, etc.

These thoughts arise from how I came to study Islam in the United States and U.S. Muslim women, because of Asian American Studies. Yet I realized I could not continue to do so as an Asian Americanist. (I'd also like to make clear in the remarks that follow herein, I address primarily the formation of Muslim American Studies instead of Arab American Studies, which has its own distinctive histories and genealogies apart from AAS.) As Bayoumi also writes, many of the tensions within AAS for the past three decades have stemmed from whether its practitioners approach the field as "origin-based" or "based on a politics of transformation." Questions as to whether AAS should be delimited to engagements with those perceived as "Asians" (or those from "Asia") within the U.S. racial imaginary, or whether AAS should continue to advance the transformative political aims, which shaped its formation and institutional inception, following the 1968 Third World Liberation Front strike at San Francisco State College. As well as subsequent struggles for the formation of a Third World College and Ethnic Studies at the University of California at Berkeley.

Though I am a strong proponent of scholarship that aspires towards social transformation, I am also realistic about academia's limits in this regard, particularly in light of the corporatization of higher education that has taken place in the last two decades.[2] Indeed, such debates around AAS's political investments initially took shape in the 1990s when I was majoring in Asian American and Ethnic Studies at UC Berkeley, and as we confronted how its institutionalization in the university was shifting the field at the start of the 2000s. There was much hand-wringing at the time regarding the increasing distance between the space of the university and the communities and grassroots struggles from which AAS emerged,[3] as well as in the cleavages between social structure and cultural theory approaches.[4] In many ways, these debates have never quite been resolved.

The attacks of 9/11 crucially impacted Asian American Studies. In the scramble to make sense of what had occurred, Asian American and other Ethnic Studies scholars quickly attempted to address new forms of racialization and state practices impacting U.S. Muslim communities through their expertise in immigration, U.S. orientalism, and histories of American imperialism. Yet many, though not all, of these engagements did so without the same types of strong grassroots engagements with the communities under siege. Thus, they were most effective in producing narratives of power, of how suddenly hypervisible communities of South Asian and Arab American Muslims came to be interpellated through the tropes of the terrorist and the veiled and oppressed woman, and how such logics shaped and undergirded the statecraft and infrastructure of the War on Terror. While AAS scholarship addressed the racialization of Muslims—and more specifically, the racialization of Asian and Arab American Muslims—it generally did not engage the lived experiences of being Muslim in the U.S., nor how people's religious views and practices were shaping and being shaped by post-9/11 logics of terror.[5]

Many of the discussions and treatments of Islam and Muslims also sidestepped or marginalized the critical role of Black Islam and African American Muslims—and thus the centrality of Blackness in American Islam—despite the fact that prior to the 1970s, the vast majority of Muslims in the United States were Black and even now, almost one-third of U.S. Muslim communities are African American.[6] In the case of my own writing and research on U.S. Muslim women's lives and subjectivities across the past century, while Asian American Studies helped form the initial of my work, I would need to immerse myself in histories of Black religion in the U.S., debates around secularism in Philosophy and Religious Studies, discourses of Islamic theology, histories of Islamic feminism in the Middle East and beyond, etc. in order to get a grasp on the story I was trying to tell.

I am well aware such multidisciplinarity is par for the course in any scholarly endeavor. However, I found that as I progressed further along with my research, the less my work seemed to "fit" in the field that had originally led me to it. This was partially due to the fact that in order to tell a history of women and American Islam in the 20th and 21st century U.S., the vast majority of my subjects were African American. Yet it was also due to a lack of research—and interest—on religion and religious subjectivities in the field (and particularly non-Christian religions), and more broadly, work addressing the intersections of race, gender, and religion.[7]

Bayoumi's call clearly warns against approaching Muslim Americans as "not solely a post-9/11 population in the United States" and proposes that we "should also be developing Muslim American Studies on its own and connecting it to African American Studies, too, as one example."[8] So my suggestions here are not to argue against the inclusion of Muslim and Arab American Studies in AAS, but simply meant to articulate the obstacles I have personally encountered over the last fifteen years of studying race, gender, and Islam in American, Asian American and Ethnic Studies fields. Thus, while I am fully supportive of any and all moves to create conversations and produce spaces in AAS in this regards, I admit I am wary about how the field's ideological origins, political legacies, and contemporary formations may foreclose upon substantive engagements with Islam as a *religion* (as opposed to a political or cultural marker), which may restrain examinations into Islam and Muslims through frameworks of race *and* religion in American life.

In addition, as I argue in my forthcoming book *Being Muslim: A Cultural History of Women of Color and American Islam* (NYU Press, forthcoming Spring 2018), "A central component of Islam's presence in the United States is its enduring presence and significance as a Black protest religion and expression of Black Cultural power." While it is incontrovertible that, as Bayoumi writes, "A large segment of the Muslim American population [has] origins from different parts of Asia."[9] It is also true that Black Muslims and histories of African American Islam are consistently elided and/or marginalized in discussions of American Islam or U.S. Muslim communities, not only in scholarship, but the larger public discourse. As such, I would simply urge care and caution in how AAS incorporates Islam and Muslims, as to not replicate these same elisions in the field, and to constantly remind our students and readers that the understandings of the U.S. Muslim experience and Islam's history in America must always exceed AAS.

The classroom is a critical site in which such dialogues can take place. For example, in Fall 2017, I will offer my course on "Islam in/and America" at Rutgers-New Brunswick for the third time. It is a survey course that approaches Islam as a lived religion and a racial-religious cultural presence in the U.S. across the past century. For the first half of the semester I focus primarily on African American Muslim communities and Islam's entanglements with Blackness in the nation's cultural imaginary. We look at the experiences of Black women who converted through the Ahmadiyya Movement in Islam—a South Asia-based Islamic missionary movement—in 1920s Chicago; consider the extensive state surveillance on the Nation of Islam (NOI); read *The Autobiography of Malcolm X*, as well as the poetry and writing of Sister Sonia Sanchez who was a member of the NOI in the 1970s. I then turn to histories of Asian and Arab immigration to the U.S., the formation of new U.S. Muslim subjectivities and communities, and how these intersect and impact existing Black American Islamic institutions and organizations.

I tell my students that these comparative histories are critical in thinking through the roles of race, gender, and religion in contemporary iterations of anti-Muslim racism as well as in understanding intra-racial and intra-ethnic relationships within U.S. Muslim communities today. I assign readings, screen films, and bring in guest speakers from AAS, African American Studies, Islamic Studies, Religious Studies, Ethnic Studies, Women's and Gender Studies, and Middle East Studies. While the course is offered through American Studies at Rutgers University, I would suggest that such a framework would also work well as a course offered through an Asian American Studies department *and* cross-listed with any or all of the other departments I named above. Such "cross-listing," I want to suggest, is critical to the ways Islam and U.S. Muslim communities are engaged in Asian American Studies. To put it another way, instead of asking, "Who gets included—and who doesn't get included—within Asian American Studies?" we should be asking, "How can Asian American Studies and its practitioners facilitate crucial dialogues between communities and disciplines?" Indeed, for me, AAS has operated as a key juncture, a critical site in the study of U.S. Muslims and American Islam.

Notes

1   Moustafa Bayoumi, "Asian American Studies, the War on Terror, and the Changing University: A Call to Respond," *Asian American Matters: A New York Anthology* (AAARI-CUNY, 2017): 21-24.

2   For example, see Nicolaus Mills, "The Corporatization of Higher Education," *Dissent* (2012), https://www.dissentmagazine.org/article/the-corporatization-of-higher-education.

3   Such sentiments are perhaps best articulated in Glenn Omatsu's 1994 essay in which he decries the erasure of "the larger goal of liberation" in AAS, which was rooted in the radical and revolutionary politics of the 1960s. See Glenn Omatsu, "The 'Four Prisons' and the Movements of Liberation: Asian American Activism from the 1960s to the 1990s," in Karin Aguilar-San Juan, ed. *The State of Asian America: Activism and Resistance in the 1990s* (Boston: South End Press, 1994).

4   As Michael Omi and Dana Takagi write in their editor's Introduction to a special 1995 issue of *Amerasia Journal* dedicated to concerns about the role of "postmodernist" theory in AAS, "This rethinking (about theory) has created a curious intellectual divide within the field. On the one hand are historians and social scientists who vigorously defend concepts of 'social structure,' and on the other are literary and cultural studies intellectuals who, heavily influenced by postmodern thought, privilege 'discursive practices'...we would argue that (this divide) profoundly affects the work produced and claims made (in Asian American Studies)." See Michael Omi and Dana Takagi, "Thinking Theory in Asian American Studies," *Amerasia Journal* 21:1-2 (UCLA Asian American Studies Center, 1995).

5   Moustafa Bayoumi's excellent *How Does It Feel to be a Problem?: Being Young and Arab in America* is an excellent exception to this critique, though as the title suggests, it focuses on the experiences of Arab Americans, as opposed to Muslim Americans. See Moustafa Bayoumi, *How Does It Feel to Be a Problem?: Being Young and Arab in America* (New York: Penguin Books, 2008).

6   An exception here is Jamillah Karim's *American Muslim Women: Negotiating Race, Class, and Gender Within the Ummah*, which examines relationships between African American and South Asian American women, and won the Association of Asian American Studies Prize for the Best Book in the Social Sciences in 2010. See Jamillah Karim, *American Muslim Women: Negotiating Race, Class, and Gender within the Ummah* (New York: NYU Press, 2008); *Ibid*.

7   This is not to say there has not been excellent scholarship on Asian American Religion, especially by those scholars involved with Asian Pacific American Religions Research Initiative (APARRI), an organization I have been proud to be affiliated with for many years. I am simply noting that though AAS does boast a significant body of work addressing Asian American Christians, and to a lesser extent, Buddhists and Buddhism in America. Asian Americanists have rarely given religion the same level of attention as scholars in other ethnic studies and race-based fields, i.e., African American, Native American, and Chicano/ Latina Studies.

8   Bayoumi, *Asian American Matters*

9   *Ibid*.

Caught in a Racial Paradox:
Middle Eastern American Identity and Islamophobia

Erik Love

The Middle Eastern American identity has been caught up in a racial paradox, with Islamophobia affecting many communities ascribed with it. Crudely applied collective terms like "Arab," "Muslim" or "Syrian" conflate ethnic, religious, and national origin groups of Middle Eastern Americans—especially in Arab, Muslim, Sikh, and South Asian American communities. Paradoxically, at the same time, the unique structural and institutional forms of American Islamophobia have not been specifically recognized as *racism*. Recognizing racism in this phenomenon is key to understanding Islamophobia in the United States as it plays out in lived experiences and in the construction of policies and practices. Yet, a discourse connecting White supremacist racism to Islamophobia has been absent from almost all mainstream discussions. Unpacking complexities like these will reveal the confounding effects of the racial paradox that renders Middle Eastern racial identity invisible.

Unfortunately, in many scholarly analyses and examinations in today's popular media, Islamophobia is described in ways that ignore the dynamics of U.S. racism. For example, after President Donald Trump introduced new policies to ban travelers and refugees from several Muslim-majority countries, analyses described the discriminatory executive orders as "Muslim bans" that created unconstitutional abridgements of religious freedom. While they indeed did just that, the motivation and sweeping effects of these "Muslim bans" were also quintessentially racist. These and other Islamophobic policies affect Muslims and other faith communities, in large part because of race.

The intention behind these cruel and ham-fisted orders was, as Trump himself proclaimed, "to keep terrorists out."[1] By positioning the policy as a "counter-terrorism" effort, Trump continued in a decades-old, racist tradition of linking terrorism exclusively to Middle Eastern and Muslim identities. And by linking national security with immigration policy, the bans deepen the conception that terrorism comes from a racially discernible "dangerous outsider." Furthermore, the "Muslim bans" draw from and reinforce long-standing racist ideas about White supremacy, American citizenship, and belonging. Similar policies and programs have frequently been cited as examples of xenophobia or anti-immigrant sentiment, but too often they are not properly understood as racism *per se*.[2]

The failure to recognize racism in Islamophobia comes about in part because of confusion surrounding the common, socially constructed racial identity that links together the most affected religious, ethnic, and national communities. For decades, the racial paradox—the racial identity that exists but is not acknowledged—has complicated civil rights and political advocacy. It has also posed a tremendous challenge for scholars attempting to understand the reproduction and development of Islamophobia. The Middle Eastern American category has been contested and unrecognized for decades, even as it has led to considerable stereotyping and discrimination. The racial paradox renders this history largely invisible in most analyses of so-called "post-9/11" Islamophobia.

The troubling symptoms of this racial paradox are relatively easy to spot. Scholars and journalists talk about "Muslims and those mistaken for Muslims" when analyzing a particular hate crime or discriminatory policy. This laborious construction comes about due to a failure to recognize the Middle Eastern American racial identity. "Those mistaken for Muslims" are, in fact, those racialized into a socially constructed identity category. Of course, it goes without saying that there is no way to actually "look like a Muslim." Nevertheless, because of the power of race in the United States, there is a racial identity category that is collectively ascribed to all those who "look Muslim."

The construction of this racial category is as uneven, dynamic, complex, and absurd as it is for all racial categories. The boundaries are unclear, contested, and shifting. In the end, though, there is no doubt that the racial identity exists, and it lies at the center of Islamophobia. It is crucial that those studying Islamophobia see past the paradox that obscures the existence of this racial identity, even if many civil rights advocates and activists use a different framework to understand it.

Consider the ways that advocates, scholars, and the media responded to the brutal murder of Balbir Singh Sodhi, a Sikh American man who was killed on September 15, 2001, by a white American who intended to, in his own words, "shoot some towel-heads" in revenge for the terrorist attacks of 9/11. Sodhi has been rightfully memorialized as the first person murdered in a "post-9/11" hate crime. Sodhi was Sikh, not Muslim. He was an immigrant from the Punjab region of India, not traditionally considered as part of the Middle East. At the time of his death, and for many years after, it was often said that he was "mistaken for Muslim." Even today, that is how this tragic story is retold—as a case of *mistaken identity*. There is scant recognition that Sodhi was murdered because his physical appearance was linked to a socially constructed racial identity which made him a target of racism.[3]

Many scholars and advocates consider the murder of Balbir Singh Sodhi, and the dozens of other recent violent attacks on South Asian and Sikh Americans, not as a manifestation of specifically racist violence, but instead as mere expressions of xenophobia or "mistaken identity." In fact, just as I was completing this essay in February 2017, yet another racist murder took place in Kansas. Srinivas Kuchibhotla was shot and killed, and two others injured, by a white American who allegedly yelled, "Get out of my country."[4] Once again, various media outlets described the murder as a case of "mistaken identity," as though racist motivation cannot be seen as linked to structural discrimination and marginalization.

Clearly this unspeakable crime was racist, and possibly Islamophobic. It was just the latest in a long line of similar crimes, including the 2010 attempted murder of taxi driver Harbhjan Singh, the 2012 massacre at a Sikh temple in Wisconsin, the beating of Professor Prabhjot Singh in 2013, and many more horrifying examples. Too often, descriptions and analyses of these attacks do not understand these incidents as examples of racist violence, carrying an intent to reinforce White supremacist ideology.

Compare the response to these recent attacks with the reaction to the 1982 murder of Vincent Chin, a Chinese American man. The murderers in this case were laid-off white American autoworkers in Michigan, angry about Japanese (not Chinese) incursions into the U.S. auto market. Amid that xenophobic climate, the attackers beat Vincent Chin to death, with one of them allegedly saying, "It's because of you little [expletives] that we're out of work." In the immediate aftermath of the killing, established civil rights organizations did not describe the attack as racially motivated, in part because the Asian American identity was, at the time, caught in a racial paradox. The attack was seen as anti-Japanese. And because Chin was Chinese, it was "simply" a case of "mistaken identity," and not an example of anti-Asian racism *per se*.

After Chin's murderers were convicted on mere manslaughter charges and given light sentences that included no jail time, newly forming Asian American advocacy organizations insisted that the case be re-tried as a murder under federal civil rights statutes. The push for a federal trial, led by journalist Helen Zia and lawyer Liza Chan, were joined by many other advocates, to establish that this was clearly a racially motivated attack. This attack affected not only the Japanese American community, but all Asian American communities. The renewed push for justice in the federal courts galvanized support from across ethnic communities—Chinese, Japanese, Korean, and many more—toward a unifying Asian American cause. Even though the legal case was ultimately not won in court, the Vincent Chin tragedy gained recognition as a racist hate crime. The advocacy effort to rally a race-based coalition in response to the race-based murder of Vincent Chin, sparked a movement that is remembered as a seminal moment in Asian American history.

The racial paradox that has trapped Middle Eastern American identity has made it difficult to organize that same kind of race-based rallying in response to the Islamophobia crisis. There is no readily accepted name for those communities most affected by Islamophobia. The term "Muslim" is used as a racialized catch-all in popular vernacular. It compounds the paradox by denoting a religious identity that includes many millions of people who are not ascribed with the racial identity of Middle Eastern American. Advocates and scholars proffer many different names for the racial identity that encompasses those most vulnerable to Islamophobia. Recently, several acronyms have been proposed, such as AMEMSA (Arab, Middle Eastern, Muslim, and South Asian), MENA (Middle Eastern and North African), and SWANA (Southwest Asian and North African). A renewed effort has been underway for several years to gain a new MENA identity category on the 2020 U.S. Census survey.

These collective terms have been met with pushback from various communities in the larger Middle Eastern American umbrella, some of whom insist that they will not willingly accept any label, except their own particular religious, national, or ethnic identity. In short, there is no consensus on a term to denote the racialized groups affected by Islamophobia. The racial paradox continues to confuse and confound, even as Islamophobia rages on, worse in 2016 and 2017 than perhaps any other time in living memory.

During the 2016 election to replace Barack Obama as President of the United States, leading candidates such as Senator Ted Cruz and Donald Trump engaged in a furious race to the bottom of the Islamophobic gutter. Shortly after Cruz suggested that local police forces form surveillance squads to "patrol and secure Muslim neighborhoods," Trump upstaged him by insisting on a "total and complete shutdown of Muslims entering the United States." These proposals, ostensibly "counter-terrorism" proposals, were profoundly racist. Quite obviously, there is no "terrorist profile," since anyone is capable of committing a terrorist act. Still, Cruz, Trump, and many other politicians believed that they could leverage the stereotype about "Muslim terrorists" and promote Islamophobia in order to win votes.

Meanwhile, officials and the media often unquestioningly categorize violence carried out by non-whites as acts of "terrorism." But politically motivated attacks carried out by whites are usually treated as aberrant or the work of "mentally ill" individuals. Once again, the racial paradox makes it much more difficult to explain how structural Islamophobic racism affects which attackers get labeled as "terrorists," and which attackers are seen as "crazy." In turn, the paradox also obscures the racism that motivates "counter-terrorism" proposals that would discriminate against Muslims.

For scholars, the racial paradox must not distract from the search for the truth. Scholars must see the full picture, and they must recognize the role of racism in Islamophobia. Other issues—gender, homophobia, religious persecution, transphobia, xenophobia, and more—almost always intersect with race in the reproduction of Islamophobia at any given moment. But that does not change the fact that racism is involved. Recognizing the role of racism requires, at a minimum, exploring the construction of the (often ignored) racial category that is collectively ascribed to Arab, Muslim, Sikh, and South Asian Americans, among other communities.

The search for the truth is of utmost importance here. After all, it is race and racism that provides much of the (usually invisible) foundation of support for American policies like torture, targeted assassinations, mass surveillance, mass deportation, and harsh immigration restrictions. How these programs and policies draw from and contribute to specifically racist stereotypes must be an area of active and ongoing research by scholars in various disciplines across the academy.

Fortunately, Moustafa Bayoumi's provocative and compelling essay does much to light a path for scholars to navigate the racial paradox surrounding Islamophobia. As Bayoumi suggests, Asian American Studies may be the most effective place for "understanding the historical and contemporary legacies of racial formation, their intersectional realities, the ways that domestic racism and international adventurism are connected, and much more."[5] It is undoubtedly true that at many institutions in North America, the disciplinary home for Asian American Studies provides the best environment for such investigations. However, because institutions vary, there will be settings in which Asian American Studies is not the best place for such scholarship. Places such as African American Studies, Ethnic Studies, Islamic Studies, Middle Eastern Studies, or Religious Studies, may be suitable alternatives.

Across and between universities and colleges, Asian American Studies institutions can and should provide some connective tissue for bringing diverse perspectives together, in cooperation with other academic institutions. There is no room for "turf wars" or other foolishness in this work—all scholars must urgently come together regardless of discipline to understand Islamophobia as thoroughly as possible. Regardless of institutional logics and power, the truth of the racist nature of Islamophobia, albeit constantly obscured by the Middle Eastern American racial paradox, must be elucidated further. This critical project—once thought to be confined to a temporary "post-9/11" era—has sadly become a permanent fixture in American politics and culture. The work to understand it must expand, and that work must reach beyond the racial paradox.

Notes

1   Sabrina Siddiqui, "Trump Signs 'Extreme Vetting' Executive Order for People Entering the US," *The Guardian* (January 27, 2017), http://theguardian.com/us-news/2017/jan/27/donald-trump-muslim-refugee-ban-executive-action/ (accessed March 7, 2017).

2   Nasar Meer, "Racialization and Religion: Race, Culture and Difference in the Study of Antisemitism and Islamophobia," *Ethnic and Racial Studies*, 36:3 (2013): 385–398; Selod, Saher and David G. Embrick, "Racialization and Muslims: Situating the Muslim Experience in Race Scholarship," *Sociology Compass* 7:8 (2013): 644–655.

3   Harriet Agerholm, "Brother of Man Murdered for Wearing Turban After 9/11 Speaks to Killer," *Independent* (2016), http://www.independent.co.uk/news/world/americas/brother-911-murder-forgives-killer-hate-crime-turban-balbir-singh-rana-sohdi-a7341896.html (accessed March 7, 2017).

4   Jim Walsh, "Killer of Sikh after 9-11 Called Ill," *Tucson Citizen* (September 3, 2003), http://tucsoncitizen.com/morgue2/2003/09/03/149112-killer-of-sikh-after-9-11-called-ill/; Jim Suhr, "Witnesses: Bar Gunman Shouted 'Get Out of My Country,'" *Kansas City Star* (February 24, 2017), http://www.kansascity.com/news/business/national-international/article134693629.html (accessed March 7, 2017).

5   Moustafa Bayoumi, "Asian American Studies, the War on Terror, and the Changing University: A Call to Respond," *Asian American Matters: A New York Anthology* (AAARI-CUNY, 2017): 21-24.

Why Asian Americans Need a New Politics of Dissent

Eric Tang

"Ultimately, the question is whether we want Asian American studies to be a scholarly practice that offers opportunity and recognition for people based on the geography of their national origins, or if we want Asian American studies to be a critical practice that is driven not primarily by a desire for recognition and inclusion but by a fundamental politics of transformation that seeks to create a more just and equitable society for everyone."

—Moustafa Bayoumi

Moustafa Bayoumi's incisive take on the future of Asian American Studies (and to this I would add, the future of Asian American politics, in general) is an urgent call for those of us in the field to rethink our long relationship with liberalism, with the regime of rights, recognition, and inclusivity—a relationship that has only led to diminishing returns since at least the mid-1980s when the field began to professionalize.[1] Bayoumi cautions against our temptation to call for the common racialization of Asian Americans based on geography or national origin, but to instead focus on what he terms a "repetition of certain racializations." President Donald Trump's exclusion of Muslims from entering the United States echoes Chinese exclusion of the nineteenth century. Present hysteria over the resettlement of Syrian refugees into the country calls to mind the hysteria that led to Japanese American internment during WWII.

Bayoumi's proposal that Asian American Studies coalesce at the specific *site* of struggle begs the question: What is it about the political conditions at these sites which allow for such repetition? I suggest that it is the absolute exercise of sovereign power—the kind of power that, with a stroke of a pen, can determine which displaced and stateless subjects are worth saving and which are disposable. It is the kind of power that renders the negotiation of liberal rights irrelevant.

Since the presidential inauguration on January 20, 2017, we have been starkly reminded that such power is real and effective. The "Muslim Ban" that Bayoumi invoked in May 2016, prior to Trump's election as president, became reality during his first week in office, executed through an executive order. However, many seem to forget that the other half of this order also involved the temporary halting of the U.S. refugee resettlement program, as well as a provision that would cut the total number of refugees entering the country during the 2017 fiscal year in half. Individual state legislatures would also have the unprecedented ability to "veto" the placement of refugees in those states. These anti-refugee provisions went largely unchallenged in the courts. A week or so later, Trump would sign a memoranda calling for the roundup, detention, and deportation of all undocumented immigrants, regardless of their supposed criminal records.

Trump's executive actions have left no room for political negotiation over rights, recognition, or inclusion, effectively targeting those who, according to Dr. A. Namoi Paik (University of Illinois at Urbana-Champaign), are rendered "rightless." These rightless who are marked as potential terrorists, will have their civil liberties stripped in any given state of emergency (to be sure, it will take only one domestic act of terrorism for the Trump administration to implement its most extreme anti-Muslim measures—many of which have likely already been drafted). The rightless are undocumented immigrants, whose very presence in the United States is criminalized, making them vulnerable to warrantless roundups, detentions, and deportations.

Upon my reading of Bayoumi's essay, he seems to ask, "Why have these issues failed to articulate as distinctly 'Asian American' concerns?" The answer itself lies within Asian America's political and intellectual fidelity to racial liberalism: The emancipation of the subject who has been racialized and gendered as perpetually foreign through full equality under the law (equal protection; equal access; political representation).

Through my own work with refugee communities, this fidelity took the form of organizing campaigns that sought "fair and equal" treatment from regimes that were constituted by racial and gendered violence—specifically, the punitive welfare state. For the past forty years, the welfare state has become increasingly contemptuous of welfare recipients. Its function is not to aid the poor, but to discipline and punish them. The contemporary welfare state cuts funding to families arbitrarily, and throws them into crisis with impunity. It also compels them to work in no-wage "workfare" programs in exchange for their monthly checks.

need something new → the refugee has known this for a long time ∠ REFUSAL

The refugees I knew were rightly skeptical of those who claimed that meaningful rights could be demanded from a state that held them in such contempt to begin with. Moreover, in giving the appearance that meaningful negotiation with the welfare state was possible, are we not instead bolstering the oppressive power we sought to challenge? The refugees then, in their own ways, seem to question how meaningful political practice could possibly emerge from political sites in which negotiation over rights is the political limit.

Asian American Studies—indeed, Asian panethnicity writ large—must find a political center of gravity other than the push for abstract rights proscribed by liberalism. I am reminded here of something Chhaya Chhoum, a community organizer from the Cambodian neighborhoods of the Bronx, once said to me. I had asked Chhaya how she understood her community organizing and advocacy with refugees in relation to broader Asian American political concerns. How did she understand the refugees' struggle with intractable poverty, a punitive welfare state, derelict housing, and chronic war-related traumas within the framework of Asian American panethnicity?

Her response: "Look, I love my Asian American people. I get what they're trying to do. But I just can't hold that right now."

Chhaya's straightforward reply, "I just can't hold that right now," is one of profound theoretical and strategic importance, one that speaks to the possibilities and limitations of Asian American activism and Asian American Studies in these times. Her words certainly point to her need to prioritize the particular over the general, the concrete over the abstract, the local over the global. And yet there remains deep regard for panethnicity. Chhaya does not repudiate that which she cannot hold. There is still "love" for what her peers are "trying to do," but for the moment she needs them to do it without her. Asian American panethnicity needs to take care of itself for now.

One might infer from Chhaya's response that she is too busy putting out fires; the exigencies of working in some of the most troubled neighborhoods has left her with little time for coalition work. But upon further discussion, it becomes clear that the matter is not one of priorities, but of epistemology. Chhaya has turned her full attention to understanding how the refugee understands the world in which she subsists; more precisely, how the refugee understands the sovereign power to which she is subjected. It is an arbitrary power that determined which stateless persons were worth saving and which were disposable. It is the same power that now proclaims that Cambodians born in Thai refugee camps, and raised in the cities of North America, are deportable "back" to a Cambodia they have never known.

for AAA

The refugee knows all too well that this power cannot be challenged by hewing closely to racial liberalism, the regime of rights. So too, those targeted as potential "terrorists," and the criminally "undocumented," know that their political challenges must go beyond the juridical appeal to civil rights. A different kind of politics is in order—one that exposes and creatively disrupts the working of arbitrary power. It is a politics of dissent that broadens what political scientist Frances Fox Piven, and sociologist Richard Cloward describe as the interval of "social dislocation," in which those in power feel vulnerable because they fear insurrections on the horizon. It is this politics which forges alliances and coalitions, and which have always been the basis of the Asian American racial identity.

AAARI Lecture Video (March 16, 2017): www.aaari.info/17-03-16Tang.htm

Note

1   Moustafa Bayoumi, "Asian American Studies, the War on Terror, and the Changing University: A Call to Respond," *Asian American Matters: A New York Anthology* (AAARI-CUNY, 2017): 21-24.

Commentary

Coalition-Building in the Inter-Disciplines and Beyond
Mariam Durrani

> "There is no such thing as a single-issue struggle,
> because we do not live single-issue lives."
>
> —Audre Lorde, "Learning from the 60s"
> *Sister Outsider: Essays & Speeches*

The question of what to include under the banner of Asian American Studies has been raised prior to Moustafa Bayoumi's 2017 essay, "Asian American Studies, the War on Terror, and the Changing University: A Call to Respond."[1] In 2006, Sunaina Maira and Magid Shihade posed similar questions about the points of intersection between Asian American Studies and Arab American Studies. They make the case that the "linking of Arab American and Asian American Studies is the necessary thing to do intellectually, politically, and morally, as a continuation of a tradition in Asian American studies of resisting empire and oppression, here and abroad," in order to build towards the ultimate agenda of developing "a fuller analysis of U.S. empire."[2] Bayoumi echoes certain similar aspects of this argument by drawing attention to the inadequacy of analyses which begin with geographic origins in an era of globalization, and the shared experience of being racialized as an immigrant "Other" in the context of U.S. imperialism.

This essay, as a response to Bayoumi, but even more so to Maira and Shihade's prescient analyses, considers the flawed results of institutional policies that create what Roderick Ferguson describes as "the *interdisciplines*," or departments organized around race, gender, and ethnicity.[3] Both Ferguson, and Maira and Shihade, explain that the creation of these kinds of departments was initially in response to the student protest movements on college campuses across northern California post-1968. These protests initiated the push for universities to create Ethnic Studies departments. For faculty and students, these spaces provided an opportunity to challenge institutional power as manifested in academia, the (settler-colonial) state, and global capitalism. Ferguson, however, argues that while Ethnic Studies was constructed as part of a resistance effort, that ultimately, despite its legacy in student movements, such minority culture and difference-based programs were appropriated and institutionalized by established networks of power. Scholar Sara Ahmad illuminates on the ways that diversity initiatives through hiring, policy changes, and even curriculum redesign, can become "about changing perceptions of whiteness rather than changing the whiteness of organizations. Changing perceptions of whiteness can be how an institution can reproduce whiteness, as that which exists but is not longer perceived."[4]

Thinking further about the "inclusion" of minority culture and difference-based programs, I draw on debates in the education field on the benefits of cross-pollinating the scholarship from culturally sustaining pedagogies, with work done on universal design learning, or seeing racism and ableism in schools in contradistinction to one another. Within this work, it is argued that "retrofitting" is a useful metaphor to think about how educational institutions handle increasing diversity.[5] Alim et al. argue that as systemic inequities—racism, ableism, homophobia—become more evident, historically "constructed" environments of educational spaces need to be retrofitted to stay standing.[6] However, this retrofitting approach is not *truly inclusive* since the initial structure was never designed to be inclusive to begin with.

Similarly, university spaces have been retrofitted to include departments for Asian American Studies, Arab American Studies, and other ethnic/race departmental programming. However, given that they were mere add-ons to already pre-existing "buildings," their impact on the university as a whole has been negligible. Such departments, instead, have been tokenized, allowing universities to congratulate themselves on their progressive intellectual ideals, while doing little to shift the nature of academic production and resource allocation.

The theme of the 2017 Association for Asian American Studies annual conference focused on care and caregiving, for and by, Asian-Americans in the U.S. and around the world, for people, and for nature. This expansive commitment by scholars echoes the transformative politics that Bayoumi espouses when he asks to see Muslim American Studies, Arab American Studies under the banner of Asian American Studies. However, the economic and political power structures that would limit such maneuvers are obfuscated, unless we recognize the fact that institutions do not see it as a net benefit to create and sustain the rise of interdisciplines.

Consequently, scholars in these spaces become pre-occupied with internal disagreements about inclusion, or the lack thereof, and compete for limited funding instead of working towards coalition-building across departments such as, but not limited to: Asian American Studies, Arab American Studies, Chicano Studies, Native Studies, Queer Studies, African American/Black Studies, and Disability Studies. Each of these departments seeks to dismantle the assimilationist and retrofitting project observable in the history of American higher education. In order to carry forward the legacy of the student protest movements of the late '60s, it may be more advantageous for us to consider the overlaps that we share across these interdisciplines in deconstructing the power structures that refuse to recognize our work, our teachings, our pedagogies, and our residence in these spaces.

Almost fifty years later, students are still fighting for legitimacy, faculty, and funding for Asian American and Pacific Islander programs across college campuses today. At Cornell University, alumni organized around the social media campaign #Fight4AAS to argue for an Asian American Studies major. At Hunter College/CUNY, the Asian American Studies Program, established in 1993, "is only able to offer a minor and has one full-time, non-tenure-track faculty who directs the program; all other faculty are adjuncts." Students at Harvard, Brandeis, Yale, Dartmouth, and other East Coast universities are also making similar demands of their institutions.[7]

For the college newspaper at the University of Pennsylvania, the Asian American Studies Undergraduate Advisory Board wrote a guest column expressing their concern over the future of the Asian American Studies department due to the recent departure of a key faculty member, and demands for more space, faculty, funding, and support from the college. The op-ed includes their explicit refusal to be the "model minority." The struggle to attain recognition and funding, index both the tertiary position of these departments (and their faculty), and what's at stake for those who wish to see these departments grow.[8] Ahmad describes this as the "effects of inhabiting institutional spaces that do not give you residence."[9] For students and faculty of color desiring full recognition in historically white institutions, the struggle continues.

To conclude, I turn to the wisdom offered by writer/activist Audre Lorde in an address on the lessons to be learned from the Civil Rights Movement. She explains that, "if there is one thing we can learn from the 60s, it is how infinitely complex any move for liberation must be."[10] While I agree with the connections made by Bayoumi and other scholars about the intersections between Asian American Studies and Arab American Studies, I ask that we push our critique beyond the mere question of inclusivity within these spaces, and towards a more radical reorganization of energy and resources within the university.

Notes

1   Moustafa Bayoumi, "Asian American Studies, the War on Terror, and the Changing University: A Call to Respond," *Asian American Matters: A New York Anthology* (AAARI-CUNY, 2017): 21-24.

2   Sunaina Maira and Magid Shihade, "Meeting Asian/Arab American Studies: Thinking Race, Empire, and Zionism in the U.S.," *Journal of Asian American Studies* 9:2 (John Hopkins University Press, June 2006): 117–140.

3   Roderick Ferguson, *The Reorder of Things: The University and Its Pedagogies of Minority Difference* (Minneapolis: University of Minnesota Press, 2012).

4   Sara Ahmad, *On Being Included: Racism and Diversity in Institutional Life* (Durham: Duke University Press, 2012): 34.

5   Federico Waitoller and Kathleen A. King Thorius, "Cross-Pollinating Culturally Sustaining Pedagogy and Universal Design for Learning: Toward an Inclusive Pedagogy That Accounts for Dis/Ability," *Harvard Educational Review*: Fall 2016, 86:3 (2016): 366–389.

6   H. Samy Alim, Susan Baglieri, Gloria Ladson-Billings, Django Paris, David H. Rose, and Joseph Michael Valente, "Responding to 'Cross-Pollinating Culturally Sustaining Pedagogy and Universal Design for Learning: Toward an Inclusive Pedagogy That Accounts for Dis/Ability,'" *Harvard Educational Review*: Spring 2017, 87:1 (2017): 4–25.

7   Frances Kai-Hwa Wang, "University Students, Alumni Fight for Growth in Asian American Studies," *NBC News* (June 10, 2016), http://www.nbcnews.com/news/asian-america/university-students-alumni-fight-increase-asian-american-studies-n589246

8   "Who Killed Asian American Studies?" *Daily Pennsylvanian* (January 31, 2017), http://www.thedp.com/article/2017/01/guest-column-asian-american-studies-893c

9   Ahmad, *On Being Included*: 176.

10 Audre Lorde, "Learning from the 60s." *In Sister Outsider: Essays & Speeches* (Berkeley, CA: Crossing Press, 2007): 138. (The author originally accessed Lorde's work on the website www.blackpast.org, an online reference guide to African American history.)

Commentary

Beneath the Surface: Academic and Practical Realities
Raymond Fong

The academic and political questions surrounding Muslim/Arab American identity, and its inclusion into Asian American Studies during this age of the "War on Terror" is both refreshing and simultaneously familiar. As Moustafa Bayoumi has stated in his essay, such issues have affected a number of ethnic groups in the past.[1] To deal with such questions, we must not only look towards a solution, but instead also recognize the contextual complexities and nuances of groups and institutions. Here, I hope to shed some light on the situation at hand.

The pigeonholing of minorities by the majority in our society is a reoccurring global phenomenon. For minorities of color in America, the evidence is everywhere. The word "Hispanic," for example, has been utilized for peoples hailing from Spanish-speaking countries in Central and Latin America. Given this already reductive label, the question then is, "What qualifies as a Latin American country?" If it is indeed a country that was colonized by Spain or Portugal, then can Macau or the Philippines be considered a part of "Latin America"? These types of historical ambiguities permeate not only the academic world, but also the practical world.

With such ambiguous labels pervading our common culture and language, the mislabeling and mishandling of "Muslim" should come as no surprise. All of these reductive labels do not follow a consistent logic in terms of geography or culture. Their only consistency is that they are expedient for the majority. The mainstream ultimately ignores the appropriate classification of Arab Americans, or the complexities of those who are part of the Muslim faith. Thus, all Muslim Americans are associated and discussed in the context of "terrorism," or more specifically 9/11. How do we then remove the stigma associated with American society's label of "Muslim"?

Japanese internment during World War II is particularly relevant when discussing the issue of Muslim Americans. Just as the U.S. government was afraid of a potential Japanese American fifth column within its borders, the current Trump administration also fears and demonizes Muslims who live in America. The state apparatus of laws, law enforcement, and ICE (Immigration and Customs Enforcement), work together to bring forth intense scrutiny upon Muslim American communities. In places where minorities have less power, essentially outside of major urban centers, this pressure is even more intense. And so, this is the narrow lens through which Muslims are viewed. This phenomenon does not have the same luxury of time that other discourses may have, simply because the less time that is spent deconstructing this lens, the more time people who fall under the label of "Muslim" will be in danger. For Muslim American communities, this is a matter of safety, and not just simply about academic discourse.

By combining academic research and organizing, we can help to combat this crisis on both academic and community levels. While the idea of placing Muslim Studies under the umbrella of Asian American Studies is flattering, the context of the decision must be considered. With the exception of a few strong graduate programs on the East and West Coasts, Asian American Studies is still a young academic discipline (close to fifty years), and is in the process of institutionalization, expanding to other universities. On paper, there are a number of universities that have Asian American Studies, but depending on their geographic location, some Asian groups are more emphasized. This being said, aside from the few strong programs that exist, Asian American Studies programs generally lack the necessary resources to adequately affect institutional change. Therefore, the larger issue is not just a matter of academic/programmatic inclusion, or exclusion.

The legacy of Asian American Studies is well documented, emerging from minority student strikes by Black, Native American, Chicano, and Asian Americans at San Francisco State College in the late 1960s. From there, it spread first to the San Francisco Bay Area universities and colleges, and later to the rest of California. Its core curriculum reflected the population of these students, namely Chinese, Japanese, and Filipinos until the 1980s. From the 1980s to 1990s, Asian American Studies expanded to include Korean American and Southeast Asian courses, followed by South Asian American classes. Today, it is not uncommon to have courses that also address issues relating to Asian Muslim immigrants from Pakistan, Bangladesh, and Sri Lanka.

Judging from the natural progression the field has taken, it seems as if the next areas of interest will also include Asian Muslim countries such as Indonesia and Malaysia, as well as the hot topic of Muslim minority ethnic groups in China. With this in mind, how can Asian American Studies address, or relate, to Islamic or Muslim Studies, and to Muslim Americans in this country? It is a double-edged sword. While it is encouraging that Muslim issues are being addressed, it is also problematic in that the discourse around Muslim issues fluctuates with local instructors. Perhaps the inclusion of Muslim American Studies within Asian American Studies solely depends on the political will of the students, instructors, and the university.

Moving forward, it is also important to note the scope (or lack thereof) of Asian American Studies, and its core mission to study topics that are relevant to Asian America. The inclusion of Muslim issues and/or topics presents an important opportunity. Aside from the innocent victims labeled "Muslim" targeted by societal prejudice, there is also an important domestic counterpart. Some of these attackers associated with Islam are actually American-raised. European Muslims, similarly, have also committed attacks in France. This would make for an extremely fitting topic for Asian American Studies to tackle as the roots of these attacks originated on American and European soil.

According to Scott Pelley of *CBS Evening News*, in their March 6, 2017 report, 78 percent of terror attacks in the United States were committed by Americans. Although the conventional explanation is that the attackers were "brainwashed" by extremist Islam teachings, the road to committing these atrocities cannot be that simple. Under academic inquiry, questions would be raised regarding the educational, political, and cultural background of these attackers. Why did they do it? How did their respective communities treat them pre-attack? Where in America are these communities located? The list goes on and on, providing a rich field for scholarly inquiry.

Going back to the question of whether Muslim or Arab American Studies should be included in Asian American Studies, I would say, "Sure, why not?" Would it be the smartest move? That is an unknown. But I do think the question of "legitimacy" per se is a meaningless one. As Bayoumi mentions, most of these ethnic and geopolitical classifications were created by Euro-centric or American interests, and so legitimacy is really up to other factors.

Whether or not inclusion would be a productive move is a multi-layered question. Is Asian American Studies institutionally strong, or savvy enough, to back Muslim Americans? Will Asian American Studies programs cooperate and unify in order to counteract the fear-infused lens that society utilizes in viewing Muslims during times of crisis? Given the great amount of academic potential, how will the different groups of Asian American Studies professors and students utilize it?

Despite the ambiguity that surrounds this issue, I believe that through this current turmoil, communities can unite to create new platforms around the ethics of equality and justice for all.

Note

1   Moustafa Bayoumi, "Asian American Studies, the War on Terror, and the Changing University: A Call to Respond," *Asian American Matters: A New York Anthology* (AAARI-CUNY, 2017): 21-24.

Authors

Moustafa Bayoumi is an award-winning writer, and Associate Professor of English at Brooklyn College/CUNY. Born in Zürich, Switzerland, and raised in Kingston, Ontario, Canada, he currently lives in Brooklyn. Bayoumi completed his Ph.D. in English and Comparative Literature at Columbia University. He is co-editor of *The Edward Said Reader* (Vintage, 2002), editor of *Midnight on the Mavi Marmara: The Attack on the Gaza Freedom Flotilla and How It Changed the Course of the Israeli/Palestine Conflict* (first published by OR Books, trade edition by Haymarket Books, 2010) and has published academic essays in publications including *Transition*, *Interventions*, the *Yale Journal of Criticism*, *Amerasia Journal*, *Arab Studies Quarterly*, and the *Journal of Asian American Studies*.

Prema Kurien is the founding director of Asian/American Studies and Professor of Sociology at Syracuse University's Maxwell School of Citizenship and Public Affairs. Dr. Kurien is a past CUNY Thomas Tam Visiting Professor at the CUNY Graduate School, 2014-2015. Her recent research focuses on race and ethnic group relations, as well as the role of religion in shaping group formation and mobilization among contemporary ethnic groups.

Dr. Kurien has received postdoctoral fellowships and grants from the National Science Foundation, The Woodrow Wilson International Center, the Carnegie Corporation, the Society for the Scientific Study of Religion, the Pew Charitable Trusts, the Center for the Study of Religion at Princeton University, the American Institute of Indian Studies, the Louisville Institute, and the New Ethnic and Immigrant Congregations Project. Her work has been recognized with a Contribution to the Field award, two national book awards, and three national article awards.

Rajini Srikanth is Professor of English in the College of Liberal Arts, and Dean of the Honors College, at the University of Massachusetts Boston. Dr. Srikanth received her Ph.D. from the State University of New York at Buffalo. Her areas of expertise include Human Rights and Literature, American Literature (including Asian American literature, Native American literature, and literature of the American South), Interdisciplinary Approaches to Literature, Literature in the Context of Comparative Race and Ethnicities, Pedagogy of Literature, and Literatures of the Middle East. She is the co-editor of *Cambridge History of Asian American Literature* (2015), and author of *Constructing the Enemy: Empathy/Antipathy in U.S. Literature and Law* (2012).

Sylvia Chan-Malik is Assistant Professor of American Studies and Women's and Gender Studies at Rutgers University-New Brunswick. She is the author of *Being Muslim: A Cultural History of Women of Color in American Islam* (NYU Press, forthcoming Spring 2018).

Erik Love is the author of the book *Islamophobia and Racism in America* (NYU Press, 2017). Erik is a Visiting Fellow at the James Weldon Johnson Institute for the Study of Race and Difference at Emory University. He also serves as Assistant Professor of Sociology at Dickinson College in Pennsylvania. He holds a Ph.D. in Sociology from the University of California, Santa Barbara.

Erik's academic interests center on race, racism, and civil rights advocacy. His research has received support from the National Science Foundation and the Center for New Racial Studies. His writing has appeared on *Al Jazeera English*, *Jadaliyya*, and in peer-reviewed academic publications.

Eric Tang is an Associate Professor in the African and African Diaspora Studies Department and faculty member in the Center for Asian American Studies at the University of Texas at Austin. He also holds a courtesy appointment in the Department of Sociology and serves as a faculty fellow with both the Institute for Urban Policy Research & Analysis and the Division of Diversity and Community Engagement. Prof. Tang was the 2016-2017 CUNY Thomas Tam Visiting Professor at the CUNY Graduate Center. *Unsettled: Cambodian Refugees in the New York City Hyperghetto* (Temple University, 2015) is his first book.

Mariam Durrani is an Assistant Professor of Anthropology at Hamilton College. She received her joint Ph.D. in Anthropology and in Education from the University of Pennsylvania and completed her postdoctoral fellowship at the Harvard Graduate School of Education. Her research focuses on higher education, Muslim youth and communities, cultural mobilities, and the gendered nature of migration.

Raymond Fong received his M.A. degree in Anthropology and Education from Teachers College, Columbia University, and B.A. in East Asian Studies from the University of Arizona. His research interests include minority student achievement, community forces, and cultural imports/exports.

2

FIFTY YEARS OF PASTS & FUTURES

"*Challenge the traditional ways of thinking in Asian and Asian American and Latino and Latin American Studies.*"
—Augusto Espiritu
CUNY FORUM 2:1 (2014)

Students mobilize for Asian Studies at City College of New York /CUNY (1974)
Photo by Mary Uyematsu Kao

"Remember, no matter what they tell you, you have as much right to be here as anyone .... And don't ever be ashamed of being Vietnamese. Be proud of who you are and where you come from."

—Sơn Ca Lâm

SHIRLEY HUNE, IN AN OVERVIEW, covers the changing intellectual landscape of the field during the last five decades and asks: "Might Asian American Studies be taught in China, India, and other Asian countries as part of transnational, diasporic, and global studies?" Concurrently, Phil Tajitsu Nash in his essay argues why Asian Americans today need liberatory education more than ever.

"Steps Along the Curved Road," with Loan Thị Đào, Peter Nien-chu Kiang, Sơn Ca Lâm, Songkhla Nguyễn, and Shirley Suet-ling Tang, offers a "community to college" mentorship model of K-12 education linked with Asian American Studies at the university level. Allan Punzalan Isaac re-examines what it means to be an individual person and student of color in a xenophobic society. Shirley Hune, in an excerpt, focuses on why East Coast Asian American Studies differs historically from the West Coast and what it can contribute to today's practice. Joyce O. Moy provides an updated report on Asian American Studies and leadership at The City University of New York, and the glaring lack of Asians at key upper-level positions.

Two scholars recount their history: Betty Lee Sung, who taught the first Asian Studies class at City College of New York, part of The City University of New York, is interviewed by Antony Wong. The late Don T. Nakanishi (1949-2016), in his speech on forty-five years of Asian American Studies at Yale University, encourages the institution to do more.

Demographics, Geographies, Institutions

The Changing Intellectual Landscape of Asian American Studies

SHIRLEY HUNE

AS WE MOVE TOWARD FIVE DECADES of the founding of Asian American Studies (AAS) on the West and East Coasts, 1969 and 1970 respectively, I consider how the field has changed. Then, as now, student demands are crucial for securing, continuing, and expanding AAS programs.

A few Asian American Studies powerhouses have emerged with sizeable faculty and endowments, especially in California. There have also been modest gains in AAS, notably in the Midwest, South, and Southwest, that reflect the increased presence of Asian Americans nationally. Still, there is uncertainty on some campuses, despite the tenacity of AAS faculty and students. The authors in Chapter Two of *Asian American Matters: A New York Anthology* share their hopes and frustrations in advancing AAS and the needs and interests of Asian American students on the East Coast. Some propose fresh thinking and practices to better situate AAS in current racial, political, and community spaces.

The world today in which AAS operates is different from fifty years ago. I use the term "intellectual landscape" to assess briefly the situation of AAS since its formation and give attention to three elements—demographics, geographies, and institutions.

Demographics

Who could have foreseen that post-1965 U.S. immigration policies and international events, such as U.S. wars in Asia, civil strife in the region, and globalization would transform Asian America from a population primarily from East Asia and the Philippines, to including major groups from South and Southeast Asia. Concomitantly, Asian Americans are no longer mainly native-born, but mostly foreign-born (66 percent in 2014), and comprise diverse ethnic groups of all ages and backgrounds. They are immigrants and refugees, with some being undocumented.[1] There are also nonimmigrant visa holders, like H-1B workers who may remain, and adoptees.

Asian American Studies has incorporated these and other demographic changes, and this is evident in its student body and faculty, courses, publications, and conference panels. Over the decades, the Asian American landscape of intellectual work has been flexible, fluid, and expansive in opening up to new groups and including their experiences and communities in teaching and scholarly endeavors.

Geographies

The initial years of Asian American Studies were understandably U.S. focused in its geography, even California-centric. Today, studies of the Asian American experience frequently encompass the perspectives of transnational, diasporic, and global studies.[2] AAS extends beyond the United States to include the geographies of Asian homelands, the Americas, and comparative studies with Asian communities elsewhere.

Asian American geographies are also being reconsidered from regional and local standpoints. Studies of Asian Americans in the U.S. South and Midwest provide distinctive findings from those on the East and West Coasts.[3] Border crossings may include rural, urban, suburban, as well as island, territorial, and mainland movements that traverse nations and states. Nor are the locations, places, and spaces of being Asian in one's declared homeland or abroad fixed; they may be temporary or continuing, but certainly evolving.

Geographies are integral to the landscape of AAS intellectual work. Locations and transitions, at times acutely disruptive, and other times deliberately chosen, have implications for how Asian Americans create new lives, seek to retain old lives, form identities, develop communities, and other adaptations.

Institutions

Asian American Studies resides within higher education institutions, another element of its intellectual landscape. AAS was established as an interdisciplinary field, a new way to organize knowledge and people. In its early years, AAS benefited from a strong U.S. economy that enabled institutions to expand, and a political climate of support for campus diversity. Recently, many campuses have faced fiscal and political challenges, resulting in serious implications for AAS.

Fiscally, with fewer resources, institutions generally provide less support for diversity matters, academic programs, and personnel. Politically, some programs are viewed as more important than others because they are revenue enhancers, and in terms of academic status, students' employment prospects, and national wellbeing. Student enrollment in classes matter more today than ever. Furthermore, Asian American concerns are often treated as less vital given the persistent belief in the model minority stereotype.

Consequently, AAS programs may not receive new faculty lines. Tenure-track positions and tenure may be elusive in institutional climates that set higher bars for Asian American faculty to succeed, and the retirement (or death) of Asian American scholars does not guarantee that their faculty lines will be replaced. AAS programs can be at risk because of changes in campus leadership, personnel, and priorities. Ironically though, campuses are now seeking to offset their reduced budgets by recruiting international students, mostly from Asia, who pay higher rates of tuition and fees.

Students advocate for support of Asian American Studies major at Hunter College/CUNY (April 2, 2017)
Photo by Amy Zheng

Higher education institutions are slow to change, but change is present. Given that institutional homes and support are essential for AAS, with programs organized largely as teaching units, how can the field position itself for the next fifty years? In my view, to grow and remain relevant, AAS needs to adapt, innovate continuously, and be proactive. Which undergraduate courses will be taught, how, and for whom (e.g., as a major, double major, minor, general education, service learning)? Not everyone seeks a graduate degree and career in AAS, but many aim to use their Asian American perspectives, knowledge base, and social justice advocacy in other fields. Students seek out skills and credentials for an ever-changing workplace and to contribute to their communities and society at large. One proposal, based on my own experiences and those of others, is to expand the field's interdisciplinarity to include disciplines and sectors of the campus, such as professional programs, that connect students and courses with practice and Asian American communities. Pathways can be developed, for example, with education, urban planning, social welfare, public health, law, and environmental studies.[4]

I also conjecture where AAS might reside in the next fifty years. The intellectual landscape of the field need not be confined to U.S. institutions. As part of global competition, Asia is developing its own higher education institutions through the benefit of its rising economies. Might Asian American Studies be taught in China, India, or other Asian countries as part of transnational, diasporic, and global studies; or perhaps as examples of majority/minority relations in other countries, as well as within American Studies—which is popular there, especially Asian American literature? Will some faculty take positions at Asian institutions in the humanities and social sciences, and teach AAS, as other faculty do now in science, engineering, and technology fields?

In closing, I have identified three elements—demographics, geographies, and institutions—that inform the intellectual landscape of Asian American Studies. My analyses here seeks to encourage new generations of scholars to be proactive and innovative in advancing AAS today and in coming decades.

Notes

1 The refugee population largely from Southeast Asia previously, now includes those from Burma/Myanmar and Bhutan. In 2011, Asians comprised one in nine unauthorized persons in the U.S., or 12 percent of the total Asian immigrant population. See Karthick Ramakrishnan and Farah Z. Ahmad, *State of Asian Americans and Pacific Islander Series: A Multifaceted Portrait of a Growing Population* (Center for American Progress, September 2014): 30–31, www.americanprogress.org.

2 For an early example of the international dimension of Asian American Studies, see "Asians in the Americas," *Amerasia Journal* 15:2 (UCLA Asian American Studies Center, 1989). Erika Lee's *The Making of Asian America: A History* (New York: Simon & Schuster, 2015) provides a new global synthesis of Asian American history.

3 Recent anthologies reevaluating Asians in the U.S. South include: Jigna Desai and Khyati Y. Joshi, eds., *Asian Americans in Dixie: Race and Migration in the South* (Champaign: University of Illinois Press, 2013); Raymond A. Mohl, John E. Van Sant, and Chizuru Saeki, eds., *Far East, Down South: Asians in the American South.* (Tuscaloosa: The University of Alabama Press, 2016). On Asians in the Midwest, see Sook Wilkinson and Victor Jew, eds., *Asian Americans in Michigan: Voices from the Midwest* (Detroit: Wayne State University Press, 2015).

4 Đào, Kiang, Nguyễn, and Tang (*Asian American Matters: A New York Anthology*, 2017), describe the links between AAS at UMass Boston and an elementary school, and how they strengthened the schooling of Southeast Asian students, community ties, AAS course and faculty development, community-based research, and publications. Through integrating Asian American topics into law programs at CUNY, and engaging students of all backgrounds using community-oriented pedagogy, Phil Tajitsu Nash (*Asian American Matters: A New York Anthology*, 2017) transformed students' understandings and relationships with Asian Americans, other immigrant groups, and their own families. My own experiences include teaching courses that were partly or exclusively about Asian Americans to largely non-Asian practitioners in master's programs in Social Welfare, Education, and Urban Planning at Hunter College/CUNY, UCLA, and the University of Washington. Designed to better prepare students for working with diverse communities, these courses also attracted Asian American students in other fields, with some going on to earn doctorates in Asian American topics.

Author

Shirley Hune is Professor Emerita of Urban Planning at UCLA and Educational Leadership & Policy Studies at the University of Washington. She served as Associate Provost of Hunter College/CUNY (1990-92), and Associate Dean of the Graduate Division at UCLA (1992-2007). Her publications are in the areas of Asian American historiography, critical race, gender, and immigration studies, and higher education issues. Her earlier research examined third world and global developments. She is a former President of the Association for Asian American Studies and has been on the editorial boards of *Amerasia Journal*, *Journal of Asian American Studies*, and *AAPI Nexus*.

Betty Lee Sung
Teaching Asian American Studies at CUNY
An Interview

ANTONY WONG

"You don't act like an Asian American woman at all!"
—City College Administrator

This interview was conducted on April 23, 2015 at the home of Prof. Betty Lee Sung.

Wong: Thank you for sitting down with us to be interviewed for *CUNY FORUM, Volume 3:1*. What is your current opinion on the state of Asian American Studies on the East Coast in 2015, and in particular within The City University of New York (CUNY)? You stated in your essay for *CUNY FORUM, Volume 1:1* back in 2013 that Asian American Studies at CUNY was "barely holding its head above water." Has your view changed within the past two years?

Sung: I still think that we have not made much headway with Asian American Studies. I taught the first courses at City College of New York back in 1970, and at that time it was completely different from what it is today. Today's people in New York are different from those in the West Coast. They're different from the Hawaiians, and they're different from the former generation that I was familiar with. There are still Asian American courses offered at Hunter College. But having been retired for twenty-three years now, I don't think I have any leverage to expand the number of courses or to do anything about it. But, I still work very hard to see if they can restore Asian American Studies somewhere because the population of Asians in New York City is over fourteen percent. We have the largest Asian American population in the country, and yet we do not have anything approaching the Asian American Studies courses that other institutions of higher learning do.

L to R: Shirley Hune (Prof. Emerita, University of Washington),
Betty Lee Sung & Russell C. Leong (Editor, CUNY FORUM)

Transcribed by Zhu-Hui Wu
Photos by Antony Wong

Wong: You are the author of *Mountain of Gold*, one of the first books on the history of the Chinese in America, and also the first teacher to initiate an Asian American Studies course in 1970 after a student demonstration, which later expanded into the Asian Studies department in 1972 at City College. What were some of the first lessons that you taught in your classes to provide the foundation for an Asian American identity in a country that didn't accept Asians as Americans?

Sung: Those times and the students were very different. Firstly, I was not familiar at all with teaching and it was a new experience for me. Yet, the students had demanded that I teach the course and City College was willing to offer such a course at that time. When I went to the library, I immediately found that there were only about five books on the Chinese in the United States. City College has one of the best libraries in the country, and yet, all they had were about five books that were all very ancient and very out of date. Most of them depicted the Chinese and Asians in a stereotypical way that I did not approve of at all. The students at that time wanted to know about their own experiences and they sort of made up the course for me. They wanted the questions that they had on their minds answered, and that was how I structured the course, giving them what they wanted at the time.

Wong: As an Asian American woman, working single-handedly in the 1970s to push for Asian American Studies at City College, were there any particular situations that come to mind where you faced an insurmountable amount of opposition to any advancement of your classes? And how did you handle it?

Sung: It was very difficult because I was the first one to offer Asian American Studies. There was nothing to go by, and I faced an insurmountable amount of opposition from the CUNY faculty, and mostly from the deans and the executive committees, who were very much against my coming into the institution at all. I had to fight against them, being the first one. I went to the executive committees and all I encountered was this opposition from the faculty that didn't want to even touch Asian, or Asian American Studies. It was very hard to counter all this opposition and the things that they said to me. Thank goodness I spoke up against them. Their remarks were: "You don't act like an Asian American woman at all!" I had to laugh at that because I think I was emboldened by the students and their stand against the regular courses that were being offered that did not have any relevance to their lives.

Wong: Were your colleagues on the West Coast receiving the same amount of difficulties?

Sung: I think some of them received some of this, but not as much. I think the first Asian American Studies course was offered at San Francisco State, and the president there was against offering it and later was shouted down. So I realized very early on that the Chinese in Hawai'i and on the West Coast were entirely different from the ones on the East Coast, which were a later generation from those that came before.

Wong: Sadly after your retirement in 1992, City College failed to continue to support Asian American Studies. Why was this so?

Sung: I think they were very happy to get rid of Asian American Studies. After I retired they immediately appointed somebody from Taiwan who had no idea what Asian American Studies was. I gave him all my course notes and materials, and he didn't understand any of it himself, so how could he teach it? I remember in one course, the enrollment immediately dropped down to six. Shortly thereafter, I guess they dropped the course and the head of the department at that time, a historian, he and I spoke and I asked why he was letting this department, one that we fought so hard to establish, be let go. He said that Asian American Studies could go into the History department. I told him that he would be the low man on the totem pole, but to him it didn't matter, and so the Asian American Studies department was dropped.

Wong: Were there no other faculty members with the qualifications to take on the duties of leading the charge for Asian American Studies in your absence?

Sung: There were very few Asian Americanists at the time, and very few studied the Chinese in the United States. They had worked in other disciplines.

Wong: What initiatives, including the formation of the Asian American Higher Education Council (AAHEC), did you and other leaders take to push for Asian American Studies once again, not only at City College, but throughout CUNY? Today, for example, Hunter College is the only college that offers a minor in Asian American Studies since 2002.

Sung: We were met with resistance everywhere we went. They kept saying Asian American Studies was not a discipline. We went to various campuses and we talked to then-CUNY Chancellor Matthew Goldstein who was very much in favor of supporting us. But somehow or other, the various colleges were reluctant.

For instance at Baruch College, we finally got a course, but the president at the time said to me, "You know, we now have the course, but nobody is enrolled, so we are dropping it." I immediately went to the student club and asked them why they weren't taking Asian American Studies when they clamored for it. I think over thirty or forty something percent of the student enrollment at Baruch is Asian, and yet, they all disclaimed any knowledge of the course. I later found out that it was listed under English or some other kind of department instead of Ethnic Studies, so nobody enrolled in it. As a result the course was canceled.

A number of colleges did offer at least one course in Asian American Studies, but Hunter was the one that was offering more, and more students were taking the courses there. I remember in late 2006/early 2007, when the president there wanted to eliminate the entire Asian American Studies Program. Hunter today is the only college that offers a minor in Asian American Studies, and yet throughout the country Asian American Studies is blossoming all over. I think we have about fifty colleges throughout the country that are offering Asian American Studies, and yet City College and CUNY does not. New York City has about fourteen percent of its population that are Asian, the largest Chinese American population there is, and yet we do not train our students who are mainly going into the city government and to jobs that will require some kind of knowledge of Asians, with courses in Asian American Studies.

Wong: After nearly a decade of requests by volunteers such as yourself, Asian faculty members, staff, and students, CUNY formed the Asian American and Asian Research Institute (AAARI) in 2001, as a central location for scholarly research and resource on policies and issues that affect Asians and Asian Americans. Almost fourteen years later, has the Institute assisted in pushing forward Asian American Studies throughout CUNY?

Sung: At that time I thought that since they weren't offering Asian American Studies, one of the very important things for Asian Americans was that there was no research being done about the situation that we were in, and so I pushed for our scholars who were doing research. Unfortunately, we lost our former founding executive director, Dr. Thomas Tam.

Since AAARI's founding though, I believe that even more research should be done. For instance, in my days, there was no adoption of Asian American children, yet this has become a big thing with the Asian American population here. Korean students, Vietnamese children, and Chinese children were being adopted into White or Black homes. These are new fields that require research. Intermarriage was a new phenomenon because it used to be forbidden by law, and yet nothing has been done on research that covers this field except for what I did back in 1990. That's a long time ago, but today the situation is entirely different. We have new groups of people coming into the country now. Back then it was only the Filipinos, the Japanese, and Chinese, but today's Asian Americans, I think, encompass more than twenty-two or more groups. The diversity of the Asian population has been growing and so we ought to do more research on the newer groups.

Wong: Your memoir will be published later this year and we are looking forward to reading it. Can you share with us a life-changing moment in your career that we don't and should know about?

Betty Lee Sung receives 2017 Association for Asian American Studies Lifetime Achievement Award
L to R: Douglas W. Lee (Founding AAAS President),
Cathy J. Schlund-Vials (2016-2018 AAAS President) & Betty Lee Sung

Sung: My memoir should be coming out soon. It is titled *[Defiant] Second Daughter: My First 90 Years*, from Advantage Press. I'm writing it because my granddaughter wanted to know a little bit about myself, and so I wrote two chapters of what I did growing up and during my college years. She and my daughter found it so fascinating that I decided to write more and went looking into my lineage, my genealogy. I found a lot about my father but I couldn't find anything about my mother, because girls at that time were non-entities. They were married into somebody else's family and assumed the identity of their husband's family, and so I found nothing. That was one of the things I lament because I felt that half of me comes from my mother and I should be able to find more about her.

Unfortunately toward my later years, my husband of almost four decades, was taken from me by my stepchildren that I helped to raise, and so that's been a sad chapter in my life. Although it's late in my life, I would like to do something for the elderly who are victims of their own families.

Wong: In regards to your career, is there anything interesting that we should know about? A pivotal moment [that you want readers to know about]?

Sung: The pivotal point in my entire life is that I was not afraid to speak out against unfairness and injustice. Asian cultures teach people to keep quiet. Suffer, rather than complain. Walk away, rather than confront. In my first ninety years, I was still combative. Can I keep this up in my later years? It's difficult, but I will try.

Wong: Thank you for your time and sharing your thoughts with *CUNY FORUM*.

AAARI Lecture Video (November 6, 2015): www.aaari.info/15-11-06Sung.htm

Interviewer

Antony Wong is Program Coordinator at the Asian American and Asian Research Institute (AAARI), of The City University of New York (CUNY). Antony received his B.A. in English from Hunter College/CUNY, and M.B.A. in Accountancy from the Zicklin School of Business at Baruch College/CUNY.

Bio

Betty Lee Sung is Prof. Emerita of City College of New York/CUNY, and co-founder and former board chair of the Asian American and Asian Research Institute, of The City University of New York. Prof. Sung received the Lifetime Achievement Award at the 2017 Association for Asian American Studies (AAAS) annual conference in Portland, Oregon.

Forty-Five Years of Asian American Studies at Yale University

DON T. NAKANISHI

Keynote Address at the
"Asian American Studies Conference at Yale University"
February 27, 2015

I. Forty-Fifth Anniversary of Asian American Studies at Yale

IT IS A GREAT HONOR and pleasure to be invited back to Yale and to participate in this important conference.

This gathering has historic significance. It was forty-five years ago during the Spring semester of 1970 when the first class in Asian American Studies was offered at Yale. It was the first Asian American Studies class offered by any Ivy League college and, along with the first class offered at City College of New York,[1] one of the first two that was taught east of the West Coast.

The class, which was titled, "The Asian American Experience," was proposed as one of the first goals of the Yale Asian American Students Association (AASA). AASA was renamed years later as the Yale Asian American Student Alliance, which had formed the previous semester in Fall 1969. That year was also noteworthy because that is when women first enrolled as undergrads at Yale. Among the 750 pioneering undergraduate women, there were eleven Asian American women: eight who transferred to the junior and sophomore classes, and three who were freshmen. The first Asian American Studies class was offered in the residential college seminar series of Timothy Dwight College at Yale. It was organized and largely taught by Yale AASA members. Prof. Chitoshi Yanaga, the first Japanese American who was tenured at Yale and a faculty member in the political science department, served as the teacher of record. A second generation *Nisei*, he shared his personal experiences of growing up in Hawai'i, his encounters with housing discrimination as a graduate student at Berkeley, and his insights on how anti-Chinese and anti-Japanese exclusion laws and hostilities in California and elsewhere had an impact on U.S.–Asia relations—his area of scholarly expertise. About twenty of the fifty-nine Asian American undergraduates[2] at Yale in 1970 took the two-hours-a-week seminar, which explored a range of historical and contemporary topics from the individual to international levels: What does it mean to be an Asian American at Yale and in American society? What was and should be the relationship between Asian Americans and the Civil Rights Movement? And how has the Vietnam War, the continuing hostilities with China, and trade tensions with Japan affected Asian Americans?

The class was not taught in a social vacuum. It was a period of extraordinary social change and conflict. It occurred during the semester when the Bobby Seale and Black Panthers trial took place in New Haven, and a massive May Day protest rally was held on the New Haven Green, which attracted thousands of demonstrators and the mobilization of the National Guard. Yale AASA issued a public statement, which was largely drafted by the future U.S. assistant attorney general for civil rights (the federal government's top civil rights official), Bill Lann Lee, a Yale junior from New York, which called for a fair trial for Seale and solidarity with Blacks and Latinos. The group also assisted Asian American restaurants and small businesses in New Haven with boarding up their front windows in anticipation of potential unrest and looting in the city, which fortunately did not occur. The class was also held when the Yale AASA organized the first-ever Asian American student conference on the East Coast in April 1970, which attracted over three hundred students from over thirty colleges. Later, in Fall 1970, AASA organized the first Asian

American Studies conference on the East Coast. AASA also successfully lobbied the Yale admissions office to recruit and admit more low-income, more public high school, and a greater diversity of Asian American students. In doing so, Yale became the first Ivy League institution to recognize Asian Americans as a historically underrepresented minority in the same manner that it did with Blacks and Latinos for the purposes of enhancing student body diversity. In short, Yale included Asian Americans in its student affirmative action efforts.

Yale AASA did more. It also worked with the Yale College dean's office to set up a special "Floating Counselor" program to assist incoming Asian American students in making the transition to Yale; initiated so-called T-groups to collectively share personal experiences of being Asian Americans; joined with groups like "Asians Against the Vietnam War" in protesting the continued military involvement of the U.S. in Southeast Asia; and collected over one thousand signatures from students at Yale's dining halls urging Congress to repeal Title II of the 1950 McCarran Act, which allowed for the mass detention of citizens, without trial, similar to what was done to Japanese Americans during World War II.[3]

In designing and taking the class, it became apparent to us that there were many limitations to the then existing literature on Asian Americans. Towards the end of the semester, a good friend of mine, Lowell Chun-Hoon, a junior from Hawai'i who would later become a prominent labor attorney in Hawai'i, and I decided that we wanted to help develop the emerging field of Asian American Studies by starting an academic journal. We agreed that we would each raise $500 during the upcoming summer and use the funds to launch the journal during our senior year. Lowell successfully raised over $1,000, but I must confess that I was too involved in doing field research for my senior thesis so that I did not live up to my commitment. Lowell, therefore, had first crack at job titles and became the first editor of our new journal, which we called *Amerasia Journal*. And although I did not raise my share of funds, I became the publisher. (As an aside, I might mention that we considered a number of names for the new publication. One that we ended up rejecting because we thought it was probably too clever and easily misunderstood was "Youth In Asia.") Along with other members of Yale AASA (like the future acclaimed architect Billie Tsien, who designed our first cover; and future distinguished civil rights attorneys Bill Lann Lee and Rocky Chin, who wrote articles on Yung Wing and New York City Chinatown, respectively, for the first issue), we published two issues of *Amerasia Journal* in New Haven before we accepted an offer to transfer the publication to the then recently established UCLA Asian American Studies Center (AASC), the first research center on Asian Americans. The AASC has supported *Amerasia Journal* since July 1971 to the present and assured its development as the premier foundational academic journal for the field of Asian American Studies.

II. A Wonderful Life Journey

Asian American Studies—and more broadly, Ethnic Studies—has served as a profoundly compelling and challenging personal, professional, and political focus of mine ever since I was a Yale undergraduate. I have been on a wonderful life journey, which I could not have foreseen traveling when I was an undergraduate, and witnessed and participated in an amazing array of dynamic and significant trends and historic events. I hope you will not mind if I share with you the importance of my Yale experience in taking my first steps on this forty-five-year trip. I think my journey provides credence to the adage that you should be open-minded in deciding on a college major and ultimately a career, and pursue what really interests you, and what you find truly meaningful and fulfilling.

*   *   *

I was born in Boyle Heights, which is a part of the city of Los Angeles, just east of the Los Angeles River and the downtown Little Tokyo, and grew up in an adjoining area called East Los Angeles. Before World War II and into the 1950s, this area had the largest concentration of American Jews in Los Angeles, the largest Japanese American community, and sizeable populations of Mexican Americans and Blacks. By the time I started elementary school, the vast majority of American Jews had moved out, especially to the San Fernando Valley and the Fairfax district of Los Angeles. Up until the second grade, I had several American Jewish classmates. After second grade, I would not have an American Jewish classmate or friend until I went to college. From second grade on, I went to racially segregated, working class schools. My high school, Theodore Roosevelt High School, one of the oldest in Los Angeles and known for its long rivalry with neighboring Garfield High School, was eighty percent Mexican American/Chicano, ten percent Asian American, and ten percent African Americans. I believe we had one White student out of a graduating class of over one thousand. Roosevelt was a wonderful place to spend my teenage years. It had lots of school spirit and tradition, active clubs, and many committed teachers. Its multiethnic, working-class student body taught me important lessons about building relationships and friendships across racial, ethnic, and class lines that have benefited me throughout my life. However, a year after I graduated, this view of Roosevelt was challenged when students at Roosevelt and neighboring Lincoln, Wilson, and Garfield high schools staged what were called the "East Los Angeles Walkouts," or the "Chicano Blowouts," to protest the unequal and culturally insensitive education Chicano students were receiving in the Los Angeles Unified School District.

My parents were both born in the U.S., but left the country with their families when they were very young and grew up in Hiroshima, Japan. In December 1939, they got married and decided to join my father's brothers, who had returned to the U.S. and had settled in Los Angeles. They opened a small grocery store in South Los Angeles. They seemed to be doing fine until the Japanese attack on Pearl Harbor on December 7, 1941. Several months later, along with over 120,000 other Japanese Americans, they were forcibly and unjustly incarcerated for over three years in concentration camps, first in Poston, Arizona, and then after they joined in protests with others over their imprisonment, they were sent to a special concentration camp called Tule Lake in Northern California. They were angry at how they were treated, sought to renounce their U.S. citizenship, and wanted to return to Japan.

Nakanishi Family (Don Nakanishi on the left)

On August 6, 1945, the U.S. dropped an atomic bomb on Hiroshima. My father's parents were both killed and my mother's parents and siblings miraculously survived while all the homes in front of, behind, and to the right and left of theirs were destroyed, and the residents were killed. My relatives attribute their survival to a bamboo fence which was in front of their house facing the epicenter of the atomic bombing. That burnt bamboo fence is on display in Hiroshima's famous Peace Museum. My parents, who by then had a young child, my older brother, realized that they should not return to a ravaged Hiroshima. They said that they begged U.S. government officials to allow them to stay in the U.S. and to remain as U.S. citizens. My parents were allowed to stay and eventually made their way back to Los Angeles. They lived in East Los Angeles for the remainder of their lives. My dad was a produce clerk at a supermarket and my mother was a seamstress in the downtown Los Angeles garment district. They tried as much as possible to raise me as a Japanese because, my mother said, it might be necessary to return to Japan if we faced difficult times. It was not possible for me to grow up fully as a Japanese. I thrived and enjoyed a multiethnic experience in East Los Angeles.

If my life had followed a more common path after graduating from Roosevelt, I would have attended UCLA or the University of Southern California, commuted to the campus from my home, majored in biology or chemistry and been fortunate to become a medical doctor, which was my long-time career goal.

If I would have enrolled at UCLA in Fall 1967, I would have found a large public university of over thirty thousand students with a student body that was nearly ninety percent White, less than ten percent Asian American, and having a very small number of Blacks and Chicanos. Two years later in 1969, Asian American and other students of color, along with their alumni and community leaders, called for the creation of ethnic studies research centers like the Asian American Studies Center. UCLA, without question, had one of the most active and influential groups of Asian American student activists and alumni in the nation, a tradition that continues to this day. However, if I had attended UCLA, I am not sure I would have become an activist or even taken an Asian American Studies class. I do not recall any of my Asian American class-mates from Roosevelt who attended UCLA becoming involved in Asian American activism there.

It was a different story for my Chicano friends who attended UCLA and other colleges. Many became leaders in the Chicano student movement. And it was through the Chicano movement that I entered Asian American Studies and the Asian American Movement. I was one of a handful of co-founding members of Yale MEChA (Movimiento Estudiantil Chican@ de Aztlán), the Chicano student group, and I was actively involved in their activities on campus during my sophomore year before I helped to co-found the Yale Asian American Students Association during the start of my junior year.[4] The agenda of activities and issues, which we pursued during Yale MEChA's first year, including admissions, a Chicano Studies class, a Chicano student conference, etc., was greatly influenced by the activities of the Black Student Alliance at Yale (BSAY), which had formed the year before. And when Yale AASA began to get organized in Fall 1969, we turned to Yale MEChA for a blueprint of initial goals and activities. In this manner, the three groups pursued similar goals and achieved success because they worked together and built strong bonds of collaboration, friendship, and support. I have sought to practice this compelling approach in academia, politics, and my daily life.

Instead of enrolling at UCLA, I attended Yale. I was the first of what would subsequently be many Roosevelt graduates to attend Yale. Although I had good grades, test scores, and extracurricular achievements, I have come to believe that my acceptance was due to a number of fortuitous and significant events. First, during the summer between my tenth and eleventh grades, Los Angeles experienced the largest and costliest urban riot during the Civil Rights era. During the Watts Riots, hundreds of businesses were burned and over forty people lost their lives during a six-day period in August 1965 in South Los Angeles. I believe this uprising, along with the growing momentum of the Civil Rights Movement and the increasing militancy of Black revolutionaries, began to have an impact on a number of institutions across the nation, including colleges and universities. Yale had just hired a young and progressive new dean of admissions, R. Inslee "Inky" Clark, who wanted to change the makeup of the Yale student body by attracting more students from schools, which traditionally had not sent students to the university, especially public high schools. At the same time, Roosevelt had an art teacher and counselor named Carmen Terrazas, a Mexican American who had graduated from the school many years before, who felt that Roosevelt students should have the same opportunities as students from private and suburban schools in attending a range of colleges. She probably was the first college adviser at any Los Angeles public high school and reached out to colleges across the country to come to Roosevelt to meet and recruit her students. It was the joining of the outreach efforts by both Terrazas and Yale in the post-Watts Riots civil rights era that resulted in Yale coming to Roosevelt to recruit students for the first time ever when I was a senior. And so it took far more than good grades and test scores for me to get to Yale. Without being overly dramatic, I think it took a righteous national social justice movement, an unprecedented urban rebellion, historic changes in laws, policies, and institutional practices—as well as the commitment of good people—for me to enter Yale.

If UCLA was a predominantly White institution in Fall 1967 with nearly ninety percent of its students being White, then what would you call Yale, which was nearly ninety-nine percent White? My freshman class was touted as the "brightest and most diverse" entering class in the college's history, going all the way back to its founding in 1701, because of the extensive outreach efforts and new admissions priorities of the new and progressive dean of admissions. There were one thousand men (Yale was all-male until my junior year), of which ten were Black, ten were Asian American, one was Pacific Islander, one was Chicano, three were Puerto Rican, and none were Native American. The remaining 975 freshmen out of 1,000 were White. Yale and Roosevelt could not be more different. However, for a number of reasons, I believed that I made the right choice in going to Yale. I loved the college, had many friends, enjoyed being on the East Coast, and had interesting professors and classes. Every day seemed like a wonderful new adventure.

I have come to believe that there were several pivotal experiences that I had during my undergraduate years that fueled and inspired my lifelong interest in Asian American Studies and Ethnic Studies, and in issues of social justice. One incident occurred a few months after I started Yale on December 7, 1967, twenty-six years after Japan bombed Pearl Harbor, which led to the entry of the U.S. into World War II. While growing up, December 7 was a day I always dreaded. It seemed like there was always at least one teacher—a history teacher, a PE teacher, it did not matter—who would ask the class, "Do you know what important event happened on this day?" The students in the class would raise their hands, a few of them would glance at the Japanese American students in the room, and one would usually answer, "This was the day the Japanese bombed Pearl Harbor." I always felt uncomfortable, even though I knew I did not have anything to do with it.

December 7 arrived during my freshman year and I wondered whether anything would happen. I attended all of my classes and none of the professors brought it up, and I went to my meals and none of my classmates made reference to it. I was relieved and thought that Yale, a place with lots of smart and socially aware people, was different. After dinner, I settled in my room and studied. At exactly 9:00 p.m., without warning, it seemed like everyone in my dorm in McClellan Hall came to my room, started to pelt me with water balloons, and loudly chanted, "Bomb Pearl Harbor! Bomb Pearl Harbor! Bomb Pearl Harbor!" While I was dripping wet and completely stunned by what was happening, a fellow student, who had been the national high school debate champ the year before, came up to me and recited by memory President Franklin Delano Roosevelt's "A date which will live in infamy" declaration of war speech. The chanting continued as if we were at a football game. Soon after, everyone left and I was left with cleaning up my room. I really did not know how I should respond. Should I just go along with my classmates, who thought it was a prank and laugh it off like they did, or should I be upset because I was being linked by ancestry to a horrendous tragedy in U.S. history that occurred many years before and that my classmates were not sensitive to or perhaps aware of what was done to my parents and other Japanese Americans during the war?

This incident weighed on me for several days of serious introspection. I did not seek guidance from my freshman counselor, college dean, or anyone. I did not think any of them would understand. I came to realize that as much as I was hurt by what had happened I really knew very little about the wartime incarceration of Japanese Americans. My parents had told me about the names of the concentration camps where they were held, but very little else. Like many other Japanese Americans who had survived the concentration camp experience, they remained stoically silent, traumatized and cautious for decades. Most did not share their memories with their children, I suspect, because their wartime treatment was so painful, disastrous and unjustified, and they did not want their children to have a discouraging outlook about their future in American society. In my K-12 schooling, I learned about Pearl Harbor, but I never learned anything about the forced incarceration. I decided that I should try to learn about what happened to my parents and went to Yale's Sterling Library, where I checked out a book titled, *Prejudice, War and the Constitution*. Written by three UC Berkeley law professors, it provided a historical and legal analysis of the decision to imprison the Japanese Americans. This was the first book I had ever read on Japanese Americans or Asian Americans.

Over the years, I have come to believe that this incident is at the core of many of my fundamental goals in teaching Asian American Studies and Ethnic Studies. For example, I think many students like me take these courses because they want to learn about the historical and current experiences of their own ethnic and racial groups, as well as those of other groups. K-12 textbooks and curricula now contain more multiethnic and multiracial content than when I was going to school, but many college students want to learn more. I also think it is important to recognize that these classes may serve to enhance awareness of self and others, especially in grappling with very complex issues of ethnic and racial identity, and the continuing significance and challenges of race in an increasingly diverse society and interconnected world. Some students, in turn, will be inspired as I was to become scholars and teachers of Ethnic Studies and affiliated fields, while others will embrace Yale's and other colleges' calls to public service and use their knowledge in becoming civil rights advocates, elected officials, social services workers, as well as leaders in community and volunteer organizations. And finally, the Pearl Harbor incident illustrates that teaching the Asian American experience is not just for the benefit of Asian Americans. We should try to share as much of the Asian American experience with as many others on our campuses and with the general public. There is so much that they can learn, just as I have gained invaluable and oftentimes alternative insights and viewpoints about American life and about myself from taking classes on and reading about African Americans, Chicanos, Native Americans, American Jews, Italian Americans and others.

At Yale during my undergraduate career, there was a very popular and large class on U.S. history, covering the period up to World War II, that was taught by a preeminent historian, Sterling Professor John Blum, who was known as a magnificent lecturer. Most students took this class during their sophomore year. On the final day of his class, he would always give a lecture on the wartime incarceration of Japanese Americans: why it was unconstitutional, unnecessary, and wrong, and why he hoped that his Yale students, many of whom would occupy significant positions of power during their adult lives, should never repeat this tragic mistake. I remember some of my dorm friends who had thrown water balloons at me during my freshman year, coming up to me after Prof. Blum's last class during our sophomore year and apologizing for what they had done and asking me questions to learn more about what my parents and other Japanese Americans had endured. Every year, I knew exactly when Prof. Blum delivered this lecture. There were always students who came up to me to learn more about the Japanese American wartime experience and more generally about Asian Americans. It is my hope that years later during their adult lives, when national crises like 9/11 occur, that they remember and apply or share the lessons that Prof. Blum tried to teach them.

III. An Unforeseen Future of Change and Growth: Asian Americans, Asian American Studies, and Yale

I have now been retired for five years. Looking back, I am very grateful to have had the opportunity to attend Yale for my undergraduate education and for igniting my interest in doing original research in Asian American Studies and Political Science; to have had the opportunity to go to that red school up north for my doctorate in Political Science; and to have spent thirty-five years as a professor and research center director of Asian American Studies at UCLA, my only employer in life. I am glad that when I was a Yale senior, I wanted to help develop Asian American Studies and Ethnic Studies, and to participate in the building of organizations and communities of color, although it definitely was not evident what the future would hold. In retrospect, I feel very fortunate to have observed, analyzed, shared and contributed to all that has unfolded for Asian Americans and Asian American Studies, as well as for Ethnic Studies and communities of color, in the years since I was an undergraduate.

For example, I witnessed the extraordinary demographic transformation that the Asian American population underwent in growing from a relatively small, regionally situated West Coast group of 1.5 million in 1970, to a national population twice its size of 3.5 million in 1980, as a result of significant changes in U.S. immigration policies. To my surprise, the population kept growing. I definitely could not have imagined that the Asian American population today would reach 18 million. The Census Bureau projects that there will be 40 million Asian Americans in 2040—nearly ten percent of the nation's population—would have seemed utterly absurd when I was an undergraduate.

I have seen Hawai'i, which was the state with the most Asian Americans in 1970, dropping below California in 1980, and now occupying the fifth spot after California, New York, Texas, and New Jersey in terms of its number of Asian Americans.

I have seen Japanese Americans, who were the largest Asian American group in 1970 with nearly forty percent of all Asian Americans, also falling down the population ladder and now being the sixth largest group after Chinese, Filipino, Asian Indian, Vietnamese and Korean Americans.

I have marveled at how the Asian American population from 1970 to 1980 completely changed from a majority U.S.-born group to a majority foreign-born population, which remains the case to this date.

I have also seen how the then controversial new concept and term of self-determination from the late 1960s, "Asian American," which was proposed to symbolize the interrelated histories of oppression and exploitation experienced by all Asian groups in U.S. society and the advantages of working together in unity to achieve common goals rather than going separate ethnic ways, has been increasingly embraced and pursued by more and more sectors of the Asian American population. There are now thousands of organizations and programs across the nation, which carry the name "Asian American."

I recall one of my first visits to New York City when I was a freshman and walking many blocks before I saw another Asian. These days, it would be difficult to avoid seeing another Asian since there are over a million of them in the city.

I remember in 1976 when I first compiled a list of Asian American elected officials for the publication we now call the *National Asian Pacific American Political Almanac,* that there were so few elected officials—and practically all were from the four West Coast states of Hawai'i, California, Washington, and Oregon—that I could literally type, xerox, and staple the list. When we released our fifteenth edition last year, after Asian Americans had substantially enhanced their political infrastructure of voters, candidates, donors, and political groups, there were four thousand Asian American elected and major appointed officials in thirty-eight different states.

And, of course, all of these changes brings to mind another familiar adage, "the more things change, the more they remain the same," be it the persistence of racial and ethnic slurs like "Chink," "Jap," and "Flip," or the amazing longevity and ramifications of the model minority stereotype that was first proposed in the 1960s.

However, with great pride, I also have witnessed the amazing, collective development and maturation of Asian American Studies during the past forty-five years. Classes are now taught at over two hundred colleges and universities. Many have undergraduate majors, minors, and concentrations. There are graduate programs, and hopefully soon, UCLA will be offering the nation's first Ph.D. in Asian American Studies. There are also a number of universities that have firmly supported and institutionalized Asian American Studies by establishing departments and research centers. Outside of higher education there are now a number of museums, theater groups, community-based organizations, civil rights groups, and film and literary associations that contribute to and benefit from Asian American Studies.

Asian American Studies has also grown substantially in terms of its scholarship and creative contributions. As the speakers will share at today's conference, there has been a tremendous growth in the research literature from historical works to literary studies, and from social science inquiries to those of professional school disciplines like law, education, and public health. After forty-five years, *Amerasia Journal* has published over thirty thousand pages of scholarship. And the number of articles published in other journals, as well as the thousands of books, policy reports, novels and films on Asian Americans can now occupy a significant section of a college library. Indeed, at one time Asian Americans were stereotyped as being only good in math and not so good in writing and verbal skills. And yet, over the past forty-five years, the field of Asian American literature—the creative writers, scholars, and critics—has been one of the most vibrant, productive, and influential areas within Asian American Studies, as well as contemporary U.S. literature.

Yale has played an important role in the development of Asian American Studies. Since 1970, when it offered its first class, Yale has offered one and sometimes several undergraduate classes each year, usually at the insistence of generations of Yale AASA members, which has helped to inspire students and faculty at other colleges, especially those on the East Coast, to seek and justify classes at their own institutions. Until 1995, when Prof. Brian Hayashi was appointed to a tenure track position in American Studies and History, Yale relied on part-time adjunct lecturers to teach these classes. Prof. Hayashi, a Ph.D. graduate of UCLA's history department, who had been long active with the UCLA Asian American Studies Center, taught several Asian American Studies classes annually and helped to design and establish the Ethnicity, Race and Migration undergraduate program while he was at Yale. After Prof. Hayashi left Yale for Kyoto University, the university hired two assistant professors to teach Asian American Studies classes. Prof. Mary Lui was one of those new hires and she subsequently became Yale's first tenured, and also the first full professor, who specializes in Asian American Studies. She has done a remarkable job. However, she remains as the only full-time professor in Asian American Studies at Yale. In contrast, UCLA, which started its many Asian American Studies efforts a year before Yale in 1969, has the largest and most renowned faculty in Asian American Studies in the nation. It has nearly sixty tenured professors in over twenty-five departments across UCLA from comparative literature to law, who teach and do research on Asian Americans and are affiliated with the Asian American Studies Center. UCLA also has a Department of Asian American Studies, of which thirty of the sixty tenured faculty are members, who offer over seventy undergraduate and graduate classes annually to support its degree programs.

Yale has not devoted sufficient resources to build Asian American Studies. However, the commitment and sacrifices of the few Asian American Studies specialists on the faculty and among graduate students over the past forty-five years, as well as other professors from departments across the university who have mentored and supervised interested undergraduates and graduate students with their senior theses and doctoral dissertations, has actually led to Yale producing a notable number of scholars for the field of Asian American Studies, as well as writers and other creative contributors for Asian America. Indeed, after UCLA and UC Berkeley, the top two producers, there may arguably be more Asian American Studies scholars who did their undergraduate and/or graduate work at Yale than any other university. Several will be speaking on panels today (Prof. Ju Yon Kim, Harvard; Prof. Janelle Wong, University of Maryland; Prof. Vijay Iyer, Harvard). Others include Prof. David Yoo, who succeeded me as director of the UCLA Asian American Studies Center, and Prof. Hiroshi Motomura of UCLA Law; Prof. Madeline Hsu, who headed the University of Texas at Austin Center for Asian American Studies; Prof. Thomas Fujita-Rony, former chair of the Asian American Studies Program, and Prof. Susie Woo of California State University Fullerton; Prof. Adria Imada of UC San Diego; Prof. Linus Yamane of the Claremont Colleges; Prof. Sandhya Shukla, University of Virginia; Prof. Adrienne Lo, University of Illinois; Prof. Claire Kim and Dorothy Fujita-Rony of UC Irvine, among many others.

I hope that Yale makes Asian American Studies a higher institutional priority in the future. Like other universities, which have succeeded in building viable programs, it will probably take the concerted efforts of students, faculty, alumni, administrators, donors and other interested leaders and individuals to advocate for this and to make it happen. Although I suspect I will not be around forty-five years from now when there may be a celebration of the ninetieth anniversary of the first Asian American Studies class at Yale, I hope we will look back on this day and this conference (and hopefully in less time than forty-five years) as a major milestone in the long-advocated growth and anchoring of Asian American Studies at Yale. I believe a first-rate Asian American Studies program would be a bright shining jewel in Yale's scholarly treasure chest.

Notes

1   Betty Lee Sung, author of *Mountain of Gold* (1967), taught the first Asian American Studies class at City College of New York in 1970.

2   Aside from the fifty-nine Yale undergraduates, there were three graduate students at Yale who played significant roles in the early development of Yale AASA: Glenn Omatsu, a graduate student in psychology; Peter Choy, a law student, who had graduated from Yale College; and Rocky Chin, a graduate student in urban planning.

3   The petition, with over one thousand signatures, was introduced into the Congressional Record by U.S. Senator Spark Matsunaga (D-HI), one of the leaders who spearheaded the campaign to successfully repeal Title II of the McCarran Act.

4   Glenn Omatsu played a major role in my involvement in Asian American Studies and the Asian American Movement. I met Glenn during the summer of 1969 when a mutual friend, Alan Kumamoto of the Japanese American Citizens League in Los Angeles, asked me to meet and answer questions that Glenn might have about Yale, where he would be starting the graduate program in social psychology in Fall 1969. When Glenn and I met, he asked me whether I was involved in any activities or clubs at Yale. I told him I was active with Yale MEChA and was recruiting Chicano students for Yale in Los Angeles during the summer. Glenn asked me, "Are the Asian American students organized at Yale?" I remember pausing a little before answering him, "Well, that's an interesting idea. No, but I will help to do that when we get back to Yale." Glenn then told me about his involvement with Asian American and Third World student activism at UC Santa Cruz, his undergraduate college. Glenn played a major role in co-founding Yale AASA when we returned to the campus in the fall. He also became very well known and influential among Asian American activists in New York City and nationally. He subsequently left Yale after a year and became the English editor for a Japanese American newspaper in San Francisco. We would join up again when he became associate editor of *Amerasia Journal* at the UCLA Asian American Studies Center.

Author

Don T. Nakanishi, Ph.D. (1949-2016), was Director Emeritus of the UCLA Asian American Studies Center, the largest and most renowned research and teaching institute in Asian American Studies in the nation, and Professor Emeritus of UCLA's departments of Asian American Studies and Education. Prior to his retirement from UCLA in 2009 after a thirty-five year professorial career at the university (and the last twenty years also as Center Director), he provided leadership and vision for the national development of the fields of Asian American Studies and Race and Ethnic Relations Scholarship for four decades.

Why Asian Pacific Americans
Need Liberatory Education More Than Ever

PHIL TAJITSU NASH

Antidotes to "Alternative Facts"

ON JANUARY 22, 2017, as Donald Trump's new administration was getting started in Washington, D.C., Presidential Advisor Kellyanne Conway defended a demonstrably false statement about the size of the Trump inauguration crowd that had been made previously by then-White House Press Secretary Sean Spicer. Speaking on the nationally broadcasted *Meet the Press* television program, Conway said that Spicer had used "alternative facts."[1] After sharp criticism from all over the global community, including members of the business community,[2] Conway later modified her words by stating that "alternative facts" were "additional facts and alternative information."[3]

Throughout the first months of the Trump presidency, Donald Trump and members of his administration have continued to stretch the truth in ways that one *Washington Post* columnist proclaimed as heralding an "alternative facts" era in American history.[4] A *Cleveland Plain Dealer* columnist lamented that, "… in Trump world, you have to run just to stand still to understand what is true and what is not. They say the truth eventually catches up with you, but at this point it's still a race to see how long the public and dogged reporters will have the energy to keep up at this pace."[5]

Rather than waiting for the truth to catch up to us, searching for some new "Geiger Counter of Truth," or creating a new training course for "How to Discern the Truth from Government Misinformation,"[6] we may want to refer back to the early days of Asian Pacific American (APA) Studies for some guidance. Designing courses that help students develop tools to critically analyze the world around them—including the words of their governmental leaders—vaccinates them against becoming passive pawns or disempowered bystanders in building a more "just, verdant, and peaceful world."[7]

Twenty-three years ago, Glenn Omatsu published "The 'Four Prisons' and the Movements of Liberation" as a chapter in Karin Aguilar-San Juan's 1994 book, *The State of Asian America: Activism and Resistance in the 1990s*.[8] Building on the work of Iranian philosopher Ali Shariati, Professor Omatsu helped me to understand the origins of APA Studies in the 1960s and '70s, and chart a way forward into the '90s and beyond. Omatsu/Shariati's analysis combined history, politics, science, and psychology to define four "prisons" that hold us back from full liberation as individuals and as a society.

> First is the prison imposed on us by [nature] and geography; from this confinement we can escape only by gaining knowledge of science and technology. Second is the prison of history; our freedom comes when we understand how historical forces operate. The third prison is our society's social and class structure; from this prison, only a revolutionary ideology can provide the way to liberation. The final prison is the self. Each of us is composed of good and bad elements, and we must each choose between them.[9]

I had been teaching APA Studies courses for ten years before the Omatsu article was published. After reading the Omatsu/Shariati framework, however, I realized that I had to more explicitly craft the course activities and outcomes so that liberation from the "Four Prisons" was not just a by-product, but a goal.

This article will start with a description of how my teaching of Asian Pacific American history, law, and public policy classes has evolved, with the first section focused on content and second section on pedagogy. The third section will describe the current state of my thinking, which is manifested in the Asian Pacific American Public Policy class that I am currently teaching at the University of Maryland. The final sections will provide ideas for others planning to follow Omatsu's liberatory model in their Asian Pacific American Studies classes, and a few ideas for classes that could be taught using the model.

While there is no guarantee that the proponents of "alternative reality" can be stopped, given their control on the levers of power at this time, liberatory education gives us both hope and provides concrete tools that build a better world, one student at a time.

I. Learning the Course Content

I got my start in teaching out of necessity. I was working as a staff attorney at the Asian American Legal Defense and Education Fund (AALDEF)[10] in New York City in the early 1980s, and public interest law didn't pay much. I applied for and received a Charles H. Revson Fellowship so that I could teach "Asian Americans and the Law" part-time at the Urban Legal Studies Program at City College of New York/CUNY, while continuing my full-time work at AALDEF.

While preparing to teach for the first time, I read many cases related to Asian immigrants in the fields of immigration, civil rights, employment, and education.[11] What was striking to me, as someone who had grown up outside of any APA community in the white suburbs of northern New Jersey, was the unrelenting tale of discrimination, violence, and sorrow that was captured in those cases. Raw racism was evident in nineteenth century cases forbidding Chinese testimony in California courtrooms. Prohibitions on Japanese immigrant land ownership were directed first at the Issei (first generation) immigrants and then at their Nisei (second generation) children, who were American citizens by birth on American soil. Cases describing every immigrant's attempt to come to these shores had unwritten back stories about his wife and kin—stories no doubt laden with separation, loneliness and loss. In the pre-Internet era, waving goodbye at the pier in Hong Kong or Yokohama often meant the start of separate lives, with kinship bonds that were unstrung and never rewoven.

I prepared a syllabus that focused on key topics in APA legal history, such as the Chinese Exclusion Act and other immigration and naturalization laws, alien land laws, education-related discrimination, employment-related discrimination, and the Japanese American internment and redress movement. Building on concepts that had been developed by APA legal services groups such as AALDEF and law students in the nascent National Asian Pacific American Law Student Association (NAPALSA),[12] I decided that the theme of the course was going to be that APAs were not just victims, but that we had fought back and, in the process, helped to vindicate civil rights and liberties for all. Each case was going to be studied in its social context, looking at APA community history and broader societal history, followed by the facts of that particular case.

Unfortunately, when I started teaching the class, I realized that I had several major burdens to overcome. While the class might have been appropriate for law students, reading several law cases each week, along with background reading for context, was too much for undergraduate students. I also found that there were no APAs enrolled in the class. And none of the white, Latino or African American students had an adequate understanding of the APA experience to allow them to tie together the cases, the context, and the concepts.

Sitting at my desk the night after my first class session, I decided to revamp the syllabus. I decided to require every student to talk to any APA that they knew, whether a restaurant owner, green grocer, or fellow student at City College (which, at the time, was located in a largely African American neighborhood at 145th Street in Manhattan). I also decided to ask them to talk to their own parents and friends to hear their impressions of APAs in their community.

The second class labored through the Chinese Exclusion Act and other immigration cases, and then I gave the students their revised assignment to talk to some APAs. Some said that they did not know any APAs well enough to ask such personal questions, but by the end of the class everyone knew what they were supposed to do.

When they returned for the third class, everything had changed. Abstract notions of immigration restrictions gave way to actual stories of mistreatment during immigration proceedings. When given permission to ask APA classmates about their lives, some class members had been invited to cramped immigrant apartments, where ignorance was replaced by knowledge of immigrant realities and a hot cup of tea.

While continuing to teach at City College, I wrote about the Japanese American redress movement for the *Yale Law Journal*,[13] which brought my City College course to the attention of APA students at Yale. Don Nakanishi and other pioneers of the APA Studies movement had studied at Yale over a decade before, but the APA History class they had pioneered had not been institutionalized. Therefore, during the Spring 1985 semester, I worked with Yale APA undergrads to modify my "APAs and the Law" class into an "APA History" class.

Learning from my experiences at City College, my new syllabus included time for guest speakers from each of the major APA communities to address the class. This strategy had the added advantage of allowing me, as someone who had never had the benefit of studying APA History in school, to sit in the back of the classroom and take notes alongside my students.

I had planned for speakers who were Chinese American, Japanese American, Filipino American, and Korean American, as these were the APA groups I was most familiar with in my community work. When learning that an Indian American student was enrolled in the class, however, I quickly invited Dr. Shamita Das-Dasgupta, a well-known psychology professor from New Jersey. When I found out that one of the students was openly gay, I invited a Filipino American gay activist from New York City to speak to the class.

Aside from surveying the APA community one national subgroup at a time, my Yale syllabus also addressed cross-group concepts such as the status of APA women. Meanwhile, because the students had little or no contact with the broader APA community, but were interested in internships and post-graduation work opportunities, a lot of their education about the APA community came during discussions before and after class.

II. The Importance of Pedagogy

So far, my teaching of APA topics had grown my knowledge of the subject matter, but my attention to pedagogy, the "how" as opposed to the "what" or "why" of teaching, had been sporadic. I had used oral histories out of necessity, but had not fully integrated them into the syllabus or the subject matter of the class.

When I started teaching traditional law topics at the CUNY School of Law in the late 1980s, however, I was introduced to Paulo Freire, a Brazilian educator whose book, *Pedagogy of the Oppressed,*[14] had spawned a global movement. This movement urged teachers at all levels of schooling to look at how they were teaching as much as what they were teaching. The goal was not to treat the students as piggy banks to be filled with coins of information that could be cashed out on a final exam. The goal was to make the subject matter relevant to the students by helping them to see themselves and their families in the context of history. Once they had the consciousness and motivation to learn more, students could be equipped with the analytical skills to understand their world, and the reading and writing skills to participate in struggles to remove injustice and inequality from their world.

In applying Freire's methods to the teaching of APA history, I realized that I had a powerful set of new tools. Instead of seeing APAs and other minorities as marginal actors in a history dominated by presidents, kings, judges, and generals, APA history should be viewed, as author/scholar Gary Okihiro so eloquently stated it, as being the mainstream, not the margin. In fact, as Okihiro pointed out in *Margins and Mainstreams*[15] (first published in 1994), the struggles of APAs, women, gays, and other minorities to vindicate their rights in the face of longstanding discrimination have been essential to the strengthening of civil rights and civil liberties for all in this country.

After two years spent as founding executive director of the Asian American Justice Center[16] in Washington, D.C., I was invited to the University of Maryland[17] to teach APA History. My new course syllabus and my new approach to teaching built on my experiences advocating for human rights for APAs, as well as Freire-inspired ideas about pedagogy. Once again, however, the syllabus and the content had to be modified to fit the students who were enrolled in the class.

Vietnamese Americans were now a large part of the student body, and their history as refugees in the 1980s and '90s had to be incorporated. Many more students were mixed-race (multiracial) or involved in cross-racial relationships, so that topic had to be addressed as well. Meanwhile, affirmative action, anti-Asian violence, transnational adoption, racial profiling, and the need to establish a formalized APA Studies program on campus, all came up as discussion topics.

Sensing a need to bring current events more explicitly into the course, I decided to give up teaching the APA History class and created a new class called "Asian Pacific American Public Policy." Instead of teaching all of APA history, I now was able to choose a few defining events and use them as teaching devices. Instead of using oral history as a tool for setting up discussion about history, I now was able to make collecting oral histories one of the objects of the course and a lesson to the students about their role as history creators and preservers. Instead of being stuck in the classroom, struggling to capture the history of millions of people and dozens of communities in fifteen weeks, I was free to take my students out into the community to show them history in the making.

III. Public Policy: A Liberatory Endeavor

The content studied in my APA Public Policy class has changed each time it has been taught, depending on who is in the class and which issues are currently affecting the APA community. However, the fundamentals of the class have remained fairly constant. The backbone of the class is the Japanese American incarceration experience during World War II and the community's struggle to gain redress thereafter. However, this topic does not come up in the first class at all.

Instead, the class begins with questions. What is public policy? Who makes it? What are the rules controlling your life right now? How can you change them?

I start with a hypothetical situation. I declare that I am going to leave class that night and drive 100 mph across campus, down a nearby road, and onto the highway to my house. Is that okay with everyone? Students note that this would be unsafe and that I might hurt someone, so I challenge them: "I don't care. It's my car and my life. I can drive 100 mph if I want to."

Soon, we are exploring who makes rules, why rules are made, how they are enforced, and the penalties that are imposed for breaking those rules. The chalkboard fills with courts, legislatures, executives, and administrative bodies. Federal jurisdiction over federal highways is distinguished from university jurisdiction over university roads. Noise complaints in the dorm have to go through a university-based process before they can be heard in a court.

Next, we watch videos of community activist Franklin Fung Chow[18] and Congressman Dalip Singh Saund.[19] Small groups discuss how each made an impact on the APA community. As a class, we discuss how each affected public policy in their own way.

Finally, we make explicit the unwritten rules we have been living under since the class began. Who has spoken? How can we create a space where all are free to speak? How can we develop tools to participate in public policy issues affecting our own lives?

In the second class, APA history and the Japanese American incarceration dominate the class. However, instead of treating those histories as derived from an immutable canon, the notion of historiography is introduced by focusing on Michi Weglyn[20] and her brave efforts to research, write, and publish *Years of Infamy*.[21] Without formal training as a lawyer, historian or researcher, Weglyn proved that there was no military necessity for the incarceration experience, and galvanized the movement for redress that led to a successful resolution in the courts and in Congress in the 1980s.

Students learn that they, too, can do the seemingly impossible to surmount the odds that were stacked against Michi every step of the way. They also look at the way that Michi used her training in the visual arts to include pictures, maps, and copies of declassified documents, which were essential in making the moral, as well as intellectual, case for Japanese American redress.

In the next few classes, students view the incarceration and redress movements through the lenses of law, legislation, executive orders, and media actions. How did media shape the incarceration and redress movement? How did redress advocates use the courts, Congress, and other venues for redress? Which strategies worked? Which could have been improved?

During the legislation discussion, students research any issue of interest to them and write a letter to their local congressmember[22] to take a stand on that issue. No one is graded on their position, but each is graded on the effectiveness of their advocacy. Several students remarked with wonder that they never expected to get a reply letter, but when it appeared, they realized that their voice had been heard and that they had played a part in some issue on the Congressional docket.

While all of this was going on, students learned the rudiments of conducting oral histories, and were assigned elders in the local APA community to interview. This year's project focused on APA federal employees, so questions focused on the work that the interviewees had done as federal workers.

Each interview was done by two students at the interviewee's home, and took about an hour. Camera equipment was available from the school, but personal equipment could be used as well. Each team had to split up the tasks of interviewing, editing a fifteen-minute excerpt, creating a transcript, and storing the finished products at the APA Studies office. Aside from technical skills, each team was required to bring an *omiyage* (small gift of flowers or candy), use professional consent forms, and write a formal thank you using a card and postage stamp. While some students did not understand this formality at first, several appreciated that they had a gift in hand when their interviewees served them food and tea, and everyone understood that the pre-Internet generation still appreciates a snail-mail card for important occasions. Cultural competence was one of the sub-themes of the class, and learning to relate to someone of another generation and background was essential in every interview.

Two field trips reinforced other subthemes of the class. A visit to the Smithsonian Institution[23] to look at barbed wire, a battered suitcase, silverware, carved objects, and other items from the Japanese American internment collection showed how history is being preserved, even if the meaning of that history is sometimes contested. Visiting the local Chinatown after a discussion of current redevelopment proposals forced students to see that the issues they were studying were still affecting living people and communities.

In some prior semesters, respect for lesbian, gay, bisexual and transgender (LGBT) people and their public policy skills have been fostered by going to the state capital in Annapolis and observing their struggle for marriage equality. While students were never told to take a position or graded on their views on any issue, they were free to express support for the LGBT community at the Annapolis event.

In the last few weeks of the class, students presented their oral history excerpts and offered critiques of their own process and products. Other students were then expected to offer constructive criticism. At first, students were hesitant to say anything critical of their own work, concerned that their grades would be lowered. When they saw that honest critique was welcomed and that everyone was expected to discuss failures as well as successes, then the flow of conversation became freer. Two reflection memos, one describing the oral history process and the other the class as a whole, were other tools designed to get the students away from their fear of constructive criticism.

The last three classes moved the discussion from the specifics of the APA experience back out to public policy issues in the broader world. In the first class, a discussion of the similarities between the Japanese American redress movement and other successful and unsuccessful redress movements around the world generated a lot of insights.

In the second class, a simulation game called "Star Power"[24] forced students to confront unfair hierarchies, using processes that featured a stacked deck and a leader who was propagating an unfair advantage for one group. In this case, the teacher himself (me, in this situation), had placed extra gold chips in the envelopes of the Square team before the game began. This "inherited wealth" was only multiplied as the game began, and I role-played a cheerleader for the "tremendous skill and insight" of the Squares as they battled the Circles and Triangles. When I decided to let the Squares create the rules of the next round of the game, and they created onerous, draconian rules, the other players revolted, and the game was stopped. Students from all groups were amazed to think that I, the trusted authority figure, would stack the deck for one group of students. This, in turn, led to a lengthy discussion about why we trust, who we trust, and why we must remain vigilant and ask who has power—and why.

In the final class, we played another game called Barnga.[25] Students played cards at four tables, but, unbeknownst to them, each table had a different set of rules. No one was allowed to talk, so when players moved from table to table, everyone started to get angry when others thought that a certain card was trump, or that Aces were high (or low), and so forth. When the roof came off again, we had another productive discussion about how rules are made, how informal rules are passed between colleagues, how the lack of speaking replicated the barriers felt by some not fluent in English in the workplace, and how we must always be constructively critical of everyone, including authority figures.

IV. Every Class a Liberatory Class

Returning to Glenn Omatsu's "Four Prisons" analysis, I believe that the current manifestation of my APA Public Policy class finally meets the criteria of a class that can help to liberate students from those prisons. Students are liberated from the confines of their current time and place through interviewing and learning about the lives of APA elders. They are liberated from the confines of historical amnesia by understanding a key event in American history—the Japanese American internment and redress movement—and analyze the many forces at work over the years. They are liberated from this society's social and class structure through role play, through deep understanding of an oppressed minority community, and through the optimism that comes from understanding that societal improvements can and will come. Finally, they are given the tools to liberate themselves from their personal prisons through structured self-criticism, critical analysis of their world, and the confidence that comes from understanding that self-worth is developed through service to others. The concrete manifestation of that service is their oral histories, which are stored at the University of Maryland as a public expression of thanks to APA community elders, and a gift to future generations seeking to understand today's APA community.

Others seeking to develop liberatory APA Studies courses can do so in any field of endeavor as long as attention is given to both content and pedagogy. Developing critical insights in students and giving them the tools and confidence to address the challenges of their generation, whatever they may be, is the best possible outcome for any liberatory academic endeavor.

V. Liberatory Classes

While the tools described in this article can be adapted for use in any class at any grade level, here are four liberatory education classes that I would like to see. They can either be taught under the auspices of an Asian American Studies program, or co-taught with colleagues from Women's Studies, Latin American Studies, Native American Studies, or other departments.

Confronting "alternative realities" should be a concern for educators across the academy, including the sciences, technology, humanities, and social sciences. The more we can collaborate to make critical thinking skills a priority for every student, the better our chance of preventing a world where "alternative realities" become unchallenged realities.

Being Yuri Kochiyama: Strong APA Women and Their Impact on History

APA activist Yuri Kochiyama[26] is best remembered in popular culture as the arms holding up a dying Malcolm X in a *Life* magazine photo taken right after he was shot in 1965. Yet Yuri had lived forty eventful years before that fateful moment, and went on to play a central role in American civil rights history for another four decades. More than a backdrop to history, Yuri played an active part and inspired many others to get involved as well.

Using Yuri as the central thread for the class, students will review twentieth century civil rights history from the viewpoint of APA women, as they took strong stands on immigration, employment, education, criminal justice, redress for Japanese Americans, anti-Asian violence, women's rights, LGBT rights, and other key civil rights issues. The lives of Patsy Mink (Title IX advocate), Michi Weglyn (redress advocate), Grace Lee Boggs (civil rights advocate), Margaret Fung (AALDEF Executive Director), Helen Zia (Vincent Chin justice advocate), Angela Oh (Los Angeles civil rights attorney), Bhairavi Desai (NY Taxi Workers Alliance Executive Director), and other women can be woven into the class, depending on the students enrolled and the interests of the teacher. Oral histories of local APA women should be used to supplement the class, and build a repository of histories that can bring APA women's stories back to where they belong—in the mainstream of American history.

From Chinese Exclusion to DREAMer Exclusion

Framing the Trump administration's current efforts to exclude and demonize Muslims in the context of the Chinese Exclusion Act of 1882, and other major immigration law changes that followed, we can examine the ways immigrants have been both welcomed to and excluded from this country. These laws include the acts of 1924, 1943, 1956, 1965, 1980, 1986, the Development, Relief, and Education for Alien Minors (DREAM) Act, as well as executive orders and other Trump-era proposals.

Use oral histories to learn the stories of local APA immigrants, and bring their stories back to the classroom to enrich the discussion. Have students visit a courthouse to informally talk to attorneys and clients waiting to have their immigration-related hearings. Visit immigrant and refugee assistance organizations to hear the latest legal and social service issues, and go to local museums to critique the ways immigrant stories are portrayed.

Finally, as the main thread of the class, have the students follow the stories of APA and Latino classmates on their own or nearby campuses who are struggling to get an education despite not having legal residency in this country. Listen to how they are adapting to work, financial aid, housing, and other issues. Brainstorm as a class, how the students would like to use their collective energy to make a difference for their classmates.

APAs and Native North Americans

Many Native Americans care deeply about land rights, fishing rights, and other treaty-related rights, as well as issues such as cultural, spiritual, and language preservation. The principled defense of water, land, and culture at the Standing Rock Sioux Reservation against the incursions of oil and gas pipeline developers in 2016 inspired the world. However, the election of Donald Trump and his actions to remove development restrictions and empower pipeline developers have caused setbacks in 2017.[27]

As a community with a high percentage of immigrants, many APAs care about immigration and naturalization issues, but also care about employment, education, and discrimination-related issues. Except for Native Hawaiians,[28] who do not view themselves as immigrants to their Hawaiian homes, most APAs do not prioritize land as a major issue, in spite of struggles to defend the International Hotel in San Francisco,[29] Chinatown in New York City,[30] and other living ethnic enclaves—driving community organizing and awareness over the decades.

While these two communities seem to have little in common, a closer examination shows many overlapping histories and issues in common. For example, in Richard Drinnon's 1987 classic, *Keeper of Concentration Camps: Dillon S. Meyer and American Racism*,[31] a well-documented connection is made between the Wartime Relocation Authority (WRA) used to control Japanese Americans, and the Bureau of Indian Affairs (BIA) used to control Native Americans.

Using Drinnon's book as a starting point, the class will explore similarities and differences in the ways APAs and Native Americans have been treated in law and popular culture, and the ways they have struggled to define themselves and fight for their rights. Individuals such as Japanese Canadian environmentalist David Suzuki, Japanese American legislator Daniel Inouye, and other APAs who had major impacts on Native American communities, will be studied. The Native Hawaiian movement, which is an indigenous rights movement focused on language and cultural preservation as well as territorial, legal, and political rights, will be another focus of the class. Issues of inclusion, exclusion, and community empowerment will be explored, whenever possible, through the use of oral histories of local Native Americans and APAs.

APAs and Native South Americans

At the same time that APA peoples have been coming to and having an impact on the United States, other Asian-derived peoples have been going to and having an impact on Central and South America. The Cuban Chinese restaurants that have fed generations of New Yorkers with *juevos foo young* and other multicultural delicacies are just one manifestation of this phenomenon. For example, immigration restrictions in the United States have meant that many Asians have gone to Cuba or other countries to become naturalized, and then immigrate under that country's immigration quotas.

Spanish and Portuguese—as Latinate languages with vowels on the ends of many words—were easier for many Asians to learn than Germanic-based English. This, and other factors, has meant that Asian-derived peoples have been able to get involved in the public affairs of their Latin American countries much earlier, and more fully, than their cousins in the United States.[32]

Following many of the threads outlined in the "APAs and Native North Americans" class, explore similarities and differences in the ways APAs and Native South and Central Americans have been treated in law and popular culture, and the ways they have struggled to define themselves and fight for their rights.

VI. Coda

Liberation is not just a goal. To escape from the "Four Prisons," promoting liberation must be a conscious part of our daily lives.

Especially as the specter of a world dominated by leaders spewing "alternative facts" becomes more and more of a reality, each of our students needs liberatory education so that they can be a protagonist in their own life, moving deliberately each day from observation to analysis, to action, to reflection.

AAARI Conference Video (May 13, 2016): www.aaari.info/2016resurgent.htm

Notes

1   A good overview of the Conway statement and its fallout can be found at https://en.wikipedia.org/wiki/Alternative_facts

2   Markets aren't kind to alternative facts, noted an investing columnist in *Bloomberg News*. https://www.bloomberg.com/view/articles/2017-01-25/markets-aren-t-kind-to-alternative-facts

3   "Alternative facts," *Wikipedia*, https://en.wikipedia.org/w/index.php?title=Alternative_facts&oldid=793357725 (accessed August 15, 2017).

4   Cleve R. Wootson Jr., "The perfect meme for the 'alternative facts' era: #seanspicersays," *The Washington Post* (January 1, 2017) https://www.washingtonpost.com/news/the-fix/wp/2017/01/22/the-perfect-meme-for-the-alternative-facts-era-seanspicer-says/ (accessed August 15, 2017).

5   Kate Brannen, "Trump's Lies Are Round the World Before Truth Puts Its Pants On," *Yahoo! News* (March 27, 2017), https://www.yahoo.com/news/trump-lies-round-world-truth-162113287.html (accessed August 15, 2017).

6   In *Manufacturing Dissent: The Political Economy of the Mass Media* (New York: Pantheon Books, 1988), Edward Herman and Noam Chomsky reminded us many years ago about the dangers of accepting every word from the mass media as the truth. https://www.amazon.com/Manufacturing-Consent-Political-Economy-Media/dp/0375714499

7   This is the tag phrase repeated many times on public radio these days in support of the work of the MacArthur Foundation, but it also summarizes the idealism of this author and many around the world. https://www.macfound.org/about/

8   Glenn Omatsu, "'The Four Prisons' and the Movements of Liberation: Asian American Activism from the 1960s to the 1990s," Karin Aguilar-San Juan, *The State of Asian America: Activism and Resistance in the 1990s* (Boston: South End Press, 1994): 19–70.

9   *Ibid.*: 56

10   Asian American Legal Defense and Education Fund (AALDEF), http://www.aaldef.org/

11   A good starting place is Hyung-chan Kim's *Asian Americans and the Supreme Court: A Documentary History* (New York: Greenwood Press, 1992).

12   National Asian Pacific American Law Student Association, http://www.napalsa.com/

13   Philip Tajitsu Nash, "BOOK REVIEW: *Moving for Redress*," *Yale Law Journal* 94 (January 1985): 743.

14   Paulo Freire (Author), Myra Bergman Ramos (Translator), and Donaldo Macedo (Introduction), *Pedagogy of the Oppressed*, 30th Anniversary Edition (New York: Bloomsbury Academic, 2000)

15   Gary Y. Okihiro, *Margins and Mainstreams: Asians in American History and Culture* (Seattle: University of Washington Press, 2014).

16   Asian Americans Advancing Justice (formerly the National Asian Pacific American Legal Consortium), http://www.advancingjustice-aajc.org/

17   University of Maryland Asian American Studies Program, http://www.aast.umd.edu/

18   Videos of Franklin Fung Chow, http://www.festival.si.edu/2010/franklin-fung-chow-chinese-cooking-techniques/. See also http://vimeo.com/63628433

19   Videos of Rep. Dalip Singh Saund, http://www.saund.org/dalipsaund/

20   Michi Weglyn, http://www.michiweglyn.com/

21   Michi Nishiura Weglyn (Author), James A. Michener (Introduction), *Years of Infamy: The Untold Story of America's Concentration Camps* Updated Edition (University of Washington Press, 1996).

22   U.S. Congress, https://www.congress.gov/

23   Smithsonian Asian Pacific American Center, http://smithsonianapa.org/

24   Simulation Training Systems, http://www.stsintl.net/schools-and-charities/products/starpower/

25 Sivasailam "Thagi" Thiagarajan with Raja Thiagarajan, *Barnga: A Simulation Game on Cultural Clashes, 25th Anniversary Edition* (Boston: Nicholas Brealey Publishing, 2006).

26 Yuri Kochiyama, *Passing It On* (Los Angeles: UCLA Asian American Studies Center Press, 2004).

27 Stand With Standing Rock, http://standwithstandingrock.net

28 Julia Carrie Wong, "Mark Zuckerberg drops lawsuits to force hundreds of Hawaiians to sell him land," *The Guardian* (January 27, 2017), https://www.theguardian.com/us-news/2017/jan/27/mark-zuckerberg-drops-hawaii-land-lawsuits (accessed August 15, 2017).

29 "International Hotel (San Francisco)," *Wikipedia*, https://en.wikipedia.org/w/index.php?title=International_Hotel_(San_Francisco)&oldid=795354582 (accessed August 15, 2017).

30 Chinatown Art Brigade, http://www.chinatownartbrigade.org/about-the-brigade

31 Richard Drinnon, *Keeper of Concentration Camps: Dillon S. Myer and American Racism* (Oakland, CA: University of California Press, 1989).

32 See, for example, the history of three Cuban Chinese generals who shaped the Cuban revolution or the ascent (and downfall) of President Alberto Fujimori in Peru. https://www.amazon.com/History-Still-Being-Written-Chinese-Cuban/dp/0873489780 and https://en.wikipedia.org/wiki/Alberto_Fujimori

Author

Phil Tajitsu Nash has served as the Founding Executive Director of the Asian American Justice Center (AAJC), Staff Attorney at the Asian American Legal Defense and Education Fund (AALDEF), Curator for the 2010 Smithsonian Folklife Festival's Asian Pacific American Program, and columnist for the *N.Y. Nichibei* and *Asian Week* newspapers. Nash has taught law, urban studies, and APA history, art, oral history, and public policy classes at UMCP, Yale, NYU, The City College of New York, and CUNY and Georgetown law schools. He is a strong believer in experiential education, and incorporates oral histories, community outreach, field trips, and group-based activities into each of his classes.

Asian Americans at The City University of New York
The Current Outlook

JOYCE O. MOY

Introduction

THERE IS A REMARKABLE LACK OF ASIAN PACIFIC AMERICANS (APAs)[1] at all levels of leadership within The City University of New York and its constituent colleges. While at the lower rungs of leadership, there are a handful of APAs, the positions are not aligned to those that influence academic programming or policies. Title and rank alone is not what is important; what matters is whether the positions allow a meaningful voice on academic programming, policy, and content, and contributes different perspectives on the direction of the University. It is also important that the positions held are on a trajectory along a career path to leadership at the University.

The City University of New York (CUNY)

The City University of New York is comprised of twenty-four campuses across the five boroughs of New York City.

CUNY is "... the nation's largest urban public university," with "... 1,400 academic programs, 200 majors leading to associate and baccalaureate degrees, and 800 graduate degree programs. With over a half million students enrolled in these programs and continuing education classes, the University offers learning opportunities at every level, from certificate courses to the Ph.D., in a single integrated system."[2]

The Asian American and Asian Research Institute (AAARI) issued a report in 2016, *Asian American Leadership at CUNY and in Higher Education* (http://aaari.info/notes/16-05-09CAALIReport.pdf), highlighting the absence of APAs in leadership positions across the twenty-four campuses at CUNY. The report was the work of the CUNY Asian American Leadership Initiative (the Initiative) which was formed in 2015 to address the lack of Asian American representation.[3]

The absence of Asian Americans in CUNY's leadership ranks came as a surprise to many for a number of reasons: a) CUNY's historic mission to educate the underserved, b) its large APA student population (20.3% in 2016, up from 19.8% in 2015), and c) its sizeable APA faculty (13.3% in 2016, up from 12.8% in 2015). CUNY is also located in New York City, arguably the most diverse city in the world. The City's APA population is estimated at 15% and growing rapidly, having doubled over the past two decades. The number of Asian Americans in leadership roles at CUNY was even more dismal than the national figures, where according to a 2012 American Council on Education report, APAs held only about 1.5% of the college and university presidencies nationally.[4] At CUNY, across twenty-four campuses, no APAs held a position as president or dean of any of the professional schools.

The report made recommendations for the development of Asian American leadership through a pipeline approach. This requires extending outreach to a greater and more diverse applicant pool, identifying and cultivating high potential Asian American candidates from within CUNY, mentorships, creating opportunities for experiential learning through appointments to interim positions, and working together with graduate and undergraduate students. It called for Asian American leadership representation in meaningful positions that influence university and college academic programming and policies, as well as student life, and service and support to the diverse communities of New York City.

The report also addressed the lack of a robust and well resourced Asian American Studies presence at CUNY which may be symptomatic of the lack of Asian Americans at the leadership table, and attention to programming and issues of importance to Asian American students, faculty and communities. As has been reiterated in research over and over again, Asian American Studies has been instrumental in the development of identity formation and self-identification as leaders for Asian American students.

The report concluded that this is a critical and opportune juncture to address leadership diversity and development of a pipeline for leadership positions at CUNY. Like many institutions nationally, CUNY faces large numbers of retirements at all levels. In view of the growing diversity of students, the recognition that diversity contributes substantially to the success of institutions, and that students benefit from culturally relatable role models, it is imperative for CUNY to focus on the issue of diversity in higher education leadership.

The report noted that CUNY was uniquely positioned to lead the change and create a national model for identifying, supporting, and growing the representation of Asian Americans and diverse academic leaders in higher education. This is because of CUNY's numerous campuses and strengths in varied disciplines from science and technology to liberal arts, humanities and social sciences, to graduate and professional schools. In addition, the three tiers of institutions from community colleges to senior colleges to graduate and professional schools, also provides a unique environment to cultivate leaders who move from different types of campuses with varying sizes of student bodies and needs, budgets and even campus environments.

The following is an update on developments since the 2016 report.

Leadership

AAARI's report did not fall on deaf ears; it was among the factors that resulted in the September 2017 announcement of the Diversifying CUNY's Leadership: A CUNY Harvard Consortium, "...a professional development program intended to cultivate a diverse group of future leaders..." AAARI is actively and aggressively recruiting aspiring Asian American and other diverse candidates for the program.[5]

In July 2017, CUNY welcomed Kevin D. Kim, an attorney and entrepreneur, to the CUNY Board of Trustees. He is the only Asian American on the fifteen member board which includes two Ex-Officio members. He was preceded by two other Asian members, Dr. Thomas Tam, founding Executive Director of AAARI who served from 1989 to 1996, and Wellington Z. Chen, from 2000 to 2017, an architect, former Commissioner on the New York City Board of Standards and Appeals, and current Executive Director of the Chinatown Partnership Local Development Corporation (CPLDC).

Since the report was released over a year ago, there remains no APA leadership representation in those positions that would have the highest impact on academic programming and policies:

> *At the Chancellery, (a total of eight positions) the highest levels of leadership at CUNY*

> *At the University-wide level (a total of eight university deans, associate deans and assistant deans)*

> *At the executive levels (twenty-four college presidents and professional school deans)*

> *At the chief academic officer/Provost (CAO) positions of any of CUNY's twenty-four senior colleges, community colleges, graduate or professional schools. There are now three (up from two) APAs with titles of Vice President and five (up from four) Assistant Vice Presidents out of 163 total positions (4.3%).*

Among the twenty-four campuses, APAs represent only 6.8% of the dean, associate dean or assistant dean ranks—twelve APAs (up from eleven) out of 174 positions (up from 171).

Faculty

APA full-time faculty representation has risen to 13.3% (up from 12.8% in 2015) not including full-time visiting and substitute faculty. The Asian American faculty has doubled from 6.7% in 2000 to 13.3% in 2016.

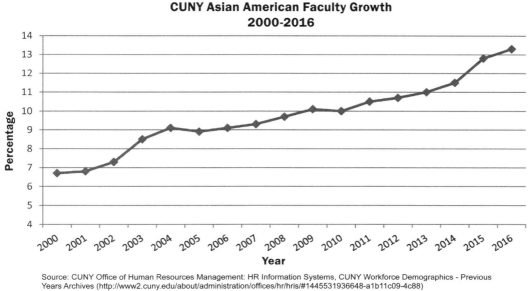

CUNY Asian American Faculty Growth 2000-2016

Source: CUNY Office of Human Resources Management: HR Information Systems, CUNY Workforce Demographics - Previous Years Archives (http://www2.cuny.edu/about/administration/offices/hr/hris/#1445531936648-a1b11c09-4c88)

Students

The Asian American student population at CUNY has seen significant growth, and that growth is expected to continue. The Asian student population at CUNY has doubled over the two past decades, reflecting the doubling of the Asian population in New York City over the past two decades.

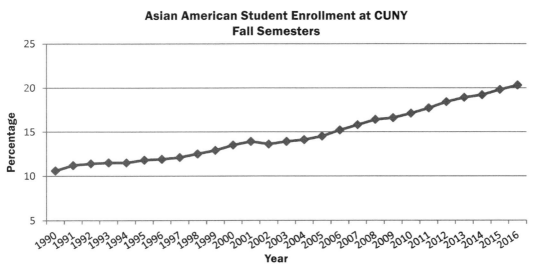

Asian American Student Enrollment at CUNY Fall Semesters

Source: CUNY Office of Institutional Research-Historical Student Data Tables (http://www.cuny.edu/irdatabook/rpts2_AY_current/ENRL_0027_RACE_UGGR_PCT_HIST.rpt.pdf)

Asian American Studies at CUNY

Asian American Studies continues to be under-resourced and largely neglected at CUNY. Even Asian Studies does not have the kind of presence or support one might expect at a university with such a diverse population, given the importance of Asia today, and the fact that 65% of the Muslim world is Asian. It would seem that Asian American and Asian Studies would be prerequisites for preparing students to enter the workforce that serves New York City and beyond.

The largest CUNY Asian American Studies program in terms of course offerings is a minor at Hunter College. The Coalition for the Revitalization of Asian American Studies at Hunter (CRAASH), a student organization, has been actively advocating over the past year for the conversion of the program and minor in Asian American Studies, into a department with full-time faculty lines and major. Asian American Studies classes have primarily been taught by part-time adjunct faculty. Through social media (www.facebook.com/huntercraash), conference panel discussions and public protests, CRAASH has forged cross-ethnic and community alliances with college and university students across the country to support their mission and engage Hunter College, CUNY alumni, and elected officials.

The Hunter College Asian American Studies Program received a five-year, $1.7 million grant from the U.S. Department of Education (DOE) through its Asian American Native American Pacific Islander Serving Institutions (AANAPISI) grant program for the Hunter College AANAPISI Project (HCAP). The funds are allocated for developing an integrated English as a Second Language/Asian American Studies curriculum, enhancing curricular and co-curricular programming on APA mental health issues, and an APA student internship program with Asian American community-based organizations. The director of the Asian American Studies Program, Jennifer Hayashida, one of the faculty instrumental in securing the grant, was notified by the Hunter administration that her contract would not be renewed. The director position was a non-tenure track faculty position. According to students and faculty, the Hunter administration does not support an Asian American Studies major, and is reviewing the creation of a center at Hunter, with the program/minor reporting to the provost. How this plays out remains to be seen.

There is an ad hoc major and minor in Asian and Asian American Studies at Baruch College, a minor in Asian American Community Studies at Queens College, and some Asian American Studies classes within some of the Asian Studies programs on other CUNY campuses.

Over the past year, the Borough of Manhattan Community College (BMCC) received and implemented a $100,000 grant from the National Endowment for the Humanities (NEH) for the "Building Asian American Studies across the Community College Classroom" project (https://buildingaas.commons.gc.cuny.edu/). Fifteen faculty from CUNY community colleges participated in a program designed to develop curricular materials for use in classrooms, and "...engage the local histories, cultures and identities of diverse, new and underrepresented Asian American communities in the New York City metropolitan area," according to Soniya Munshi, assistant professor of Sociology at BMCC.

Nationally, more and more students are advocating for Asian American Studies. With the DOE and NEH having recognized the importance of Asian American Studies through their funding of Hunter's AANAPISI Project, earlier funding for the development of the Asian American Community Studies program at Queens College, and BMCC's classroom project, CUNY should be encouraged to allocate more resources to support Asian American Studies at CUNY.

The Future for Asian Americans at CUNY

The lack of APAs in CUNY Leadership creates a serious anomaly in the CUNY system because the data clearly indicates that there is a qualified pool of potential APA applicants available at every level from leadership to faculty. CUNY would be expected to be able to identify and hire more APAs in leadership positions.

AAARI and the Initiative will continue:

- To call for CUNY to formally institutionalize the CUNY Asian American Leadership Initiative and the recommendations of its report

- Raise awareness of the lack of Asian Pacific American representation in leadership positions in the CUNY system

- Raise awareness of the large and growing APA student population and addressing their needs—both within CUNY and New York City

- Identify institutional, societal, and cultural barriers to APAs in gaining leadership appointments in the CUNY system

- Recommend actionable steps to remove barriers and to increase APA representation in CUNY and its colleges

- Create infrastructure to implement recommendations, including seeking resources and monetary support from the University (vs. just recommending) and ensuring sustainability

- Constitute a committee to monitor change in CUNY hiring/appointment practices, as well as make colleges accountable to the committee (vs. just recommending)

- Establish demonstratively effective practices that will contribute to the national dialogue and solutions to the issue of lack of APAs and other underrepresented groups in higher education leadership

Notes

1 Defined by the U.S. Department of Labor Office of Federal Contract Compliance Programs as "A person with origins in any of the original peoples of the Far East, Southeast Asia, the Indian subcontinent, or the Pacific Islands."

2 https://www.cuny.edu/academics.html

3 The terms "APA" and "Asian Americans" are used interchangeably herein.

4 *Raising Voices, Lifting Leaders: Empowering Asian Pacific Islander American Leadership In Higher Education* (American Council on Education, 2012), https://bookstore.acenet.edu/products/raising-voices-lifting-leaders-empowering-asian-pacific-islander-american-leadership-higher

5 http://www2.cuny.edu/academics/faculty-affairs/faculty-development-across-cuny/diversifying-cunys-leadership/

Author

JOYCE O. MOY is the Executive Director of the Asian American and Asian Research Institute (AAARI), of The City University of New York (CUNY). Ms. Moy's field of focus is economic development and entrepreneurship, with an emphasis on small and medium enterprises (SMEs). She is also a professor at CUNY and has taught entrepreneurship, management, and business law. She has developed curriculum in financial education which has been adopted by the Cities for Financial Empowerment as a national model for training counselors working with the poor, working poor and others seeking to get out of debt, improve their financial conditions, and work toward building assets. She was the first Asian American director of a U.S. Small Business Administration funded New York State Small Business Development Center (SBDC). She was one of the early instructors in the Asian American Studies Program at Cornell University, teaching a course on "Asian Americans and the Law," jointly with the Cornell University School of Law and undergraduate program.

Steps Along the Curved Road

LOAN THỊ ĐÀO
PETER NIEN-CHU KIANG (江念祖)
SƠN CA LÂM
SONGKHLA NGUYỄN
SHIRLEY SUET-LING TANG (鄧雪齡)

Introduction

IN OCTOBER 1986, an invited gaggle of fifty faculty and students convened at Cornell University for a historic East Coast Asian American Scholars Conference to lay the initial groundwork for an Asian American Studies network "East of California." Resolutions unanimously passed by participants included statements of support for institutionalizing an Asian American Studies program at UMass Boston and an Inter-College Research Institute in Asian American Studies at The City University of New York (CUNY), along with a call to reconvene in the future to assess the progress of East Coast Asian American Studies programs.[1] Russell Leong, then editor of UCLA's *Amerasia Journal*, was one of two non-East Coast participants. We greatly appreciate Russell's fresh invitation from *CUNY FORUM* after all these years.

Prior to 1986, only one course with dedicated Asian American Studies content had been offered at UMass Boston. Created in the 1970s by the pioneering Nisei sociologist, T. Scott Miyakawa, the course remained dormant following his death in 1981 until Peter Kiang revitalized it in Spring 1987 as part of a local, long-term, community capacity-building plan to firmly establish Asian American Studies at the region's urban public university.[2] Step by step since then, a critical mass of core faculty has developed a range of individual and collective strategies to:

- Facilitate socio-culturally responsive and academically relevant learning communities that support student persistence, mentoring, and connection at our urban working-class commuter university;

- Document significant issues, needs, and interventions in local Asian American communities and on campus, recognizing that our own students and alumni are themselves members and participants within local neighborhoods, workplaces, and community-based institutions;

- Build research and development capacities in local Asian American communities through connecting ethnic studies perspectives, interdisciplinary methodologies, and analytic frameworks with students' and alumni's diasporic social networks and cultural/linguistic knowledge;

- Produce and preserve original collections of locally-relevant source materials, such as oral histories, digital stories, spoken word performances, directories, maps, and photo/video/print archives.

Meanwhile, our esteemed campus colleagues, Rajini Srikanth, Karen Suyemoto, and Paul Watanabe also played presidential or co-founding leadership roles nationally for the Association for Asian American Studies, the Asian American Psychological Association, and the Asian American and Pacific Islander Policy Research Consortium. Their contributions ensured that expressive arts, empirical social science, clinical practice, policy impact, and the interests of marginalized populations were mutually and integratively advanced by Asian American Studies agendas nationally, as well as in our own program.[3]

In these and other ways, we have worked to sustain the transformative revolutionary intentions of the field's founders,[4] while grounding our efforts in the never-ending realities of trauma and healing shared by our original core constituencies: refugees and veterans from the wars in Southeast Asia. Their painful, yet purposeful steps to and from our urban public university created many important educational pathways for newer generations to follow and extend.[5] This article briefly describes one such example that illustrates our strategic commitment to share and deepen the impact of our curricular frameworks, pedagogical practices, and student/family/community/alumni engagements in Asian American Studies. Though framed here as a straight-forward progression of steps, the path has often curved with many "MIS[SED] STOPS" along the way.

Pathway Steps

UMass Boston Asian American Studies students in Songkhla Nguyễn's Vietnamese Structured English Immersion second-grade classroom at Mather Elementary in Boston, March 2014
Photo By Peter Kiang

Step One

More than twenty years ago during the 1993-94 school year, Ngọc Lan Nguyễn, a second-wave refugee who fled Vietnam by boat, was in her first year of teaching fourth grade in the Vietnamese bilingual education program at Mather Elementary School in Boston. Reflecting the neighborhood profile, one third of the children at Mather Elementary came from Vietnamese refugee/immigrant families, like Lan herself. Having just graduated from UMass Boston in Education and Asian American Studies, Lan had been promised by the Asian American Studies faculty that we would assist her as much as possible during her first year of teaching. By her second month on the job, she returned to the campus after school and implored:

> Some of my kids just got into a fight with older boys who were harassing a younger Vietnamese student on the way home from school. It happens every day and I get so angry. People need to know about it. Sometimes I just want to shout, "DON'T IGNORE IT!" to the school and the community.

Lan's urgent need compelled us to design a collaborative four-month harassment documentation project for her classroom. Though outraged by the extent of violence documented each week, Lan found the process educational and empowering, as did her students. One child reflected at the time, "I feel good studying the problems so next time if I see that problem again I will know what to do."[6] Although two decades have passed since then, Vietnamese immigrant children still comprise over thirty percent of Mather Elementary today, and Lan is still there teaching.

Step Two

After her first week taking an undergraduate Asian American Studies course at UMass Boston in 2006, co-author Sơn Ca Lâm reflected, "I haven't felt this way since bilingual class in elementary school. Everything is connected in our class. Home. School. Family. Community. I haven't felt this way for a long time." Sơn Ca's profound insight led to further realizations about why her memories of bilingual education were so precious. She recalled that her first critical discussions regarding racism and identifying as Vietnamese American, rather than Vietnamese, took place in fourth grade at Mather Elementary, and her teacher was Ngọc Lan Nguyễn. Sơn Ca quickly recognized that many other Vietnamese American college students in Asian American Studies at UMass Boston also had memories of bilingual classes at Mather Elementary with Cô ("Teacher") Lan. It became clear that an emerging public educational pathway for the Vietnamese community, from elementary school to college, featured some distinctive directional markers and reference points from Asian American Studies along the way. More were also needed, however, and Sơn Ca was inspired to create her Mather Elementary memory performance poem, "MIS[SED] STOPS," which accompanies this essay.

Step Three

In 2007, co-author Songkhla Nguyễn, together with Sơn Ca Lâm and twenty other undergraduate classmates took the course *AsAmSt 294: Resources for Vietnamese American Studies*, which that semester focused on the post-Katrina rebuilding process of Gulf Coast Vietnamese communities, including one week of direct participation with projects in New Orleans and Biloxi during spring break.[7] Following this course, Songkhla and Sơn Ca, both of whom had strong science and Asian American Studies backgrounds, jointly designed and implemented a community science education summer program in Biloxi in 2008, to connect youth with Vietnamese American family and community cultural contexts involving aquaculture, environmental justice, recycling, gardening, and other areas of science, technology, ecology, and health. Co-authors Shirley Tang, Peter Kiang and others, wrote at the time that these curricular and community connections between Boston and the Gulf Coast showed, both conceptually and concretely, that the development of Vietnamese American Studies as a field, could freshly articulate the foundational intentions of Asian American Studies.[8]

Step Four

Sơn Ca and Songkhla both stayed at UMass Boston to continue as graduate students while working in the Asian American Studies Program. After completing her M.A. in Applied Linguistics and teaching her first Asian American Studies course as an adjunct instructor in Summer 2013, Sơn Ca entered a Ph.D. program in Geography at Clark University in Worcester, MA, with the intention to return as a professor in Asian American Studies. Meanwhile, after receiving her M.Ed. in Elementary Education in 2010, Songkhla was immediately hired to teach second grade with Vietnamese immigrant children at Mather Elementary. Like the programmatic promise made to Ngọc Lan Nguyễn in 1993, the Asian American Studies faculty agreed to support Songkhla in her first year of teaching and beyond at Mather Elementary. More recently, two other UMass Boston Vietnamese American alumni from Education and Asian American Studies, Linda Nguyễn and Tuyết Đinh, were also hired as kindergarten teachers at Mather Elementary—creating a critical mass of dedicated teaching faculty across grade levels who are also grounded in our curricular commitments and pedagogical practices.

Step Five

With this remarkable core of Vietnamese American alumni teaching at Mather Elementary, and with co-author Loan Đào hired in 2011 as a tenure stream faculty in Asian American Studies, our intersections with Mather Elementary can now occur daily through curricular articulation, tutoring assistance, family literacy support, parent translation, classroom-based research, supervised internships, and intergenerational story production. Working closely with children and families in Songkhla Nguyễn's second grade classroom, in particular, faculty and student projects and processes in Asian American Studies courses taught respectively by co-authors Tang, Kiang, and Đào, in 2013 and 2014, have also garnered grant support from the university's Civic Engagement Scholars Initiative (CESI) as effective models of curriculum design with civic-centered outcomes. Among many new resources being developed currently are original children's storybooks with Vietnamese American Studies themes based on family, community, and elder stories.

For example, one storybook, *Vy's First Time at the Nail Salon*, produced by undergraduates Mya Nguyễn and Judy Ngô in the Spring 2013 course, "Southeast Asians in the US," focuses on a young girl, Vy, who, one day, goes to her mom's workplace at a nail salon because there is no other childcare option. Vy soon discovers the dangers of nail polish remover (acetone and other chemicals), as well as the sharp tools and hot sterilizer machine that are used. The story shows that the nail salon is not a playground, even though Vy truly enjoys being with her mom who works long hours away from home—much like the daily life story for many families in the Vietnamese community.

A second example from the same Asian American Studies course, produced by Cam Vân Trân titled, *The Question of Thương,* features a Vietnamese American girl named Thương (whose name means "Love") who wonders if her father loves her at all because he does not hug her affectionately like the families of some of her friends. The story promotes inter-generational communication and understanding in culturally relevant ways for Vietnamese American families. The author/illustrator, Vân, was also a student in the Vietnamese bilingual program in Boston, and interned in Ngọc Lan Nguyễn's third grade classroom at Mather Elementary with plans to become a teacher herself.

Impact and Next Steps

As Asian American Studies undergraduates create such products and share them directly with Vietnamese immigrant children in Mather Elementary's classrooms, critical educational pathways become more clearly defined. Second graders are engaged and inspired by college students (fourteenth graders) who attend the university down the street where their teachers also went to college. In turn, some of the college students follow their own pathways toward careers and graduate degrees in Education or other Asian American Studies-related fields. The long-term capacity of families, schools, communities, and the Asian American Studies Program itself continues to expand across generations. Indeed, one generation of Vietnamese bilingual students from Ngọc Lan Nguyễn's classes at Mather Elementary has already graduated from UMass Boston, and we expect children from Songkhla Nguyễn's current second grade classroom to take Asian American Studies at UMass Boston in 2024 and beyond.

Beyond pathways and cross-generational relationships, however, engaging with Mather Elementary as both a public educational site and Vietnamese community site, also reflects the political/policy reality facing bilingual education. In 2002, following passage of Proposition 227 in California, lobbyist businessman Ron Unz similarly financed a statewide referendum to eliminate bilingual education in Massachusetts. Aggressively promoted through Mitt Romney's victorious gubernatorial campaign, the Unz referendum forced the dismantling of Boston's well-established transitional bilingual education programs, including Mather Elementary's Vietnamese bilingual program in 2003.[9] Several years of dysfunctional restructuring then followed until the city eventually implemented the Structured English Immersion (SEI) model for all of its target languages, including Chinese and Vietnamese. With a student profile that remains over thirty percent Vietnamese, Mather Elementary provides the largest and most stable Vietnamese structured English immersion program of any public elementary school in the city and state.

The cumulative impact of the non-linear steps described above also address several longstanding critiques of the Asian American Studies field, such as weak investments in the development of Southeast Asian American students and communities, and failure to engage seriously with the domain of K-12 education.[10] Furthermore, while the Mather Elementary example is highlighted here, we have comparable twenty-year examples of pathway development and impact for Khmer and Chinese student/faculty/alumni/community contexts as well.

Finally, other strategic commitments for our program currently include:

- Master's and doctoral level program building with our sister ethnic studies academic units and research institutes under the transdisciplinary conceptual umbrellas of Transnational Cultural Community Studies (TCCS) and Global Inclusion and Social Development (GISD) graduate programs.

- Modeling faculty/student/alumni/community engagement with relevant research and development in critical areas besides K-12 education, such as health disparities, disabilities, civic participation, and transnational leadership.

- Providing direction as a federally-designated and funded Asian American Native American and Pacific Islander Serving Institution (AANAPISI) and deeply engaging with what it means to be an East Coast AANAPISI research university.[11]

We clearly have much more to share and many more steps to take. We look forward to learning from other contributors and respondents to this and future issues of *CUNY FORUM*.[12]

MIS[SED]STOPS by Sơn Ca Lâm

1. SFX: [Bus noise, doors shutting, bus moving]

SƠN CA

When you're eight years old and in the third grade, going home from school on the same bus with your friends is very important.

My friend, *Mỹ*, is Ms. O'Brien's favorite Asian. She has really really light skin, her English is perfect and she knows big words, so she got moved to the regular class in the first grade. She's the go-between for us in bilingual class, and the other kids.

Then there's *Thảo*, who always shares her chips at snack time when someone forgets to bring something. She's the one to go to for food. She jumps rope pretty well too.

And *Minh*, he has the loudest mouth ever! All he talks about is cars. He talks to me in class all the time and gets me in trouble because his mom knows my mom, so we are supposed to be friends.

All of us had a responsibility on the bus – to always take care of each other.

Everyone is sandwiched into the leathery green seats except for Ms. O'Brien. Ms. O'Brien always got a seat all to herself. Her meat droops down her arms like jell-o when she wags her blimpy fingers and hollers out our seats. We're like little trolls around her. And her hair is curly and white like my grandma's, but she wears these huge glasses that make her bulging eyes pop out even more. We were all terrified of her.

MISS O'BRIEN

Hurry up and move in!

You sit here.

No, you two can't sit together!

(Turns around) Quiet down back there!

What do you have there? A note? Give it to me!

SƠN CA

We have a new student named Khum. Khum is darker than the rest of us, but he's still Vietnamese because he's in our class. He just came to America.

(whispers) FOBs we call them.

and he doesn't know any English, so we decided that he would be squished in the dreaded middle today. We will protect him there.

Hi, your name is Khum right? I'm Sơn Ca.

(In Vietnamese: What's Việt Nam like? Are there more Vietnamese people than in our class? Well, there's not many of us here so don't go anywhere by yourself. One time, there was a girl who just came here, and the other kids picked on her . . .)

Ở Việt Nam ra sao vậy? Có nhiều người Việt hơn õ bên đây không? Ở đay ít người Việt, Khum đừng đi đâu một mình nhe. Hồi đó có một bạn cũng mới qua . . . bị máy đứa kia ăn hiếp . . . .

MISS O'BRIEN
Speak English!

SƠN CA
But he just came here, he doesn't know how to yet . . .

MISS O'BRIEN
Speak English!

SƠN CA
And we rode the rest of the way home in silence . . . .

---

2. SFX: [Bus]

1975—The war ended in *Việt Nam*. My parents said we lost, which is why we had to leave *Việt Nam*—refugees they called us. But before fleeing *Việt Nam*, my father was fighting in the war for five years, then toiling in the fields of the reeducation camp for another ten. My mom and sister, *chị Khuê*, had to prepare months ahead just to make a weeklong journey by train, mud, and then foot to see him for a day. *chị Khuê* said that after having to live for so long without a father, she forgot who he was, and found it weird when *ba* wanted to sit next to her and hold her. She was eight then.

Then we made our way to the refugee camp in the Philippines, where I was born. And finally, we came to America, where it was supposed to be easier. But my parents still had to work so much that I never got to see them, and I started to call my sister mom—"má Khuê."

One day, *ba* had to replace his hip joint, and aside from the fact that it was just hurting, no one knows why or what happened to it, not even him. Despite all the struggles that my parents have had to endure, they were still called names like "gook" and "chink." We are like weeds and leeches in America—taking what isn't ours: space, chances, life.

MISS O'BRIEN
Speak English!

---

3. SFX: [Bus]

SƠN CA

When I was twelve, my parents took me out of school to become "naturalized." Apparently, all this time, I had been a fake? Usually, the kid doesn't have to go, but since they didn't speak much English, I was supposed to be their interpreter. We were nervous about the interview—what if America rejects me? The naturalization officer began plunging into his questions, and I was trying my best to fulfill my responsibility.

(in Vietnamese: He asked how long have you been here? What is our address? How many people are in your family?)

Ô ̉ng hỏi ba với mẹ ở đây bao lâu rồi?

Địa chỉ ở đâu?

Gia đình mình có mấy người?

Then he looked at me and said . . .

NATURALIZATION OFFICER:

I am talking to your parents, not to you.

(Turns to parents) How long have you been here?

Is this your biological child?

DID. YOU. BIRTH. THIS. CHILD?

SƠN CA

He talked to them as if they were retarded children. But even retarded children in America are treated with more dignity than what my parents received that day. And I just sat there, in that small glass room—in silence, swallowing all the shame, anger and humiliation that we were taught so carefully to hide. While my parents incessantly thanked this white man who had degraded them. All for me to become an American citizen.

But if I could go back to that day, I would say to him:

You have no right talking to my parents that way. They are American citizens and work just as hard as you do, if not harder. And you're treating them like scum. We have as much of a right to be here as anyone else does . . .

---

4. SFX: [Bus]

MISS O'BRIEN
Speak English!

SƠN CA

We rode the rest of the way home in silence. I can only imagine Khum—one of his first few experiences in the U.S. was to keep silent and quiet. Even though he didn't understand what was going on, he must have felt so terrible and lost.

If I hadn't just remained silent that day, if I had just ignored Miss O'Brien:

Ở trong lớp, khi nào Khum cần đi tiểu, Khum phải giơ tay lên hỏi cô giáo nhe. Nhớ đừng nói chuyện lớn, hoặc chạy trong hallway. In class, when you need to go to the bathroom, you have to raise your hand and ask the teacher. You can't talk or run in the hallway. When we speak Vietnamese outside of class, everyone else thinks we're saying bad things about them. But remember, no matter what they tell you, you have as much right to be here as anyone. My father always told me that if you don't speak up for yourself, no one else will, so don't let anyone disrespect you. And don't ever be ashamed of being Vietnamese. Be proud of who you are and where you come from.

---

5. *SFX: [Bus stops, doors open]*

SƠN CA
(reaches hand out to Khum) We're home.

Notes

1   Lee C. Lee, "Asian American Studies: Contemporary Issues," *East Coast Asian American Scholars Conference Proceedings* (Cornell University, October 24-26, 1986): 31–32.

2   See: Peter N. Kiang, "Bringing it All Back Home: New Views of Asian American Studies and the Community" in G.M. Nomura, R. Endo, S.H. Sumida, R.C. Leong (eds.) *Frontiers of Asian American Studies* (Pullman: Washington State University Press, 1989): 305–314; Peter N. Kiang, "The New Wave: Developing Asian American Studies on the East Coast," in Gary Y. Okihiro, Shirley Hune, Arthur Hansen, and John M. Liu (eds.) *Reflections Through Windows of Shattered Glass* (Pullman: Washington State University Press, 1988): 43–50.

3   See, for example: Rajini Srikanth and Esther Y. Iwanaga, *Bold Words: A Century of Asian American Writing* (New Brunswick, NJ: Rutgers University Press, 2001); Haeok Lee, Peter N. Kiang, Paul Y. Watanabe, Patricia Halon, Ling Shi & Daniel Church, "Hepatitis B Virus Infection and Immunizations Among Asian American College Students: Infection, Exposure, and Immunity Rates," *Journal of American College Health* 61:2 (2013): 67–74; and Karen L. Suyemoto, Grace S. Kim, Miwa Tanabe, John Tawa & Stephanie C. Day, "Challenging the Model Minority Myth: Engaging Asian American Students in Research on Asian American College Student Experiences," in S. D. Museus (ed.) *Conducting Research on Asian Americans in Higher Education: New Directions in Institutional Research* (San Francisco: Jossey-Bass, 2009): 41–55.

4   Shirley Suet-ling Tang, "Community-Centered Research as Knowledge/Capacity-Building in Immigrant and Refugee Communities" in Charles R. Hale (ed.) *Engaging Contradictions: Theory, Politics and Methods of Activist Scholarship* (Berkeley: University of California Press, 2008): 237–263; Peter N. Kiang, "Crouching Activists, Hidden Scholars: Reflections on Research and Development with Students and Communities in Asian American Studies" in Charles R. Hale. (ed.) *Engaging Contradictions: Theory, Politics, and Methods of Activist Scholarship* (Berkeley: University of California Press, 2008): 299–318; Peter N. Kiang, Karen L. Suyemoto & Shirley S. Tang, "Developing and Sustaining Community Research Methods and Meanings in Asian American Studies Coursework at an Urban Public University," in Timothy P. Fong (ed.) *Handbook of Ethnic Studies Research: Approaches and Perspectives* (Lanham: Rowman & Littlefield, 2008): 367–398.

5   See, for example: Loan Thị Đào, "Hai Bà Trưng Project: Building Vietnamese (American) Female Student Leadership at the University of Massachusetts Boston," in Amefil Agbayani, Samuel Museus, and Doris Ching (eds.) *Underserved Asian Americans and Pacific Islanders in Higher Education* (Manoa: University of Hawai'i Press, 2014); Shirley S. Tang and Peter N. Kiang, "Refugees, Veterans, and Continuing Pedagogies of PTSD in Asian American Studies," in An Integrative Analysis Approach to Diversity in the Classroom. Special issue. *New Directions for Teaching and Learning* 125 (San Francisco: Jossey–Bass, 2011): 77–87; Peter N. Kiang, "Pedagogies of PTSD: Circles of Healing with Refugees and Veterans in Asian American Studies," in Lin Zhan (ed.) *Asian Americans: Vulnerable Populations, Model Interventions, Clarifying Agendas* (Sudbury: Jones & Bartlett, 2003): 197–222; Peter N. Kiang, "Pedagogies of Life and Death: Transforming Immigrant/Refugee Students and Asian American Studies," *positions: asia critique* 5(2) (Duke University Press, 1997): 529–555; Peter N. Kiang, "A Thematic Analysis of Persistence and Long-term Educational Engagement with Southeast Asian American College Students," in L. Zhan (ed.) *Asian American Voices: Engaging, Empowering, and Enabling* (NY: National League for Nursing, 2009): 21–58.

6   Peter N. Kiang, Nguyen Ngoc Lan & Richard L. Sheehan, "Don't Ignore It!: Documenting Racial Harassment in a Fourth-Grade Vietnamese Bilingual Classroom," *Equity and Excellence in Education*, 28:1 (1995): 31–35.

7   An Asian American Studies Program video about the 2007 AsAmSt 294 course and students' Gulf Coast community rebuilding focus can be viewed at http://www.youtube.com/watch?v=dKgrwkT0X1o

8   James Điền Bùi, Peter Nien-chu Kiang, Shirley Suet-ling Tang, Janet Hồng Võ, "Cá Trí Nhớ: Roles of Vietnamese American Studies and Education Post-Katrina," in L. Zhan (ed.) *Asian American Voices: Engaging, Empowering, and Enabling.* (NY: National League for Nursing, 2009): 171–190.

9   Mandira Kala, Peter Nien-chu Kiang, Nicole Lavan, and Faye Karp, "English Learners in Boston Public Schools: Enrollment and Educational Outcomes of Native Speakers of Vietnamese," *Gastón Institute Publications* Paper 141 (2009), http://scholarworks.umb.edu/gaston_pubs/141

10   Peter N. Kiang, "Checking Southeast Asian American Realities in Pan-Asian American Agendas," *AAPI Nexus: Policy, Practice & Community* 2:1 (2004): 48–76; Peter N. Kiang, "Linking Strategies and Interventions in Asian American Studies to K-12 Classrooms and Teacher Preparation," *International Journal of Qualitative Studies in Education*. 17:2 (2004): 199–225.

11 An Asian American Studies Program video produced by Sơn Ca Lâm, "What Does it Mean to be an AAPI-Serving Institution?" is viewable at http://www.youtube.com/watch?v=-W63C5kl6gA

12 For more information about UMass Boston's Asian American Studies Program, see: http://www.umb.edu/asamst and https://www.facebook.com/UMB.AsAmSt

Authors

Loan Thị Đào is an Associate Professor of Asian American Studies at the University of Massachusetts Boston. She specializes in Southeast Asian refugee migration and community development, immigrant and refugee youth, and social movements. Her most recent publication is "Out and Asian: How Undocu/DACAmented Asian Americans and Pacific Islander Youth Navigate Dual Liminality in the Immigrant Rights Movement" in *Societies* 2017, 7(3), 17; doi:10.3390/soc7030017.

Peter Nien-chu Kiang (江念祖) is Professor and Director of the Asian American Studies Program at the University of Massachusetts Boston where he has taught since 1987, focusing on research, curriculum development, and advocacy in both K-12 and higher education with Asian American immigrant/refugee students and communities. His most recent single-authored article is "Asian American Studies Praxis and the Educational Power of Boston's Public Chinese Burial Grounds" (2016).

Sơn Ca Lâm is a Ph.D. student in the Department of Geography at Clark University in Worcester, MA. She holds an M.A. in Applied Linguistics and B.A. in both Earth, Environmental & Ocean Sciences and Comparative Ethnic Studies from the University of Massachusetts Boston. Her areas of research focus on: displacement, ethnic studies, language/culture/identity, community building & development, the environment, and place. Her 2010 chapbook of poetry is titled *Uncaught Bullets*.

Songkhla Nguyễn is a second-grade teacher in the Vietnamese Structured English Immersion Program at Mather Elementary School in Boston. She holds an M.Ed. in Elementary Education from the University of Massachusetts Boston, as well as a B.S. in Biology with a concentration in Asian American Studies. Her research interests include: bilingual literacy development, models of holistic education, Vietnamese American Studies, and Asian American narratives.

Shirley Suet-ling Tang (鄧雪齡) is Associate Professor of Asian American Studies in the School for Global Inclusion and Social Development at the University of Massachusetts Boston. She is a co-Principal Investigator for a five-year, $1.75 million, grant award from the U.S. Department of Education Asian American Native American Pacific Islander Minority-Serving Institution (AANAPISI) Program, and received the 2016 Chancellor's Award for Distinguished Teaching at UMass Boston. She holds a Ph.D. in American Studies from SUNY Buffalo, and a B.A. in English with Honors from Chinese University Hong Kong. Her most recent publication is "Digital Stories in Asian American Studies and Co-Producer Knowledge in AANAPISI Contexts" (2017).

Standing Beside
A Comparative Racial Critique

ALLAN PUNZALAN ISAAC

Following is an edited keynote presentation from the conference on Comparative Racialization and the Futures of Asian American Studies, at the Hunter College/CUNY Roosevelt House Public Policy Institute, on December 9, 2016, sponsored by Mapping of Asian Americans in New York (MAANY) and NYU A/P/A Institute.

Consciousness on Campus

What is the value today of human lives—be they African American, Asian American, Latino, Native American or White American? *Al Jazeera* reported in November 2016 that according to FBI statistics, hate crimes against Muslims in the United States shot up 67 percent in 2015 to their highest levels since the aftermath of the September 11, 2001 attacks.[1] The Southern Poverty Law Center reported 867 hate incidents occurring around the country just ten days after the 2016 presidential election.[2] New York City has seen the highest number of reported incidents. Many of these incidents have happened right on our campuses—sites of our work and not coincidentally, what philosopher Louis Althusser has termed an Ideological State Apparatus (ISA).

Poster on Howard Street, Manhattan
Photo by Antony Wong

Individual action and governmental policies continue to underscore the differential value of human lives, a crisis made visible by the Black Lives Matter movement. Black Lives Matter is an insurgent movement against white supremacy. For many the castigatory taunt of "Trump, Trump" or "Build the Wall" during and right after the election is an assertion of propertied whiteness and the extension of that whiteness to the space that the sound attempts to fill. What I also hear from the taunt is the resounding erosion of the value in whiteness and its proclaimed territory. If such whiteness needs to constantly and insistently assert itself, this implies that various insurgencies are in fact chipping away at this power. The white taunt, much like the racial epithet, must continually produce itself in its pronouncement to insist and accrue value to what it believes to be its right.

Racial Critique

The conference theme—Comparative Racialization and the Futures of Asian American Studies—upon which this edited commentary is based, suggests a relationship between comparison of our racial histories as scholarly method and our political futures. For many of us, our research and the culture work we perform in our classrooms seek to make space for imagining different futures, with social justice always in view, and with race as an analytical lens.

I want to think through some rough-spots in our work life to consider how we produce the notion of value-making in a moment when popular nationalism is at a fevered pitch. How do we, as educators, witness responsibly? What is our responsibility when we encounter the daily questioning of the value of human lives, in which some of us become more disposable than others—"life unworthy of life," to disturbingly echo the words of Nazi Germany. What does it mean when many bodies, including our own, are on the line? The moment means that we *must* put our bodies on the line.

Spatial and Political Possibilities

The insistence on the border wall is founded upon white settler claims of territoriality. But, why is there the need for sonic repetition as a disciplinary tactic? The physical presence of the immigrant figure violates the spatial and temporal trajectory of whiteness itself. Beneficiaries of DACA (Deferred Action for Childhood Arrivals), the undocumented, and H-1B visa holders threaten the space and place of whiteness. The taunt exclaims, "I must put you in your place so I can be sure of mine." Excludable and disposable labor, as exemplified by the Southwest, East and South Asian immigrant, is supposed to create value for the white settler and then leave the territory. To paraphrase historian Ranajit Guha: "Read as an immigrant—with the perfect prefix im—to register the change in her status as one no longer waiting outside—the sense of time she brings with her is the child of another temporality."[3] The immigrant figure brings with her a different history and threatens to transform the time and space of the U.S. nation-state.

Thus, the immigrant figure's presence changes the naturalized trajectory of whiteness. Thinking historically, we know *this* is a 250-year struggle—since 1790 when the only alien eligible for citizenship was the free white man. A young woman in a Black Lives Matter protest refuses to be exclusive and contained labor-property so that the liberal humanist subject can orient his humanity and self-possession—*this*, we know, is a 400-year old struggle. Native peoples of Standing Rock changed briefly the seemingly inevitable march of capital progress and settler colonialism to imprint the globe—*this*, we know, is a 500-year struggle. These long-term struggles reveal the possibility and the fact that white symbolic power can be detached from white material power.

In this longue durée, the body on the line is a site of production of meaning and value. This is one of the founding principles in the struggle for ethnic studies in the late 1960s. In its political alliances and anti-war movement, Ethnic Studies' founding was comparative and international in scope. As sociologist Robyn Rodriguez has argued, this messy founding was an epistemological standpoint, and relatedly, a methodological approach that privileges the embodied subjectivities of marginalized groups as a form of knowledge and a particular kind of engagement in their lives as crucial to knowledge production. Early thinkers in the field forged alliances through intimate connection and most significantly, *commitment*. And we're not simply talking about solidarity: "I support you; I'm in solidarity with you." To choose proximity, to choose to stand beside, is to commit. These are relationships that were built on affection, love and pleasure, *not* towards inclusion but towards transformation. To stand beside is an affective and emotional connection that one makes towards a futurity.

"'Beside,'" gender studies scholar Eve Sedgwick suggests, "comprises a wide range of desiring, identifying, representing, repelling, paralleling, differentiating, rivaling, leaning, twisting, mimicking, withdrawing, attracting, aggressing, warping, and other relations." If we take any one of her gerunds, each forges both a relationship and a temporality. These relations lay open a range that we can imagine against the so-called march of time. The effort involved in choosing proximity is to open up frictive, messy histories. Yet, this labor makes possible engagements and visions involved in being beside something. In these frictive histories, tense proximities, and chosen kinships with other groups, beside-ness generates ethical and temporal formations.

Beside Labor

I wish to illustrate a troubling scenario. The protest walkout for sanctuary designation at my Rutgers University campus had a good turnout—multi-racial and multi-ethnic as Rutgers is. Behind me I noticed a group of students quietly holding up a large banner that read "Trump 2016." Some were wearing the signature red caps. Some Black and Latino students were speaking to the group. Many held camera phones, ready in case any violence ensued. One member of the Rutgers police, a young white man, stood by watching with gun in holster. Upon second look, I noticed that half the Trump supporters were East and South

Asian American students. This disturbed me, but I was not surprised, given the range of local Trump supporters spouting anti-Muslim, Hindu-right rhetoric, as well as anti-abortion Catholic stances over the past few weeks. What is it, I wondered, about the socially mobile Asian American student who desired to take his place in capital extension and its liberal promise in our public institutions.

Iyko Day's work, *Alien Labor*, has helped me to think about settler colonialism, Asianness, and capital. As Day has astutely analyzed, commodity and money are different expressions of value under capitalism, namely, use-value and exchange value. Yet, they are treated in error as divergent entities since both are derived from abstracted socially necessary labor-time. Material commodity, according to Day, becomes the expression of concrete labor, and money becomes the expression of abstract labor. Each becomes racialized in settler colonial logic: concrete (moral) labor comes to be attached to whiteness, while money as abstract (immoral) labor comes to be attached to the Asian foreign other. In Day's formulation, contracted labor and the H-1B visa holder, the highly skilled worker, become agents of globalization that threaten white power, value, place, and territory.

These mistaken conflations are learned by my students at Rutgers. When they stand with Trump supporters, I understand that they identify with the idea of concrete moral meritorious labor, even though many are most likely first or second generation Americans, whose parents were H-1B workers in central New Jersey's tech, communications, and petrochemical corridor. However, the Asian racial form emerging in a moment of crisis would slot them into the abstract circulation of money that is believed to take away value from whiteness.

In *Intimacies of Four Continents*, Lisa Lowe signals how the Asian racial form can serve as the erasure of bodies and history. Historically, she argues, the Asian body's constructed proximity to whiteness and colonial authorities makes possible the obscuring of the divide between enslavement and freedom. That is, the fantasy projected upon the Asian body both opens and erases the historical and material range of coerced and voluntary labor. While supplementing slavery, disposable and excludable labor becomes a fantasy of transition, as well as enables forgetting and the erasure of inequities.

This erasure and ultimate misrecognition produces not only the liberal human subject, but I would also argue the only imaginable trajectory for the future as the citizen-subject. In the ISA called the university, we form the imagination of many students who do not believe themselves vulnerable. Herein lies where I think the imagination of my students become stymied. Many students cannot believe that they themselves could be made vulnerable, because there is only one path to become economic citizen-subjects: through a process of forgetting and the erasure of difference.

Beside Commitment

Many students believe that university education creates value in their bodies and skills only if this education is translatable into capital returns. How can we make possible and intelligible to our students the creation and embodiment of value, a value in themselves outside of market forces? That their time spent in our classrooms is not mere "workforce preparation"?

Marx defines labor-time as the abstracted duration of human labor necessary to create value for commodity. However, Marx's labor-time only *conceptually* translates human activity and signification into capital value. Historian Dipesh Chakrabarty's classic work *Provincializing Europe* reminds us that every activity produces multiple relations, meanings, and temporalities. That is to say, human activity is just activity. Some labor-time is channeled to serve capitalist needs; some are not. Temporalities and various durations live beside each other, but not necessarily towards some kind of capitalist value-making.

In this more expanded notion of labor-time, there is a possibility of hearing a different language of value at the edges of this translation of human activity—in recognizing multiple socialities, even tentative and transitory belonging and allegiances to create value beyond capitalist demands. Without physical commodities to manufacture in the U.S. anymore, theorist Franco Berardi calls post-Fordist modes of production, semiocapitalism, which "takes the mind, language and creativity as its primary tools for the production of value."[4] Chakrabarty suggests that, as with all translations, this shift contains traces in humanistic endeavors of mind, language, and creativity. These traces thrive beside and along capital relations as living paracapitalist formations, often dependent on, but not necessary to, capitalist production.

This is what I hope my students can hear and imagine in my classes as a place of a different sort of labor-time. We teach colonizable skills, but we also communicate value-making outside of capital. When we teach that poem, that story, that reading, other significations besides market value are being produced. We teach against certainty and inevitability. At the very least, we teach the feeling of ambivalence against the certainty of the good subject-citizen.

Ambivalence is a structure of feeling that dis-articulates the body with multiple meanings (valences). Ambivalence acts upon the body by asking of the "here" and "now" as well as the "there" and "then": What could have been? What should be? What is all that remains to be resuscitated? What can be cobbled anew? Thus, to think and feel ambivalence is to think and feel different temporalities and the multiple ways of marking time. To feel ambivalence is to experience the body differently as a site that can generate value and meaning.

Beside Time and Space
Racial capitalism attempts to vacate bodies and lands of meanings that do not serve capitalist ends. Erasure and forgetting promise their obverse: recall and disruption. Different racial forms create histories, and when they rub up against each other, they mess up time. When we think comparatively, besideness forces us to rethink our intellectual labor, to think about how we can recognize and create values and conditions of possibility that would exceed capitalist narratives and their claims of inevitability.

Frictive histories make visible these disruptions to narratives of inevitability. In a sense, comparative and frictive histories make us think against time. By imagining and uncovering values that are outside value-making of capital, we also accomplish another important aspect: we take away value in whiteness and white supremacy, symbolic and material. The historical and contemporary responses to this unrelenting violence and racial capitalism is about care and commitment in our chosen proximities and our chosen alliances. To stand beside. To put our bodies on the line. To take what is considered value-less and create conditions of possibility—*this* is occupying the world, *this* is making space, and *this* is taking time.

Notes

1   "FBI: Hate Crimes Against Muslims in US Surge 67%," *Al Jazeera* (November 14, 2016), http://www.aljazeera.com/news/2016/11/fbi-hate-crimes-muslims-surge-67-percent-161114175259237.html

2   Cassie Miller and Alexandra Werner-Winslow, "Ten Days After: Harassment and Intimidation in the Aftermath of the Election," *Southern Poverty Law Center* (November 29, 2016), https://www.splcenter.org/20161129/ten-days-after-harass-ment-and-intimidation-aftermath-election

3   Ranajit Guha, "Migrant's Time," Saloni Mathur, ed., *The Migrant's Time: Rethinking Art History and Diaspora* (Williamstown: Cark Art Institute, 2011): 4.

4   Franco Berardi, *The Soul at Work: From Alienation to Autonomy* (Los Angeles: Semiotexte, 2009): 21.

Author

Allan Punzalan Isaac is Chair of American Studies, and Associate Professor of American Studies and English at Rutgers University, The State University of New Jersey. Dr. Isaac received his B.A. from Williams College, and Ph.D. in Comparative Literature from New York University. He specializes in Asian American, comparative ethnic and postcolonial aspects of contemporary American literary and cultural studies. His book *American Tropics: Articulating Filipino America* (University of Minnesota Press, 2006) is the recipient of the Association for Asian American Studies Cultural Studies Book Award.

East Coast Asian American Studies

SHIRLEY HUNE

Parts of this commentary are extracted from "Origins: The First Asian American Course at the University of Maryland, College Park," from CUNY FORUM, Volume 4:1 (2016).

IT HAS NOW BEEN FORTY YEARS since I taught my first Asian American Studies (AAS) course. My academic sojourns in different regions—Mid-Atlantic (University of the District of Columbia, two years), East Coast (The City University of New York, fourteen years), California (UCLA, fifteen years), and the Pacific Northwest (University of Washington, eight years); as well as being a 2.5 generation Chinese Canadian from Toronto, Canada, a multiethnic city that is part Midwest and part East Coast, have all enhanced my study of the Asian American experience.

Differences in Asian migration patterns and timing to various regions of the U.S. (and other Americas, and elsewhere) have intersected with local histories, economies, and racial dynamics, as well as national policies and practices. Asians in America have also created their own lives, spaces, and places utilizing their culture, skills, and aspirations within the context of opportunities and constraints that are offered to them.

East Coast Asian American experiences have made unique contributions to Asian American Studies, and I highlight three here briefly:

1. As regional studies are part of U.S. history, so we might consider this approach in Asian American Studies. Many Asians of various national origins came directly to the East Coast and their history of interactions with local populations are revealing. The absence of anti-miscegenation laws in New York and other Northeast and Midwest states, for example, resulted in Chinese and South Asian family formations with Whites, Blacks, and those from the Caribbean during the mid-nineteenth through early twentieth centuries.[1] These intersections and other dynamics (see item 2 below) challenge the notion of a West Coast Asian American experience as an encompassing framework that can speak for all Asians in the United States. Regional experiences shed new light on the study of Asian Americans, their history, diversity, and complexities.

2. East Coast global links with the North Atlantic, Caribbean, and Latin America, past and present, reveal distinctive Asian American settlements, economic development, and culture, such as the pan-Asian ethnic enclaves in Flushing, Queens; a "global immigrant neighborhood" in Sunset Park, Brooklyn; as well as Cuban Chinese restaurants, West Indian curry shops, and Korean fish markets in non-Asian areas.[2] As a site of international finance and other enterprises, highly paid and busy professionals have contributed to a growth of services, including pricey restaurants with cloth napkins and affordable nail salons provided by Asian entrepreneurs who cater to a wide range of clientele. These and other characteristics provide opportunities to expand and build upon Asian American comparative studies.

3. The East Coast has its own record, from the 1970s to present day, of community activism and student protests in response to racism and other inequalities, including demands for Asian American Studies, as part of a larger Asian American movement for social justice.[2] As Asian American Studies became identified as a West Coast, specifically California, phenomenon in its first decades, East Coast AAS supporters initiated actions to establish their positionality in the field.

Two such actions were the founding of the East of California Initiative at Cornell University in October 1986; and the hosting of the Association of Asian American Studies (AAAS) sixth national conference at Hunter College/CUNY in June 1989. Participants of the East of California Initiative sought greater recognition for East Coast Asian American experiences, to support community struggles, and to advance research on the region.[3] The Initiative's networking model was adopted by the Association for Asian American Studies, and is reflected in its regional, ethnic group, and subject matter caucuses (now called sections). By hosting its conference outside of the West Coast, AAAS helped to establish itself as a national organization with significant participation from the East Coast, Midwest, West Coast and Hawai'i. The conference theme of "Comparative and Global Perspectives of the Asian Diaspora," was prescient in broadening the context of Asian American Studies, from a largely U.S.-based focus, to one that acknowledged more fully the transnational landscape of its ethnic groups and locations, concepts that are now well represented in the field.[4] And so, here just two examples that demonstrate the East Coast's exceptional role in developing AAS and strengthening the Association for Asian American Studies' credibility.

Consequently, the Asian American experience is multivariable, similar, yet different. Asian American Studies on the East Coast reflects these and other challenges in making its mark in the academy, and in being relevant to and an advocate for its communities.

Notes

1   On earlier historical periods, see, Vivek Bald, *Bengali Harlem and the Lost Histories of South Asian Americans* (Cambridge: Harvard University Press, 2013); Mary Ting Yi Lui, *The Chinatown Trunk Mystery: Murder, Miscegenation and Other Dangerous Encounters in Turn-of-the-Century New York City* (Princeton: Princeton University Press, 2005); and John Kuo Wei Tchen, *New York before Chinatown: Orientalism and the Shaping of American Culture 1776-1882* (Baltimore: The Johns Hopkins University Press, 1999).

2   For aspects of contemporary Asian American communities, including their role in the economy, see Eric Tang, *Unsettled: Cambodian Refugees in the New York City Hyperghetto* (Philadelphia: Temple University Press, 2015); Tarry Hum, *Making a Global Immigrant Neighborhood: Brooklyn's Sunset Park* (Philadelphia, PA: Temple University Press, 2014); and Margaret M. Chin, *Sewing Women: Immigration and the New York City Garment Industry* (New York: Columbia University Press, 2005).

3   Lee C. Lee, ed. "Asian American Studies: Contemporary Issues," *East Coast Asian American Scholars Conference Proceedings* (Cornell University, 1987). About fifty scholars and students from private and public institutions (almost exclusively from the region) met to strengthen ties in developing AAS, given their relatively small numbers on any campus.

4   I was present at the first East of California Initiative meeting as a faculty member from Hunter College/CUNY. At the time of the Association of Asian American Studies conference at Hunter College, which was supported by the Asian/American Center at Queens College/CUNY and City College of New York/CUNY, I was President of AAAS and Chair of the Hunter College Conference Committee. Several contributors to *Asian American Matters: A New York Anthology* (AAARI-CUNY, 2017) were also present at both events. Margaret M. Chin who served as Conference Coordinator, later attended graduate school, and is presently an Associate Professor of Sociology at Hunter College. There are many examples of transnational understandings of AAS in this anthology.

Author
Shirley Hune is Professor Emerita of Urban Planning at UCLA and Educational Leadership & Policy Studies at the University of Washington. She served as Associate Provost of Hunter College/CUNY (1990-92) and Associate Dean of the Graduate Division at UCLA (1992-2007). Her publications are in the areas of Asian American historiography, critical race, gender, and immigration studies, and higher education issues. Her earlier research examined third world and global developments. She is a former President of the Association for Asian American Studies and has been on the editorial boards of *Amerasia Journal*, *Journal of Asian American Studies*, and *AAPI Nexus*.

3

WRITING ACROSS, AGAINST AND BEYOND BORDERS

"*Everyone lives in a story...because stories are all there are to live in, it was just a question of which you chose.*"

—Amitav Ghosh
The Shadow Lines (1988)

"Around Town 1," Digital C-Print (2012)
Concept and performance by Anida Yoeu Ali
Photo by Masahiro Sugano

THE ASIAN AMERICAN EXPERIENCE has always taken transnational cues; Asians today may belong to two or more ethnicities, races, religions, languages, and communities. Ming Xia describes his intellectual training and journey from mainland China to the U.S., his being banned from China, and his subsequent exploration of India, South Asia and Islam, and his ideas around a broader, pan-Asian vantage.

Meena Alexander, herself educated in Africa, France, England and the U.S., describes her recent journey to Palestine as a poet-in residence at Al-Quds University. She experiences both Palestine and Jerusalem on both sides of the separation wall.

Judy Yung recounts the poignant stories of Chinese detainees and their poems written on the walls of Ellis Island. Yung, together with the late Him Mark Lai, are known for their translations of earlier poems written on the walls of Angel Island in San Francisco Bay, but few have known or seen the expressions by Asians on Ellis Island. Vinay Lal explores the gray areas of Asian American Studies—its ambivalences especially in relation to South Asians.

Also included here is a report on "A Third Literature of the Americas," with Evelyn Hu-DeHart, Kathleen Lopez, Maan Lin, Yibing Huang & Wen Jin, put together by Russell C. Leong. Yibing Huang also shares his poem, "Copper." Luis H. Francia contributes three poems on politics, faith, and war in the Philippines.

For further reading, see:

- Reza Aslan, *Tablet & Pen: Literary Landscapes from the Modern Middle East* (*Words Without Borders*) (New York: WW Norton, 2010)
- Erika Lee and Judy Yung, *Angel Island: Immigrant Gateway to America* (New York: Oxford University Press, 2010)
- Meena Alexander, *Fault Lines: A Memoir* (New York: The Feminist Press at CUNY, 2003)
- King-Kok Cheung, *Chinese American Literature without Borders, Gender, Genre, and Form* (New York: Palgrave Macmillan, 2016)

A China Scholar's Rendezvous with Islam

MING XIA

Towards Atman and Brahman

AS A SCHOLAR, my mind has always run the risk of stretching towards and being torn apart by the two extremes of the abstraction ladder: towards a lower level of abstracting the finer analysis of the concretus; or, towards a grander generalization of the abstractus.[1] Within the teachings of Hinduism, a deeper look inwards into the mind may ultimately lead to a higher level of transcendence. Thus, Atman and Brahman, Self and Universe, come into one union; the individual nature of things or events, also lies in their interconnectedness.[2]

Jama Masjid, Delhi

Like many specialists on East Asia/China in the U.S., I started my professional journey as an area/region expert. And despite my age, I cannot believe that I must constantly reinvent myself, now looking into the relevancy of Islam to East Asia/China studies. Raised an atheist in Communist China and trained as a specialist on the West, during the first decade of my academic career I developed my research interests from Matthew Arnold's concept of Hellenism and Hebraism (knowing and doing).[3]

In order to have a more thorough understanding of the origin and essence of Western civilization, my research focus shifted clockwise, first to continental Europe (Roman era and modern/contemporary France), Great Britain, and then the U.S. This smooth journey, however, was interrupted by my departure for the U.S. in 1989, forced upon me by the Tiananmen Square Massacre. While in the West, becoming a "China specialist" was the new expectation of me, a new identity my six-year Ph.D. training was designed for, under the sponsorship of a caring and wise "China hand."

Since China itself constitutes a civilization, its history and language training often deters China specialists from stretching into other regions, and even into countries such as Japan and Korea. During the first fifteen years of my scholarly experiences in the U.S., my attention, culture-wise, was monocular. Under the pressure of the orthodox paradigm of positivism in American political science, the push to polish one's "quant" skills took precedence over diversifying cultural literacy. This normalcy, however, was punctured by the September 11 terrorist attacks.

In a new preface for the reprint of his book, *Jihad versus McWorld: How Globalism and Tribalism Are Reshaping the World*, political scientist Benjamin Barber wrote sarcastically that, "statistics may help us count the bodies, but it will do little to prevent the slaughter."[4] Barber's clarion call though did not cause an immediate impact upon my research agenda. At the time, I had been straddling both comparative politics and international relations—Asian studies and international political economy. The academic logic of paying attention to the Middle East and Islamic Studies did not occur to me yet.

Islam, China, and the U.S.

Besides the ubiquitous talk of Islam and Muslims—reaching the level of Islamophobia—here in the U.S., three events have converged upon my purview that remind me of how, the issue of Islam, has been posing more questions to my understanding of China and the East.

The Chinese state-sponsored project of assimilating Muslims and Islam into "Chinese-ness" has become a source of contention in Chinese politics. Regarding how to treat Muslims, China and the U.S. share some similarities, despite the fact that the pair form a contrast of autocracy versus democracy. For example, the process of both "localization" and "nationalization" has created a strange phenomenon in China. Many Chinese (those who share basic ethnic features of the Han Chinese) are classified as non-Han "minority nationalities," mainly due to their faith in Islam. Among fifty-five so-called "minority nationalities," ten are Muslim, accounting for seventeen million people.

The third largest one, the "Hui nationality" (close to ten million), is scattered among the Han people. Using Islamic faith as the main foundation for classifying several such "minority nationalities" makes it difficult for Islam to spread among non-believer Han Chinese. To some extent, the U.S. has "naturalized" the Muslim American "into an ethnicity" in the same fashion.[5]

I am not certain whether this parallel can be attributed to an American degenerative imitation of China, or a common imperial logic from the center toward the periphery. However, the twentieth century concept of "Chinese nation" was constructed mostly from a Han Chinese (accounting for 92% of the total population) perspective to subsume all fifty-six nationalities under this category. Understandably, this umbrella concept for nation-building has been contested by major minority nationalities, mainly Tibetans, Uighurs and others living in China's Far West.

Through the Lens of Islam

Under its entire course of communist rule, the Chinese central government in Beijing has had persistent tensions with Tibetans and Muslim minorities in the Far West. This drastic deterioration of relationships, however, only just happened recently within the new century, in particular, after 2008, where it reached its worst. Unfortunately, the securitization of Islamic affairs, and the ensuing demonization of Muslims in the U.S. under the guise of the global War on Terror, has offered a convenient pretext for the Chinese government to place Tibetans and Uighur Muslims under de jure, or de facto martial law (in 2008 and 2009 respectively).

The Chinese Party-state has charged these groups against three particular crimes: "extremism, terrorism, and splittism." Ironically, these three charges are a perfect indictment of the Party-state itself which follows ideological extremism, implements state-sponsored terrorism, and drives centrifugal forces into accelerated splittism (as seen with Xinjiang, Tibet, Taiwan, and Hong Kong). China has become a significant part in the long fault line of conflicts between Islam, and all other major civilizations, as dramatized by political scientist Samuel P. Huntington. To fully understand the cruel nature of the Chinese stability-maintenance regime, depends upon your knowledge of Islam and the Muslims in China.

According to the Chinese government, there are "five anti-China poisons" overseas—namely, the Democracy Movement, Taiwan, Tibetans, Uighurs, and the Falun Gong. Naturally, China's democratization must involve participants from all five forces. Being among this loose community in the West, I have been asked and pressured by some Uighur activists to address their grievances and needs, having been both scolded and helped by them, to understand the subtleties of Islamic religion and culture.

For example, Wu'er Kaixi, a legendary student leader in the 1989 Beijing Student Movement, and a Uighur himself, proposed that the National Committee of the China Democracy Party recognize and award, Ilham Tohti, a moderate Uighur economist imprisoned for life by the Chinese government. At numerous forums that I have organized, representatives from the Uighur American Association, Europe East Turkistan Union, and the Ilham Tohti Initiative in Europe, all have shed light upon the current crises in China and its future projection from a Muslim perspective. As a Han Chinese, I have gradually adjusted myself by offering some accommodations to my Muslim colleagues, such as adding Halal food to conference refreshments; using East Turkistan/Xinjiang simultaneously; and developing a fuller understanding of Muslims' grievances and identity, respecting and being sympathetic to their endeavors.

The increasing frequency and fatality of violent clashes between the State and Uighurs—as a byproduct, the rising tensions between Han Chinese and Muslims beyond Xinjiang, between China and Islamic states (Turkey and Malaysia, for example)—offer a compelling reason to assess the rise, or the demise, of the Chinese Communist regime as a multiethnic empire through the lens of Islam.

Freedom from the Known

As China has shifted its standpoint away from an erstwhile outward-looking attitude toward universal values, into an atavistic China, concerned with exceptionalism and "the great rejuvenation of the Chinese nation," my anti-regime standpoint was sharpened further by my inadvertent involvement with an Oscar-nominated film, *China's Unnatural Disaster: The Tears of Sichuan Province*. This critical documentary covered the collapse of school buildings during the 2008 earthquake, and questioned construction standards which angered the government.

Due to the film, together with my old disloyalty to the Party-state in 1989, and my newfound friendship with His Holiness the 14th Dalai Lama, the Chinese government decided to place me on a blacklist, denying my entry to China. My oppositional standpoint gave me an unexpected vantage point to "see the reality 'behind,' 'beneath' and 'from outside' the oppressors' institutionalized vision."[6]

After the Chinese government slammed its China door on me, it unintentionally brought me a new gift: freedom from the known.[7] After having secured my tenure and promotion to full professor, I plunged into Indo-Tibetan Studies, a vast field that has long entreated and intimidated me at the same time. To some degree, this big plunge was cushioned by my excursion into Southeast Asia. The more liberal and pluralistic Islamic culture, in both India and Southeast Asia, offered me a less culturally risky entry into Muslim lives and Islam.

During my first sabbatical in 2003-2004 at the Woodrow Wilson Center for International Scholars, I was invited for an exclusive lunch with Benazir Bhutto, the late former Prime Minister of Pakistan and the first woman to head a Muslim majority nation. This was the first time in my life that a Muslim woman in a hijab personally explained her points of view to me on global and regional affairs.

During the last third of my sabbatical at the National University of Singapore, ethnic and religious riots broke out from the provinces of Narathiwat, Yala and Pattani at the Thai-Malay borders, over the deaths of eighty Muslim protesters who suffocated during their detention and transport in overheated army trucks. To defuse tensions and re-build peace, the Thai Prime Minister at the time, Thaksin Shinawatra, ordered military airplanes to drop, not bombs, but instead, a hundred million paper origami cranes with peace messages.

Shinawatra's counterpart at the time, Lee Kuan Yew, and his attitudes on ethnic relationship, in particular between Chinese and Malay Muslims in Singapore, were noted against this big backdrop. Lee reflected that among his generation, Muslims and Chinese integrated well. Referring to his Muslim colleagues, Lee said: "We drank beer, we went canvassing, we went electioneering, we ate together. Now they say, 'Are the plates clean?' I said, 'You know, same washing machine.' Halal, non-Halal and so on, I mean, they are all divisive."[8]

Former Prime Minister of Malaysia, Mahathir bin Mohamad, had harsh criticisms of political Islam. However, conservative influences from the Arab world upon Southeast Asia were increasing. For many countries in my East Asian and Southeast Asian Politics teaching, the Islamic angle and *The Qu'ran* have become a prerequisite for a comprehensive understanding of the political development and underdevelopment there (in addition to Indonesia, Malaysia, Thailand, Burma, and the Philippines).

When I spent my second sabbatical in Singapore in 2011, I was given two books as gifts at a book fair: *Translation of the Meanings of The Noble Qu'ran in the English Language*, by Muhammad Taqi-ud-Din al-Hilali and Muhammad Muhsin Khan; and *Revelation, Rationality, Knowledge and Truth*, by Mirza Tahir Ahmad.[9] Although I have read *The Qu'ran* in both Chinese and English, as well as other books on Islam before, these two books plus Manzooruddin Ahmed's *Islamic Political System in the Modern Age*[10] boosted my confidence to venture into Muslim politics and to introduce such topics in my undergraduate teaching.

One unforgettable experience was when I wandered over to a mosque on top of a hill nearby the National University of Singapore faculty living compound during prayer time. The Imam invited me in, prepared me and guided me through the entire prayer process. The worshippers helped chant and pray in Arabic for me, and later I was invited to join their dinner. Although I had some reservations about Lee Kuan Yew's neo-authoritarian politics in Singapore, I appreciated his policy on multi-religious and cultural tolerance and integration. And so, as a non-Muslim, I was able to experience firsthand the whole process of Islamic worship.

Rendezvous – Asian and Islamic Studies

Circumstantial factors, serendipity and my own curiosity led me to embrace Islam, not as a believer, but as a scholar. For me, it has become a natural rendezvous for Asian Studies (even for China Studies) and Islamic Studies. It is worth pointing out that the concept of "the East" as defined by the Chinese orthodox scholarship, has become equivalent to Chinese-ness and China. However, the East constitutes a whole, only after we start treating China and the Sinic countries—Japan, ASEAN (Association of Southeast Asian Nations) countries, India, and Islamic countries (Iran and Turkey, for example)—as legitimate parts of Asian Studies, a *Pancaskandha* under Pan-Asianism.

MIng Xia at the National Islamic Center of Malaysia

In 2013, while standing on Galata Koprusu gazing at the skyline of Istanbul and the sparkling water of the Bosphorus strait, I realized that my global intellectual journey had completed a full clockwise circle. Therefore, I do agree with Moustafa Bayoumi's proposition to include and recognize Islamic and Muslim Studies in Asian Studies, in order to expand its ontology and critically examine the epistemology practiced in the field. Elaborating on Bayoumi's argument on the subsumption of Asian Studies into the "National Security lens," and the "opportunity and recognition" for scholars on Asia (myself, having already included Islamic and Muslim Studies), I can certainly see a connection between the two.[11]

Under the American-centric National Security lens, traditional Area/Regional Studies can never rid itself of the auxiliary role in social sciences that privilege those disciplines and sub-disciplines on the U.S. Nor can it challenge the hegemonic status for a group of mostly American-born scholars, keeping "foreigners" off limits. A hierarchy exists in terms of nations and regions, which therefore pervades academic disciplines and scholarly subjects as well. I had the experience once of being told by a former coordinator that I was not qualified to teach "Comparative Human Rights," after a retired professor had asked me to keep running the course. This coordinator's rationale was that I did not have the knowledge about the U.S. Constitution and civil rights, even though I trained for ten years as a comparativist of Western political systems in China, and took American Politics as one of my Ph.D. comprehensive exams.

A Politics of Transformation

How do we redress such a subtle racialized slight? I believe it is important to introduce a "fundamental politics of transformation" in Asian and Asian American Studies, not only for scholars like us to have a "more just and equitable society," but also, as I feel, for people living in the ancestral/motherlands we have left behind, to be able to enjoy justice and equity.

But, how can we achieve such ambitious transformations? Differing from the common goal to redress "an internalized racial logic" as identified by Bayoumi,[12] I would like to replace such a defensive strategy, by forming a united front with an active and ambitious enterprise to succeed for the sake of its intrinsic value and importance. I also think that the increasingly complex regional conflicts in Asia (Zomia Studies)[13] and the world (the "clash of civilizations," the West vs. the rest—namely the Confucian-Islamic nexus identified by Samuel P. Huntington, of course is debatable)[14] force us to identify the sources and solutions of these conflicts in the context of traditional Asian and Islamic Studies.

The Shanghai Cooperation Organization, led by China and Russia, has been offering an anti-West authoritarian bastion in the Eurasian continent, appealing especially to Iran, Pakistan, and Turkey. How can we Asian specialists offer some ideas for solving these fundamental challenges facing the U.S. and the world, including the conflicts arising from racial, religious, and ethnic factors? Huntington believed that, "Asia is the cauldron of civilizations. East Asia alone contains societies belonging to six civilizations— Japanese, Sinic, Orthodox, Buddhist, Muslim, and Western—and South Asia adds Hinduism."[15]

Turning away from the Judeo-Christian bias lurking in Huntington's writings, towards a positive attitude, if we can realize that Asia has offered many social laboratories, and therefore, opportunities to understand and resolve the grand clash of civilizations, we can then easily transcend the Bermuda triangle of conflicts among the three Abrahamic monotheistic religions that thwart many promising plans for peace. We must move away from the Western-centric zero-sum solution and try to contribute a non-zero sum remedy from the Asian repertoire of wisdom for conducting war and building peace.

The relationship between Islam and other religions, at least in monsoon Asia, had not been part of the Western discourse on national security. Therefore, it did not have the antagonism of absolute ideologies. The most impressive, and, for many Western observers, unthinkable fact, is that India has had three Muslim presidents, a Sikh prime minister, an Italian Catholic president of the National Congress Party, and a Christian defense minister in the cabinet. The "Father of the Indian Constitution," B.R. Ambedkar, converted to Buddhism. As a Hindu, philosopher Sri Ramakrishna "experimented with different faiths," studying Christianity and meditating on *The Qu'ran*.[16] According to Ramakrishna, "I have practiced all religions—Hinduism, Islam, Christianity—and I have also followed the paths of the different Hindu sects. I have found that it is the same God toward whom all are directing their steps, though along different paths."[17]

This inclusive embrace of all religions influenced Mahatma Gandhi, who said: "In the morning I used to read the Gita and at noon, mostly the Qu'ran. In the evening I taught the Bible."[18] "I consider myself a Hindu, Christian, Muslim, Jew, Buddhist, and Confucian."[19] Both Hinduism and Buddhism (see the Dalai Lama's *Beyond Religion: Ethics for a Whole World*),[20] share a common understanding of "secularism," which philosopher S. Radhakrishnan explains: "It does not mean opposition to religion. It does not mean disrespect to religion. It only means that the State as such is not identified with any particular religion but tolerates every religion, appreciates every religion, respects all religions—Hindu, Buddhist, Muslim, Christian, etc."[21]

If we can somehow inherit this Hindu-Buddhist solution and its version of secularism, we may possibly do away with the crusading spirit against Islam and non-Abrahamic religions, and offer an Asian solution to global conflict. If we are able to accomplish such a collective success through the cross-fertilization of combining Asian with Islamic Studies, it will surely elevate the standing of Asian Studies, enhancing the respect it enjoys in the social sciences and humanities.

* * *

"Transformation" can be seen and understood in terms of Asian Americans, the U.S. and the world, especially the ancestral/motherlands of researchers in Area/Regional Studies. Most importantly, this success may be a precursor for the coming of an Asian Renaissance under a liberal, democratic, and cosmopolitan framework—a goal for which many Asian specialists (at least this author) have aspired. This may be the highest politics of transformation.

AAARI Lecture Video (September 29, 2017): www.aaari.info/17-09-29Xia.htm

Notes

1   S. I. Hayakawa and Alan R. Hayakawa, *Language in Thought and Action*, 5th ed. (New York: Harcourt Brace, 1990): 84–85.

2   Fritjof Capra, *The Tao of Physics: An Exploration of the Parallels between Modern Physics and Eastern Mysticism* (Boston: Shambhala, 2010); Fritjof Capra, *The Web of Life: A New Scientific Understanding of Living System* (New York: Anchor Books, 1997).

3   Matthew Arnold, *Culture and Anarchy* (Cambridge: Cambridge University Press, 1955): Chap. 4.

4   Benjamin Barber, *Jihad versus McWorld* (New York: Ballantine, 2001): XXV.

5   Moustafa Bayoumi, "Asian American Studies, the War on Terror, and the Changing University: A Call to Respond," *Asian American Matters: A New York Anthology* (AAARI-CUNY, 2017): 21.

6   Sandra Hardin, "Philosophy and Standpoint Theory," in George Steinmetz, ed., *The Politics of Method in the Human Science* (Durham: Duke University Press, 2005): 355.

7   J. Krishnamurti, *Total Freedom: The Essential Krishnamurti* (New York: HarperOne, 1996): 109.

8   Lee Kuan Yew, *Hard Truths: To Keep Singapore Going"* (Singapore: Strait Times, 2011): 228–229.

9   Mirza Tahir Ahmad, *Revelation, Rationality, Knowledge and Truth* (UK: Islam International Publications Limited, 1998).

10   Manzooruddin Ahmed, *Islamic Political System in the Modern Age: Theory and Practice* (New Delhi: Adam Publishers and Distributors, 2006).

11   Bayoumi, *Asian American Matters*: 23.

12   *Ibid.*

13   James Scott, *The Art of Not Being Governed: An Anarchist History of Upland Southeast Asia* (New Haven: Yale University Press, 2009).

14   Samuel P. Huntington, *The Clash of Civilizations and the Remaking of World Order* (New York: Touchstone Books, 1996).

15   *Ibid.*: 219.

16   S. Radhakrishnan, *Eastern Religions and Western Thought* (New Delhi: Oxford University Press, 2010 [1940]).

17   Swami Nikhilananda, "The Gospel of Sri Ramakrishna," *Ramakrishna Math and Ramarishna Mission*, http://www.belur-math.org/gospel/introduction.htm (accessed February 18, 2017).

18   *Wikisource*, https://en.m.wikisource.org/wiki/Page:Speeches_And_Writings_MKGandhi.djvu/251 (accessed February 18, 2017).

19   Lawrence J. Peter, *Peter's Quotations* (New York: William Morrow, 1977): 428.

20   Dalai Lama, *Beyond Religion: Ethics for a Whole World* (Boston: Houghton Mifflin Harcourt, 2011).

21   S. Radhakrishnan, *Our Heritage* (New Delhi: Orient Paperbacks, 1994 [1973]): 148–149.

Author

Ming Xia is a Professor of Political Science at the College of Staten Island/CUNY, and a doctoral faculty member at the CUNY Graduate Center. Dr. Xia previously taught at Fudan University (1988-1991) and served as a residential research fellow at the Sigur Center for Asian Studies at George Washington University (2003), and the Woodrow Wilson International Center for Scholars (2004). At the National University of Singapore, he worked as a visiting research fellow (2004) and a senior visiting research fellow (2011) at the East Asian Institute, and a visiting senior research fellow (2012) at the Asian Research Institute. Dr. Xia's research interests include political governance and transition in China, organized crime, international political economy, globalization, Asian women in politics, and a comparison of China and India.

Impossible Grace
Poems and a Journey

MEENA ALEXANDER

"There is a way in which beauty can heal."

I.

IT KEPT RINGING IN MY HEAD: I am going to Jerusalem. I was a child again, sitting between my parents in the car, speeding past no man's land. The U.N. flag fluttering. I remember stones, dry earth, barbed wire. And in the city we had left behind, tiny streets, the glowing hunched buildings, donkeys with their burden, pilgrims stooped on Via Dolorosa, the misty darkness and glory of the church of the Holy Sepulchre. In those days with an Indian passport there were two countries one couldn't travel to: South Africa and Israel. So we came through Jordan. My parents wanted to attend Easter services in Jerusalem. After that came the Six-Day War. I left my childhood behind and moved on.

While Jerusalem remained with me in memory, I had no hope of going there. Then quite by chance, in May 2010, in the mountains of Shimla at the Indian Institute for Advanced Studies, I met the philosopher Sari Nusseibeh. We were all gathered there for a conference on History and Memory. I remember a group of us riding up in a minivan through the twisting mountain roads. Sari was sitting near me.

Do you know the poetry of Fadwa Touqan? I asked him. The memoir *Mountainous Journey* was vivid in my mind. Do you teach her work at your university?

I must find out he said, if we teach her work. Then he counseled me to read Al Khansa's poetry. There is something mystical about it, he said. She had a very close relationship with her brother.

I would love to come to Palestine someday. I said this never thinking it could happen.

You will come as our guest, he said.

So it was that time opened up and with his kind invitation I was able to spend a month in Palestine—as Poet in Residence at Al-Quds University. And I was invited by my friend the Egyptian novelist Ahdaf Souief to join the Palestine Festival of Literature (PalFest) which was to take place towards the end of my month in Palestine.

*

Preparing for my journey I started dreaming of the separation wall. It invaded my dreams. All over the world walls were coming down, and here was one that was built to cut a people away from the earth.

*

Sometimes poems have a life of their own. So it was with 'Impossible Grace.' On the night of April 4, 2011, just a few days after I arrived in Jerusalem, I wrote the poem. I wanted to evoke the many gates of the city of Jerusalem, and for each gate I wanted a flower, but in the end the poem turned out differently and there is only the wild iris in it, its color blue-mauve like the sky in the early morning above the hills of Jerusalem.

In some ways it's a love poem. I wrote it in the dead of night in the Indian Hospice where I was staying, my bedroom cut out of the rock face, right next to the hole where the thirteenth century mystic Baba Farid had lived for forty days and nights meditating on God. I wrote it in the city of golden stones and of many faiths, the city of countless gates.

Rock Garden Courtyard at Indian Hospice in Jerusalem, Israel

In my notebook I wrote: *Why was the gate of Mercy sealed?*

That line did not make it into the poem which was composed in tight couplets. I heard music in my head as I wrote the poem. I read it the next morning to Sari when I saw him on campus. I had called him earlier before I started the poem to ask about the gates of Jerusalem. In the poem the old man who guides the speaker towards the fountain is a real person who sometimes takes visitors around the city. And Raimon's café, is a real place.

Later it troubled me to see the Israeli soldiers sitting on the parapet by the cafe, just inside Damascus gate, swinging their feet. How young the soldiers were, as two by two they patrolled the old city. I was often stopped and asked the question: Are you a Muslim? Sometimes the soldiers barred my way. I did not reply. I would instead try to tell them where I was going. Coming from a country founded on secular principles I felt my religion was no one's business but my own. No doubt it was not just the way I looked, but also the fact that I was wearing *churidar-kameez* with a *dupatta* that made them ask the question.

I gave a talk at Al-Quds and I spoke of Gandhi and how my mother's parents had been followers of his non-violent movement and the fierce belief they had that India would be freed from the yoke of British colonialism. I spoke of Palestine and how people all over the world hoped there would be a peaceful future.

I read out my poem 'Impossible Grace' on the last day of the Palestine Literary Festival. It happened quite by accident. It was not meant to be like that. The reading in the tent in Silwan—where settlers were destroying Palestinian homes—was meant to be for the townspeople to read their own work and the members of PalFest would be their audience. That was the idea, but the evening had gone badly.

When we got there, after a reception at the American Colony Hotel, the street was filled with the acrid scent of tear gas. Earlier that evening, April 20, 2011, the Israeli army had lobbed tear gas at the tent, trying to get rid of the people in it. Close to Silwan the bus stopped. We left the bus and walked in a group. The dark was illuminated by lights from a few shops, and we could see the glowing lights in the houses nearby. A cluster of people stood there, as we figured out what to do. Onions helped, cut onions that were passed around, scarves, scraps of tissue, anything to ease the fumes of tear gas. There were broken stones on the road, and from the houses nearby the people were chanting *Allāh u Akbar*. Whistles came in the dark. There were soldiers on the hillside nearby, though we could not immediately see them.

How dark the tent was as we stumbled in. A cheer went up as the lights came on. Plastic chairs were rearranged quickly. The man from the Silwan Solidarity Committee who welcomed us spoke in very moving fashion. We had wanted to welcome you, he said, in our own way and with the poems of a thirteen-year-old poet, but see we now welcome you with tear gas. One of the signs in the tent read—'Israel wants to demolish the houses of 1,500 years. We will not give up our houses—Bustan Committee.'

There was supposed to be an open mic so the people of Silwan could read and share their work, but because of the tear gas, the parents had taken their children to the relative safety of home.

Read something Meena, Ahdaf said to me.

All I had was my notebook. I pulled it out of my bag, opened it and found 'Impossible Grace.' So that was how I came to read 'Impossible Grace' for the very first time in public. Ahdaf translated the poem, on the spot into Arabic, stanza by stanza. I was glad that the poem was composed in short, terse couplets, perhaps that would make her task easier, I thought. Then Gary Younge, *The Guardian* reporter read, as did several other writers. Some in our group who had delicate lung conditions were forced to leave—the tear gas was hurting them. Others stayed till the end and the Palestinian rap group DAM brought the house down with their songs. The first song was in English. It had lines about a man in an elevator with a beautiful woman who trained her sub-machine gun at him. The singer had on a T-shirt with a teddy bear with an eyepatch. Why the eyepatch? I asked. He looked straight at me, laughed and said—Just like that.

Six months later, I was in Delhi. My cell phone rang. It was Petra Klose calling from Vienna to ask if I would give permission for the poem 'Impossible Grace' to be used as the lyric base for the First Al-Quds Composition Award. I remember us talking that evening in Delhi, over a really bad phone line. I heard music in my head as I was composing the poem, I told Petra.

In October 2012 I traveled from New York for the premiere performance. As the baritone Christian Oldenburg sang in the theater of Hind Husseini College, my eyes filled with tears. I seemed to smell again, the tear gas that had invaded our eyes, the first time that poem found its way into public space. And I thought of how we had stood on a terrace at Al-Quds, the separation wall was so very close, it stood there like a backdrop. Above it floated clouds.

One of these days that wall will dissolve away, I had said out loud for anyone who was willing to listen —just like the clouds. It was what I believed and still do.

Impossible Grace

At Herod's gate
I heap flowers in a crate

Poppies, moist lilies—
It's dusk, I wait.
*
Wild iris—
The color of your eyes before you were born

That hard winter
And your mother brought you to Damascus gate.
*
My desire silent as a cloud,
It floats through New gate

Over the fists
Of the beardless boy-soldiers.
*
You stopped for me at Lion's gate,
Feet wet with dew

From the torn flagstones
Of Jerusalem.
*
Love, I was forced to approach you
Through Dung gate

My hands the color
Of the broken houses of Silwan.
*
At Zion's gate I knelt and wept.
An old man, half lame—

He kept house in Raimon's café,
Led me to the fountain.
*
At Golden gate,
Where rooftops ring with music

I glimpse your face.
You have a coat of many colors—impossible grace.

Music video: https://youtu.be/XoHz_gynDoo
Composed by Stefan Heckel

Impossible Grace (Arabic Version)

الرحمة المستحيلة

I.

عند باب الساهرة

أكوم زهورا في سحارة

شقائق النعمان والزنبق الرطب

وصلت فترة الغسق فانتظرت

II.

السوسن البري

لون عيونك قبل أن تولد

وذلك الشتاء القاسي

عندما اتت بك امك الى باب العمود

III.

طافت رغبتي الصامتة كالسحابة

عبر باب الجديد.

فوق قبضات

الجنود اليافعين الملساء

IV.

توقفت لتنتظرني عند باب الاسباط

وقدماك مبللان بالندى

من أحجار

القدس

V.

حبي، اضطررت أن اتي اليك عبر

باب المغاربه

ويدايا مصبوغة بلون

بيوت سلوان المدمرة

VI.

عند باب الاسباط ركعت وبكيت

وقادني الرجل العجوز الاعرج

الساكن في قهوة ريمون

الى النافورة

VII.

وعند الباب الذهبي

حيث تملأ الموسيقى الاجواء

لمحت وجهك

لديك معطف ملون بألوان كثيرة – الرحمة المستحيلة

Separation Wall in Bethlehem, Palestine

II.

I was getting ready for my journey to Jerusalem. March 31, 2011, I stood in a cold ill-lit portion of the Rome airport. Behind me was a woman, young and pale, a baby on her back, another woman tugging her child along. Long skirts. One mother pulling a blue plastic truck. The men behind them, dark in Jewish skull caps.

Were they Indian? Were they from Kerala, my home state? With a start I realized they were speaking Hebrew, not Malayalam.

How time was looping in my head. What should I say when the immigration people faced me at the Tel Aviv airport? Friends had told me not to say that I was going to a Palestinian institution. I am going to Jerusalem. I am going to see my husband's Jewish cousins. I am going to give poetry readings. Perhaps if I said some of this they would not take my notes away from me, take away my computer. I had heard stories of friends who were visiting Palestine losing so much in the Tel Aviv airport. I tucked my notebook away, tightly in my purse.

Pigeons distracted me. Pigeons inside Terminal H of Fiumicino Airport, swooping low by the D&G sign. Bird wings outstretched and fluttering over the neon signs: Dolce & Gabbana.

Later in my notebook I wrote:

"I am flying into my own fate."

It was dark when the plane landed at Ben Gurion Airport. Navtej Sarna had graciously arranged for me to stay at the Indian Hospice in the old walled city of Jerusalem, just inside Herod's Gate. It was to be my home for many days to come. Outside the airport the driver was waiting for me. A burly middle-aged man, he engaged me in small talk and as we drove in the darkness. He pointed out, by the apartments built on the hill, an ugly scarring thing, brightly lit, a concrete hulk.

The wall! he said. On this side Israel. On this side Palestine. He moved his right hand off the steering wheel and swiftly gestured back and forth.

Meena Alexander with two students on the Al-Quds campus

Slowly we drove towards the ancient city of Jerusalem. Nazeer the son of Sheik Ansari, was waiting for me at Herod's Gate. It's called Baab al Zehra—the flower gate, he said. He had been waiting for me in the half-darkness a long time. I did not want you to arrive and no one to welcome you, he said. His great-great-grandfather came from India. For well over a hundred years his family had been there. They married Palestinian women. All this he told me as we walked through the ancient stones of Herod's Gate, up the steps towards a large green metal gate that he opened swiftly. There was a long pathway with tall thin trees on either side. I glanced at my watch. It was 2am.

Why was clock time so important? I jotted it down in my notebook. Time, something to hold onto.

My bedroom was cut out of Jerusalem rock. It was whitewashed, cool, and had a curved roof with two beds, a mirror and an attached bathroom. I felt safe in that room and woke to hear the muezzin from the Al Aqsa mosque calling the faithful to prayer. I walked out in my dressing gown in bare feet and made my way to a well made of golden stones. In a room just a few feet from mine were a set of steps leading down into the hole where Baba Farid the thirteenth century mystic had come all the way from India. It is said he stood in that hole for forty days and nights singing praises to God.

I sat by the well side. I felt as I had died and returned to where I was meant to be.

I made friends with the elder daughter of the house and she told me her story. As our friendship deepened she showed me her misshapen ankle—a bit of bone cut out. She explained how bombs fell on the Indian Hospice in 1967 killing her grandmother, aunt, and aunt's seven-year-old son.

She said: I had bone cut out of my foot. Mother would not let the doctors amputate the foot, though they wanted to. Why do I need a girl without a foot? mother said. So they patched up the bone. They kept bombing from the sky, and when we ran to this other side of the courtyard, the bombs followed us. Where is Sheikh Ansari they asked—the soldiers who came to find him. They wanted to kill him. Don't kill him, mother cried out. My father was covered in burns. It was napalm they used. I hate war. O how I hate war!

Then she put out her hand and drew me forward. She led me down into the hole in Jerusalem rock where the saint Baba Farid stood for forty days and nights without food. How dark it was inside the hole. Bit by bit my eyes adjusted and I could make out rock and what felt like a spider's web. Surely there were tiny creatures of the earth scurrying there.

My friend had a parrot in a cage. She set the cage on the warm cobblestones of the courtyard. The parrot calls her Tutu. Tutu, Tutu, it cried. On and on it cried. There were other birds too in the courtyard of the Indian Hospice, and each morning I woke to their warbling. In the courtyard there was a lemon tree with golden fruit, an olive tree and pots of flowers, jasmine and a purple headed bloom whose name I did not know. Also the blood red flower, red anemone—Shaqqiq An-Numan (the wounds of Numan). One sees it everywhere in Palestine, amongst the rocks, in dry dark soil.

Once I saw a scarlet clump, right by the separation wall that cuts through the Al-Quds campus in Abu Dis. I was led there by two young women students who befriended me. Please tell our story to the world they said. We are dear friends and after the wall was built we could no longer visit each other. She has a blue card and I have a green one. We are not allowed to meet each other. How can this be?

Another young student said to me. We have no freedom of movement. Why shouldn't we live our lives in freedom? He was escorting me through the museum of prisoners showing me the diaries, the fragile artwork that the political prisoners had made.

There came a moment when I could not bear what human beings were doing to others. So I turned to flowers.

The professor of botany at Al-Quds took me through the land around and showed me so many flowers and shrubs and trees. It was there that I discovered the dark glory of the black iris, a regal, lonely flower. I knelt beside it on the stones and gazed at it for a long time.

There is a way in which beauty can heal. I put the black iris in my poem about Baba Farid. The poem which follows is called 'Indian Hospice.'

*

Indian Hospice

Yesterday it rained so hard
Lemons spilt from the lemon tree
And rolled all over cobble stones in my Jerusalem courtyard.

I thought of Baba Farid
Who came on a pilgrimage centuries ago.
In a hole cut from rock by the room where I sleep

He stood for forty days and nights
Without food or drink. Nothing for him was strange
In the way his body slipped into a hole in the ground
And nothing was not.
Rust in the stones and blood at the rim of his tongue.
In the humming dark

He heard bird beaks stitching webs of dew
Sharp hiss of breath let out from a throat,
Whose throat he did not know.

Was it his mother crying out O Farid, where are you now?
She had done that when he swung
Up and down, knees in a mango tree,

Head in the mouth of a well
Singing praises to God.
Crawling out of his hole there were welts on his cheeks

Underfoot in bedrock — visionary recalcitrance.
A lemon tree shook in a high wind.
Under it, glistening in its own musk, the black iris of Abu Dis.

Wild with the scents of iris and lemon he sang — O Farid
This world is a muddy garden
Stone, fruit and flesh all flaming with love.

AAARI Lecture Video (October 18, 2013): www.aaari.info/13-10-18Alexander.htm

Note

Grateful acknowledgment is made to the journals where these poems were first published. TriQuarterly: 'Impossible Grace'; The Hindu Literary Supplement and Postcolonial Text: 'Indian Hospice.' Both poems appeared in the limited edition chapbook *Impossible Grace* (Jerusalem: Center for Jerusalem Studies, Al-Quds University, 2012). The poems also appeared in *Birthplace with Buried Stones* (Evanston: TriQuarterly Books/ Northwestern University Press, 2013). The music for the poem 'Impossible Grace,' composed by Stefan Heckel, was performed in Jerusalem, and is the winner of the First Al-Quds Composition Award.

Author

Meena Alexander is Distinguished Professor of English at the CUNY Graduate Center and Hunter College/CUNY. Prof. Alexander has two new books forthcoming in 2018: her eighth book of poetry *Atmospheric Embroidery* (TriQuarterly Books/ Northwestern U Press), and the anthology she edited: *Name Me a Word: Indian Writers Reflect on Writing* (Yale U Press). Her awards include those from the John Simon Guggenheim Foundation, the Fulbright Foundation, the Rockefeller Foundations and the Arts Council of England. She has also received the PEN Open Book Award and the Imbongi Yesizwe International Poetry Award from South Africa. In 2011, she was Poet-in-Residence at Al Quds University in Jerusalem, and took part in the Palestine Festival of Literature (PalFest). www.meenaalexander.com

Aerial view of Ellis Island's dormitory building (largest building at top of photo) where Chinese poems were found
Courtesy of Harry H. Laughlin Papers, Special Collections Department, Picker Memorial Library, Truman State University

在家千日好，　A thousand days at home are easy;
出外半天難。　Half a day abroad is hard.[1]

Translated by Charles Egan

Journey to the West
Poems and Stories of Chinese Detainees on Ellis Island

JUDY YUNG

IN 1985, DURING THE RENOVATION of the immigration station at Ellis Island in New York City, preservationists uncovered more than 400 square feet of inscriptions in eleven languages on the walls, columns, partitions, and doors left by detained aliens sometime between 1901 and 1954. There were messages of hope and despair. One Italian immigrant wrote, "Damned is the day that I left my homeland." There were also drawings of boats, birds, flags, and people. Others simply put their hand on the wall and drew its outline as evidence that they had been there.[2]

Among the new discoveries found on the third floor of the Baggage and Dormitory Building were several Chinese poems and inscriptions etched on the marble partitions of the men's bathroom stalls. Some of the poems were partially illegible. One political slogan, "Long live China! Victory to the people! China will overthrow imperialism!" was dated June 17, 1952. None of the other poems were signed or dated, although one poem made reference to the Sino-Japanese War (1937-1945).

Written in the classical style of Chinese poetry with four or eight lines per poem and five or seven characters per line, the poems bear a strong resemblance in content, tone, and language to those found carved into the wooden barracks at Angel Island in San Francisco Bay. This should come as no surprise since the writers were from the same socioeconomic strata and geographic region in China, and all were given similar cold receptions by U.S. immigration officers intent on enforcing the Chinese Exclusion Act.[3]

思念故鄉眼淚流，	Thinking of home, my tears begin to flow;
不知何日可無憂。	I wonder, when I can ever be free of worry?
父母伯叔妻兒散，	Parents, uncles, wives, and children scattered;
樓房屋宇變成溝。	Our houses and rooms completely leveled.
命大如天花旗到，	Luckily I landed in the Flowery Flag,
以為安寧可無愁。	Thinking I would be safe and free of sadness.
誰知移民將我捕，	Who knew that I'd be seized by immigration officials?
不由分說入拘留。	They threw me in detention, ignoring my protests.
何能解決苛條例，	How can I gain relief from these oppressive laws?
待期勝利可自由。	I await the time of our victory, for then we can be free.
亦望同群齊合力，	I hope compatriots will join together, pool their strength,
捐輸回國殺我仇。	Donate funds, and return home to kill our enemies.[4]
得見父母妻兒會，	Then, when I'm reunited with my parents, wife, and children,
笑口吟吟講西遊。	With laughter I'll describe my journey to the West.[5]

Translated by Charles Egan[6]

Adhering to the structure of regulated verse, this poem echoes the same themes and sentiments as found in the Angel Island poems—war and poverty that drove Chinese immigrants overseas, resentment at being detained and confined, and the desire for China to become a free and strong country capable of defending its citizens abroad.

There was one major difference in the backgrounds of Chinese detainees at Angel Island versus Ellis Island—the predominance of Chinese seamen who had been arrested for desertion and were awaiting deportation at Ellis Island—as many as 206 men in 1925 and 300 in 1943.[7] Most of them were poor, uneducated, and from Guangdong Province. Some hailed from Fujian, Shanghai, and Hainan Island. This second poem, a quatrain, was most likely written by one of these sailors.

長監苦困壽命長，　Though imprisonment is long and bitter, my life will be long;

去船恐有身受傷。　When I landed from the ship, I feared bodily harm.

勸君莫怕移民例，　I urge you: don't be afraid of immigration laws—

定有安然放我歸。　It's certain we'll be freed to go home in peace.

Translated by Charles Egan[8]

Another translation of this poem in *The New York Times* interpreted the second line differently: "But I suffer not like I may suffer if I were back on the ship, where they might hurt me if I were to return."[9] This makes sense given that many Chinese seamen at this time were complaining about racial discrimination and cruel treatment on board the foreign vessels they served.

Away from home for six months at a stretch and lonely for female companionship, Chinese sailors were probably also the ones who drew the lewd sketches of nude women and wrote the following poem—a muddled version of a well-known folk rhyme of the late-Qing dynasty. According to Mr. Chow, who was detained at Ellis Island for two weeks in 1950, drawing graffiti on the bathroom walls was one way for the men to relieve their frustration and loneliness. Chow remembered seeing a young man trying to etch the following poem on the bathroom wall. He noticed mistakes in the poem and tried to suggest corrections, but to no avail.[10] No such drawings or poems of a sexual nature were found among the 300 Chinese inscriptions and graphics on the barrack walls at Angel Island.[11]

二八佳人巧樣貌，　A girl just sixteen, of dazzling beauty,

一雙玉手千人枕。　A pair of jade arms, and a pillow for a thousand heads.

伴點脂唇萬客帛，　The dot of rouge on her lips has been tasted by countless men;

洞房晚晚換新郎。　Each night, her bridal bower welcomes a new bridegroom.

Translated by Charles Egan[12]

The original poem of eight lines come from *Qianlong xia Jiangnan* (*Emperor Qianlong Travels to the South*), a novel that describes the romantic and martial adventures of Prince Bao before he ascended the throne as Emperor Qianlong. In Chapter Eighteen, the prince, dressed as a commoner, asks a favored courtesan to write him a poem, and she offers the following:

二八佳人巧樣妝，　A girl just sixteen, with dazzling makeup;

洞房夜夜換新郎。　Her bridal bower, each night, welcomes a new bridegroom.

一雙玉臂千人忱，　A pair of jade arms, and a pillow for a thousand heads.

半點來唇萬客嘗。　The dot of rouge on her lips has been tasted by countless men;

做就幾番嬌媚態，　How many times has she cast a coquettish glance,

裝成一片假心腸。　And pretended a love that was false?

迎來送往知多少？She welcomes them in, and ushers them out – who knows how many?

慣作相思淚兩行。Experienced in love, her tears fall in lines.

Translated by Charles Egan

The literary quality of these poems pales in comparison to the Angel Island poems, which were rendered in beautiful calligraphy on the walls. The absence of literary allusions and historical references in the first two poems and the errors made in the third poem, are indications that Chinese detainees at Ellis Island were probably less educated than those at Angel Island.

*   *   *

Who might these anonymous poets have been? How did they end up at Ellis Island instead of Angel Island, where the overwhelming majority of Chinese immigrants were detained and processed? And what do their poems, oral histories, and immigration records tell us about their treatment at Ellis Island as compared to that of Chinese immigrants at Angel Island?

It all started in 1882 at the height of the anti-Chinese movement brought on by economic recessions, labor strife, and white racism. That year Congress passed the Chinese Exclusion Act, barring the further immigration of Chinese laborers to this country and denying Chinese aliens the right to naturalization. The Exclusion Act marked the end of an open door immigration policy and laid the foundation for subsequent laws that excluded other Asian immigrants and restricted immigration from southern and eastern European countries. It also firmly established the immigration apparatus needed to enforce the immigration laws—inspection and detention sites, inspection policies, and federal documentation such as passports, visas, and "green cards."

Built in 1892, the immigration station at Ellis Island was indisputably the busiest and most important immigrant portal to the United States. Until it closed in 1954, 12 million immigrants, mainly Europeans, were quickly inspected and processed through at the rate of 5,000 people per day. The newcomers were given a cursory physical exam and asked a total of twenty-nine questions to make sure they were not convicted criminals, lunatics, prostitutes, dangerous radicals, or "liable to become a public charge." Twenty percent of the 12 million had to be detained overnight or at most for a week or two because of legal or medical issues. In the end, only 1 percent were denied entry and deported. The exceptions to this pattern were Chinese immigrants, who, like at Angel Island, were thoroughly examined and often detained for weeks and months at a time. According to a newspaper reporter, "Chinese boys seem to spend the longest periods on the island."[13]

Ellis Island may have been the busiest port of entry, but because there was no direct line of ships between China and New York, there were fewer Chinese applicants to inspect at Ellis Island than at Angel Island. From 1900 to 1930, 100,000 Chinese applicants were processed through San Francisco and Angel Island, as compared to 40,000 at Port Townsend and Seattle, 20,000 at Honolulu, and only 5,000 at Ellis Island. Compared to Angel Island, detention time was shorter for the Chinese at Ellis Island and there were fewer exclusions and appeals, mainly because of the higher class of travelers (merchants, students, and government officials) who were coming to New York from Europe, Cuba, Trinidad, and Mexico. As was true at Angel Island, first- and second-class passengers were usually inspected on board the ship and did not have to even step foot on Ellis Island. Only 5 percent of the Chinese applicants who were denied entry at Ellis Island appealed their cases as compared to 25 percent at Angel Island, but the deportation rate for the Chinese at Ellis Island was twice as high—12 percent as compared to 6 percent at Angel Island.[14]

Based on a list of 4,142 Chinese exclusion case files from Ellis Island at the National Archives in New York, I estimate that 90 percent of the detainees were male, 40 percent claimed U.S. citizenship, 20 percent claimed merchant status, 8 percent were students, and 5 percent were seamen or stowaways awaiting deportation.[15] Many of the Chinese immigrants had come to Ellis Island by way of Hong Kong,

Vancouver, Montreal, and Halifax. Upon arrival, they were turned over to immigrant inspectors in the Chinese Division of the U.S. Immigration Service. These so-called "Chinese inspectors" were well aware of the devious methods that the Chinese were employing to evade the Chinese exclusion laws and gain admission into the country—by smuggling across the Canadian border, falsely claiming to be members of the exempt classes, or surrendering themselves at the border for arrest and trial under the guise of being natives of the United States. Their job was to prevent the illegal entry of Chinese immigrants into the country. Immigrant inspectors held all Chinese claims for right of admission suspect until the applicant's identity and asserted relationship could be verified through cross examination on matters of common knowledge between the applicant and his witnesses. The burden of proof was on the applicant.[16]

The Case of Native Sons

The *Commissioner-General of Immigration (CGI) Annual Report* for FY1936/37 noted that most Chinese seeking permanent residence at that time were claiming the right to enter as American citizens, either by reason of birth in the U.S. or as the foreign-born children of citizens, as the following three cases show.

In 1939, after a tearful parting with his mother in Toishan City, sixteen-year-old William Yee left for Hong Kong, where he boarded the *Empress of China* bound for Vancouver. Summoned by his father, who was living in New York at the time, he was leaving home to avoid conscription and to escape the ravages of the Sino-Japanese War. "I'm actually a fourth-generation American," he said in an interview with the Ellis Island Oral History Program.[17] In 1869, the year that the transcontinental railroad was completed, his great-grandfather became the first in the family to go abroad to seek his fortune. He found work as a sheep rancher in Wyoming and returned to China, where he died. William's grandfather also went to America to try his luck, but he died within two years of some illness. William's own father had better luck. He first worked in the canneries of California and Alaska before settling down in New York City. Now it was William's turn to continue the tradition of going overseas to make a better living.

From Vancouver, William took the Trans-Canadian Railroad to Montreal and made his way to Halifax, where he got on a cruise ship headed for New York. "Looking at the Statue of Liberty," he recalled, "I know I'm here, [I've arrived]." His father was at the port to meet him, but he was not free to go with him. Instead, William was taken to Ellis Island by ferry for immigration inspection. Unlike Angel Island, he was not subjected to a blood and stool examination for parasitic diseases, but his eyes were probably checked for signs of trachoma. Then he had to wait three weeks before he was called for a hearing before a Board of Special Inquiry (BSI) consisting of two immigrant inspectors, a stenographer, and a Chinese interpreter—just like at Angel Island.

When asked to describe his stay at Ellis Island, William replied, "Ellis Island is a confined space [with] a guard outside your dormitory and you stay within the confines of your dormitory." He recalled that the dormitory, where the Chinese men were kept segregated from women and other races, was almost full. As to the food he was served in the dining hall, William vaguely remembered there was rice and Chinese food, "no hamburgers or anything like that."[18] Unlike the Chinese detainees at Angel Island who all complained that the Chinese food was inedible, William had no complaints. To pass the time, he said, they could participate in arts and craft classes run by volunteers. The rest of the time he spent waiting to be called for the interrogation. "Some people came back crying because they had answered wrong, and some people were very depressed. I just felt numb the whole time, waiting to get out of there."

Gem Hoy "Harry" Lew, who was detained at Ellis Island for two months in 1951, also claimed to be the son of a U.S. citizen. Fifteen years old at the time, he had come by plane via Calcutta, London, and Newfoundland to join his father, a laundryman in New York. During his oral history interview, he had this to add about detention life:

Gem Hoy "Harry" Lew at age 16
Courtesy of the Ellis Island Oral History Program, Ellis Island Immigration Museum

There had to be at least two hundred Chinese, ninety-five percent from Hong Kong or Toishan, all speaking the same dialect. We slept in a room that had fifty guys, in bunk beds one on top of each other. We're never allowed outside, always stay in the same room. Go to the dining hall, they feed us, we go back to our living quarters or hang out in the corridor area. We play chess, play cards, play ball, try to kill time, see? That's all the pastime we can have. Boring for two months. [Sometimes fighting would break out] just like in prison. These guys who have been there for months get tense and aggravated. They gather together, they talk something insulting, and they start fighting. I had a good time because we had nothing to do. In fact, when I left Hong Kong I was less than a hundred pounds. When I get out of Ellis Island I weigh a hundred and fifteen. I gained fifteen pounds. They fed us, and nothing to do.[19]

Like many other Chinese immigrants at the time who were trying to circumvent the Chinese Exclusion Act, William Yee took the "crooked path" by assuming the false identity of a son of a U.S. citizen. Constantly on the lookout for these "paper sons," the Board of Special Inquiry asked him many questions about the layout of his village, his neighbors, his family and relatives in order to verify his true identity and relationship to the sponsor. The same questions were asked of his alleged father, who evidently gave the same answers. William had done his homework in studying carefully the coaching book that had come with the purchase of his false identity. "I was successful at the interrogation because I have a good memory of what I'm supposed to say, see. So that's why I'm here today." He passed the test and was landed soon after his hearing. William would go on to graduate from high school and serve in the all-Chinese 14th Air Corps during World War II. He met and married Catherine Chan in Shanghai, and was able to bring her to America under the War Brides Act. The couple settled in New York City, where William ran a successful business importing Chinese art goods and raised a family of two children. As to what became of Harry Lew, he graduated from Fordham University with a pharmacy degree and opened the Chung Wah Pharmacy on Mott Street in New York's Chinatown.

Fourteen-year-old Chin You Fun, who was detained at Ellis Island for two months in 1936, was not as lucky.[20] He also claimed to be the son of a U.S. citizen, but he was grilled for two days and asked 119 detailed questions about his family background, the layout of his village and house, and his voyage to America. His alleged father and brother served as witnesses and were asked the

Chin You Fun's Certificate of Identity
Scan by Vincent Chin

same questions. Their answers were also compared to those given by family members in previous investigations. While the BSI conceded that the alleged father was a U.S. citizen and that he could have sired the applicant on a return visit to China, they excluded Chin You Fun because of certain discrepancies in their answers that put the claimed relationship in doubt. In particular, the alleged father had reported in 1920 prior to his departure for China that his wife had died. So how could the applicant, born in 1923, be his blood son? In addition, the BSI pointed out twenty other discrepancies in their answers as proof that the applicant, father, and brother lacked knowledge that they should have possessed.

The family retained a very smart attorney to appeal the ruling to the Secretary of Labor. He was able to successfully argue point-by-point that the evidence presented by the BSI in their summary judgment was immaterial and inconsequential to the case. For example, he said, the father had forgotten to mention he had a granddaughter because he had never seen her, she having been born at a time subsequent to his last visit to China. No one in the family knew the whereabouts of the oldest son because he had been out of touch with the family for around twelve years. As to the father's reporting the death of his wife in 1920, the attorney argued that it was most likely a misunderstanding because in subsequent hearings, he always asserted that his wife was still alive in China. Then in a brilliant move, the attorney pointed out the many instances of agreement in the testimony, even with respect to the location of the official post office in the Sin Loong grocery store owned by one Chin Sun Kai, as conclusive proof that father and son were related as claimed. Chin You Fun's case shows how meticulous and difficult some of the immigrant inspectors were at Ellis Island, but also how appeals could be won through the judicial system.

The Case of Chinese Seamen

As noted in the CGI annual reports through the years, many Chinese were employed as seamen on foreign ships because China had no merchant marine and the Chinese could be hired at lower wages. Once on U.S. soil, all seamen were allowed sixty days of shore leave and were not subject to U.S. immigration laws. The Immigration Service was well aware of how many Chinese were using this privilege to gain illegal entry into the country, either as disguised seamen or as deserters. The *CGI Annual Report* for FY1915/16 noted that out of 8,047 Chinese seamen on 396 vessels, 67 escaped and only 5 were apprehended. With the outbreak of World War I, desertions doubled due to the dangers of shipping in the war zone and to dissatisfaction with the low wages.

During the 1920s and 1930s, immigration officers frequently conducted raids in Chinatown looking for illegal aliens. In 1925, in an effort to put a stop to the tong wars as well as deal with the rise in desertions, officers rounded up 600 illegal aliens, many of whom were seamen who had overstayed their leaves. Two hundred of them were detained at Ellis Island for weeks and months while awaiting hearings and deportation. During the Great Depression, with thousands of native seamen unemployed, the Seamen's International Union applied pressure on the Immigration Service to arrest and deport any and all Chinese seamen who were illegally in the U.S. As a result, more than 200 were caught, confined at Ellis Island, and ultimately deported.[21]

DESCRIPTION OF PERSON DEPORTED

Lee You before deportation from Ellis Island
Courtesy of National Archives at New York

In 1924, Lee You, a former seaman, was apprehended in one such raid after the Immigration Service was tipped off that his employer, Reliance Fireproof Door Company in Long Island, New York, employed illegal aliens. During his BSI hearing at Ellis Island, Lee You revealed that he was twenty-eight years old and born in Kiangsu Province. He had been a seaman for eleven years and first came to the U.S. in 1917 on a Norwegian ship from Calcutta. His last trip was on a Dutch vessel that landed in Brooklyn, New York. When he could not find work on another ship, he decided to stay in the U.S. and started working at Reliance, dipping metal and wooden frames into paint for sixty-five cents an hour—"unpleasant work nobody wants to do," according to the investigator. The BSI ordered him deported for engaging in labor, which violated the Chinese Exclusion Act, and in addition for being illiterate, and therefore inadmissible according to the Immigration Act of 1917.

Most Chinese seamen at that time did not have the funds or support to hire an attorney to appeal their cases, but Lee You did. However, his appeal to the Secretary of Labor failed. Unable to furnish a bond in the amount of $3,000, he was confined at Ellis Island for three months before he was deported to China via San Francisco.[22] There was a deportation train that took deportees from Ellis Island to San Francisco every six weeks, but in the case of Lee You, he was put on the *S.S. Comus* in New York on January 24 and deported from San Francisco on February 7, 1925.

Again in 1943, immigration officers, at the behest of British and Dutch shipmasters, arrested 170 Chinese seamen for jumping ship and illegal entry. They were sent to Ellis Island and held there without bail for over three months. Still they refused to go back to work until their demands for better treatment and equal wages were met. When the House of Representatives passed a bill to have them deported to England, they petitioned Congress to deport them to China instead, pointing out that they would be severely punished if returned to England. Representative Samuel Dickstein of New York, after receiving repeated protests from supporters and going to Ellis Island to hear from the seamen themselves, agreed there was merit in their grievances. He proceeded to help pass legislation in Congress to prohibit the deportation of alien seamen to another country without the consent of their home government. In the case of the Chinese sailors, they would not be deported to England but to China.[23]

How did this group of Chinese sailors find life in detention at Ellis Island? According to their petition, "We have been fed with very poor food, and slightest protest brings immediate reprisal. We cannot receive any telephone messages. We are closely watched all the time."[24] They might have passed their time at Ellis Island doing arts and craft projects, playing cards or ball, gambling (possibly by betting on which fly or insect would be the first into a circle drawn on a wall), or writing graffiti on the bathroom walls.[25] One of them might have written this Chinese couplet that is still visible on the walls at Ellis Island today. It aptly sums up the hardships suffered by Chinese detainees at Ellis Island.

在家千日好， A thousand days at home are easy;

出外半天難。 Half a day abroad is hard.

Translated by Charles Egan[26]

In 1943, Congress repealed the Chinese Exclusion Act as a goodwill gesture to China, a U.S. ally in World War II. Chinese aliens could finally become U.S. citizens, but only 105 Chinese per year were permitted to immigrate to the United States. It was not until Congress passed the Immigration and Nationality Act of 1965 that the last vestige of racism was removed from our immigration laws, putting every country on an equal footing. The broken immigration system was finally fixed. Thousands upon thousands of Chinese immigrants were admitted based on a preference system that favored family reunification and skilled and professional labor. As a result, families that had been separated for decades were finally reunited and America benefited by the large influx of high-tech and professional workers. The Chinese American population grew from 0.5 million in 1970, to 4 million in 2010.

Yet today, fifty-two years later, we find ourselves embroiled in another immigration debate—what to do about the 11 million undocumented immigrants living in the shadows of society; the 400,000 immigrants and refugees detained annually in government and private prison facilities for longer periods and in far worse conditions than Angel Island or Ellis Island; and the long waiting line of applicants trying to join their families in America, get a work visa, or seek political asylum. Meanwhile, we have a newly-elected president who is bent on banning all Muslims and refugees, deporting all undocumented immigrants, and slashing legal immigration in half by favoring English-speaking and highly-educated workers over family reunification. As we search for a way to fix our broken immigration system, we would do well to heed the tragic consequences of the Chinese Exclusion Act. If we are to maintain our lead in the global economy while remaining true to our values as a nation of immigrants, Congress needs to step up to the plate and pass comprehensive immigration reform that will protect our borders and all U.S. workers, provide a legalization process for undocumented but worthy immigrants, and allow us to do our part to help the "huddled masses yearning to breathe free."

AAARI Lecture Video (March 6, 2015): www.aaari.info/15-03-06Yung.htm

Notes

1   Him Mark Lai, Genny Lim, and Judy Yung, eds., *Island: Poetry and History of Chinese Immigrants on Angel Island, 1910-1940*, 2nd ed. (Seattle: University of Washington Press, 2014): 182–83.

2   George Bayliss, "At Ellis Island, Memories Found in Graffiti," *Philadelphia Inquirer* (April 2, 1989): 8-A; Barry Moreno, *The Illustrated Encyclopedia of Ellis Island* (Westport: Greenwood Press, 2004): 97–98.

3   Him Mark Lai, "Chinese Detainees at NY's Ellis Island Also Wrote Poems on Barrack Walls," *East/West* (November 8, 1985): 1; Yuan Guoqiang, "The sorrows of Chinese immigrants on Ellis Island linger for a hundred years," *Zhong Bao*, (August 30, 1985).

4   Japan invaded China in 1937, sparking the Sino-Japanese War.

5   *Journey to the West* (Xiyou ji) is a favorite novel among the Chinese, who often entertained one another with narrations of scenes during their leisure time.

6   Lai, Lim, and Yung, *Island*: 180–81.

7   "72 More Chinese Ordered Deported, 206 Now at Ellis Island," *The New York Times* (September 20, 1925): 1; Liu Liang-mo, "China Speaks: China is Fighting as an Ally, But She is Not Being Treated as One," *Pittsburgh Courier* (March 27, 1943).

8   Lai, Lim, and Yung, *Island*: 180–81.

9   Albert J. Parisi, "Anxiety, Not Fear," *The New York Times* (July 7, 1985).

10   "Unbearable memories in Ellis Island immigrant poems," *Huaqiao Ribao* (August 5, 1985).

11   Architectural Resources Group, "Poetry and Inscriptions: Translation and Analysis," prepared by Charles Egan, Wan Liu, Newton Liu, and Xing Chu Wang for the California Department of Parks and Recreation and Angel Island Immigration Station Foundation, San Francisco, 2004.

12   Lai, Lim, and Yung, *Island*: 182–83.

13   Libby Lackman, "Aid Immigrants at Ellis Island," *The New York Times* (March 2, 1941).

14   These comparative statistics were compiled from tables on "Chinese Seeking Admission to the United States," found in the annual reports of the Commissioner-General of Immigration (CGI) from 1900 to 1930.

15 "New York Chinese Exclusion Case Files," National Archives at New York City. This list includes immigration case files in the New York District Office that date from 1882 to 1960 and is not complete, as many case files may have been lost, destroyed, or moved to other locations through the years. I am indebted to Vincent Chin for sharing the list with me.

16 *CGI Annual Report* FY1927/28: 15–16.

17 William Yee, interview with Janet Levine, July 18, 1994, Ellis Island Oral History Program, Ellis Island Immigration Museum.

18 There is no evidence that Chinese food was ever served at Ellis Island. According to Moreno's *Encyclopedia of Ellis Island*, a typical meal consisted of boiled beef, potatoes, lentil soup, succotash, bread and butter, and tea (150).

19 Gem Hoy "Harry" Lew, interview with Paul E. Sigrist, May 17, 1993, Ellis Island Oral History Program, Ellis Island Immigration Museum. According to the description of the dormitories in the *CGI Annual Report* for FY 1927/1928, they were much nicer than the Chinese quarters at Angel Island: "The quarters occupied by detained aliens consist of large, light, well-ventilated rooms with floors and dados of Dutch or white glazed tile. Each person is allotted a white enameled single bed with woven-wire spring, good quality mattress, pillow, blankets, and clean linen. Bathrooms have built-in porcelain tubs as well as showers (27)."

20 Chin You Fun (You Ah Foo), File 169/194, Box 504, Chinese Exclusion Case Files, Record Group 85, Records of the Immigration and Naturalization Service, National Archives at New York City.

21 *CGI Annual Report* FY 1915/16: 179; *CGI Annual Report* FY 1916/17, 179-80; "Chinatown Cowers as Raids Continue," *The New York Times* (September 16, 1925); Peter Kwong, *Chinatown, N.Y.: Labor and Politics, 1930-1950* (New York: Monthly Review Press, 1979):119.

22 Lee You (Lee Ah Foo), File 55/153, Box 253, Chinese Exclusion Case Files, Record Group 85, Records of the Immigration and Naturalization Service, National Archives at New York City.

23 Liu Liang-mo, "China Speaks," *Pittsburgh Courier* (March 27, 1943); "Chinese Seamen to be Released," *Gazette and Daily*, May 31, 1943; "Chinese Seamen Win Long Fight," *Gazette and Daily* (July 9, 1943).

24 "Chinese Seamen to be Released," *Gazette and Daily* (May 31, 1943).

25 The gambling game played by Chinese men at Ellis Island is described in Meyer Berger's article, "6 Guards Out, 26 Accused in Ellis Island Graft Case," *The New York Times* (February 14, 1952).

26 Lai, Lim, and Yung, *Island*: 182-83.

Author

Judy Yung, Professor Emerita, University of California, Santa Cruz, was born and raised in San Francisco's Chinatown. She received her B.A. in English Literature and Chinese Language from San Francisco State University, and her Master's in Library Science and Ph.D. in Ethnic Studies from the University of California, Berkeley. As Professor of American Studies at the University of California, Santa Cruz, she taught courses in Asian American Studies, women's history, oral history, and mixed race. Her publications include: *Island: Poetry and History of Chinese Immigrants on Angel Island, 1910-1940*; *Unbound Feet: A Social History of Chinese Women in San Francisco*; *Chinese American Voices: From the Gold Rush to the Present*; *The Adventures of Eddie Fung: Chinatown Kid, Texas Cowboy, Prisoner of War*; and *Angel Island: Immigrant Gateway to America*.

"We're Here Because You Were There"
Asian American Studies and Its Ambivalences

VINAY LAL

"Asian American" and "Indians": Vignettes

NEARLY A DECADE AGO, the Asian American Studies Center at UCLA published my book, *The Other Indians: A Cultural and Political History of South Asians in America*.[1] The title of my book alluded, in part, to the difficulties inherent in speaking of South Asian "Indians" in the U.S. Growing up in India, the only Indians that I knew of in "the land of the free and home of the brave," were those who had been mowed down by the white man. We called them "Red Indians," if only because they were so described in the American comics found in lending libraries. It was an accident of history, one of many such ill-fated accidents in European adventurism that shaped the world, that would lead to the characterization of America's indigenous people as "Indians."

Transitioning to the category of "Asian American" was no easy matter either for what the U.S. Census now recognizes as "Asian Indians." In Britain, the term "Asian" indexes most often Indians, Pakistanis, and Bangladeshis—among them Indians who often knew nothing of India, and had only arrived in Britain in the wake of their expulsion from East Africa.[2] The Chinese, Vietnamese, Japanese, and Koreans in Britain are something of an afterthought. The "Asians," on the other hand, were instantiations of what postcolonial scholars and anti-colonial activists characterized as "the Empire striking back." "We're here because you were there," the Asians told the Whites. The Asian in England had become so ubiquitous by the early 1980s, as the inheritor of the proverbial corner shop, that "Mr. Patel" could even find a place in one author's admittedly "idiosyncratic" companion to England and Englishness.[3]

Contrariwise, in the U.S., Indians seemed for a long time to have no place in that umbrella grouping known as "Asian American," and this was not because the Chinese and Japanese at least had a foothold in the U.S. many years before Indians first made their presence known on the West Coast around 1890. To Ralph Waldo Emerson and Henry David Thoreau, the chief progenitors of American Transcendentalism in the 19th century, the 'Orient' may have signified mainly India. But to the other literati, and in the common imagination, the 'Orient' brought to mind the Far East, or China and Japan.[4] Then there is the matter of Indians having tried, though without success, to pass as Caucasian—thus white. And so the impulse to grant Indians a place within the family of "Asian Americans" was not altogether palpable.

Invisible Asia(n)s

For a long time, Indians in the U.S. have complained of their 'invisibility.' Among them, the feeling persists that India is generally ignored, only making it to the news as the site of religious killings, endemic poverty, and uncontrollable pollution. Indian Americans are not the only community among Asian Americans of whom it can be said, in the words of a recent article in *The Atlantic*, that they "remain mostly invisible in the American political debate."[5] But, from the perspective of Indian Americans, their invisibility reflects India's marginality to global geopolitics. It is also especially acute and disturbing because Indian Americans are disproportionately well-educated and, on that very questionable view, should be deserving of more attention.[6]

There is, then, a pervasive anxiety of influence among Indian Americans.[7] As in India, where the most militant adherents of Hinduism secretly admire Islam as a rational, monotheistic, muscular, simple and highly organized faith, while they publicly berate it as an intolerant, puritan, and terrorist-driven religion, Indian Americans here too are envious of the extraordinary media coverage that Islam has been receiving over the last two decades.

Similarly, though the practitioners of Asian American Studies may have become more accommodating in the last decade, many in the Indian community have asked me whether Asian American Studies is really any more ecumenical than it was in the past. Is it any less dominated today, than it has been since its inception, by Chinese-Americans or Japanese-Americans? Whose 'Asia' is being invoked, to what end, and what are the parameters and contours of the Asia embedded in 'Asian American Studies'?

The Politics of Speaking of "South Asians"

The somewhat more astute members of the Indian-American community question what is the politics of deploying the term 'South Asian.' "Progressive" scholars and activists have insisted that the political and socio-cultural realities of the Indian sub-continent are best captured by speaking of "South Asia" as a single entity. Better still, to signify the possibilities of solidarity among Pakistanis, Bangladeshis, and Indians, their shared histories, and their common subjection to racism and discrimination in the United States, they deploy the term '*desis*' (from '*desh*,' country, or, more tellingly, 'mother country').[8] However, most Indian Americans from the community are not in the least keen on having India lumped, and thus confused, with Pakistan. They point to the fact that Pakistan has often been described, by the United States and commentators around the world, as a "failed state." But if this may appear to characterize a good many countries, they call attention to the common branding of Pakistan as the breeding ground for Muslim extremists.

Islam in South Asia and Muslim Americans

If the place of Indians, and more broadly South Asians, within the fabric of Asian American Studies remains uncertain, how should we deliberate over Moustafa Bayoumi's call for a conception of Asian American Studies that is still more inclusive and responsive to the increasing presence of Arab Americans and Muslim Americans? "The complexity of the Muslim American experience," he avers, "is something that Asian American studies has never really grappled with, I believe."[9] One can hardly disagree, except to ask if there is any other field of study, or discipline, that has "grappled with" the "complexity of the Muslim American experience"? Sadly, as the following remarks will suggest, even Islamic Studies programs in the American academy, have done little to reflect the "complexity of the Muslim American experience," judging at least from the narrow conception of Islam peddled by such programs.

Some Asian American scholars will likely balk at Bayoumi's suggestion that their field encompass the histories and experience of Muslim Americans, even if one takes to heart his plea that "Asian American Studies is not about the geography of Asia, really, but about the ways in which people are interpellated and organized and come together within the United States as different types of 'Asians.'"[10] According to Bayoumi, the place where one is, is really a function of the psychogeography to which one has habituated oneself. Bayoumi does not abide by geographical determinism, yet the geographical coordinates are not altogether indeterminate, and so we find him suggesting that Asian American Studies should "at least include those Arab Americans who hail from West Asia and those Muslim Americans who hail from Asia generally."[11] So in what respect is Asian American Studies *not* incipiently about "the geography of Asia"?

Varieties of Islam

Before we speak of Muslim Americans, whether they be Arabs, North Africans, or South Asians—all candidates, it seems, for being viewed as "Asian American," no doubt alongside Muslim Americans with origins from Indonesia, Malaysia, China, and elsewhere—it would be fruitful to advert to the problems that inhere in speaking of Islam as such. In the United States, especially, the Middle East, or what is otherwise called West Asia, is assumed to be the 'natural' and 'authentic' home of Islam. It comes as a surprise to most Americans when told that South Asia is home to the largest Muslim population in the world. India, where fewer than 15% of the people are Muslims; and Pakistan, which is overwhelmingly a Muslim-majority state, each have around 180-200 million Muslims.

Demography has its own politics; but numbers aside, by far the more germane consideration is that Islam developed in South Asia over a course of a millennium along considerably different trajectories than in West Asia. The tendency in the West however has been to altogether ignore Islamic South Asia. The tacitly held view is that Islam in South Asia is something of a deviant form, an inauthentic and bastardized version of the true faith housed in the Arab world.

The consequence of this disposition is not merely that one becomes oblivious to what we might call the varieties of Islam. There are many more disturbing implications of such ignorance. Pakistan is assuredly a part of the Muslim world, but it is as much, however difficult it may be for orthodox Muslims in Pakistan to concede this, a part of the Indic world. Over the course of the second millennium C.E., the Indo-Islamic cultural synthesis that was forged in the Indian sub-continent led to the brilliant efflorescence of music, architecture, cuisine, art, literature, and religious expression.

Pakistani Muslims have, however, increasingly been drilled with the idea, most particularly following the Islamicization policies of General Muhammad Zia-ul-Haq, President of Pakistan from 1978-1988, that their practices of Islam have been contaminated through centuries of close proximity to Hinduism. By turning their gaze westward, towards the historic homeland of the Prophet Muhammad, Muslims will be liberating themselves from the cunning tyranny of effete Hindus. The targets of these Islamic terrorists who have been wreaking havoc on the streets of Pakistan are not just religious minorities, but also, just as ominously, those Muslims who in various ways have defied the creeping drumbeat of a Wahhabi-infused Islam, which has now taken a vise-like grip over growing arenas of Pakistani society.

The Radicalization of Islam

Hindu nationalists, whose writ runs large in much of India today, have amply demonstrated that Islamic extremists are scarcely alone in their vicious instrumentalization of religion to political ends. What is these days termed the "radicalization" of Muslims is, moreover, increasingly on display in India as well. Both the indifference of the state to the marginalization of Muslims, as well as the provocations to which they are subjected by belligerent Hindus, are likely to accentuate the trend toward such "radicalization."

Nevertheless, as many commentators in and outside India have noted, Indian Muslims have remained strikingly unreceptive to calls to global jihad. "India, with 180 million Muslims, has produced almost no jihadis." So ran a recent headline in the *Indian Express*, a major English-language daily, which continues in this vein: "Muslims here see stake in political system."[12]

The stodgy if highly respected *The Economist*, which cannot be accused of being partial to India, ran a 2014 article entitled, "Why India's Muslims are so Moderate." While noting that "India's Muslims generally have reasons for some gloom," enduring, for example, lower levels of education and poorer employment prospects in comparison with Hindus, the article also highlights the repudiation of violence across a broad swathe of Indian Muslim communities, and their engagement with members of other religions. "The contrast with the sectarian bloodletting, growing radicalism and deepening conservatism in Pakistan next door," states the author, "is striking."[13]

Can South Asian Muslims Mediate?

One would not know any of this from a reading of contemporary Western 'authorities' on the politics of Muslim societies. Gilles Keppel's *The War for Muslim Minds: Islam and the West* (2004), makes absolutely no reference to India.[14] I fear similarly that when "Muslim Americans" are invoked, it is a certain kind of Muslim, the so-called "authentic" Muslim who is of 'Middle Eastern' provenance, that is generally being brought to mind. There is little, if any, cognizance of just who these Muslim Americans are, and very little acknowledgement that they are the inheritors of a great many different, and often conflicting, traditions and histories.

Ten percent of the Asian Indian population of around four million in the U.S. is comprised of Muslims, though they are barely mentioned in the voluminous commentary on Muslims that appears in the press every day—even if they are, as I have suggested, perhaps uniquely positioned to mediate between Asian Americans and Muslim Americans, as well as between Muslim Americans and American society at large. While Bayoumi's attempt to briefly complicate the history of Muslim Americans is commendable, South Asian Muslims appear nowhere in his commentary. If we are to speak of the possibilities of multi-racial coalitions between South Asians, Arabs, and American Muslims, how can we overlook the role of Ahmadiyya preachers who arrived to the U.S. in the 1920s from what was then undivided India? They gave Islam in the U.S. a new lease of life and overcame, as one scholar has put it trenchantly, "racial and ethnic separation that existed not only in the Muslim community, but the U.S. and globally."[15]

South Asians, Muslim Americans, and the Politics of Identity

In the week following the September 11, 2001 attacks on the World Trade Center and the Pentagon, the non-profit advocacy group, South Asian Americans Leading Together (SAALT), which aims for a "more just and inclusive society in the United States," recorded 645 hate crimes against South Asians, Sikhs, and Muslims.[16] In all likelihood, many more hate crimes probably went unreported. Not one of the nineteen hijackers involved in the September 11 attacks was of South Asian origin. On the morning of September 15, 2001, Balbir Singh Sodhi, a Sikh man from Mesa, Arizona, was shot dead in front of his gas station. His killer, Frank Roque, had reportedly told his friends the previous day that he was "going to go out and shoot some towel-heads." As he was being arrested, Roque shouted, "I am a patriot! I stand for America all the way!"[17] Roque saw only a bearded and turbaned man in front of him; he "mistook" him for a Middle Easterner, an Osama bin Laden look-alike. Sodhi would have the unfortunate distinction of being the first victim in the United States of a retaliatory hate crime after September 11.

Sixteen years later, just weeks into the presidency of Donald J. Trump, and shortly after an executive order popularly dubbed as the 'Muslim Ban' was issued, an Indian software engineer, Srinivas Kuchib-hotla, was shot dead at a bar in Olathe, Kansas, by a Navy veteran, Adam W. Purinton. Kuchibhotla's companion and fellow Indian, Alok Madasani, escaped with a slight bullet injury. Kuchibhotla would become the first victim in the country whose death might justly be described as having been precipitated by Trump's executive order barring the citizens of seven Muslim-majority countries from entering the United States.[18] The killer, *The New York Times* reported, was "tossing ethnic slurs at the two men and suggesting they did not belong in the United States."[19] Witnesses stated that they heard Purinton shout, "Get out of my country," before he opened fire on the two Indians. Purinton told a bartender hours later that he had shot dead two "Middle Eastern" men.[20]

Iran, India, Iraq: they're all the same anyhow. Their names sound alike. The assassin sees no difference. Three countries that lie east of the Suez Canal, some would be so bold to say east of civilization, just seem to elide into each other. Sunni, Shia, Hindu, Jain, Vaishnava, Shaivite, Buddhist, Nichiren, Parsi, Sufi, Alawite, Sikh: in the vast archipelago of ignorance, differences are easily smothered. Some South Asian Americans might have been tempted into taking comfort from their identity and assumed that they would not be the targets of white rage. Perhaps many thought that they could be mere bystanders, if unwilling ones, to the slug-fest between Islam and the West. But they have, time and again, been rudely awoken to the fact that their identity will not be their salvation.

Every brown-skinned person is perforce a Muslim—at least for now. It is not only American Muslims, of course, who have historically had to confront racial discrimination and xenophobic outrage. Islam perhaps generates anxieties that are distinct in the Christian West, and in Anglo-Saxon America. Christianity and Islam are uniquely the two proselytizing religions; they are in competition with each other from the eschatological standpoint, trying to save souls and winning converts.

The Christian West's anxieties over Islam have now become everyone's anxieties. South Asian Americans and Arab Americans; Hindus, Muslims and Sikhs: are all subjects of a surveillance regime. That may be one reason why Muslim Americans should perhaps be welcomed under the ambit of 'Asian Americans.' "Within National Security Studies," Bayoumi explains, "we can see how the U.S. government is already establishing an infrastructure to study Muslims and Muslim Americans, and I don't want to be studied solely by the government. The study of Asian Americans, Muslim Americans, and Arab Americans must be critical work that is decoupled from an exclusive National Security lens…"[21]

I understand the spirit in which Bayoumi asserts that he "doesn't want to be studied solely by the government": he knows for a fact that the likes of him, and me, will be studied; and if that is to happen, the state and its functionaries should not monopolize the narrative by which both of us are defined. Of course, as the editor of *The Edward Said Reader*, Bayoumi is all too aware that the parties that have been complicit in Orientalism—and now "National Security Studies"—extend well beyond the state to the academy, experts, policy institutes, the corporatized media, and a great many more people who represent the sinews of power. Does one want to be studied at all?

Whatever the bizarrely-worded "War on Terror" means, it has necessitated a fundamental reassessment of the assumptions about identity, security, and the state. Bayoumi's plea that the imperatives of the National Security State should not be permitted to influence the study of Muslim Americans can be justifiably extended to other areas of scholarly inquiry and academic research. Much has been written by scholars about the origins of Asian American Studies, and ethnic studies more broadly. It would not be untrue to say that, fifty years after these initiatives were launched, most students, and even many mature scholars, still derive their politics from their identity. The election of Mr. Trump to the White House shows that is unequivocally the case for most white Americans as well, not only for hyphenated-Americans. The American university will become a truly politically enabling institution when it is able to help most students and scholars derive their identity from their politics.

Notes

1   Vinay Lal, *The Other Indians: A Political and Cultural History of South Asians in America* (Los Angeles: UCLA Asian American Studies Center Press; New Delhi: HarperCollins, 2008).

2   See, for example, Neil Berry, "Britain's Asians," *Toronto South Asian Review* 6, no. 2 (Fall 1987-Winter 1988): 28–35; Rozina Visram, *Ayahs, Lascars and Princes: Indians in Britain 1700-1947* (London: Pluto Press, 1986), commences her study thus: "This book traces the history of Asian settlement in Britain from 1700 to 1947. . . . The term 'Asian' as used here refers to the people from the Indian subcontinent. I have used the terms 'Asian' and 'Indian' interchangeably; I use 'black' in a political sense to refer to peoples of Afro-Caribbean and Asian origin" (vii).

3   Godfrey Smith, *The English Companion: An Idiosyncratic A-Z of England and Englishness* (London: Pavilion/Michael Joseph, 1984): 184–85.

4   Alan D. Hodder, "'Ex Oriente Lux': Thoreau's Ecstasies and the Hindu Texts," *The Harvard Theological Review* 86, no. 4 (October 1993): 403–38; Vinay Lal, "Emerson and India," Unpublished MA Thesis (The Humanities Center: The Johns Hopkins University, 1982); David Weir, *American Orient: Imagining the East from the Colonial Era through the Twentieth Century* (Amherst: University of Massachusetts Press, 2011).

5   Alex Wagner, "Why Are Asian Americans Politically Invisible?," *The Atlantic* (September 12, 2016), https://www.theatlantic.com/politics/archive/2016/09/why-dont-asians-count/498893/ (accessed March 23, 2017).

6   Michael Safi, "Reza Aslan outrages Hindus by eating human brains," *The Guardian* (March 10, 2017), https://www.theguardian.com/world/2017/mar/10/reza-aslan-criticised-for-documentary-on-cannibalistic-hindus (accessed March 23, 2017).

7   I have addressed this question at length in "A Bloated Hinduism: North American Hindus and the Imagination of a Vanguard," in *Accommodating Diversity: Ideas and Institutional Practices*, ed. Gurpreet Mahajan (Delhi: Oxford University Press, 2011): 265–88.

8   See, as an illustration, Vijay Prashad, *Uncle Swami: South Asians in America Today* (New York: New Press, 2012).

9   Moustafa Bayoumi, "Asian American Studies, the War on Terror, and the Changing University: A Call to Respond," *Asian American Matters: A New York Anthology* (AAARI-CUNY, 2017): 22.

10   *Ibid.*

11   *Ibid.*

12 "India, with 180 million Muslims, has produced almost no Jihadis," *Indian Express* (February 5, 2017), http://indianexpress.com/article/india/india-with-180-million-muslims-has-produced-almost-no-jihadis-muslims-here-see-stake-in-political-system-bernard-haykel-4508136/ (accessed March 28, 2017).

13 A.R., "Why India's Muslims are so Moderate," *The Economist* (September 8, 2014), http://www.economist.com/blogs/economist-explains/2014/09/economist-explains-3 (accessed March 29, 2017); This is much the same conclusion reached by *The New York Times* correspondent, Jake Flanagin, who shortly thereafter wrote on "Why India's Muslims Haven't Radicalized" (October 16, 2014).

14 Gilles Keppel, *The War for Muslim Minds: Islam and the West* (Cambridge: The Belknap Press of Harvard University Press, 2004).

15 Junaid Rana, "Islam and Black America: The Story of Islamophobia," *Souls* 9, no. 2 (April–June 2007): 156.

16 South Asian Americans Leading Together, *American Backlash: Terrorists Bring War Home in More Ways Than One* (Washington, DC: SAALT, 2001): 3; The FBI in its annual survey of hate crimes recorded a lower number of "hate crimes" targeting "people of Middle Eastern descent, Muslims, and South Asians," while conceding that the attacks had spiraled from "just 28" in 2000 to 481 in 2001. See U.S. Commission on Civil Rights report, http://www.usccr.gov/pubs/sac/dc0603/ch6.htm (accessed March 29, 2017).

17 http://www.usccr.gov/pubs/sac/dc0603/ch6.htm (accessed March 29, 2017).

18 At the other end of the world, in India, one prominent English-language daily did not hesitate to venture forth with the opinion that "Kuchibhotla is possibly the first casualty of the religious, racial and ethnic divisiveness that has swept the U.S. following the election of President Donald Trump . . ." See Yashwant Raj & Srinivasa Rao Apparasu, "Hyderabad Engineer Srinivas Kuchibhotla shot dead in US," *Hindustan Times* (February 24, 2017): 1.

19 John Eligon, Alan Blinder, and Nida Najar, "Drinks at a Bar, Ethnic Insults, Then Gunshots," *The New York Times* (February 25, 2017): A1, A17.

20 Mark Berman and Samantha Schmidt, "He yelled, 'Get out of my country,'" *The Washington Post* (February 24, 2017).

21 Bayoumi, *Asian American Matters*: 23.

Author

Vinay Lal is a writer, blogger, cultural critic, public commentator, and Professor of History and Asian American Studies at UCLA. His seventeen authored and edited books include *The Empire of Knowledge: Culture and Plurality in the New Global Economy* (Pluto Press, 2002), *The History of History: Politics and Scholarship in Modern India* (Oxford, 2005), *Political Hinduism: The Religious Imagination in Public Spheres* (Oxford, 2009), the two-volume *Oxford Anthology of the Modern Indian City* (2013), and most recently, *A Passionate Life: Writings by and on Kamaladevi Chattopadhyay* (co-edited, Zubaan Books, 2017).

Prof. Lal's intellectual interests include Indian history, global politics, historiography, popular culture, cinema, and the politics of knowledge systems. His lecture courses, now with over a million viewers, are available in their entirety at youtube.com/dillichalo; and he blogs at vinaylal.wordpress.com

A Third Literature of the Americas
With Evelyn Hu-DeHart, Kathleen López, Maan Lin, Yibing Huang & Wen Jin

RUSSELL C. LEONG

"America is a hemispheric concept—
it includes Central, North, and Latin America"
—Evelyn Hu-DeHart

LITERATURE CHANGES AS IT TRAVELS, creating new languages, new ideas, and new critics. Literature may even create a "third space" for telling stories differently than before. Thus, as Indian novelist Amitav Ghosh has stated, "stories are all there are to live in, it was just a question of which one you chose."

Forty years ago, writers including Maxine Hong Kingston, David Henry Hwang, Frank Chin, Bienvenido Santos, Hisaye Yamamoto, Jessica Hagedorn, Milton Murayama and others through their creative works laid the groundwork for what is now broadly—and generically—termed "Asian American literature." Such literature was limited to writing in English solely within the borders of the United States. Since then, novels, poetry, and plays by Filipino, South Asian, Korean, Burmese, Vietnamese, Hawaiian, Samoan and other Asian and Pacific Americans have been produced across the Americas. No longer generic, the complexity of writers' backgrounds together with the stories they tell raise new questions, including:

1. What and whom should be included as Asian American?

2. Does this just include writing in English—or can it include literatures in other languages such as Spanish—or Vietnamese—or Pidgin?

3. What is the history of Asians in the Americas—Central, North and South, and how does the literature reflect this?

4. What are the implications of "third literature" that reflects more than "East" or "West?" For example, Chinese in Cuba may draw upon both their Chinese and African American roots.

5. What is the relationship between Asian American, Pacific Islander, and diasporic literatures?

This report focuses on the realm of Chinese American literature. We hope that our efforts will spur others to examine the literatures of other Asian and Pacific groups of the Americas and the Pacific region, thus helping to form and augment what we have broadly named "A Third Literature of the Americas."

It is fitting that the term "third literature" was inspired by—and derived from—the late Teshome Gabriel's writing on "Third Cinema" which broke new ground in looking at cinema from a decolonized, post-1950s Third World perspective. Gabriel was an Ethiopian poet and literature and film scholar at UCLA, and I was fortunate to take graduate film classes from him in the '80s. Gabriel had a vital role in introducing African, Asian, and Latin viewpoints on culture, cinema, and literature to his students and colleagues internationally. Thus his legacy lives on in the works that Asian, Asian American, and African scholars, filmmakers, and activists create.

Today, readers and scholars alike have discovered that "Chinese American literature" can no longer be confined to works written in English alone. Due to a number of factors including the rise of China, the ascendance of Latin America, the institutionalization of Ethnic Studies, and new critical scholarship on both sides of the Pacific, we are finding that the twenty-first century signals a "third Chinese literature of

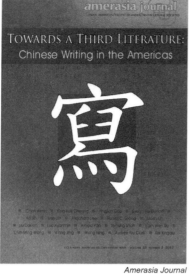

the Americas"—novels, stories, and poems written in English, Chinese, and Spanish. These new developments resulted in a first-time international collaboration among editors and scholars in the U.S. and in China. In 2012, a volume of *Amerasia Journal* (38:2) was published by the UCLA Asian American Studies Center entitled "Towards a Third Literature: Chinese Writing in the Americas," edited by Evelyn Hu-DeHart (Professor of History and Ethnic Studies at Brown University); Wang Ning (Professor of English and Comparative Literature at Tsinghua University, Beijing), and myself, at UCLA.

Subsequently, in December 2012, The City University of New York's Asian American and Asian Research Institute (AAARI) in conjunction with UCLA's Asian American Studies Center held and videotaped a trilingual program in New York City to bring scholars from the East and West Coasts, and from the U.S. and China, together to discuss the creation of a "third literature." Two of the editors and contributors to this special volume of *Amerasia Journal*, together with invited scholars in Latin and Caribbean American Literature and Modern Chinese Literature, discussed the implications of a "third Chinese literature of the Americas," which is available for public viewing online at www.aaari.info/12-12-14Literature.htm.

A Hemispheric Concept

"America is a hemispheric concept—it includes Central, North, and Latin America" is how noted Ethnic Studies historian Evelyn Hu-DeHart framed her opening keynote remarks. Contrary to the belief that the first Asians first settled in the Americas in the mid-nineteenth century, Hu-DeHart briefly outlined four stages in the history of Asians in the Americas. She argues that the unbroken Manila Galleon trade, from 1565 to 1815, first brought the "Indios" of China and Manila to Mexico City, and to Lima, Peru in the sixteenth century.

By the early seventeenth century, according to Hu-DeHart, Japanese could also be found in Guadalajara, Mexico. The second stage, the nineteenth century, was the *hua gong* or workers' period which utilized Chinese indentured labor to replace African slaves, especially in Cuba and Peru. Between 1847-1875, there were about 250,000 who entered. Third, from 1882, the time of the Chinese Exclusion Act to 1965, the phase most familiar to North Americans, was when Chinese entered the U.S. in much larger numbers. After this period, here was a re-entry, of sorts, of Chinese immigrants entering and investing in Latin America.

Hu-DeHart states in *Amerasia Journal* that "by the late-twentieth and early-twenty-first centuries, however, Chinese outside of China had become cosmopolitan and globalized on different levels, with their attendant cultural and literary identities taking on diverse forms, including 'multicultural' and 'pluralistic' forms in liberal democracies, or in postcolonial forms in the nations of Central and Latin America."

Migration, individual histories, and education and language determined to a great extent what form such literary and cultural offerings would take: these included poetry, short story, novella and novel, and theatrical works. Actually, according to Hu-DeHart, Latin American and Caribbean literature is the very definition of multicultural; representing Spanish, Portuguese, British, French and other European colonials, Blacks both slave and free, native peoples from all corners, and Asian immigrants spanning the origins spectrum from East Indians to Middle Easterners, Japanese to Chinese. She cites V.S. Naipaul of Trinidad as the best known writer, and Japanese Peruvian poet Jose Watanabe and Japanese Bolivian poet Pedro Shimose, as adding to the spectrum of Asian writers of the Americas.

Chinese Afro-Cubans

In studying the transcultural and mixed-racial heritage of the Chinese in Cuba, Kathleen López, a scholar of Latin American and Caribbean history at Rutgers University talked about how a new theoretical framework—that of a third literature of the Americas—could be applied. She pointed to two major waves: the first was the coolie trade of 1847-1874 in which 125,000 indentured laborers went to Cuba and almost half died. The remainder

Chinese Cuban Youth Demonstrating Martial Arts in Havana, Cuba (2007)
Photo by Kathleen López

mostly worked in agriculture and intermarried with Afro-Cubans. The second phase was between 1902-1959 during the Republican period to the 1959 Revolution. The 1949 Chinese Revolution also resulted in an exodus of Chinese to Cuba, as well as Taiwan and elsewhere. After 1959, some small businessmen, with their enterprises nationalized, fled to Florida and other parts of the U.S.

The first community history of Chinese Cubans was published in Havana in 1927 according to López, and its author, Antonio Chuffat Latour, was the son of a Chinese merchant and a Cuban woman of African descent. "Chuffat drew on the histories of both Blacks and Chinese in Cuba to shape his political consciousness."

López believes that the sources for defining a "third" literature of Cuba and of the Americas should include newspapers, plantation records, Chinese association (huiguan) records, poetry, letters, novels, paintings, and ephemera. These informal sources often provide a rich and textured history of the process of migration, adaptation—and creation, of a layered Chinese Afro-Cuban identity. She states: "these kinds of sources lend us access to individual and communal understandings of the Chinese Cuban past."

Siu Kam Wen

Maan Lin (Jenny Lin Martínez), originally from Taiwan, now teaches Spanish at Queensborough Community College/CUNY. At the forum she shared the process of her English and Chinese translations of a short story by award-winning Peruvian Chinese writer Siu Kam Wen, who won Peru's highest literary award in 1986 for his collection entitled *El Tramo Final* (The Final Stretch). The subject of several dissertations in the field of Spanish language and literature (including Maan Lin's), Siu writes with raw emotion, including anger and frustration about growing up in Lima's barrio chino (Chinatown), the child of immigrant parents who own and operate a small grocery store relying strictly on family labor. The story Lin translated was Siu's rendition of the traditional Chinese "martial arts" or swordsman story (wuxia xiaoshuo).

National Cultures and Minority Relations

Wen Jin, who has taught comparative literature at Columbia University and also at Fudan University in Shanghai, explored the theoretical implications of a "third literature" of the Americas. In addition to tagging it as ethnic literature, Asian American literature written by 2nd and 3rd generations, or diasporic Chinese writing, Wen Jin expands the dimensions of Third Literature of the Americas to include:

1. Having to do with translations and literature traveling across nations

2. Internal comparisons, e.g. of minority literatures and majority literatures

3. Third literature as a mode of critique, and a way of analyzing the role of race and ethnicity

4. As a space for how ideas and literature circulates—between national cultures and spaces

Wen Jin brought up the example of Aku Wuwu, a poet and member of the Yi ethnic minority—one of 55 ethnic minorities in China. His works reflect his visits with Native American peoples in the U.S. Complementing Wen Jin's viewpoints, poet Mai Mang (Yibing Huang of Connecticut College) raised

Chinese, English, Spanish: Writing a Third Literature of the Americas (December 14, 2012)
L to R: Evelyn Hu-DeHart, Kathleen López, Wen Jin, Yibing Huang & Maan Lin
Photo by William Tam

questions regarding his own status as a nationally-honored contemporary bilingual "Chinese poet." In fact, Mai Mang revealed that he too was a "Tujia," a member of a minority group in Hunan province. Moreover, having lived half of his life in China and the other half abroad, mainly in the United States, what label should he affix to himself, if any—Chinese, Chinese American, minority . . . or?

As seen from the preceding discussion, the concept of a "third literature" is truly a term which, traveling both within and among the Americas and Asia, forces us to "rewrite" a literary history of the Americas. Such a rewriting and consideration of works written in English, Spanish, or Chinese, opens a window into Sino-American and Latin American relations. This process documents the independent intellectual and political positions the Chinese outside of China have taken, and continue to take in the world, transcending the boundaries of race and nation and trespassing narrow lines of ethnic chauvinism.

Mai Mang's poem "Copper," written in Peru in 2013, is a part of these evolving "third stories" of the Americas.

Author

Russell C. Leong believes in the power of words to free the future. During his 33-year tenure as an academic editor at UCLA, he edited the first books and journals on Asian Pacific media and film, on Asian American sexualities, on Asian Americans post 9/11, and on Asian American transcultural studies. Between 1977-2010, Leong was the editor of the foremost journal in Asian American Studies, *Amerasia Journal*, published by the UCLA Asian American Studies Center. There, he served as an adjunct professor of English and Asian American Studies. His stories (*Phoenix Eyes* [2000]) and poetry (*Country of Dreams and Dust* [1993]) received an American Book Award and PEN Josephine Miles Award. Leong, educated in the U.S. and Taiwan in film and comparative literature, is a consulting senior editor for International Projects at UCLA and the founding editor of CUNY FORUM, for The City University of New York's Asian American and Asian Research Institute.

铜 Copper

麦芒 MAI MANG (YIBING HUANG)

我梦见很多我不认识但与我相似的人，
像铜一样被挖出来，
又重新被埋进去，
埋进地球黑暗的深处。

I dreamt of those whom I did not know
but who looked just like me,
dug out like copper,
and buried again,
back into the source of the earth.

January 10, 2013, one night in Mina Tintaya (an open-pit copper mine located at an elevation of about 13,400 feet), Espinar, Cusco, Peru

Author
Yibing Huang is associate professor of Chinese, and curator of the Chu-Griffis Asian Art Collection at Connecticut College, in New London.

"Langit, Lupa, Impierno" (Heaven, Earth, Hell)
2013, 2017 © Copyright by Artist: Jun-Jun Sta. Ana

Requiem for the Common Tao and Other Poems

LUIS H. FRANCIA

Requiem for the Common Tao*

They did him in for
what he did, though
      he had not.

Did him in, they did, didn't
they, though he had no
    sin, did he now,

for all he had

was running on
empty
     belly
empty
     veins
empty
     mind and pocket

e   m   p   t   y
in excelsis Deo!

O miracle most
obscene, emptying
him who no
    longer had
anything
to be emptied!

and where was the

Maker of they who
did, where was the
    Angel of he

who didn't?

Un-make the Maker
Un-frock the angel
Un-sin the sinner

Un-die the dead, the dying
Un-nail the nailed
Un-do the deed or

the deed will do
us dead.

The drug wars

Dig on,
Dig on

darker deeper than
any grave

Manila 2017
Tao = Filipino for person

Dream of the Ascetic

Have I been holy too long?
Poisoned by saintliness, I need to
detoxify, and bathe in the world
and the waters of its gaudy ways.
I need to reacquaint myself with

the language of the flesh and its oily alphabets.
Has the world missed me, will it say,
yes, you are one of us, the elect?
Touch me and feel the fever of my virtue.
I need to get off my sanctimonious knees,

my artful ways of deceiving, and forswear
my worship of someone so caught up in torture!
What is it I want of Jesus but to mark me as a brother,
uncrucify himself and disobey his father
As all sons must. We could talk man to man over

cups of unmiracled wine, in the company we prefer,
of whores and poets and honest thieves, away
from the patriarchs, the Pharisees, and the holy men.
I'll seize him up close, note his nose
may not be so fine after all, his skin darker

than his publicist lets on.
We won't talk about his divinity, his
platform as the Son of God.
I will warn him, but he will know, about
the eternal struggle between fathers and

sons, how the begotten must kill the begetter.
I will tell him to ignore his campaign promises,
and savor the extraordinariness of being mortal,
human, of bleeding, having sex, singing songs.
We will walk the streets and argue about

the infernal in him, and the celestial in me.
We will visit churches built in his
honor, so he can have a good laugh.
You are the devil, I'll tease him,
and you my father's bastard, he'll reply.

We will stop in front of a tree, and,
having sampled the pleasures of the city,
this man, this carpenter's son and magnificent Jew
will ask me to hammer him once more
into the wood. Arm around my shoulders

he will whisper, "Prove your
love, brother, and crucify me!
Let my flesh be the fruit and
the cross the new tree of knowledge.
One bite to make everything right!"

At once will I understand and say,
as I take up the hammer,
this is the way we are, mon frère,
each nail, each blow, each
thorn, a full measure of love, that

you may sit with our father forever in
glory, and I, secret sharer in the divine,
will be murderer and savior once more:
Judas to your Christ,
Cain to your Abel.

Contemplating a Statue of
Douglas MacArthur on Corregidor Island

Evening star, still star, brilliant gleam in
The sky how I wish Douglas never returned

Had taken that slow boat to China instead
By way of Okinawa, by way of Japan.

Doggone Dugout Doug, what was in
That pipe you smoked, thinking you
Were our jut-jawed liberator when you

Were the oppressor, when the dreams
You handed the little brown brothers
Were as fleeting as corn-cob smoke

When all there is to show for it in the
Monsoon air of Corregidor, this lair
Of Chinese corsairs, Spanish jailers
And Yankee officers, is this bald-headed

Expatriate Minnesotan in the boots of
His occupier father determined to keep
These islands slices of American pie?

He is in love with the guns now silent
And his twisted odes on freedom
Lie as flotsam on the dark waters of
History, in love with the ruins of a life
That never was.

Corregidor, June 5, 2011

Author
Luis H. Francia is an online columnist for the *Philippine Daily Inquirer,* and teaches at New York University and Hunter College/CUNY. Luis has written five collections of poetry: *Her Beauty Likes Me Well* (co-authored with David Friedman, 1975); *The Arctic Archipelago and Other Poems* (1992); *Museum of Absences* (2005); *The Beauty of Ghosts* (2010); and *Tattered Boat* (2014). He is the author of a memoir *Eye of the Fish: A Personal Archipela*go (2001), and *A History of the Philippines: From Indios Bravos to Filipinos* (2010/2014). He has edited three anthologies, including *Brown River, White Ocean: An Anthology of Twentieth-Century Philippine Literature* in English (1993). He is the winner of the 2002 PEN Open Book Award, and 2002 Asian American Writers' Workshop Literary Award.

4

ACTIVISM, ART & MEDIA

> legacy:
> the clarity of our own vision
> what we choose to do with our own lives
> will bear fruit to that
> work/spirit.

—From "Parents," a poem by Fay Chiang

Asian American Arts Alliance Town Hall (December 3, 2013)
L to R: Corky Lee, Susan Yung, Elizabeth Young, Nina Kuo,
Rockwell Chin, Robert Lee, Russell C. Leong & Fay Chiang
Photo by Antony Wong

Fay Chiang (1952-2017), an alumnae of Hunter College/CUNY, was a poet, visual artist, community and cultural activist in Manhattan's Chinatown and the Lower East Side for over forty years. In the 1970s, Fay was executive director of the Basement Workshop, the first Asian American multidisciplinary cultural organization in New York City. Most recently Fay was the programming/development director for Project Reach, a youth and adult-run, multiracial, multi-gender, substance abuse prevention and anti-discrimination training center. Her publications include: *Miwa's Song* (1982), *The City of Contradictions* (1979), *A railroad on Gold mountain (Spotlight books)* (1997), and *7 Continents 9 Lives* (2010).

"Beyond the working class immigrant generation's basic needs of clothing, shelter for survival, I believe culture is the psychological weapon for the survival of our future generations."

—Fay Chiang

GLENN OMATSU CHALLENGES US to look at new types of political and cultural movements based on local needs, but with global implications. Asian American Studies and communities, he argues, are defined today by the growing gap between highly educated and well-off professionals, and larger communities without rights: refugee families, immigrant workers, undocumented students and workers, poor seniors, and those who are incarcerated.

Included here is Robert Lee's manifesto for cultural and fiscal equity for New York City's artists of color. Tomie Arai presents a portfolio of family portraits derived from the World War II internment camps. Her artwork also graces this book's cover.

The global impact of organizing and activism can be found in two related pieces: Vinit Parmar's quest for environmental sustainability from "Bihar to Brooklyn, to Berlin," reinforces the goals of the Paris Climate Accord. Shahidul Alam, the noted Bangladeshi photojournalist, utilizes his poetry and images to aid the ongoing global protest to "Save Sundarbans." Mary Uyematsu Kao provides a personal account of Yuri Kochiyama and her enduring impact on today's generation of youth.

David K. Song comments on the films of Sundance-award winning Korean American filmmaker Andrew Ahn, who explores both immigrant and gay identity in his films.

Envisioning the Next Revolutions
How Today's Asian American Movements Connect to Worldwide Activism

GLENN OMATSU

"We live in a period of world history that is filled with both destruction and also human possibilities."

IN THE EARLY 1990s, I ended my article, "The Four Prisons and the Movements of Liberation," about the state of Asian American activism with a series of questions: Will we fight only for ourselves, or will we embrace the concerns of all oppressed people? Will we overcome our own oppression and help to create a new society, or will we become a new exploiter group in the present American hierarchy of inequality? Will we define our empowerment solely in terms of individual advancement for a few, or as the collective liberation for all people?[1]

Two decades ago, these were urgent questions facing Asian American activists, and today they are even more urgent due to changes that occurred worldwide and within our communities. These include several major wars, economic upheavals, increasing inequality between rich and poor, environmental disasters driven by corporate greed, and assaults on human rights in nearly every nation. Not as obvious is the emergence of numerous grassroots movements across the globe as ordinary people organize against these attacks on humanity and envision alternative ways of living. Understanding this dialectic—between that of powerful political and economic forces destroying human lives and that of people mobilizing collectively to respond to these attacks—is the crucial starting point for activists to grapple with the questions of oppression, exploitation, empowerment and liberation today.

Within Asian American communities, there is an additional dialectic that activists are addressing: the growing gap between those who are relatively well off and those who are poor. This gap mirrors the worldwide trend, and increasingly it is not only economic inequality, but more fundamentally a divide between those with privileges, rights, and power to access and control resources, and those without rights and power. In several regions of the world, this divide means the denial of basic rights such as access to water and other necessities to growing numbers of people, and the emergence of modern forms of slavery including human trafficking. On a smaller scale, this division between those with rights and privileges, and those without them, is found within Asian American communities.

The mainstream narrative of the Asian American experience focuses on the sectors that are relatively privileged, who have successfully dealt with some barriers to rise up, and become part of the existing social structure. These are the families with incomes and assets surpassing those of many Whites. They are the young people who are found in record numbers in elite private and public universities. In the workforce, they are the highly-educated individuals who have achieved careers in a number of professions, serving in the roles of highly-skilled specialists and managers.

During the past two decades, one of the important contributions of activists in our communities is to focus organizing on the other and often forgotten sector: those without rights. They include immigrant workers, refugee families, undocumented immigrants, high school dropouts and youth not in college, small business people, senior citizens in poverty, and incarcerated people. In Los Angeles, for example, activists have founded several organizations that have redefined core Asian American issues to include the voices of the unheard people. These organizations include Koreatown Immigrant Workers Alliance (KIWA), Pilipino Workers Center (PWC), Southeast Asian Community Alliance, South Asian Network, API Equality, and Kizuna.

These organizations do not easily fit into mainstream definitions of activist organizations. Like activist formations in the broader society, they are involved in grassroots organizing, advocacy, community education, empowerment of low-income people, and important campaigns against powerful oppressors and exploiters. But they also do much more. One of their most valuable functions is to provide a political space for people to come together to envision new ways to respond to community needs and new forms of human relationships. Because these organizations involve activists, they serve as places for not only envisioning but also for enacting. Through creative experiments launched in recent years, activists are now asking a sharper and deeper question than I raised twenty years ago: If we do not define our community empowerment or human liberation in terms of the existing social structure, then what alternatives do we envision, and how do we use our current work to attain these alternatives?

Transforming Our Communities Through Grassroots Organizing

In this short essay, I highlight five grassroots initiatives created by activists in Los Angeles and Southern California in recent years. By highlighting five initiatives, I am not stating that they are the most important, but only that I am more familiar with them than with other undertakings. I also focus on these recent initiatives because they are not as well known as older activist formations. Highlighting these will hopefully encourage people to identify and appreciate similar experiments within their own communities, and also to create political spaces to envision and initiate their own experiments.

The five initiatives are all relatively new, and some emerged only within the past five years. They focus on different issues, ranging from grassroots organizing on neighborhood issues, to arts and culture, to community entrepreneurship. Yet, what they have in common is that they were all founded by activists who define their work as part of the global grassroots movements for social change. In other words, these five examples help us understand the process of social change in this period, and how activists in grassroots movements are enabling people to create alternative social and political relationships not found in the current social structure.

Chinatown Community for Equitable Development (CCED) arose in 2012 to fill the void of nearly four decades in Los Angeles Chinatown of having no grassroots activist voice on issues. Although Los Angeles is the home to many Chinese American activists, it was not until the formation of CCED that the historic enclave had a powerful activist presence. CCED emerged as an alliance of activists with residents and small business people to oppose the opening of Wal-Mart in their neighborhood. Although CCED was not successful in stopping Wal-Mart, its grassroots mobilization within Chinatown and its coalition with other organizations in the city, blocked the project for more than half a year and also forced public officials to scrutinize the giant corporation's often hidden practices for securing business permits, skirting environmental regulations, and exploiting low-wage workers. Currently, CCED is taking up issues common to other historic ethnic enclaves: gentrification, rising rents, and evictions of long-time residents and small businesses.

Like other effective grassroots campaigns in Asian American communities throughout the U.S., CCED is a multiethnic and inter-generational formation. Veteran activists from the Asian American Movement of the late 1960s and early 1970s work closely with younger activists and interact with Chinese, Vietnamese, Cambodian, and Latino residents, small business people, and senior citizens. From the beginning of its campaign against Wal-Mart, CCED members realized that it was not enough to mobilize people against oppression but to also help people envision an alternative Chinatown based on equity, justice, and respect for the rights of all people. Beginning with its campaign against Wal-Mart and continuing in its current work protecting tenant rights, CCED members are creating spaces in Chinatown where people's lives and human dignity matter more than corporate profits or property values.

K.W. Lee (2007), Photos by Hyungwon Kang
Featured in *CUNY FORUM Volume 2:1*

The K.W. Lee Center for Leadership in Koreatown is not as well known as other activist organizations in the ethnic enclave, despite bearing the name of one of the most famous Korean immigrants in the U.S. K.W. Lee is a celebrated journalist, who in his long newspaper career, garnered numerous awards for his investigative reporting. Following his retirement from the mainstream press, he initiated an English language edition for *The Korea Times* during the turbulent period of the 1992 Los Angeles Riots and Uprisings. Together with his multiethnic staff of young writers, he focused on the stories of humanity coming out of the upheaval, refusing to accept the simplistic, mainstream lens of Black-Korean conflict. Civil rights attorney Do Kim founded the K.W. Lee Center for Leadership in 2003, not only to recognize Lee's achievements in journalism, but to spotlight his ideas for changing Korean American consciousness, especially among youth. Lee and Kim believe that Korean Americans—and, more broadly, all Asian Americans—need to understand the corrosive effects of materialism and individualism that are becoming embedded in the community through the obsession of immigrant parents to get their children into elite universities. Lee believes that this singular pursuit is creating highly-educated professionals who attain positions of power, but who lack compassion and understanding for others.

On the homepage for the K.W. Lee Center for Leadership, Do Kim posted an essay by K.W. Lee explaining the alternative community consciousness needed by young people today. In his essay which he calls "A Cautionary Tale," Lee focuses on two well-known figures in the Korean diaspora of the early twentieth century—Dosan Ahn Chang Ho and Charles Ho Kim—and notes that their contributions to the Korean liberation movement against Japanese colonialism, and to Korean American history, were attained without college degrees. He contrasts their life values and enduring legacy to Syngman Rhee, an Ivy League graduate who rose to power as South Korea's first president but became a dictator and was finally ousted by a democratic movement led by young people. For Lee, the lesson for Korean American youth and their parents is clear: the values of community service and compassion must replace the prevailing focus on materialism and individualism. "Individually we are powerless and dysfunctional," states Lee. "YOU must be the generation to create a new value system—one of community consciousness—to break away from the past."[2]

Tuesday Night Project (TNP) in Little Tokyo has in recent years gained recognition in mainstream Los Angeles cultural circles where it is commonly classified as "an outdoor performance space" for Asian American poets and other artists. In contrast, those intimately involved with TNP know that it is much more. Founded in 1999 by Traci Kato-Kiriyama, TNP arose as part of a movement of young Asian American and Pacific Islander poets and artists to use spoken word, music and performance art to both raise awareness of community issues and to encourage young people to speak out in our communities.

Traci Kato-Kiriyama was a young activist who was influenced by mentors who had participated in the Asian American Movement of the late 1960s and early 1970s. She grew up with the ideal of serving the community and participated in community struggles to practice this value. She discovered her passion for poetry and performance while in college through her involvement with community groups. When she held her first events called Tuesday Night Café in a small courtyard in Little Tokyo, the neighborhood had no nightlife—the result of years of corporate devastation of small businesses and low-cost housing through redevelopment. Kato-Kiriyama chose to locate TNP in Little Tokyo, both to acknowledge its connection

Taxi and Boxer, Thai Town street art, Hollywood, CA
Photo by Russell C. Leong

to the long tradition of poetry and arts in the Japanese American community, and also to help transform the neighborhood into a center for vibrant youth culture.

Today, with the resurrection of Little Tokyo as a trendy neighborhood, it is easy to overlook the earlier impact—and continuing presence—of TNP in community transformation. Kato-Kiriyama's vision of the neighborhood also stands in contrast to that of mainstream business and community leaders. For example, she defined TNP as a free performance event to subvert the increasing corporate-driven effort to turn arts, culture and performers into commodities for profits. She also opened TNP to both established performers and newcomers to break down the prevailing belief in western societies that only highly talented people can produce art and engage in cultural performances. Finally, while focusing on the development of Asian Pacific Islander voices, especially youth, she conceived of TNP as a multiethnic and inter-generational gathering place to enable participants to experience what our communities can become when they are built around values such as service, gratitude, and human dignity.

In the Echo Park and historic Filipinotown area bordering downtown Los Angeles is The Park's Finest, a Filipino barbeque and fusion restaurant founded in 2012. Five activists who grew up in immigrant families in the neighborhood created this restaurant as an extension of their work in community groups serving low-income Filipino immigrants, and supporting democratic movements in the Philippines. One of the founders, Johneric Concordia, grew up eating his father's barbeque feasts for family and friends, and learned to contribute his own talents in cooking to the community groups he joined, notably Tuesday Night Project. Following early TNP performances, he cooked meals for volunteers and then started a catering business that served as the basis for the restaurant founded with his friends.

From the beginning, the five founders envisioned The Park's Finest as more than a restaurant or a business. They linked its mission to community groups that they are a part of and helped promote awareness of Filipino culture and Filipino American history. For Concordia especially, the restaurant connects his love for his community and the values in his life to those of his immigrant parents and the earlier Manong generation, specifically pioneer labor leader Philip Vera Cruz. Concordia also draws from his background with TNP and understands the importance for activists to transform physical spaces in our communities, including businesses, into gathering places for people to experience richer forms of human relationships than is found in the prevailing social order.

More than a hundred miles to the south of The Park's Finest is a smaller but similar community business founded by an activist. From the outside, the Filipino Food & Bakery shop in a small strip mall in San Diego looks like any other Filipino "point-point" fast food restaurant. A steady stream of customers, many from the nearby naval base, drive up and quickly carry out their meals, attracted by the good food, reasonable prices and warm hospitality of staff. But this small business is no ordinary restaurant. At various times of the day, the restaurant becomes an informal meeting place for activists involved in the Filipino community and multiethnic coalitions. On certain evenings, the restaurant transforms into a venue for spoken word and musical performances by young people who use these art forms to both express their ideas, and identify issues of importance within the community. This restaurant is the creation of activist Lily Prijoles, an alumna of UC Berkeley's Ethnic Studies program who returned to her hometown to give back to her community. By redefining her restaurant as a multi-purpose community space, she is continuing the long tradition within our immigrant communities of small businesses serving as informal neighborhood centers. Also as a hub for activism, her restaurant is a political space for promoting community building through inter-generational dialogue, social change, and youth empowerment.

In this time period of growing exploitation and also capitalist crisis, what does social change look like? What do revolutionary movements look like? According to veteran activist Grace Lee Boggs, the next revolutions will be very different from those of the twentieth century that involved seizure of state power by powerful political parties. She believes that the precursors for the next revolutions can be seen in the political activity of numerous grassroots movements across the globe. Unlike past movements, today's grassroots organizations are not created as extensions of an overarching political party. Instead, they are locally based and informally networked, and they periodically come together to share experiences and resources and coordinate campaigns. Today's pre-revolutionary groups focus on multiple issues ranging from promoting sustainable local economies, to upholding workers' rights and dignity, to militantly organizing against giant corporations for protection of rights and resources.

Boggs also believes that today's movements are different from those of the past because of their emphasis on being simultaneously structure changing and people transforming. According to Boggs, the revolutionary movements of the past century believed problems in people's lives and enduring problems, such as racism and sexism, could not be effectively addressed until material conditions in their lives were changed through gaining control of resources and creating a new social structure. In contrast, today's movements do not organize people to "demand more" or focus on gaining material wealth to live comfortable lives, but are focused on building community and human relationships around values that reject the forces of militarism and materialism that dehumanize people and destroy communities. As a result, these new formations emphasize the importance of what some call new revolutionary values, such as compassion, service, and human dignity.

Building Our Grassroots Movements Around New Revolutionary Values

But what does a grassroots movement focusing on building communities and human relationships through values such as compassion actually look like? For Asian American activists, it is common to look for models of social change in other parts of the world, but in this period it is better to look inward at our own communities. The five grassroots initiatives that I highlighted earlier in this essay are among the many projects that emphasize community building and forging human relationships different from the prevailing values of materialism and individualism. By highlighting these initiatives, I do not want to over-estimate their importance, but I do want to show the contributions that Asian American activists are making in this period to the worldwide movement for social change and human transformation.

Significantly, there is also one grassroots movement organized around the values of love and compassion, led by a young Asian American woman with roots in Asian American activism, that has gained recognition beyond our communities. Ai-jen Poo is a leader of the organizing efforts to gain rights and dignity for domestic workers and caregivers. This is a nationwide movement that networks numerous local groups focusing on empowering caregivers, including the Pilipino Workers Center in Los Angeles. For Poo, grassroots organizing based on love and compassion does not mean the absence of conflict and confrontation—similar to the insights of Martin Luther King, Jr., who stated that peace does not mean the absence of war, or that nonviolence does not simply mean the absence of violence. Foregrounding love and compassion as organizing principles transforms human interactions, while simultaneously enabling people to confront and change institutions from this new perspective. Today's movements based on love and compassion are no less militant than those of the past, but their goals for social change are intimately connected to how participants engage in the process of changing society.

Los Angeles Chinese Newspaper (September 7, 2017)
Photo by Russell C. Leong

I believe that the valuable work of activists like Ai-jen Poo and other young Asian American activists also is connected to the rich, historical tradition of activism within our communities, especially that of early Asian immigrant workers. Early activists in our communities pioneered two important practices that I believe younger activists have embraced, practiced in their daily work, and can also now share with others outside our communities. One is what I call "militant humility," and the second is what I call "shared leadership." Both emerged from the particular historical experiences of Asian immigrant workers who were excluded from the U.S. labor movement and, as a result, created their own community-based movements through worker centers. As a result, the campaigns initiated by early immigrant workers prefigure some of the key features of today's grassroots movements, especially the emphasis on envisioning and practicing richer forms of human interactions based on new revolutionary values. The concepts of "militant humility" and "shared leadership" were practiced by immigrant workers in this broader context.

In U.S. mainstream society, and even within progressive organizations, the quality of being humble is regarded as being weak, and humility is not associated with movements for social change. Instead, most activists focus on militancy and are trained—both consciously and unconsciously—to see political power and social change in terms of militant struggle. In contrast, the tradition of Asian American activism —born from the struggles of early immigrant workers who were excluded from the labor movement—integrally linked militancy with humility. This tradition of militant humility enabled them to fiercely fight for equality and justice while also developing patience for the challenging process involved in grassroots organizing. Practicing militant humility is not easy and requires ongoing ideological clarity. Community elders caution us to be militant towards those who oppress our communities but humble to those we serve. Otherwise, without ideological clarity, we can find ourselves humbly respecting powerful authorities while ignoring or defying the people we should be serving. In other words, practicing militant humility is part of the ongoing process of learning how to change society while simultaneously transforming our own lives.

Similarly, the concept of shared leadership stands in contrast to the prevailing model of leadership in the western world and is generally associated with the military, corporations, government and other hierarchical institutions. The prevailing model sees leadership as an individual attribute found in charismatic people who are able to command others. Historically, the prevailing model is based on western colonialism and related to the development of racism, patriarchy, and other forms of colonial domination. Leadership training programs based on the prevailing model focus on the development of assertiveness in a select number of individuals, independent decision-making, and the ability to manage large numbers of people.

In contrast, the alternative model of shared leadership is based on the understanding that all people within a community are leaders, and leadership best works when all are able to contribute their particular skills. In addition, communities organized around shared leadership also emphasize leadership training as part of everyday life with all in the community helping each individual develop new leadership skills. The alternative model is not unique to Asian Americans but is part of the traditions of many indigenous peoples, and also found in anti-colonial movements of the past five centuries. Those who practice shared leadership value qualities not found in the dominant western model: the capacity for nurturing others, the ability to mediate conflict, the qualities of compassion and empathy, and the talent for encouraging different viewpoints while upholding one's own core principles. This approach does not regard leadership as a special characteristic in a few individuals, but as a collective attribute that emerges and develops within a community, especially through struggles for justice. Thus, for Asian American and other activists, implementing shared leadership is an important part of empowering people, and also transforming our communities, around the values of dignity, justice and compassion.

Currently, we live in a period of world history that is filled with both destruction and also human possibilities. From a global perspective, Asian Americans are a very small population whose experiences of oppression and resistance may seem insignificant when compared to larger groups. Yet, the initiatives created by Asian American activists in this period are valuable because they provide insights into how to transform communities, and people's individual lives, through revolutionary values. Ultimately, together with other grassroots struggles across the globe, the movements created by Asian Americans can help manifest on a larger scale the rich possibilities for human liberation in this time period.

Notes

1   Glenn Omatsu, "'The Four Prisons' and the Movements of Liberation: Asian American Activism from the 1960s to the 1990s," Karin Aguilar-San Juan, *The State of Asian America: Activism and Resistance in the 1990s* (Boston: South End Press, 1994): 19–70.

2   "Writings of K.W. Lee," *K.W. Lee Center for Leadership*, http://www.kwleecenter.org/kwwritings/

Author

Glenn Omatsu teaches at the Asian American Studies and the Educational Opportunity Program (EOP) at California State University, Northridge, where he works with first-generation freshmen from low-income families. He also serves as coordinator of the Faculty Mentor Program and the College of Humanities Peer Mentor Project. He is active with community and labor groups, and national solidarity networks.

Robert Lee doing taijiquan at Columbus Park Pavilion, Manhattan Chinatown (March 29, 2017)
Photo by Antony Wong

Cultural and Racial Equity in Practice
Current Policy and Research and the Future of NYC

ROBERT LEE

Following is a response by Robert Lee, co-founder and executive director of Asian American Arts Centre (AAAC), and his personal observations to an event hosted by the New York Community Trust, at the Museo del Barrio, on November 16, 2016, regarding New York City's first-ever comprehensive cultural plan, CreateNYC. Not all aspects of the cultural plan are addressed by the author's comments.

Background: In June 2015, Mayor Bill de Blasio signed legislation requiring New York City to produce *CreateNYC*, a roadmap to guide the future of arts and culture. The NYC Department of Cultural Affairs (DCLA) worked together with artists, cultural organizations, New York City agencies, arts and culture experts, and community residents to collect data and public input to inform the cultural plan. In Fall 2016, the *CreateNYC* team hosted a variety of opportunities for public input to develop a clear picture of the experiences, values, and cultural priorities of New Yorkers from all walks of life.

In Spring 2017, a draft plan was released for public review and comment. In response to the draft plan, artists and activists released *The People's Cultural Plan* (www.peoplesculturalplan.org).

The final *CreateNYC* cultural plan was released on July 19, 2017, and is available online at www.createnyc.org.

TOWARDS THE CONCLUSION of this event I realized a large part of the discussion dealt with policies and practices, elaborating the administrative system to be able to make the arts accessible to all parts of the city. What was being overlooked became clear when questions were taken from the audience. When asked about the needs of a thirty-four year old community organization, one speaker's reply was that her foundation saw such groups as having a natural life cycle. And therefore, no sustainability program would be undertaken to support such groups.

Cultural Inequity and a "Natural Life Cycle"?

The idea that a natural life cycle could be applied to community cultural organizations was striking, given that the development of a comprehensive cultural plan for New York City is based on several decades of cultural inequity. This can hardly be called a "natural process." Fixing the system's approach has failed to zoom in and see how the arts are actually transmitted under conditions of racial and cultural neglect.

A systems approach takes no responsibility for individual people of color (POC) organizations, and sees them only in terms of their "life cycle." Their skills and achievements configured under difficult and daunting conditions, their devotion to their arts and their communities are then easily diminished, and disregarded. It becomes conceivable that a system of transfer to an established larger organization, can learn to serve their audience, present their arts, and even gain a community's trust.

Organizations of Color

When a natural development took place in the 1980s, artists of color created the major cultural phenomena known as multiculturalism, which has persisted for over twenty years. Throughout the country, when community groups sought increased support to accommodate audiences, the funding community chose instead to create a major funding program called New Audiences, where funds to showcase these new artists were given to established institutions. As artists attracted larger audiences, they were moved from community venues that nourished them, to mainstream institutions pushing their notion of "multiculturalism."

Why were community venues not supported? Because we were not trusted. We were organizations of color—not white. Sharing power with us was unthinkable. This is an example of the intentional racial and cultural neglect that community members may not have known, nor realized, its impact on the POC community. Despite this, artists such as Martin Wong, Zhang Hongtu, Mel Chin, Danny N.T. Yung, Xu Bing, Lily Yeh, Indira Freitas Johnson, Zarina Hashmi, Tseng Kwong Chi, Gu Wenda, Natvar Bhavsar, Ai Weiwei, and more recently Wafaa Bilal and Simone Leigh, all were exhibited early in their careers at the Asian American Arts Centre (AAAC), and came to be recognized as important to the visual life of this society and the international community. This is one of the many ways that indicate the significant value of community cultural organizations.

Min, Yong Soon
Defining Moments 4/6
20x16 inches (h x w x d)
1992
Photo montage
www.artasiamerica.org/artist/detail/80

Another aspect of arts organizations was raised by comparing them to public libraries. Libraries bring many of its users to public hearings to substantiate their request for funds, while arts groups bring few, if any. This difference offers no insight into the issue of arts organizations. Public hearings are themselves a questionable way of relating to communities for whom racial and cultural neglect has become a norm. Local audiences did not pound on the door of AAAC to initiate a program to support unknown artists.

Different Yet Equal

In the 1980s, a small group of devoted artists were responsible for envisioning arts programming. They did that when nobody cared. I could have asked artists we exhibited to come to city hearings, but I doubt any would have come since officials weren't listening then, and I'm afraid the plan is to not listen now.

If teaching mainstream institutions how to replace community arts organizations becomes the outcome of this public process, then the problem of inequity will continue. You may teach people to attend public hearings, but it may just be another attempt at assimilation. POC don't want to be assimilated. We want to retain our difference. We want to be equal.

Nationally, neo-liberalism has formed the policies geared towards POC. In New York State, this led to the creation of a funding department for community arts called Ghetto Arts, which then proceeded to fund New York City's community arts organizations peanuts for four decades. Just as the center has its periphery, and the periphery has its fringe, it is on the fringe where POC have existed. The harmful effects of this decades-old policy should, as much as possible, be reversed.

What We Believe and Trust

A systems approach can never serve the purpose of what the arts represent. Equity for POC is not just about equal access to the arts, or problems with resource distribution systems. Art is about real human contact, people who want to share, enjoy, and touch what we touch. It's about the transmission of what moves us, what animates us, and what we come to feel because the artist/teacher feels with us.

Ultimately, it's about what we believe and trust. That's what artists/performers do, what good teachers do, and what community arts groups do. It's that bond of trust that sparks and fosters participation and identity. The best thing a systems approach can do is to move out of the way. It should let those motivated to create, present, transmit, care for and preserve the arts and the culture it grows—the arts in situ—embody our living culture. Such arts motivate people, and are already in place with years of demonstrated commitment to their community and their work.

Do we have the will to take responsibility for decades of neglect, and policies that have alienated both those on the right, and those in diverse communities? Now, after the 2016 presidential election, a different stance needs to be realized. Diversity needs to be affirmed. But can this call for equity realize the next step in doing what's right?

Forty Years of Neglect

We need to reverse forty years of neglect, and send a message to Trump that New York City affirms the value of diversity. We value and affirm our neighborhoods, and the diverse cultures of all ethnic peoples. The goal of cultural equity, strengthening neighborhoods, communities, ethnic groups, is nothing less than the goal of making the entire city great. This deep commitment comes first before real estate, land use, and the temptation to gentrify communities. Further discussion may be necessary on this issue; however, the colonization of settled neighborhoods must be stopped, or else equity is meaningless.

The challenge that Trump presents us is to embrace diversity. We need to embrace our differences, rather than show how liberal or tolerant we would like to see ourselves. We need to truly believe diverse cultures endow us with the energy and rhythms that New York City is known for. White ethnics have their neighborhoods as well, and can be embraced too for what they contribute to the mix. Their pride and their culture should never be neglected as POC have been, and should not be confused with the biases and hostilities that they have been taught to identify as theirs. Demagoguery can be challenged once we are clear that it is in our neighborhoods, in real people, and not in systems and profits. That is where the strength and beauty of our city lie.

Transform Neo-Liberalism

Beyond legal rights and token tolerance, POC and all ethnic groups want to feel recognized, welcomed, and accepted by the larger city. Towards this goal, embracing our diversity could be made tangible by some form of legitimization, such as issuing a certificate for display, or an entitlement that enables a clearer path to funding and support. However, such a piece of parchment, even if issued, will mean nothing unless the quest for cultural equity is the first step in an ongoing move to transform neo-liberalism.

People in the arts who endure in small localized communities that may have been uprooted, who acquire a faith that lasts and carries them through, and whose arts may never come to be recognized for the strength and meaning it has for their communities and for our nation—these are examples of exceptional people. Contrary to celebrity culture, these people and what they do, should be seen as exceptional investments. I suggest a different, not necessarily expanded role, for our government—motivated with strengthening culture and fulfilling the inner well-being of people, not just for its economic material enhancement.

Contemporary society can express its desire and appreciation of other traditional ethnic cultures and their wisdoms as the birthright of every grandfather and grandmother, to be seen and regarded, given their wise, loving presence. Neo-liberalism can recognize its excesses; its inequity; its reliance on youth culture; its drive for power and money; its use of science to replace what is felt; its preference for legalities rather than its humanity; and its material secularisms that leave little space for a valid role for the spirituality of every faith. And so, in closing, I suggest the following when pursuing a comprehensive cultural plan for New York City:

1. Equity must be at the center of the eight questions posed to guide the procedures of all public meetings so New Yorkers can grasp the implications for their communities.

2. A cultural plan that affirms New York City's commitment to the value of our neighborhoods and the diverse cultures of all ethnic peoples. A city is as strong as its communities.

3. A cultural plan that issues a certificate, or entitlement, to community groups that establish a clear and direct path to funding and support.

Postscript

At the Cultural Equity Group (CEG) Cultural Equity and Diversity Meeting on April 21, 2015, where the DCLA commissioner was invited, a key issue was funding succession for elder POC arts organizations, whose infrastructures are over thirty years in the making. With the conclusion of two years of research and outreach culminating in the *CreateNYC* cultural plan, which is now public, clearly the government has shown it listens selectively, ignoring the voices of people of color, and the arts leaders who have represented these communities for decades.

No concern is expressed for the demise of elder POC cultural organizations. Mayor de Blasio is solely focused on the Cultural Institutions Group (CIG), mainstream organizations, and the ethnic reflection of their staff—essentially a repetition of the failed New Audiences program in the '90s.

Asian Americans, people of color: This ten year cultural plan is an opportunity to recognize that liberal government will never support the strengthening of our communities, is not capable of offering us justice, the truth, nor the freedom embedded in our arts. We can play the games of the mainstream, but if we want to survive, if we want our cultures and communities to survive, we must organize and strengthen our communities locally through coalition building. The City will continue to fail us, as they have for the past forty years.

Author

Robert Lee is the Executive Director/Curator of Asian American Arts Centre (www.artspiral.org) where he initiated the Art Centre's visual arts programming in 1978, drawing attention to Asian American artists as a field of special study. He has focused on artists who, since 1945, demonstrate the historic cultural presence of several generations of Asian Americans in the U.S. He has taught a course on this subject at the Parsons School of Design in 1997.

Many well-known artists today were exhibited at the Arts Centre early in their career, such as: Dinh Q. Le, Lily Yeh, Mel Chin, Zhang Hongtu, Martin Wong, Charles Yuen, Ik Joong Kang, Ai Weiwei, Ming Fay, Choong Sup Lim, Albert Chong, Tseng Kwong Chi, Yong Soon Min, Kip Fulbeck, Kwok Man Ho, Mike Kanemitsu, Alfonso Ossorio, VC Igarta, Tara Sabharwal, Anna Kuo, Natvar Bhavsar, Zarina Hashmi, Tam Van Tran, Amy Loewan, Younghee Paik, Emily Cheng, Suikang Zhao, Indira Freitas Johnson, In Sook Hwang, Corky Lee, Tomie Arai, Wafaa Bilal, Simone Leigh, Mariam Ghani and Chitra Ganesh, Rumiko Tsuda, Santiago Bose, Roger Shimomura, Ushio Shinohara and Patti Warashina.

Robert served eight years (1985-1993) on the board of The Association of American Cultures (TAAC) advocacy organization for people of color in the arts. As a founding member (1983) of the Asian American Arts Alliance, he oversaw its operations for six years. He is also a member of the Chinatown Working Group, Cultural Equity Group, and People's Cultural Plan.

Editor's Note

Robert Lee is an artist, activist, archivist, and a force of nature—a proponent and developer of community-based art, artists, and institutions in New York City during the past forty years. He is best known as the co-founder and executive director of the Asian American Arts Centre, a vital force in discovering, exhibiting, and disseminating the work of Asian American and Asian artists.

"Bob," as he is more commonly known, is the son of a Chinese laundryman who had a business in North New Jersey—located just three blocks from the Newark Uprising of 1968. When I interviewed him on March 2, 2017, Bob was wearing what appeared to be a hipster's white shirt with a block print of hanging laundry. I complimented him on it, and then he told me about his family work as a youngster folding shirts in the laundry. He had spied the shirt in a small street market on Houston Street and bought it because it reminded him of his origins. Though the laundry was a common occupation for Chinese immigrant families, doing such work did not automatically give him a broader Chinese or Asian American identity. Yet art, according to Bob, was not merely a high note in an opera or a one-time acrobatic stunt; rather, Asian American art always needed, and demanded, a social context for its lifeblood.

Bob went on to say in this interview (full video, https://youtu.be/yASV0WHdRNI) that it was not until he moved to Manhattan's Chinatown in the late 1960s that, "I began to see where I fit into the present moment."

Bob himself is a product of the polyglot, "hothouse cultures" (in his words) of the New York region, buffered also by the "winds of Asia." According to him, the community aspect of the Asian American arts movement started with the Basement Workshop—in an actual basement on Elizabeth Street. In the early days, his whole family was involved, including his wife, the choreographer Eleanor Yung, and her brother, Danny N.T. Yung, who was then studying at Columbia University.

Bob began showcasing artists in 1982, and as exhibitions and spaces overlapped with his wife's Asian American dance programming—they merged, moving to a loft and applied for funding. The 1980s, as he recalls, was a decade of identity politics, setting the stage for multiculturalism in the 1990s, a term that was picked up by mainstream institutions, who ironically received most of the available funding through the philanthropy community's New Audiences programs.

So, whether it was the memorable "June 4th" (1989) show which travelled the U.S. —a first for the Asian American community; "Ancestors" (1995), a collaboration with Kenkeleba House that examined ancestral ties between Africans and Asians; or the more recent "Detained" (2006) that focused on race, exclusion, and spirituality among Arab and Asian Americans, Bob has pushed the envelope, opening artistic and political spaces that mainstream museums, galleries, and exhibitors hardly touch.

Yet even so, Bob and the Asian American Arts Centre has remained in the trenches, struggling for funding, exhibition space, and wider recognition of their extraordinary service to Asian and Asian American artists, and other artists of color. To this day, Robert Lee's willingness to confront the art establishment, and the status quo, has made him an articulate model and mentor for emerging activists, curators, and scholars. His response to New York City's *CreateNYC* cultural plan attests to that.

* For more on the contested origins of alternative Asian American art spaces, see Bob's 2010 interview by Herb Tam in *Alternative Histories: New York Art Spaces, 1960-2010* (Cambridge: MIT Press, 2012).

Momotaro/Peach Boy
A Portfolio

TOMIE ARAI

"Momotaro is a story of possibilities and second chances,
retold to explain the cycle of hope and grief brought about by war."

MOMOTARO/PEACH BOY IS A PORTFOLIO of nine prints based on the popular Japanese folk tale about a baby boy who emerges from a giant peach and grows up to become a hero. The prints in this series form the pages of a fictional narrative, inspired by family memories of the forced incarceration of Japanese Americans and the experiences of Japanese American GIs in World War II. Each of the prints incorporate photographs of my father, grandfather and son, as well as cartoon characters, material from the National Archives, traditional Japanese motifs and illustrations appropriated from magazines and children's books.

As a third generation Japanese American, I was interested in constructing a contemporary Japanese American folk tale that explores the relationship between art and history by combining autobiography, oral history, and portraiture in the art making process. I am particularly interested in oral traditions and folk histories that have been created to explain historical events and have been passed down over several generations.

Momotaro is a classic adventure tale with many readings. During World War II, the Japanese government used Momotaro as a propaganda vehicle for promoting nationalism and imperialist expansion overseas. In the original folk tale an old couple nearing the end of their lives dream of having a child. They discover a giant peach floating in the river, and when they open the peach a baby boy leaps out. They name the baby Momotaro, or Peach Boy. When the boy grows up he goes off to fight the monsters who have been terrorizing his village. On his journey to Onigashima, the island of the ogres, he meets a pheasant, a dog and a monkey who agree to help him. Together, they defeat the wicked ogres and return to Momotaro's village laden with riches. In both the traditional and contemporary versions of this story, the elderly couple is rewarded for a lifetime of hard work and self-sacrifice with a perfect child. Momotaro's brave deeds redeem his aging parents in the eyes of society. The peach, an Asian symbol of longevity and fertility, is woven into Momotaro's clothing in the form of a crest and appears as an ever-present reminder of the importance of family and community.

Momotaro was told to me as a young child, and it was not difficult to see my father as the brave young boy who goes off to fight the wicked ogres. I have tried to retell this story from both a child's and an adult's point of view. The story presented here is not a celebration of my father's heroic deeds, but an examination of the ways in which we create folk heroes and share stories of survival by bending the truth, fictionalizing history, and embellishing memory. In the retelling, Momotaro becomes a story of possibilities and second chances generated by desperate acts, told and retold as a way to explain the endless cycle of hope, expectation, and grief brought about by war.

Grief features a portrait of a survivor of the bombing of Hiroshima, taken by the Japanese photographer Yamahata Yosuke in 1945. A giant wave or tsunami threatens to envelop this woman. In my story of Momotaro, the barren landscape of pre- and post- war Japan becomes a metaphor for the childless couple who are overcome by grief and the desire for a more hopeful future.

Momotaro/Peach Boy, Nine solar plate etchings – a portfolio printed by the artist at the Women's Studio Workshop, NY 2014, 2017 © Copyright by Tomie Arai

In **Possibility**, a young boy emerges from a giant peach that is floating in a universe of manga characters and toys. The new world he finds himself in is a reference to the post-war Super Flat movement founded by artist Takashi Murakami, where the boundaries of class, privilege, pop art and fine art are flattened to produce a consumer culture driven by materialism and the ambition to succeed.

Fathers and Sons is a portrait of my grandfather, Juhei Arai, and my father, set against the backdrop of the Topaz Relocation Center in Utah, where my father's family was incarcerated for the duration of World War II.

Peach Boy is based on a studio portrait of my uncle, Aaron Arai, taken in Sacramento, California, circa 1924. Dressed as a cowboy, this photograph of my uncle seemed to capture both the irony of the assimilation experiences of the Japanese community, and the determination of the descendants of Japanese immigrants to claim a place for themselves in America. The artist's models seen lined at the bottom of the print, symbolize the aesthetics of 'measuring up' to our ideals of proportion and beauty.

A Soldier's Story comes from the title of the play by the same name, by Charles Fuller, which addresses the deeply conflicting feelings about race and racism within the African American community. As a parallel narrative, the Japanese American soldier in this print is pictured struggling with the decision to prove his patriotism to the country that has denied his family their rights as American citizens. The retelling of Momotaro, with my family as the central characters, is an exploration of the ultimate price that was paid by these young men to win acceptance and approval.

Artist

Tomie Arai is a public artist who lives and works in New York City. Her recent projects include banner designs for the Smithsonian's A/P/A Folklife Festival on the National Mall, public artwork for the new Central Subway Chinatown Station in San Francisco, and a community collaboration entitled "Portraits of New York Chinatown" recently on view at the Museum of Chinese in America.

Tomie's work has been exhibited nationally and is in the collections of the Library of Congress, the Bronx Museum of the Arts, the Japanese American National Museum, the Williams College Museum of Art, the Museum of Modern Art, and the Whitney Museum of American Art. She is a recipient of two New York Foundation for the Arts Fellowships, a Joan Mitchell Visual Arts Grant, a National Endowment for the Arts Visual Arts Fellowship for Works on Paper, and three MidAtlantic Arts Foundation Visual Artists Residency Grants. In 1997, she was one of ten women nationwide to receive an Anonymous Was a Woman Award for achievement in the visual arts.

In 2015, Tomie was awarded a Lifetime Achievement Award in the Visual Arts from the Women's Caucus for Art. As a co-founder of the Chinatown Art Brigade, a cultural collective of artists and activists, she received a 2016 A Blade of Grass Fellowship, a 2017 LMCC Creative Engagement grant, and an Arts and Activism grant from the Asian Women's Giving Circle for the public art project, "Here to Stay."

From Bihar to Brooklyn, to Berlin
A Quest for Sustainability and Soul

VINIT PARMAR

> "In the era of global warming, nothing is really far away; there is no place where the orderly expectations of bourgeois life hold unchallenged sway."
>
> —Amitav Ghosh, *The Great Derangement: Climate Change and the Unthinkable* (2016)

I. In My Grandfather's House

BLACK LIKE COAL. From the air and into my being. One could not wipe it away. Beads of sweat drew streaks of coal dust that stubbornly stuck to damp skin. Did I wash my hands? asked my grandmother before allowing me to eat. Yes. But I could not scrub away the grit embedded under my nails. Did I wash my feet? Yes. But now the towels were gray. Did I wash my mouth? Yes. But a gargle that could not shake the ooze stuck in my nose. I associated that coal with visits to my grandfather's home during Dhunbad summers in Bihar, India. His cement home was made ugly by the industry that supported his comfortable life from the 1950s to 1970s.

My grandfather retired from the energy industry, having made a small fortune selling unrefined coal for thirty years. Like him, many unskilled entrepreneurs gained from supporting the country's northeast coal industry. The last one hundred years of capital clamor for coal extraction fueled the development of the city, but at the same time it spawned the expansion of the city of Kolkata. Dhunbad's coal illuminated Kolkata's twenty million faces but left it in the dust.

I was born from this dust. One cannot imagine how a lotus flower rising out of the water sits in the muck of life. How could a town covered in dust ever reach greatness? Food. Dhunbad was famous for its street vendors as families dined around cartloads of Chat, Gol-Guppa, and Aloo-Patties, all scrumptious traditional Gujarati dishes.

Life was sweet corn in our backyard. I sharpened my teeth peeling sugarcane stalks and squeezing out the last drops of glucose. Guava-bearing trees promised a basket of savory fruit. It never occurred to me that this goodness came from the muck.

*   *   *

Brown like the color of my skin. I could not wipe it away. Early in my youth, my parents uprooted me from dusty Bihar only to stick me into an uninviting Forest Hills classroom in Queens, New York. Could I scrape off the color? asked a classmate. No, it would not rub off. From where did I come? India. Why did I smell like this? I don't know. I did not know I was different. Nothing in my seven years of life prepared me to fend off bullying and humiliation: A sudden push down the stairs. The disappearance of my lunchbox. The regular theft of my bike. Garbage stuffed in my desk. My name topped a not-so-secret list of "The Ugliest" in the class. What was worse, being covered in the coal-laced grime that killed everything or the desolation of an all-Caucasian school where nothing could survive as I knew it?

We're familiar with how a butterfly's wings may flap to move mountains. The bullying I experienced as a stranger in a landscape of intolerance affected me for decades as I searched for something meaningful. My loneliness birthed a need to seek order.

My adolescent life was based on adhering to rules. Rules offered control. One rule I tried to follow came from my father's civil engineering practice. He applied a yardstick to gauge everything, and not just buildings: Be accurate and efficient as a machine—a saying at a time when computers were not invented. Even my hobby of photography exhibited a fascination for order, in line, mass and shape.

I pursued this principle in studying the applied science of chemistry. A chemical could be quantified and life was simple. Then, I saw Ingmar Bergman's *Persona*. The notion that the identities of a nurse and her patient could clash to create a riveting story made me cast aside my ideal of structure and embrace film as a medium for expression. I discarded my hobby of photography, which then seemed passive, and started to create stories.

A second value I picked up in my adolescence was to fulfill my duty. Like the Puritan ethic of hard work, it came from our family's Hindu-based belief in karma. Hence, my duty was to obey my parents; as the student, to succeed academically; and as the believer, to submit to the Hindu scriptures in Vedic texts. It did not matter that I could not understand—the duty-bound need not know what lies beyond the horizon to be the good follower. Now, with Bergman, Michelangelo Antonioni, Federico Fellini and Woody Allen pre-occupying my time, measuring success through this ocular scope, my life came up short.

The more provocative questions remained unanswered: Was duty still to be upheld when the parent was wrong, science was ambiguous, and the pundit obsolete? And, when society repeated history by following the parent, religion, and science with the same errors? Swarming with these thoughts, I still felt incomplete until graduate school came along. Enrolling in law school was the turn in the forked road towards a certain freedom from the strict definitions of duty and rules. The right path would have been filmmaking, but that had to wait until later. Comprehending law empowered me. Within the classroom walls, I found comfort in relating with victims of the disparately treated, sharing in the history of women and people of color deemed as property, and finding common ground in the diminished Asian identity as told through histories of Chinese slavery and Japanese internment.

The inner strength I sought was found sitting behind the desk of the chief administrative judge for whom I clerked during law school. Somehow, intellectual reflexivity was born while crafting legal arguments, and it helped that my legal reasoning was afforded the power of a court's stamp of approval. As a practicing New York attorney for seven years, I did my rounds. My career as a trial lawyer on Wall Street helped to heal the inner child who had been hurt from years of battling bullying and humiliation in America.

Green like greed. It smelled like money, looked like money, but none of it was within my grasp. For all my logged hours for trial dates and court battles under my charge as an in-house lawyer, what were the fruits of my one hundred-hour-a-week efforts? I worked to fill the corporate coffers. So I quit my $4 billion corporate insurance gig on Wall Street to work as a Grip on a film set in Pennsylvania for $50 a week.

II. A Grip on Reality
Few lives may be as convoluted, a mish-mash of unanticipated turns and discoveries, as mine. Yet these were the seminal events that propelled my life as I pursued my destiny as an adult.

I returned to Bihar four decades later to make documentary films about the environment and social justice, and about how development impacts people. Looking back at this history confirms how the past has led me to first document Bihar's coal industry; then, the present-day ecology of the Ganges; and then, to document renewable energy issues on the remote Sundarban islands of India. In all of this, I realized, we human beings must come to terms with the consequences of our actions.

It was easy to transition from life under the dim fluorescence of the office and courtroom, to the verve of sunlight, actors, and a vibrant film set. I worked through the various film crew roles quickly until I landed in field sound recording. What seemed to be an anomalous craft to others, seemed facile to me with my affinity for detail and process. There was no job too far away—circling New York State for a documentary, a theater play in Cairo, a tourism commercial in Malaysia, a music video in Utah, a submarine for a short film, and back to New York City's *Saturday Night Live* set. Already by age thirty-five, my body was hitting the physical limits of an arduous travel schedule, fourteen-hour days at six-week stretches. My lifestyle was not sustainable, and so I switched gears for a routine that applied intellect, as well as technical skills, as a professor at Brooklyn College/CUNY.

III. Quest for Answers

Film still from *Quest for Energy*

I traveled to Chennai, India, for a three-day Fulbright seminar on how industries impact our health and environment. I traveled across India's railways to a dozen towns and cities over forty-five days. But I felt the story was still untold.

The trip was an eye-opener. The cheapest ways to travel were also the most "clean," like trains as opposed to planes, and rickshaws compared to taxis. Development was rampant, but so was the pollution. Systems like industrial production, large-scale logistical transportation, and fossil fuel companies that depended the heaviest on energy, were the least accountable.

Does not everyone want to solve health and pollution problems? No one would say no. However, while NGO leaders confirmed my film *Living River*'s accurate rendition of the facts, they admitted it might create a public uproar. Public administrators asked to shelve the film until industry leaders were culled to abide by environmental laws. Academics complained the film was an outsider's point of view of a domestic problem.

The seminar ended, but I didn't return home. I hit the road again for more filming on how development trumps health and environmental causes. Eight years of toil and trouble produced *Living River* (2012, re-edited and released on iTunes in 2015). The upshot of *Living River* is that the Ganges River carried its karma in the form of waste and chemicals that the people dumped into it.

I had not felt positive about making *Living River*. The accusatory words of a passerby stung, stopping me from acquiring focus on my lens, "Who are you, a foreigner, to present India in a bad light?" Suddenly, one comment from a stranger shined light on an old issue: I was the stranger, but this time in a familiar land, what I had called my own land. So then who was I, and where did I belong?

On a plane heading back "home" to Brooklyn, I asked in the most objective voice I could muster: Was the perspective in *Living River* not too different from a paparazzi's fleeting fascination with the plight of those trying to improve their standard of living? Didn't *Living River* simplistically point a guilty finger at a failing government? Unable or perhaps unwilling to answer my own questions, I looked the other way for a distraction.

No sooner had I dusted off my camera when a campus colleague entered my office and invited me to help him change the world with a film. I hopped on board. Little did I realize at the time that this new project would become my redemption from *Living River* by highlighting positive stories of Indians reducing their carbon-footprint while increasing their living standards. *Quest for Energy* (SnagFilms, 2012) was a collaboration with Professors Micha Tomkiewicz (Brooklyn College/CUNY) and Ryoya Terao (New York City College of Technology/CUNY). We later then embarked on *Carbon-2-Green* to extend *Quest for Energy* by illustrating the carbon-footprint impact of micro-renewable projects in developing and developed nations.

While filming in India again to assist another colleague, Prof. Tansen Sen (Baruch College/CUNY), I disappeared into narrow Chinatown alleys to document the shrinking Chinese population in *The Tanneries of Tangra* (15 minutes). One afternoon, a dozen drunk, unemployed laborers surrounded my rental car, pulled me out, took my camera, and held me at knifepoint. Pressed against the wall and facing impending death, I experienced a flash of memories and thought, "What was the purpose of saving the planet from global warming if it's now at the cost of my life?"

Cornered, their interrogation tried to expose my guilt so that I would pay for my penalties. Did I get government authorization to film? No, and I didn't need a permit, but... Did I seek their permission to film their property? No, it was not their land, but... To this desperate bunch, I was not within their caste, class, creed, or national origin. I was simply a wealthy foreigner for their picking. To their disappointment, my pockets were empty. As their blood cooled and the hot afternoon's canteen of whiskey diluted in their veins, this cadre eased their grip on me. Eventually I was released without harm.

So, did I not belong where I was born? *Quest for Energy* answered this question. The film was only as relevant as those who may be inspired to change themselves. In screenings, viewers wondered how they might try to make a difference. Berliners appreciated the Indian efforts and hoped to assist others in their position. Indians were proud of how their fellow islanders fared. Slovakians felt inspired that technology was the answer. Viewers across the U.S. were inspired by the tenacity of the uneducated farmers to work toward a common cause.

In Berlin, Germany, I saw residents shrinking their per capita footprint by eliminating nuclear energy and banking on renewables as their sole reliance of energy by mid-century, leading the world in establishing the highest bar on efficiency toward emission-free living. This past year, Germans spent an unprecedented billion Euros to install wind turbines in their northern Baltic waters.

My own quest however continued. When would the journey to find a voice be over? When would I become a citizen of the world, borderless, undefined by country, religion, political party, or class? In making *Carbon-2-Green*, this inquiry resolved itself.

IV. Sustainability: East/West Differences

In the East, sustainability is not a concept, but living within one's means is. The outcome is the same, considering the valuations are different. What we choose to include in our value system is based on what is important to us, what we need, and how much we are willing to pay for it. As a practical matter, sustainability is more a function of economy and feasibility than thinking green thoughts.

What do you need when you go camping? A tank of propane gas for cooking, a fully charged flashlight, a lamp powered by the car, and bottles of potable water. Asian Indians outside of urban areas live like they camp out every day, and they must set aside time and funds to acquire access to electricity, gas, and water. Fifteen percent of their income goes to energy and natural resource acquisition, compared to three percent for those living in urban areas.[1] One can say that their problem is the problem of the underdeveloped world. Their financial burden underscores the unsubsidized cost of energy and resources. The relative higher cost of these necessities has promoted a frugality amongst the villagers and rural communities. Here are a few examples:

Water

My aunt will use just a half-gallon of fresh water to wash all the utensils, pots, and pans used to cook dinner for four. Her morning shower taps only a single five-gallon bucket of fresh water. Why do Indians consume less? Are water meters measuring their usage? No, a measuring infrastructure has not been built and there is no regulation on society's use of water. Do they have to pay for it? No, water runs freely from the open tap. The concept is simple: what we do not use today, we may use tomorrow. With scarce resources, little is taken for granted.

Sun

Resources like the sun are forms of energy. Hindus personify the sun's energy with the God Surya, Lord Varuna for water, and God Vayu for wind. Even stones and soil in Indian mythology carry God-like significance. The subtext of respect and reverence underscores the use of any resource as it is God-given. And, what God giveth today may be taken away tomorrow. One conserves water so as not to abuse a precious gift. Thus, conservation is engrained into anyone using these resources. Oddly, fossil fuels have no omnificent personification.

Beliefs

Religion fills another important function. The power of belief overcomes physical limits. Every two years my New York-licensed family physician, a native Indian, returns with his family to his homeland. He never misses a chance to visit the holy waters of the Ganges River. There, he takes a dip, washes his body, and sips from the river. Did he not watch my film, *Living River*, to realize that both domestic and industrial pollution course through that river? The level of coliform, a factor that measures fecal matter, exceeds normal limits by two hundred times, and the chromium level is ten thousand times higher than maximum tolerable levels. Visitors to the river may not be wise to the degree of pollution silently flowing through its waters, but it does not stop a million visitors each year from bathing in it or sipping its water in the belief that its touch strengthens the spirit and cleanses the soul by vanquishing negative karma. I have always wondered if, by the strength of one's conviction, we could surpass the boundaries of physical reality. Can this belief, a vital component of the will, change one's relationship to nature?

The same cannot be said for an American household, regardless of the fervor of religious engagement. America continues to lead us, perhaps in the wrong direction. Americans make up five percent of the world's population.[2] Yet, Americans consume more than twenty-four percent of the world's goods and natural resources.[3] Currently, per capita in India, consumption is one tenth that of an American, but that is rising.[4] It is expected that India will consume as much as Americans do, as they model Western behavior to achieve greater heights of development. In his book *Hot, Flat, and Crowded* (2009), Thomas Friedman asks how many Americas can the world's resources support.

To offset unsustainable growth like America's rise, no nation-state wishes to impose economic caps or limits on its people's freedom for capital gains. However, careful government control of the price of oil and gas has curbed its use—for example, in Europe. Feeling a financial pinch will also invite technological innovation for low or no-energy appliances and goods, or ones that are self-sustaining. It may open up opportunities for companies to seek out and leverage government incentives to do research and development. Nothing drives the economy better and faster than government incentives and a plan to reassure the investing public that their investments are secured with a market of consumers waiting to buy.[5]

In the West, we see these separate forces working collaboratively toward one single interest in increasing the social good of our planet. To this end, September 21, 2014 marked the People's Climate March to focus the world's attention on the dire need for solutions in our Green Revolution. New Yorkers, Berliners, and Delhians all gathered to spell out a collective "Yes" message. In the East, the idea of development is directly tied to these solutions; while in the West, the renewable trend is exactly that, something perceived as a fad that one may voluntarily purchase, like organic soybeans. No such choices exist in the true heartland of India. The real question is, what can I afford and how quickly may I get it?

V. Sundarbans: Off-the-Grid Technology

To visit the Sundarbans region located in the State of West Bengal in India is to take a vacation off-the-grid; no running tap water and no electricity. A visitor may stay on just one or two of the fifty inhabited islands, out of a total of one hundred and two scattered in the largest urban wetland that pours the grand Ganges Basin's Himalayan ice melt into the delta between India and Bangladesh. Known as a World Heritage site,[6] the Sundarbans is the home to nearly two hundred and seventy-three rarely seen Bengal white tigers.[7] The local folk do not yet know that climate change will submerge fifteen percent of this tender region by 2020, and seventy five percent by the end of the century.[8] But they have witnessed two islands that have been submerged, and know something is wrong.[9]

Before 1997, kerosene lamps illuminated the lives of four million residents. Although underdeveloped, democracy functioned, and the elected village chiefs, or "Panchayats"[10] from each island's several districts, voiced their need for electricity at monthly council meetings. In the 1990s, Dr. S. P. Gon Chowdhury attended a meeting and heard their voices. He was the director of the state's Renewable Energy Development Agency, charged with the task of supplying clean energy to that region.[11] With his guidance, government subsidies, and support by a unanimous vote to adopt renewable technology to access electricity, the island began to switch from kerosene to clean electricity.

Actually, the technical know-how was inspired by American technology developed before the Bush Administration cut domestic energy program funding. Colorado-based National Renewable Energy Laboratories within the U.S. Department of Energy had created a prototype for a hybrid biomass-diesel "Gasifier," which was installed in the Sundarbans. This micro-grid facility generated emission-free electricity to support six hundred homes and businesses from 5 p.m. to 11 p.m. everyday without fail. Suddenly, the electrified township of Gosaba sparked with life and the community was inspired.

Children no longer breathed burned kerosene oil to study at night. Mothers watched national news on television sets. Relatives enjoyed Bollywood films acquired from DVD-rental stores. Fathers brought home restaurant food and treats. Hospitals provided surgical care, stored vaccines, and preserved blood in cold banks. Offices offered computer classes. Businesses boomed. Employment increased and the standard of living rose. And, an imperceptible change occurred. The birth rate declined, as observed by Dr. Gon Chowdhury, as the villagers became preoccupied with their new evening distractions.

A grandmother proudly showed me her recently purchased manure-gas fermenter bought for $400 with government subsidies. She put seventy-five pounds of manure from her two cows into a cement pit. The next day, she turned on her two-stack oven to cook with natural gas emitted from her fermenter. Her gas was free. And she was happy to not inhale fumes usually produced from burning wood while cooking.

A local cook invited me into his home to share his story. He installed seventy-five watt solar panels, at $325 a piece with subsidies, into each of his ten-rooms of his newly built residence. His business plan was to run an eco-hostel and attract environmentally conscious tourists to the Sundarbans region.

Most however could not afford these relatively expensive investments. A rented rechargeable twelve volt battery powered a fan, light, and television every night for about $1 a week. A $35 portable self-powered solar lamp illuminated an entire house or all the merchandise in a store. In the town's garbage dump site, I found discarded diesel generators, kerosene lamps and tanks. Gone was fossil fuel, replaced by renewable technology. This was upward mobility and development-in-action on a grass-roots level.

Now, during a short visit in Berla, in central India, even my father had been inspired by my work to include technology into his project. He established a not-for-profit school operated by a Gurukul, a local NGO. Here, typically off-the-grid, the educational and cultural institution relies on solar power for most every aspect of energy they use for water heaters, electro-voltaic panels, cookers, and lamps. Villagers may not be able to read in their own native language but they were aware of energy and living sustainably.

On the rural islands, as with most off-the-grid places around the world, there is a direct connection to the land's resources; food is just one of the many uses to those living off the land. Wood from wild trees are a source for cooking fuel. Manure mixed with hay and other natural elements, when dried, make discs for fuel. Hay is also used as a source for energy and heat when burned.

Forest products are used for a variety of economic, hygienic, and medical uses. Some examples: Certain types of bark and twig clean the teeth. Bamboo are useful in gardens and construction. Nuts are a food source used to tan leather or used for medicine. Limestone and other materials are valuable for building materials. Medicinal herbs and plants, reptiles, amphibians, and some birds are traded, driven by outside demand.[12]

The traditional forms of fuel acquisition within the Indian household are based on cheap and easy access to energy. Usually it is a task for the housewife or female who collects the dung and prepares it to be burned as dried discs. Let there be no mistake that there is no environmental advantage to burning manure discs—it was developed to economize for a lack of wild tree wood. Burning discs has only one benefit in that it conserves existing crops of thick, aged trees, and sprawls of mangrove forestry.

Where energy innovation is lacking, conservation practices excel, like in Bihar. When technological advances are available in places like Brooklyn, conservation practices decline. We need the best from both worlds. Even then, we still have an uphill battle, where conservation and climate change may be the easiest challenges that will pale in comparison to other struggles we must face.

VI. Paths of Sustainability

Prof. Johan Rockström (Stockholm University) tells us that we may be able to let the environment guide us toward a better path of sustainability.[13] Scientists grappling with this issue identify ten parameters that determine life on the planet: the level of nitrogen, the degree of biodiversity, the quantity of chemical pollution, the amount of aerosol pollution, the amount of fresh water, the quantity of natural forestry, climate change, and some other elements. He theorizes that our existence on the planet depends on all elements, meaning that a circle divided in sections for each element makes up the pie. The outer limit of the pie is the boundary as defined by the finite limit for each element. Exceeding the boundary means over-consuming or over-producing in that one category. However, there is an unavoidable connection between the components on which the planet hinges to maintain balance. Any three parameters taken to its extreme may push the balance of the earth toward a lower state of resilience and toward a downward precipice of instability. He argues that we must focus on all the fronts in which we created imbalances. Climate change through sustainable efforts is just one of our goals.

Oxfam argues that meeting basic necessities of life ought to be mixed into Rockström's circle of the Earth's target boundaries. Meaning, that the circle ought to be seen as a double donut, where its inner circle is formed by the lack of daily necessities for nearly four billion people around the world. Access to clean water, education, shelter, the basic food groups, and a few other elements are what prevents the development of a significant population—which imposes on Rockström's elements. For example, if the degree of poverty and the number of those in poverty were reduced, there would be less slash-and-burn of forests, and thus less imposition on climate change, wood resources, levels of nitrogen, and fresh water use.

Prof. Noam Chomsky (Massachusetts Institute of Technology) asserts that, in this decade, we face the hardest part of our challenge, and that is to grapple with a swift change or swerve of the collective will towards effective action on a global scale. Meaning, one country cannot change the course of humanity. It will take the collective will of over two hundred countries acting in unison to agree on plans of action. If the eradication of poverty is any example of the United Nations' success, the only governing body that may be equipped to take on this task, then can we let the U.N. guide us much further as they have in reducing the problems of the poor?

Communities are already providing us answers. Helmfeld, just fifteen miles north of Berlin, is Germany's first self-sustaining town. Returning to Brooklyn is a return to a land of unregulated capitalism, where growth of corporate value is held higher than quality of life for those working within these entities. But I am also returning to a place where hope springs with opportunity to change. I return to complete filming for *Carbon-2-Green*, where I am documenting a Brooklyn chiropractor who reduced his carbon footprint nearly to zero. He solarized his house, removed carbon-producing appliances, and powers his electric car from the sun. Herein lies this individual's pursuit for happiness. An entrepreneurial renewable energy company found the right plan, and cutting-edge and affordable merchandise for his idea. The government subsidized nearly half the cost of his solar switch. The bank approved his home equity loan to cover all other costs. In just under a decade, his electric bill reduced from $200 a month to zero, and he paid off his loan from the savings. He pursued his idea and achieved a zero footprint. It is also a land where waste and biomass are turned into electricity, and where families are beginning to value conservation and take solar as both a good investment and the right value-based choice.

Bihar gave me a taste of what the world will be like if we continue with coal. Brooklyn holds a mixed bag of possibilities. On the one extreme, excess is what the world wishes to copy. But its grassroots start-ups, from eco-gardening to socially conscious activism, that exemplify the heart of the American spirit to thrive and capitalize community life. Berlin showed me the direction the world ought to be heading. Berla offered a chance to apply in rural India what has worked elsewhere.

What is the color of a harmonious, sustaining life? Is it a particular shade of "green?" I argue that we ought to discard the use of the color "green" in decarbonizing our society. Reducing our carbon dependency is a matter of survival and a way to conduct every aspect of our lives. It's more than a matter of semantics. When one tries to be "green," one tries to incorporate new practices through a trial-and-error process, constantly trying to learn from the prior experience. This learning may take a lifetime, a time frame humans can no longer enjoy to fix what is wrong in the world. Full integration of "green" or zero-emission life cannot be a matter of choice, where one voluntarily signs up to try it out. As long as it remains as an externality, it will never be digested and incorporated. In theory, "green" or emission-free living ought to be a necessity, as an internal driving force, to diminish the footprint to its minimal size possible.

The future is about changing how we see the world by altering how we value all objects and material goods we make and use. If all the objects we extracted from the Earth included the value of energy it took to deliver them to the consumer—the maintenance of the ecology and reconstruction for the auxiliary damage to the environment, and health of workers—then we may reach the right cost to society that the consumer must pay.

An increased value of goods may also create an incentive to seriously adopt the "cradle-to-cradle" concept. For every product we use, manufacture, design, process and deliver, recirculation into the cycle will change. It will include the use of recycled energy and products from beginning to end. In some sense, it is energy extracted and reinserted into the next usable object, like reincarnation of material goods.

Some of us are paying attention to our "karmic energy." People must resolve how to live harmoniously within a finite planet. We only have two choices, and it is no longer about whether to live or die, but to sustainably live or die trying. As caretakers of the living planet, Gaia, we human beings are accountable for all life, not just our own.

Notes

1   M. Alam, J. Sathaye, and D. Barnes, "Urban Household Energy Use in India: Efficiency and Policy Implications," *The Berkeley-India Joint Leadership on Energy and the Environment E-Library*: LBNL-43942 (1998): 4, http://www.sciencedirect.com/science/article/pii/S0301421598000081; R. Bacon, S. Battacharya, and M. Kojima, "Expenditure of Low-Income Households on Energy," *Extractive Industries Development Series* #16 (The World Bank, June 2010): 79, http://siteresources.worldbank.org/EXTOGMC/Resources/336929-1266963339030/eifd16_expenditure.pdf

2   "U.S. and World Population Clock," *United States Census Bureau*, http://www.census.gov/popclock/

3   American Consumption, http://www.mindfully.org/Sustainability/Americans-Consume-24percent.htm, and http://www.worldwatch.org/node/810

4   "The State of Consumption Today," *Worldwatch Institute*, http://www.worldwatch.org/node/810

5   By embedding actual cost to the environment into the manufacture and operation of all appliances, goods and human activities, we may begin to account for the true value of the ecological loss and maintenance, loss and capture of biodiversity, and environmental degradation and repair.

Economists have externalized costs of fossil fuels, in that the price of iron ore used to make ships to deliver the fuel are not included in the price to deliver the oil. The cost of extraction and operation, maintenance of the coal mine, and health and safety equipment is far removed from the cost of gas to the consumer.

Could we really afford fossil fuels if their total true cost was included in the final price? What was the cost of displacing the earthen rock bed to extract metals from the ground? What was the cost to fix the environmental and ecological damage over a span of time to compensate for the loss of such metals? Including these and other real costs will enable consumers to take financial responsibility for consumption choices.

6 "The Sundarbans," *UNESCO World Heritage Centre*, http://whc.unesco.org/en/list/798

7 Sundarbans National Park, http://www.sundarbansnationalpark.com/

8 Report: "Mixed Picture on Human Development West Bengal Releases Three District Human Development Reports," *United Nations Development Programme* (July 12, 2010), http://www.in.undp.org/content/dam/india/docs/pr_human_development_west_bengal_releases_three_district_hdr.pdf

9 Subir Bhaumik, "Fears Rise in Sinking Sundarbans," *BBC News* (September 15, 2003), http://news.bbc.co.uk/2/hi/south_asia/3102948.stm

10 "Town Panchayat (T.P)," *Wikipedia*, http://en.wikipedia.org/wiki/Town_Panchayat_(T.P.)

11 West Bengal Renewable Energy Development Agency, http://www.wbreda.org/

12 R. K. Puri and O. C. Maxwell, "Forest Use and Natural Resource Management in Two Villages Adjacent to Pu Luong Nature Reserve and Cuc Phuong National Park, Vietnam," *Academia* (March 15, 2002): 44, http://www.academia.edu/1924316

13 Johan Rockström, "Let the environment guide our development," *TED Talks*, https://www.youtube.com/watch?v=Rgq-trlixYR4

Author

Vinit Parmar is Associate Professor of Film at Brooklyn College/CUNY. His expertise is in professional audio mixing and location sound recording for film, television, and commercials. He is also a former civil rights, immigration, entertainment, and copyright lawyer, as well as an award-winning documentary filmmaker having made several Asian works that focus on the impact of technology and development on the environment. His films include *Living River*, *Quest for Energy*, and *Tanneries in Tangra*. He is currently filming in Berlin for two documentaries on refugee/migrant stories.

Photo by Shahidul Alam/Drik/Majority World

The Price of Gratitude

You sheltered our millions while many stood by
We remain grateful
You trained freedom fighters, never asking why
We remain grateful
You stood by us, campaigned by our side
We remain grateful
Nigh fifty years on from carnage and genocide
We remain grateful

But then

You built a dam, starving farmers of water
You built a fence, imprisoning a nation
You killed Falani, acquitting the killers
We remain grateful?

Trade agreements unfair
Loan agreements unjust
Transit terms unequal
We remain grateful?

More dams to be built
More rivers to be linked
More civilians to be killed
We remain grateful?

And now

You will sell your coal, pollute our air
You will suffocate our fish, warm rivers without care
You will destroy our forest, preserving your own
Investment we'll share, liabilities mine alone

Your banks will profit, your machinery will sell
Your own laws you'll break, it's Bangladesh what the hell
Grateful we've been, for a war together won
But this land is ours, for generations to own

—Shahidul Alam
25th November 2016

Save Sundarbans: Global Protest 2017

SHAHIDUL ALAM

Note: "Save Sundarbans," is a global protest in which activists, artists, and photojournalists, including Shahidul Alam, played a part.

It is where the Bengal Tiger, now close to extinction, still stalks. It is where deer roam and hummingbirds fly. It is the richest terrestrial and aquatic ecosystem anywhere. Sundarbans ('beautiful forest' in Bangla), the world's largest single tract mangrove forest is a UNESCO-declared World Heritage Site that has sheltered 50 million coastal people from ravaging storms. The beautiful forest is in danger. The joint project of PDB (Bangladesh) and NTPC (India) for 1320 MW Rampal coal-fired power plant spells disaster for Bangladesh. Thousands have taken to the streets in protest, braving arrest and torture, but the government, who has already killed protesters of other energy projects are determined to bludgeon through. We need you and we need you now.

On the 7th January 2017, we have called for a global protest. You have a role to play. Join the movement.

Stage demonstrations/human chains and send written appeals to the embassies of Bangladesh and India.

Organise bicycle rallies, boat rallies, use theatre, songs, cartoons, masks or just hold up placards. Send us your protest/solidarity video messages and photographs.

Appeal to United Nations.

Campaign to International Press/Media.

Find other creative ways to resist.

My Journey as a Witness
Shahidul Alam

Author

Shahidul Alam is a photographer, writer, curator and activist. Alam obtained a Ph.D. in chemistry at London University before switching to photography. He returned to his hometown Dhaka in 1984, where he photographed the democratic struggle to remove General Ershad. Alam set up the award winning Drik agency, the Bangladesh Photographic Institute and Pathshala, the South Asian Media Institute—considered one of the finest schools of photography in the world. The director of the Chobi Mela festival and chairman of Majority World agency, Alam has been exhibited in galleries such as MOMA in New York, the Centre Georges Pompidou in Paris, the Royal Albert Hall and Tate Modern in London, and The Museum of Contemporary Arts in Tehran. He has also been a speaker at U.S. universities Harvard, Stanford and UCLA; Oxford and Cambridge universities in the U.K.; and the Powerhouse Museum in Brisbane. His book *My Journey as a Witness* was listed in the "Best Photo Books of 2011." In 2015, he was awarded the Shilpakala Padak by the President of Bangladesh for his contribution to the arts.

URL: www.shahidulalam.com

Yuri Kochiyama at 125th Street subway station in New York City
Photo courtesy of the Kochiyama Family

Taking a Stand with Yuri Kochiyama

MARY UYEMATSU KAO

Yuri Kochiyama: Rites of Passage

One of the unspoken rites of passage for a third generation Japanese American (Sansei) from the 1970s Los Angeles Asian American Movement was to visit the Kochiyama Family in New York City. For many Sansei getting their feet wet in the Movement, the Kochiyama's embraced us as family and introduced us to a whirlwind of all kinds of people. The Kochiyama's apartment might well have been described as "Movement Central."

Since the early 1960s, every Saturday night was an open house at the Kochiyama's where neighbors, foreign students, aspiring entertainers, professional athletes, civil rights workers, friends, out-of-towners, and parent activists would congregate, sometimes with as many as 100 people. The Kochiyama open house tradition was a breeding ground for "decolonizing your mind." Visitors were thrust into a diverse mix of persons who were involved in struggles from local to international, and injustices from past to present.

Yuri Kochiyama at anti-war rally in the early 1970s
(per credit from Diane Fujino's book cover)
Photo courtesy of Phil Tajitsu Nash

One of my first impressions of Yuri was from a 1974 anti-war march in midtown Manhattan. We (maybe 2,000 people) were confined to marching three abreast on the city's sidewalks. When we were suddenly besieged by New York's "finest" on horses, they charged at us right on a street corner so as to split the march in two. Being from Los Angeles and having never seen cops on horses before, no less being reared at up against the wall, it was pretty intimidating. But amongst the mass confusion of the disassembled march, we found Yuri. And like a seasoned combatant, she said these kinds of police attacks could be countered by throwing down marbles on the street to make the horses lose their balance. That was my first lesson in street fighting with the cops.

I will always remember Yuri for her dedication and allegiance to Malcolm X—continuing not just his memory, but more importantly supporting his work. Malcolm kept alive Paul Robeson's strategy to put the U.S. government on trial for its human rights violations against its African American citizens. Malcolm kept alive Robert F. Williams' example of defending Black people "by any means necessary," which helped spur the Black Liberation Movement into being.

There was hope in the air. Yuri learned from all the great fighters of the African American revolutionary tradition, from Frederick Douglass to Mumia Abu-Jamal—that U.S. imperialism was not going down through the ballot box. Revolutionary change in the U.S. is not a dinner party by people of color in the White House. Yuri lived a very full life teaching young people these hard-earned history lessons.

Yuri's final rite of passage is shared with precious company—Mabel Williams (widow of Robert F. Williams) and now Ruby Dee (widow of Ossie Davis). These have been the living greats of our generation.

Sister Yuri makes us proud to be who we are, and to stand up for that. Her actions spoke louder than her words.

Afterword

L to R: Kathleen, Katie & Melinda (March 2017)
Photo by Chuck Diep

It will be going on three years now since Yuri Kochiyama moved on to the next life. I recently received an e-mail from Chuck Diep, a fellow UCLA alum, who I met when he was a graduate student in education studies. Diep is now a middle school teacher at Temple Intermediate in Rosemead, and three of his 8th grade history students had entered the Los Angeles County 2017 National History Day competition.

This year's theme was "Taking a Stand in History." Diep's students—Kathleen, Katie, and Melinda, all second generation Chinese Vietnamese—after looking through the book *Rad American Women A-Z*, were intrigued by Yuri, "an Asian American woman who fought for Black rights." The following is an excerpt from the center panel of their history project:

"Yuri Kochiyama was a Japanese American woman who dedicated her life to fighting for a just society. Yuri took a stand through concrete political actions and by challenging people to be conscious of injustices. Interned during WWII, she experienced injustice firsthand and in the 1960s, she took great risk by becoming friends with the controversial Malcolm X. Inspired by Malcolm's teachings, she worked tirelessly for oppressed people—opening her home to organizing meetings, leading protests, and even occupying the Statue of Liberty in support of Puerto Rican political prisoners. She attended and spoke at rallies until she was in her 90s—her unrelenting fight making her a folk hero. In her prime she bridged communities by working across color boundaries—making her a symbol of unity. The memory of her efforts inspires young people, especially Asian Americans, to become more socially and politically engaged in the continuous struggle for social justice.

Yuri did the community building necessary to sustain movements. Her work planted seeds that inspired future generations to be involved too. Her quote, 'Consciousness is power' encourages us to always be aware, to know our history so we won't be too divided. 2017 marks the 75th anniversary of Japanese internment. Today, Trump wants to ban Muslim immigration and register Muslims living in the U.S. Trump supporters have used internment as a precedent to justify his proposal. Yuri's actions are more important now than ever. She encourages us to challenge injustices like this, and others, while working together despite race."

Katie, Kathleen, and Melinda's submission to the National History Day competition is a reassuring reminder that Yuri planted "something of value" for Asian Americans and Pacific Islanders to follow and continue the fight for human rights of all oppressed people.

Author
Mary Uyematsu Kao is the long-time publications coordinator of the UCLA Asian American Studies Center Press. Through her documentary photography and writing, she continues her involvement with the Asian American Movement and with Asian American communities.

Andrew Ahn's *Spa Night* and A Certain Korean American Space

DAVID K. SONG

SCRAWLED ON THE SIDEWALK between two barren planters not too far from my apartment: "K-Town is the New Mecca." A prepositional phrase is missing, I think, but the declaration of sentiment is pretty clear. It's a signpost, the destination straight ahead—"Visit Koreatown!" I've been in the neighborhood long enough to know that over the years, papers have trumpeted the discovery, or the transformation, or the trendiness of this enclave. An urban bohemia. Still a bit grimy and beaten down like any good fixer-upper, but oh so much potential, centrally located in the heart of the metropolis that is Los Angeles. The nightlife teems, especially in the afterhours. Hidden bars, cafes, and eateries serve up drinks and dishes for culinary pornographers. "Visit K-Town!" Drive down Olympic and admire the red wooden lamp posts—inspired by Korean architectural tradition and sponsored by the Community Redevelopment Agency—lighting the concourse for the weary pilgrims of the world.

A food critic once waxed nostalgically of *his* Koreatown, an enclave of fire escapes festooned with Napa cabbage leaves where the "rhythmic pounding of garlic in wooden mortars" roused this groggy gastronome to break his fast each dawn. Not improbable, I suppose, in one of the densest neighborhoods in the city, that such a quaint configuration of tenants and morning routines existed at some point. Somewhere in a senior housing complex, a few *halmeonis* dutifully arising in pre-dawn light to assail garlic cloves as their foremothers had, and their foremothers before them. A time-honored rite handed down from the antiquity of the Goryeo Dynasty in an undisturbed genealogy of culinary preparation. It's a conveniently vacuum-packed portrait of a neighborhood, begging for descriptions of pansori street buskers performing over the clamor of fire engines and the 720 bus line, for those unfamiliar with the neighborhood and wholly dependent on one writer's depiction. While Korean residents are one of the largest groups representing a single national origin (the Greater L.A. area itself represents the largest concentration of ethnic Koreans outside of the peninsula), the overwhelming majority of Koreatown residents are drawn from a global pool of immigrants, other Asian nations, and hemispherical neighbors such as Mexico, El Salvador, and Guatemala. Other enclaves have even been carved out of this one, such as the official designation of a slice of 3rd Street as Little Bangladesh.

Film still from *Spa Night*

In the twenty-five years since *Sa-i-gu* (the Los Angeles Rebellion, April 29, 1992), the neighborhood has metamorphosed: burned-out lots have been rebuilt with an eye towards securitized architecture; and as urban centers become attractive, old hotels and eateries have been dusted off and new veneers applied in the decades following the Rodney King verdict. And yet, the fascination for a specific K-Town tourist/consumer experience has persisted. Major publications, even *The New York Times* and *The Wall Street Journal*, have had at least one titillating first-person exposé on the bizarre practices of K-Town's nightlife culture—from "booking" (forced socialization between men and women at night clubs), to room salons, to *doumis*.

As a second generation Korean American who has lived in the neighborhood for most of my adult life, I can appreciate the spectacle of temptation, the temptation of the spectacle, and each opportunity to mark off my bingo card of dutiful K-Town tropes. (One square is set aside for the techno-orientalist *Blade Runner* reference when referring to that one electronic billboard on Wilshire and Serrano, which really, should now embrace its meta destiny and go full-homage and project a pill-popping woman in a hanbok.) So, here is *your* K-Town, all swaying palm trees and mini-mall signboards marked with indecipherable sticks and circles of pulsing neon. Yet, when re-treading such familiar representational territory though, how do those choices reflect not only upon the space, but also the inhabitants who labor under those burdens?

Enter here Andrew Ahn's first feature-length film *Spa Night*, a meditative work that debuted at the 2016 Sundance Film Festival. The film's narrative follows the life of David, a teenage Korean American son of working class immigrants and who is still in the closet. While David's sexuality is one of the film's central concerns, *Spa Night* also explores another essential aspect of David's character: his and his family's identities as Korean/Korean Americans living and working in Koreatown. The film presents the neighborhood as an actual community, rather than just a tourist or commercial site for simple consumer voyeuristic pleasure.

Space figures largely in Ahn's works, establishing context for the narrative arcs of his characters. Consider that Ahn originally wanted to shoot his first short film *Andy* at Koreatown Plaza, but the unexpected costs of securing shooting rights meant that Antelope Valley Mall would serve as a stand-in instead—but the choice of such a venerable Western Avenue institution, such as K-Town Plaza and its vendor kiosks, would've been appropriate.

Andrew Ahn (Left) on set of *Spa Night*

Individual locales within Koreatown resonate with even more significance in *Spa Night*. The twenty-four hour spa is already a common fixture alongside the cafes, restaurants, grocery stores, dry cleaners, and churches throughout the neighborhood. In *Spa Night*, however, the spa functions as a critical site through which the narrative unfolds. From the outset, David clearly perceives the spa as a family space, based on the practice and all its attendant meanings that have been transplanted from Korea.

The film opens with a spa scene: David and his father take turns scrubbing each other's backs. They meet up afterwards with David's mother in the spa's co-ed resting area. And while the family shares a giant bowl of shaved ice, David's mother contemplates a future in which, a "pretty Korean girl," can also partake in this ritual together with them. While the spa is initially presented as a family space for David, it also offers a suggestive avenue to explore his sexuality. But, does it offer a safe outlet for such desires?

Film stills from *Spa Night*

In the film, David spends the weekend shadowing a former church friend at their college campus. David goes to a house party and then a drunken foray at the *noraebang*, another time honored K-Town practice, complete with compulsory singing and mangled rapping. Dancing and flirting with members of the opposite sex (awkwardly, in David's case), David and his newfound friends participate in activities that are ostensibly and performatively heterosexual, including a drinking game of "gay chicken" with soju shots for the loser. The night concludes with a trip to the spa where the genders must split up. While relaxing in the sauna, David's gaze lingers on his friend's body—not the first of the night, but particularly damning while they are all sitting in the buff—and is met with hostility. "What are you looking at?"

Film still from *Spa Night*

The ritual of the spa is both familiar and familial for those who partake in it regularly. As a microcosm of Koreatown, the spa is also a space shared with intrigued outsiders who can inscribe their own meanings and rites within its parameters. That isn't a conceit unique to *Spa Night*—scandalous narratives of K-Town nightclub indulgence have coexisted comfortably with stories of some spas developing reputations as hot spots for gay cruising, especially when rumors involve certain closeted Hollywood personalities. And so, both ordinary folks and incognito celebrities have patronized such establishments with the goal of finding company, alongside *ajeossis* who are there simply because that's just what they have always been doing. It's their thing.

The film's spa similarly reflects a diverse clientele: Black, Latino, Asian, White, each with their own agendas, sometimes conflicting, which David observes when he takes on a part-time job there to support his family after they lose their restaurant. In one scene, two Latino men seeking privacy are interrupted when an oblivious Korean man wanders into their sauna room. In another, a police officer attempts to mediate a dispute between two spa patrons, one speaking in Spanish and the other in Korean—the latter demanding a refund from the spa owner, accusing the other of doing "bad things." Though these patrons are simply passing through, they are not cognizant of how the spa is a much more complicated space for someone like David, which suggests that perhaps such identities can't be so neatly divided.

While the spa serves as a conduit for David to explore his family and sexual identity, other Koreatown scenes set in restaurants, church, and side streets further round out his Korean American identity. A defining experience of a diaspora can center on the difficulties of migration, or displacement, along with the challenges of acculturation wrought by relocation: working to stay afloat, conforming to new cultural expectations, forcing the tongue to an unfamiliar language, and raising resentful offspring. And so, if the difficulty of these tribulations is *supposed* to be justified by the material success of the second-generation (as a newly-minted white-collar professional or the progenitor of a heteronormative nuclear family—ideally both) to prove that the alienating shit-show of immigration was totally worthwhile—what does it mean for David's parents then, immigrants whose only child does not seem college-bound nor interested in bringing home a *saeksi* willing to scrub *ddae* off her mother-in-law's back?

Film stills from *Spa Night*

Understandably, David's parents want to funnel their resources towards the best possible future for their child: "You're better than that," says David's father in frustration, after their disastrous temporary gig as movers. "We didn't move here so that you could move furniture." From his father's perspective, David needs to go to college. And so his parents send him to a cram school, another common fixture of Asian American enclaves, mini-mall reminders of how immigrants have pooled ethnic capital to build a thriving industry around standardized test prep, tutoring, and college counseling to polish students for the Ivy League—for a price—and to ensure that their displacement from the motherland had not been in vain.

Having spent a decade in the cram school industry as a part-time instructor for the [**INSERT STAN-DARDIZED EXAM HERE**], I can attest to the varied demographics of the students who've wandered into my classroom. Not everyone came from an affluent family with disposable income to burn for some bootleg exams photocopied from *Barron's SAT* (at worst). For those living around Koreatown, especially, I've known students whose parents worked extra hours as cab drivers or restaurant servers, just to cover the monthly tuition bill, in the hopes that test prep was their children's avenue towards success.

David's parents are also in a similarly fraught situation. The film, which features the perspective of a native-born Asian American, could've easily resorted to stereotypes of domineering tiger parents, or even overprivilege a narrative of second-generation self-actualization. Instead of shrill SAT-obsessed caricatures, David's parents are portrayed sympathetically as they deal with the disintegration of the American Dream and its threat to undermine their family. The then-childless twenty-something year old immigrants who landed in Los Angeles, could not have anticipated that after years of toil, that they would lose their business and need to work for others.

"We were so excited to be here," David's mother reflects, as she and David stand in front of an empty apartment building closed off by a chain-link fence. The newly-arrived couple's first residence in America was supposed to have been "the perfect place," in the words of David's father, but was now abandoned and waiting to rise from stucco ashes as yet another overpriced, obscene Faux-talian luxury condo. Their former home, another K-Town casualty of gentrification.

Showcasing familiar locations and practices, *Spa Night* avoids taking the guidebook route in its depictions. The film avoids gratuitous voyeurism, and viewing requires more engagement than expecting *Lonely Planet*-style predigested pieces of information. Over two-thirds of *Spa Night* is in Korean, a noteworthy attribute considering that the film was featured in the U.S. Dramatic Competition category at Sundance, and that the actors themselves spoke Korean fluently. The natural quality of speech for the actors, whether in Korean or English, helped to sustain the credibility of the film. Ahn's casting decisions have precedent in his past work though, notably in his 2011 student thesis short *Dol (First Birthday)*.

Film still from *Dol (First Birthday)*

Running 11-minutes in length, *Dol* uses the traditional Korean celebration around a child's first birthday (a tradition that makes a thematically resonant appearance in *Spa Night* as well) to allow its character Nick—also closeted to most of his family—to reflect upon his sexual identity. When it comes to the birthday celebration, especially, *Dol* has the candor of a home video. There is no intrusive exposition on the nature of the *doljanchi*, either in voice-over or dialogue. The event stands on its own, and the partici-pants seem completely natural in their roles. (Of course, it turned out that Ahn had actually cast his own family members for this project, but it wouldn't be until after *Dol*'s completion that they would learn that this was also his way of coming out to his parents.)

While the family seemed at ease throughout *Dol*, Nick is visibly vexed, and the short closes with a deeply affecting scene that only underscores his emotional turmoil and uncertainty. *Spa Night*, on the other hand, takes a different route in which clear decisions are made: as David explores his sexuality at the spa, a close encounter with a White patron in the sauna is ultimately circumscribed by David's admon-ishment of "no touching." Near the end of *Spa Night*, David finds himself again in a similar position with another man—this time, someone who is also Asian. "Are you Korean?" David asks. "Me too," he responds. Even after such deliberation, his first fully-realized experience is not without its challenges: he confronts complicated and unresolved feelings, scrubbing himself raw until he draws blood.

By the end though, some of David's hesitancy seems to have fallen away. He seems defiant even after getting caught by his boss, throwing his key down on the table as he quits his job. He remains standing during church service after the rest of the congrega-tion has taken their seats. And when he goes running one last time before the film fades to black, it is no longer the slow jog and static vista of Koreatown in

Film still from *Spa Night*

the background that we have been seeing previously. Instead, David now runs harder than ever before, the camera tracking his movement down the sidewalk, as if trying to outrun his problems—home, the SAT, and sexual identity.

Spa Night doesn't necessarily offer any tidy conclusion for David as he commits to this other layer of himself, and that's the point. David's experiences and values are interwoven together and that complexity of identity—informed by an intersection of race, ethnicity, sexuality, gender, class, and so on—can often be overlooked in a popular discourse that seeks to project only one specific aspect at the expense of the others. Similarly, Koreatown, like any other neighborhood, vibrant and alive, continually rewrites itself, even as others continue to insert their own inscriptions.

Although the narrative is fictional, *Spa Night*'s representation of space is a comparatively more thoughtful slice of life in Koreatown than some reductive perspectives that have come before. But that's the way it is, I guess. Limitations of the medium. Lived experiences at odds with the expectations of the outsiders.

AAARI Lecture Video (March 17, 2017): www.aaari.info/17-03-17Ahn.htm

Author
David K. Song is a second generation Korean American and longtime resident of Los Angeles Koreatown. He graduated from UCLA's Asian American Studies M.A. program and is currently an associate professor of Asian American Studies at East Los Angeles College. He also serves as board member of the Korean Resource Center, a Los Angeles-based non-profit community organization empowering low-income, immigrant, Asian American and Pacific Islander, and other communities of color throughout Southern California.

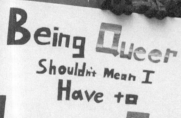

COMMUNITY RESEARCH AND
ONLINE METHODOLOGIES

"Asian American Studies matters as research methodology, as critical historiography, and especially as a generative framework for articulating new terrains of activism and coalition work (made necessary by the 'War on Terror')."

—J. Mayor

COMMUNITY-BASED RESEARCH is paired together here with guides to useful, and mostly free, digital and online learning tools which can democratize our access to knowledge and information.

In "Tales from the Field," New York-based faculty Tarry Hum, Margaret M. Chin, Zai Liang, John J. Chin, and the late Peter Kwong, share their community-based research field notes that cover quantitative and qualitative methodologies. John J. Chin in "Jitneys in Manila," links his own marginalization as a gay Korean American male growing up in the Midwest, with his specific research interests in health advocacy.

Tarry Hum and Samuel Stein present new data and examine how migration and capital from China is changing Chinese enclaves in Manhattan, Brooklyn, and Queens. Kevin L. Nadal updates his guide to micro-aggressions in light of today's social media wars.

In separate guides, Antony Wong, and Raymond Pun with Molly Higgins, provide digital archives and tools for education and open-source learning.

Tales from the Field
Research Methods and Approaches to Studying Community

JOHN J. CHIN, MARGARET M. CHIN,
TARRY HUM, PETER KWONG & ZAI LIANG

L to R: Tarry Hum (Queens College/CUNY), Peter Kwong (Hunter College/CUNY),
Margaret M. Chin (Hunter College/CUNY), Zai Liang (SUNY Albany) & John J. Chin (Hunter College/CUNY)
Photo by Antony Wong

MAPPING OF ASIAN AMERICANS IN NEW YORK (MAANY), is a CUNY-based interdisciplinary research collective, which aims to compile current knowledge, initiate collaborative projects and disseminate information about Asian American communities in New York City. Its current focus is on presenting lectures and holding seminars to start building a dynamic intellectual platform that brings together academics, artists, community activists, and advocates.

Tarry Hum (Urban Studies, Queens College/CUNY)
"What are the challenges and joys of community-based research?"

Beginning in Fall 2014, when Peter Kwong first convened the "Mapping of Asian Americans in New York," comprised of a group of Asian Americanists from across various CUNY campuses, one of our goals has been to provide a space for us to share our research and have an opportunity to get feedback from one another. This is the final event of the semester and we are finally getting an opportunity to do that through this dialogue: Tales from the Field (December 15, 2014).

My name is Tarry Hum, a faculty member at Queens College and the moderator for this afternoon's talk at Baruch College. This afternoon we have four presenters, three from CUNY and one from SUNY Albany. For this conversation, we posed a number of questions:

1. Describe your research interests and/or current projects.

2. What motivates your research and scholarship?

3. What research methods do you use? Strengths and weaknesses?

4. What are the challenges and joys of community-based research?

5. What are some surprising/unexpected experiences and/or findings?

6. How would you advise junior academic/activists?

Let's begin with John Chin, who's an associate professor and currently on leave as director of the graduate urban planning program in the Urban Policy & Planning department at Hunter College.

Transcribed by Antony Wong & Zhu-Hui Wu

John J. Chin (Urban Policy & Planning, Hunter College/CUNY)
"I joke about my work moving from the sacred to the profane."

Thinking about the questions that have been posed for this seminar, maybe it would help for me to also talk a little bit about my career trajectory, because that sort of explains how I got where I am in the field. I have a doctorate in urban planning. That's my discipline, which is already an interdisciplinary field. But I got my doctorate at Columbia University, and a lot of my mentors were sociologists. I was really open to lots of things when I went to graduate school. I was open to anything applied and policy-related, or urban planning-related. I remember being at a party with some professors and grad students, and one of my professors was like, "John, do you really want to be a professor?" And I was kind of taken aback, but I realize in hindsight what that was about. I didn't want to be a professor like they were, very academic, very high-level thinkers. I was much more of an applied kind of person. I wanted my work to take place more in the real world.

I didn't feel so out-of-place at Columbia. I think I did okay over there, but my professor's comment was sort of a clarifying moment for me, I think, for my career. I have a long history of working in non-profits. I helped co-found an organization called Asian and Pacific Islander Coalition on HIV/AIDS (APICHA) in 1989. Some time later, I was on staff there for eight years. I've been involved with the organization now for about twenty-five years. By the time I got my first academic job in 2007, I'd been mostly doing non-profit work, and then later grant-funded research at the New York Academy of Medicine, for fifteen to twenty years.

When I got my first academic job, I felt like I wasn't really working because I was just writing, doing some teaching, and doing research. I really felt like I wasn't really working. It was very uncomfortable for me, and over the years, I really have gotten used to that fact that this is my job. I'm a researcher, a writer and a teacher, and that's my job. About the difficulties of doing community-based research, one for me is that sometimes I want to be more involved in the service end of the community work that I'm doing. Right now, I'm really very much on the research end. A lot of the impact that I have is around developing new knowledge, hoping it will disseminate into the community work, and then shape that work. But sometimes I do have the desire to be more directly involved, so there is kind of a tension there.

Most of my work has been in HIV. In grad school I think I really wanted to move away from that and study ethnic economies, looking at Chinatown and that kind of thing. Peter Kwong was actually one of my professors, and he helped me do some projects in that area. But I really found it very hard to do my dissertation on that because I was working at APICHA almost full-time and just had a hard time trying to do two separate things. So my dissertation ended up being on New York City's HIV planning process, where the city allocated more than $100 million in funding for HIV care each year, looking at that policy process and how the community got involved in planning for those funds. That kind of set the path for me, and ever since then I was thinking that one day I would do my real work outside of HIV, outside of health, and more on what I started with. But twenty years later, you find that you're still doing what you have been doing, and then you realize maybe that this is actually what I like to be doing.

I'm working on several research projects now. I just finished a five-year study looking at Chinese immigrant religious organizations and their views on HIV. I have five years of data that I'm trying to publish on. My new study is looking at sexually-oriented massage parlors in New York City and Los Angeles, with my colleague Lois Takahashi at UCLA. I joke about moving from the sacred to the profane, but there is a common theme here, which is going to one of Tarry's questions on what motivates my research. I'm very curious about the underside of things. With religious institutions, I think of them in both positive and negative ways. They are very good for the community, but they are also the kind of institutions that dictate what behaviors and views are right and wrong, often to the detriment of certain subgroups. So I am very curious about what they are really thinking. They have these great beautiful, peaceful spaces, people rely on them for lots of support. But what is really going on in those institutions? And then with the massage parlors, they're popping up all over the place. There's three in my neighborhood, and I'm really wondering what's going on there, especially if illegal stuff is happening.

How are they really operating? What's going on there? That leads to one of my surprising findings with the massage parlors. Number one, that there are a lot of them in New York. We documented 475 sexually-oriented massage parlors in the five boroughs of New York City. I think that we probably didn't hit all of them, and those are the ones with the storefronts, the ones that you can see on the street and have a door. There is additional activity that's occurring in residential apartments, activity that we're not easily able to see or document. This was an HIV-funded study, and one of the surprising things is that there is not as much HIV risk as we might have thought because there are a lot of "hand jobs." So from a health perspective, that's not that risky. There is a fringe that's doing pretty risky stuff, so we want to look more into that.

Regarding condoms, when doing riskier stuff, they are not necessarily using them. So yes, that's a problem. There are stories of women who get offered a thousand dollars not to use a condom and that kind of offer is hard to turn down. We might assume that people do this out of economic necessity, and that kind of thing is true, but the women also developed interesting rationales for why they're doing what they're doing. One woman told us that she thinks she's doing a community service. She said that some of the men she works with are quite angry and aggressive, and just think how much worse they'd be if they didn't have her to go to and help relieve some of the stress. Whether that is a rationalization to make her feel better about what she is doing or whether she really believes in it, it's hard to say. But it's kind of an interesting idea.

Zai Liang (Sociology, University at Albany – SUNY)
"How do you do community research both in China and the U.S.?"
I want to thank my CUNY colleagues for providing me the opportunity to share my work. I was teaching at Queens College a long time ago from 1993 to 2002. In Fall 2002, I moved from Queens College to SUNY Albany, the capital of New York State. So this year I'm spending one year at the Russell Sage Foundation to do research. My training is primarily in quantitative sociology and also demography, although I am increasingly more appreciative of the qualitative ethnographic type of research.

I first moved to New York in 1993, my first year as an assistant professor at Queens College. I was doing research on international migration in my doctoral dissertation, and then I was doing a two year post-doc at Brown University, from 1992 to 1994. So in my second year of post-doc I got a job offer from Queens College, but I had something very much in my head that I wanted to do research on the international migrants here in New York. The natural starting point for me is to look for a topic that is connected to the community—Chinatown, for example. But then in 1993, in the spring, we all heard about the Golden Venture episode, the tragic event where a lot of people died. Essentially that brought a lot of international media attention to the issue of undocumented migrants from China's Fujian province. From my perspective, I thought I could study that topic. I had some friends, professors from China who are from Fujian. So why not go to Fujian and go take a look at what the community looks like, back in the early 1990s?

So that was my starting point. Regarding the approach you're going to take in your research project, that depends on what kind of research questions you want to address, but also depends on the financial resources—sometimes you have brilliant ideas, but you really can't do it until later. I think my initial goal was pretty modest. I told myself, "What can we learn from the data we collect in China by the Chinese government?" That [information] was free from my perspective. I was an assistant professor. I didn't have a lot of money. So I know the data pretty well. So we run all the tables. The thing is, there's limited information about international migration in the Chinese survey and census data. But the major thing is that we can get a pretty good idea; for example, one of the major provinces sending migrants to other countries like the U.S., for example. We can say, Beijing for example, Shanghai, and Guangdong traditionally, are major migrant-sending provinces. And then the other thing, looking at data from China, over time you can actually see pretty clearly that international migrants from Fujian went out very, very quickly. And the nice thing about using data from China was that you can actually compare with people who left, and people who remained in China. What are their characteristics? What are their occupations prior to leaving for the United States? Their marital status? You learn something about that process.

I think perhaps the most important thing I learned in that project was that there was a critical time, a major shifting from urban-based international migration to rural-based. In Fujian, the data clearly shows that pattern. And that transition is very important because we know that the rural part is much larger. If you see that trend going to the rural-sending migrant places, you're going to have a big pool of potential workers to come, right? In fact that's what clearly happened, some years later we observed that. And the other thing about rural-origin migrants is that rural-origin migrants tend to have a very dense network. They have much stronger ties than the urban-based migrants, and that matters in terms of trust, money, so on and so forth, studying business once they're in the U.S. So that was my initial take on the Fujian migration.

And then I wasn't entirely happy with what I did at that point. I thought that I could do a little more. I was getting a little more ambitious and said to myself, "I know about the province very well. I know the literature pretty well, but I wanted to be doing a bigger project, a larger sample, and in both China and the U.S." So I was investigating whether that was possible, and did some fieldwork. Then I wrote some proposals and luckily I got some funding to carry out that idea. So you can draw a China-based migrant-sending community sample. I had maybe around 2,800 households, and we carried out that survey in 2002 or 2003, and 2004. And meanwhile, we also carried out the survey in [Manhattan's] Chinatown.

So speaking about community, how do you do community kind of research in China and the U.S.? I think from China's perspective, at least at that time, it was a lot more difficult because the undocumented migrant story was not something the Chinese government was very proud of. To accomplish my research objectives, essentially, I had to work very closely with my Chinese collaborators. The thing is that if you want to go to a village and talk to some people in a village, that's probably okay—but doing a massive survey, you had to work through the system somehow. So eventually we were able to get it done with the help of my collaborators. I remember at an earlier conference some people said, "Oh, you can't do a survey of that magnitude in China on this topic. That's just too sensitive." But eventually we were able to do it.

Back in New York—the survey we did—we talked to about 410 immigrants from Fuzhou. Essentially, we were working closely with the Fukien American Association on East Broadway, so they were very helpful. We rented an office with money I had from the project to pay the rent. I had [bilingual] speaking students that carried out the interviews. The timing was fortunate from my perspective because it was right after 9/11; many were unemployed and they needed time to talk, and plus I provided a little bit of financial incentive for the interviews.

The third project that I'm working on right now, starting around 2010, looks at how the immigrants from Fujian province came to New York and moved to other places. The idea actually came from an earlier project. When I did the major survey in Chinatown in 2003 and 2004, while looking at their labor history, seeing what kind of jobs they got, my earlier perception was that they were going to tell me that they had jobs in Manhattan or Brooklyn. But to my surprise when you look at their history from the long questionnaire, the majority of job histories were not here in New York but in all other places. This was very interesting because all the books that we read about Chinatown, what all the researchers think about, study, pretty much have a conception about immigrants, is based in one location, right? New York City, Los Angeles, and San Francisco—not quite thinking beyond that. The Fuzhou story is interesting because we need to rethink about what is happening to that story when a large number of immigrants move and work outside of New York. So I thought maybe that was something that I could do, and so I wrote a proposal to the Russell Sage Foundation, an idea to track down some of these immigrant's work outside of New York.

And so from that beginning, we carried out a survey of employment agencies in Chinatown. We surveyed around thirteen employment agencies in Chinatown, and from that survey, we tabulated every single job posted in the employment agency: their current location, how much they're getting paid, and what kind of job is being posted, especially the location. So we were able to map the locations and salary, and meanwhile we were mapping the Chinatown bus [routes] because it forms a very coherent story. Basically the maps overlapped, especially locations with immigrant jobs, and then the Chinatown bus lines in the different parts of the country.

So that's where I am right now, trying to wrap up the story to see what we can learn. Maybe the final thing I want to say is that we also carried out a survey of entrepreneurs who went to other places in the U.S. We did a survey of six states, five to six entrepreneurs in each state, so we have done questionnaires and very in-depth interviews. Some surprising stories, one person in Texas was saying, "Money was very easy to make here. Come here."

Maybe I'll stop here and we can talk later.

Margaret M. Chin (Sociology, Hunter College/CUNY)
"My heart has always been with the working people of New York City."

I'll start off the way John Chin did too, and share a little bit about my background. When you hear the titles of my books and know more about my background, you'll know why I'm interested in these topics. My Ph.D. dissertation was on garment workers, comparing Chinese and Latino garment workers, and that book is called *Sewing Women* (2005). I also wrote about the garment workers and their transformation after 9/11 into home health aide workers and what happened to Chinatown after 9/11—that was in a chapter called *Moving On* (2005). I have a small study on ethnic media that I haven't finished yet, but I'm still working on. And now my newest work is called *Working the Real World*, which is on Asian American college graduates who are the second generation—the ones who were born here.

My own life and work are connected throughout. I was born in New York City and not in Chinatown, surprisingly, but on the Upper West Side of Manhattan. If any of you know Lincoln Center, and know the projects there, that's where I was born. My mother was a garment worker and my father was a restaurant worker. I grew up in those projects in a working class community, always attending public school. I went to Stuyvesant High School. At that time when I grew up in the projects, my neighbors were mostly African American and Latino. There were some Asian Americans, mostly Japanese Americans and Chinese Americans. We all went to the neighborhood public schools. Since the public schools were half African American, my class was also half African American, and many of us went to Stuyvesant together. It was a very different time at Stuyvesant High School. So I grew up differently. Also, at that time the projects were in a community that was gentrifying, so the schools were actually pretty good because we had middle class, upper class wealthy folks attending, as well as the kids from the projects, all going together to school. And so, we as a whole, were able to have a better education and access to places like Stuyvesant High School. Some of the kids I went to school with who came from the projects went off to Brooklyn Tech, Stuyvesant, Stanford, Swarthmore, and they're African American and Latino. We still keep in contact.

This is how I grew up and so my heart has always been with the working people of New York City, because I grew up with working people. When I went to college, I went up to Harvard and I started off as a math major, and I never finished as a math major. I started off as a math major, and because I went to Stuyvesant everybody thought I was good in math! You know, I was good at math, but when I got to Harvard I realized you need a lot more passion to be able to write those proofs, to prove those things in math. In Harvard, to graduate with a math degree you needed to write a thesis, and my heart was not into writing a thesis on math. By my junior year, I thought, "Can I just not get an honors degree or not do a thesis?" But they basically said, "If you want a math degree, you need to write a thesis. But what you can do is to graduate in something else." And so I ended up graduating with an applied math degree. And so I tell my students and everybody else too, that you can change your mind many, many times in your career. So I did not graduate with a math degree, I graduated with an applied math degree, and ended taking some classes in sociology, statistics, and in computer science.

I ended up doing just fine, and I ended up going into the work world—not in sociology, but in the work world. I ended up working for IBM for six years before getting my Ph.D. because I had an applied math degree, and a pretty good knowledge of computer science. That's where that "work in the real world" comes in my latest study, because I'm actually also interested in professionals and Asian Americans. Because when I went to IBM, I was one of very few Asian Americans. There were more that came in later, but I was one of very few among the minority group of African Americans and Latinos, whom, just like me, had the advantage of affirmative action in the workplace. We were sent to many different places to train, but we were also given mentors, given sponsors in these workplaces. I have found that today a lot of young folks in the work world don't have the kinds of mentors I had when I went to work in the professional world.

After a number of years, I also realized that IBM wasn't quite my passion either. Deep down inside I realized there wasn't a lot written, other than Peter Kwong's work, about the people in Chinatown at that time. So this was in the '80s and '90s, and I went to grad school in the '90s at Columbia University with John—we were there together. We knew each other through Chinatown, volunteering at the Chinese Progressive Association. When I was thinking of graduate school, I said, "Okay, I want to study the garment workers in the community because nobody had really been thinking about them, or even the restaurant workers." So I asked myself, "Well, how do I do this?" I didn't even know at that point that I wanted to do sociology. I went to different departments. I went to history and they said that I had to study a period, not contemporary Chinese. I went to anthropology and they said I couldn't study just New York with California, but had to study overseas. So this is what I'm telling you, that it's okay if you're an undergrad or whatever, that it's fine to do a little exploration.

So what advice would I give? You can do your exploration, you can change your majors and you do whatever, and then you end up doing what you want to do. So I ended up in sociology because I knocked on Herbert Gans' door. He said, "You want to study what? Why don't you do this program?" So I went to IBM and told them I wanted to apply to graduate school. "Is it possible for me to do this?" And they said, "You know what, take a two-year sabbatical and think about it." So that's the kind of support that I actually got, even in the corporate work world. I think it was a different time. So I went off and actually stayed and never went back to IBM.

I got my Ph.D. at Columbia and finished in 1998. Before that, I took a few years to write my dissertation on Chinese garment workers. I compared them with Latino garment workers in New York City, who were mostly Mexican, Ecuadorian, and Dominican at that time. And I looked at the Chinese garment industry in Chinatown. I looked at the differences, how they hired, and why the Chinese industry workers were paid less although they were unionized. At the same time, the Latino workers were paid hourly and actually got more, and plus, there were a few who were undocumented. And so I tried to figure out why. One of the reasons for the Chinese was that it was actually something they were all complicit at. It was a way of letting the Chinese women workers work and take care of the kids, balance their work hours, and get union benefits. But at the same time, the workers knew they were kind of exploited, but they wouldn't say it out in those many words, but they knew they were. But if they didn't do it this way, they wouldn't be able to take care of the kids, wouldn't be able to run in and out of the shops, and wouldn't be able to get the health benefits. So it was kind of like an agreement that they had with each other and the shop owners, whereas the Latino workers, they didn't have their families or have too many kids here at that time. So they worked their hourly wages, and they knew that they were being exploited too, but they were going to take advantage of it. If they weren't at least getting paid the minimum wage they would just leave their shop and go to another because at that time in the mid-1990s, the garment industry was still pretty strong here in New York City.

So I did that for my dissertation. And then when I left, I actually worked with Katherine S. Newman. I did a study on the working poor, looking at Blacks and Latinos transitioning out of welfare. So that was done basically with people who lived in the projects, kind of like the people who I grew up with, so it was easier to get in to work with them. If you can't tell by now I don't use any of my math background. I actually do qualitative fieldwork. I go in and I interview. I do fieldwork inside the garment shops, go visit people in their homes, and interview people at their jobs as well. So my stuff is all qualitative these days.

My latest study is on Asian American college graduates, those who are born here and those who came underneath the age of thirteen, and looking at how their family and college experiences have basically shaped their trajectory in the work world. So I'm kind of looking at the glass ceilings and where a majority of Asian Americans are at now. It's a brand new study, so you can ask me questions about what I'm finding a little bit later.

So I'll close off and let Peter speak.

Peter Kwong (Asian American Studies & Urban Policy & Planning, Hunter College/CUNY)
"When I was a kid I read too many martial arts novels—it's always about fighting against injustice."
I came to the States to attend college in the 1960s. Like most of my peers who were educated in Taiwan, we were all channeled into studying science. I followed my dad's wish to major in engineering. I came here at the height of the Civil Rights Movement and understood quickly that it was a struggle not just for Blacks, but for all colored minorities—me included. Not wanting to be treated just as another Asian nerd, nor willing to be marginalized and ignored, I switched to political science as soon as I got my B.S. in civil engineering.

Once I got into political science I was very excited, studying comparative politics: China, Japan, and the Soviet Union. I was really having a good time but then realized that all these abstract things had no relevance to the real world around me. My aim to study was a personal desire to see people respect and understand each other. But the books I'd come across were all written in a remote professional style, detached of the author's emotion and vision. I felt that my fellow students—China specialists, Russian specialists—were arrogant and racist, and did not have much stake in what they were studying.

I was lucky to be living at the right time to join the anti-war movement, and later, the student strike in 1968 at Columbia, which helped channel my studies to the "real world," so to speak. My master's thesis was on the Red Guards. As the student movement was unfolding, it was also the Red Guards as we understood it in those days, fighting for equality, fighting for the rights of sons and daughters of poor peasants and workers. And this was the time that we were fighting for affirmative action for minorities. My master's essay was a way to link what was going on in China and the U.S. at the time.

After that, I slowly drifted into becoming a full-time activist; from campus anti-war movements to city-wide civil rights actions, then the Asian American Movement. Eventually I realized that I needed a base to do real political work; that was when I moved to Chinatown around 1970 and really got involved full-time in community organizing. I dropped out of the Ph.D. program. I was involved in the forming of the city's Third World Coalition, Chinatown's Food Co-op, anti-Taiwan government movement (Taiyutai Movement), and demonstrated for affirmative action on various campuses. It was a really exciting time. We really thought a revolution was coming. But it didn't come. Everyone went back to do their regular stuff. All the radicals were going back to graduate school. I realized that all the community work I did in the community didn't pan out. And then I realized that it was not enough just being active without having theories and a more in-depth knowledge. That's when I went back to graduate school.

I said to my department, "Why not do something about mobilization in Chinatown in the 1930s, which mirrors very much of what was going on in the 1960s?" They told me that there weren't any specialists on ethnic studies, much less on Chinese Americans, and wouldn't let me do it. So then I went to Charles V. Hamilton, the only African American professor in the political science department, who was willing to help out minority students. So I did my thesis under him and finally got my degree. But what happened at that point was that I realized that my life had changed, and realized the role I could play by balancing being an activist and being a scholar.

So from that point on I really didn't compromise much, although with great negative consequence to my career. But I stuck to three things: First, I do research based on my own activist activities. I was working with restaurant workers, so I wrote about restaurant workers in Chinatown. The sweatshop workers, later on the garment workers, the immigrant workers, etc. So I stick to the thing that I'm actually working on. To some this is a no-no in the academic field. "How could you be actively involved in this kind of work?" And this was one of the things that I was punished for, again and again. Nevertheless, I always thought there was a hidden truth, another dimensional truth that regular scholars did not see. In other words, you could study in the library, you could talk and interview people, but things are not the same for a group on account of what they believe, what they say, and what they want to do. But when in an actual struggle, it's not the same thing. The kind of issues that come up challenges all that stuff. Now these are facts, they are not political positions. So this is the area that I think was very important to capture. The second thing that I thought was important was that even though I'm an activist, I always want to bring out a theoretical understanding about these struggles.

The third perspective is that I'm not interested in writing academic books. I'm interested in reaching out to as many people as possible. This has led me on a very different type of trajectory. Even though I'm an activist/scholar, I don't want to be an observer. I want to write about things I'm actually involved in and actually participating in. So in my written works I prefer to write for a mass audience. So the books I published are all through trade publishers, they're not academic stuff. The advantage to that is reaching out to more people. Most of my books have a lot more circulation. In *The New Chinatown*—it was published in 1987 and I'm still getting royalties. People would say, "You know Peter, I became an activist because I read this book." So it clearly shows that the work has impact and is different from others.

I write for mass publications. I struggle so hard. You know I'm a foreigner. English is not my first language. My English grammar oftentimes has problems, but I wanted to write for mass publications. I struggled with trying to make my sentences shorter, not using big words, trying to digest things and present them in a way that people could understand. I was fortunate enough to write for *The Nation* and *The Village Voice*. At one point I actually thought I was going to quit teaching. And then later my articles were published in the *International Herald Tribune* and many places. For a while I was doing a lot of things that didn't have anything to do with my field anymore. As you know, the Korean American/African American problems in the late 1980s—I was practically the only Asian American writing articles about that at the beginning. I would go to the African American community and they would tell me that they didn't want to talk to Koreans and to get out of there. So I wrote this whole series of articles and one of them is about the riots after 1992 in Los Angeles, and that was nominated for a Pulitzer Prize.

I have published very few articles in a refereed journal because the kind of stuff I write would just get people upset. "Where's the source? There's not enough quotes!" All that kind of nonsense. But I did publish tons of articles that were actually published in edited academic books and encyclopedias.

Another dimension to my work is as an activist/scholar. I try to get my knowledge out there. One of the things I do, even until this day, is to constantly be interviewed through magazines and through media. As some of you know, I'm often quoted, giving a long discourse to these reporters. Then they would quote me one or two sentences that had nothing to do with anything. But anyway, that's what I do. Some knowledge did rub off from the process.

There's another hat I wear that you probably don't know, along the line of mass distribution—I got involved with documentary filmmaking back in 1974. Over the years I've helped to produce over thirty documentaries and four co-productions. Many of them received international awards. One of them was nominated for an Academy Award in 2010. So again, this is my way of trying to get my work through to people. The reason I first got into documentaries was because I was teaching at Old Westbury College. The Rockefellers at that time wanted to give money to "minorities" and so they built this college, which recruited the worst possibly prepared kids in the city, and brought them into Old Westbury, Long Island, one of the most prestigious neighborhoods in the area. We had a whole bunch of idealistic faculty that thought that we could change them. At that time you couldn't lecture because the kids couldn't concentrate on you, and you couldn't ask them to write things. So eventually I started talking to them about where they're from, what problems they had. Once I did that they had tons of stuff that came out. This was when I first started to use documentaries to get these kids to be interested and to be motivated to learn. And through that process I recruited half a dozen people, including Amy Goodman, a top producer, and another person who received an Academy Award.

So I was lucky enough, published enough, to get tenure and get promoted. At the same time, I was able to do things other people didn't have the time or inclination to do. So sometimes my work will be a combination of the three. Chinatown restaurant workers for example. I first started talking about them on the "Today Show" on NBC. From there, I wrote and published many articles, and from that I wrote *The New Chinatown*. In *The New Chinatown*, one of the things I did was I try to understand the structure of the Chinese community. I was the one writing about *tongs*, organized crime, put in the context of Chinese communities. And subsequently, a lot of reporters didn't want to know anything else I wrote about in Chinatown. They always wanted me to talk about organized crime, *tongs* and stuff.

What I did was to get into film, as well as into journals, mass journals, constantly trying to see myself as both a filmmaker and a scholar. I'm always trying to inject some theoretical content, and this is where I get into fights with my editors, with filmmakers. Jon Alpert is one of the leading filmmakers that I have worked with and we always have fights. I said, "This shit doesn't have any context. You've got to have some perspective in it." He would say, "Our viewers are not interested in talking heads. You have to do the story [that] would make people want to watch and listen." I guess since I'm not a good enough artist to achieve that, we always have to disagree and compromise to come to an optimal outcome.

My work actually ranges from obviously Chinatown, to human rights issues in China. There's the documentary that got nominated for an Academy Award. It's basically in that spirit. I was working for NBC and PBS during the June 4th massacre. A lot of you don't know what it is, but that was more than twenty-five years ago.

What is my theoretical approach? Political economy is my foundation; I see political economy as what drives things. I'm also very mindful that things are always in a process of change, evolving from something to something else in the future. I also emphasize history, with a dash of sociology. As humans we group together and form institutions. This is what people call culture, and I call it, "stickiness of reality." In other words, you do things for a certain state or purpose and then you get stuck, and that becomes a pattern of behavior. In that sense, dabbling in sociology can explain certain things but also makes things difficult to change.

Finally, why am I doing all of this? I have never understood why, except that I think when I was a kid I read too many martial arts novels. It's always about fighting against injustice, fighting against government, fighting against the rich, the nasty merchants, and against the greedy landlords. It's always about standing up for the little guy. This is what kung fu movies are all about. I always pick the side that I think is being abused, taken advantage of, being lied to. This is what my analysis is often classified as. In another way, I am a very classical Chinese scholar. The Chinese scholar is supposed to be and should be, the first one to worry about things before everybody else understands. He is also the last person to relax during the crisis.

So in this sense, I'm supposed to be a critic. I'm a social critic, I have nothing good to say about anything. I'm very judgmental and a pain in the ass. Thank you, that's it.

MAANY Seminar Video (December 15, 2014): www.aaari.info/14-12-15mapping.htm

Authors

John J. Chin is a Professor of Urban Policy & Planning at Hunter College/CUNY. Professor Chin's research focuses on urban health, immigrant communities and the role of community institutions in community planning and in the delivery of social and health services. He is also interested in how key community-based institutions in immigrant and minority communities shape community values and norms, particularly in relation to controversial or sensitive topics, like HIV.

Prior to coming to Hunter College, Prof. Chin was a Senior Research Associate at the New York Academy of Medicine, an Assistant Professor of Clinical Sociomedical Sciences at Columbia University (Mailman School of Public Health), and a Visiting Assistant Research Scientist at the University of California, San Francisco. He was a co-founder and Deputy Executive Director of the Asian & Pacific Islander Coalition on HIV/AIDS (APICHA). He has also worked for the NYC Commission on Human Rights and the NYC Comptroller's Office.

Margaret M. Chin joined the Sociology Department at Hunter College/CUNY in September 2001, and is the author of *Sewing Women: Immigrants and the New York City Garment Industry* (Columbia University Press, 2005). Prof. Chin's research interests focus on new immigrants, working poor families, race and ethnicity, and Asian Americans. Her current research projects include a book manuscript on how Asian ethnic media is used by first and second generation Asians and Asian Americans; a comparative chapter on differences and similarities among Brooklyn's Chinatown, Flushing's Asiantown and Manhattan's Chinatown; and a paper on how young student parents balance parenting and school.

Tarry Hum is a Professor of Urban Studies at Queens College/CUNY and the CUNY Graduate Center. She is the author of *Making a Global Immigrant Neighborhood: Brooklyn's Sunset Park* which received a 2015 Honorable Mention for the Association of Collegiate Schools of Planning's Paul Davidoff Award. Hum is co-editing a forthcoming volume from Temple University Press, *Immigrant Crossroads: Globalization, Incorporation, and Placemaking in Queens, NY.*

Peter Kwong (1941-2017) was Distinguished Professor of Urban Policy & Planning at Hunter College/CUNY, and Professor of Sociology at the CUNY Graduate Center. He was a pioneer in Asian American Studies, a leading scholar of immigration, and an award-winning journalist and filmmaker, widely recognized for his passionate commitment to human rights and social justice. As a scholar, he was best known for his work on Chinese Americans and on modern Chinese politics. As a journalist, his exposés of Chinese drug syndicates and Los Angeles racial riots had been nominated for the Pulitzer Prize. As a documentary filmmaker, he was a recipient of a CINE Golden Eagle Award, and a co-producer of *China's Unnatural Disaster: The Tears of Sichuan Province* for HBO, which was nominated for an Academy Award in 2010.

Zai Liang is Professor of Sociology at University at Albany – SUNY. His current research is the study of how migrant children fare in China's history-making migration and urbanization process. Specifically, he studies equality of educational opportunity, access to health service, and health outcomes such as self rated health, mental health, and mortality for children in destination cities as well as for migrant children left behind in rural China using the latest data from censuses and surveys. He is one of the first researchers to study contemporary Chinese migration patterns in the age of market transition in China.

Riding "Jitneys in Manila"
Down My Own Community Research Path

JOHN J. CHIN

Why Jitneys?

WHILE IN GRADUATE SCHOOL AT COLUMBIA UNIVERSITY pursuing a Ph.D. in urban planning, I was naturally drawn to particular topics of study, but being insecure, I grasped for the "correct" way of choosing a research project. One of my professors in our doctoral seminar used the catchphrase "jitneys in Manila" as a shorthand way of critiquing students' research ideas if he thought they were merely about amassing information, and not answering vital scholarly questions. Aside from suggesting a casual dismissal of knowledge about the lives of Asian working people, his admonition made me anxious for other reasons, which I've spent my entire research career exploring.

Over the years, "jitneys in Manila" has stuck with me like a faint shadow over all of my work as a researcher. Various forms of the same argument have been thrown at me by grant reviewers, journal editors, and colleagues whenever I studied and wrote about Asian American communities. I've wrestled with that shadow, defied it, and also in some respects, made peace with it. If there was a hierarchy of research approaches in the social sciences, with the jitneys at the bottom, I had a better understanding of why they sat there and why they shouldn't be dismissed so easily.

Three Lessons

My understanding is inextricably linked to the lessons I've learned about how Asian American and other marginalized communities have asserted their power. My research path parallels three lessons I've learned from my experiences with building organizations and from the political activists I've admired:

1. Autonomous organizing: The need to focus on one's own work and not try to fit in with the priorities of others. This was a lesson I learned from activists organizing black, gay communities in the 1980s—a lesson that extends to the importance of building strong "indigenous" community organizations.

2. The power of data to support the need for the work of community organizations: Generating data involves devoting time and resources to studying issues and populations that are largely invisible or ignored.

3. Expanding beyond and bridging the gap of understanding: This is more than the simple need to speak effectively to those who hold the purse strings. It's also about the need to build a strong civil society in which we move beyond political maneuvering and towards true understanding.

When a people or a phenomenon are marginalized or invisible, simply pointing to its existence—by describing those "jitneys in Manila"—is an essential first step. Moving beyond that level of inquiry may be a privilege that early on I didn't think there was time for. Over the years, however, as the community organizations I helped to build grew, and my research career matured, I've come to better understand the challenge our professor presented to us when he used his problematic catchphrase. Of course, it's only in hindsight that I can make some sense of the path I followed. There was very little in terms of advanced planning. I followed the path of my own personal anxieties, interests, and burning questions, all of which somehow outweighed the admonitions about "jitneys in Manila," and found a way to develop a research career.

Behind my choice of research topics may have been a wish to understand myself within the larger story of the Asian American experience. And beyond that, a yearning to find remedies for the isolation and injustices endured by marginalized and invisible people who were like me. Could I have been the kind of person who starts first with the scientific purpose, shapes a grand and universal research question, and coolly designs a study to answer it? Perhaps, if I had a different life experience, felt less alone and invisible growing up as Korean-American, and gay, in a suburb of 1970s Pittsburgh.

Growing up Korean American in Pittsburgh

My father was a biochemist and I think I inherited some of his scientific habits, a satisfaction in cataloguing and categorizing, and systematically pursuing answers to questions. My mother didn't work outside of home, but she loved to paint and sing when my siblings and I were young. I think I also inherited some of that love towards more creative approaches to the world's questions. It would make sense then that my research often relied on mixed methods, drawing on both quantitative and qualitative data and analysis.

Neither of my parents was particularly politically or social justice-minded, but they weren't pushovers either. As children and young adults, they had lived through Japanese colonialism, World War II, and the Korean War. They immigrated from Korea in the late 1950s to Hawai'i—my mother as part of a larger family move, and my father on a student visa. Hawai'i was a relative haven for Asians in the U.S., and my parents were surrounded by friends, family members and other Koreans who had come over around the same time. My parents met and married in Hawai'i, and then in early 1967, just a few months after I was born, my father finished graduate school and found a job on the mainland, requiring our family of four at the time to move to an almost entirely white suburb of Pittsburgh.

It would be an understatement to say that this transition was a shock for my parents, especially my mother, who was the youngest of five children and who had slept in her mother's bed until the day she married my father. Unlike Hawai'i, Pittsburgh had winter, and our neighborhood had just one other Asian family. We made do, networking with the few Korean families in the greater Pittsburgh area and periodically attending the Korean church or stopping by the tiny Asian grocery, both in downtown Pittsburgh, about a 20-mile drive away.

Because of the distance and the limited offerings of the Asian grocery, my mother made much of our Korean food herself. To prepare a season's supply of kimchee, she started by soaking heads of Napa cabbage in trash cans filled with salt water. She grew bean sprouts in the moist shade of the bathtub. My older brother, younger sister and I sat around the kitchen table helping her seal up a mix of pork and vegetables inside of mandoo dumpling wrappers, learning to use the slippery egg whites as glue. In the privacy of our home, we were a Korean family.

Before my first day of kindergarten, the first time I would spend substantial time away from my family, my parents and older brother sat me down and taught me some essential survival tools, such as how to ask to go to the bathroom in English and not in my baby Korean. This was the start of a brave new world of assimilation. The concepts of bilingualism and multiculturalism hadn't yet reached the mainstream of my parents' social circles.

Pittsburgh was my hometown, and I loved it, being all I really knew until age twelve. I loved the Steelers and the Pirates. I still have the hockey puck I retrieved at a Penguins game after it flew into the crowd, a sign that I really belonged. In grade school, during our annual school trip to Kennywood Park to ride the roller coasters, the local TV news personalities had set up a booth where they greeted fans and gave out signed photos of themselves. I eagerly collected their photos like baseball cards, and marveled at my good fortune to make physical contact with those I had imagined as being part of Pittsburgh's inner circles.

I loved my hometown even though one of the primary realities of living there was the normality of being different. Since there weren't many Asians in our area, we were seen more as curiosities than as a threat. Still, hostility was sometimes more overt, and as I learned from my parents, one didn't need to be silent about it, which my father once stunningly demonstrated.

Soon after moving to Pittsburgh, we lived in a nondescript, lower-middle-class development made up of rows of interconnected two-story rental units. A neighborhood boy, a young teenager, began ringing our doorbell and then running away. After a few evenings of this, my father waited quietly inside by the door, and when the boy approached, he swung the door open, grabbed him by the shirt and dragged him into our apartment. As the rest of my family sat there at the dinner table, mouths agape and most likely chopsticks in mid-air with food on the way to our open mouths, my father berated the terrified boy before letting him go. Needless to say he never came calling again.

Despite the indelibleness of that scene and my satisfaction at seeing this harasser thwarted, there was a sense of loneliness to it, a smallness to it—just my young mother and three small children eating our Korean dinner at dusk, watching my father scold a teenage white boy who was probably mostly harmless, but up to no good for the moment—a drop of assertion in a sea of whiteness.

Similarly, in the larger Korean community in the area, the resistance and coping I saw was primarily interpersonal and social. Koreans gathered together for mutual social support, through churches and social circles, but their activities were rarely directed outwardly and collectively towards political systems. My parents and their Korean friends had created an important and comfortable space, but it also felt isolating. Pittsburgh, Pennsylvania, USA, was the only home I knew, and living inside a Korean bubble wouldn't be the answer that would allow me to fully inhabit my home. This became even clearer as it dawned on me that I might be gay.

Civil Rights, Ethnic Studies & LGBT Movements

From my childhood vantage point, this budding awareness of my sexuality presented an unsolvable problem. Other than silence and invisibility, I couldn't see another type of response that could result in anything good. When I discovered ethnic studies and political movements in college, I experienced a visceral relief, learning about workable models for navigating the world as a fully visible adult.

Being able to develop a viable professional and academic career path that connected to my personal history was a luxury afforded to me by the Civil Rights Movement and the various identity-based movements that followed, including the development of Asian American Studies and other ethnic studies. As is common among American-born Asians who grew up in mostly white neighborhoods, I didn't awaken to an Asian American identity until college. Aside from the Korean church I intermittently attended with my parents, I never had the opportunity to be around so many other Asian Americans. The isolation I felt growing up seemed to have a remedy, and I wanted to know more about my Asian American self, and Asian America, more broadly.

Because our Asian American Studies program was just getting started during the middle of my undergraduate studies at Cornell University, I took courses in the Africana Studies department, learning about the Civil Rights Movement. In the Women's Studies department, I learned about the ways that commonly accepted social norms supported economic and political power structures. I wrote my senior thesis on Vincent Chin's murder and anti-Asian violence. I was mentored, personally and academically, by Prof. Lee C. Lee, who tenaciously and successfully fought for the start of my school's Asian American Studies program. I grabbed onto the intellectual lifelines provided by scholars like Peter Kwong (*The New Chinatown*), and documentary filmmakers like Christine Choy and Renee Tajima-Peña (*Who Killed Vincent Chin?*), and Arthur Dong (*Forbidden City, USA*), who followed their own "jitneys in Manila," benefiting all of us.

I also got involved in the gay student organizations on campus, particularly Gays, Bisexuals and Lesbians of Color (GBLOC). As part of GBLOC, I helped to organize a conference that provided a pivotal moment in my political awakening. I had the opportunity to meet various social movement and community leaders, as well as academics writing about the experiences of LGBT people of color and organizing in our communities. One lesson in particular stuck with me during a talk by Gil Gerald, who at the time was the executive director of the National Coalition of Black Lesbians and Gays. Gil introduced me to the concept of autonomous organizing—the notion that one should build a power base within one's own community to provide the strength needed to fight for justice and rights on the outside. I witnessed this concept in action when I later helped found an Asian American HIV/AIDS organization in New York City.

HIV/AIDS Awareness

In the mid-1980s, when the AIDS epidemic started to enter mainstream consciousness and reached the ivy-covered walls of Cornell, I met a force of nature by the name of Suki Ports, a Japanese American, early AIDS activist, who was the director of the first minority AIDS organization in New York City. I invited her to come to my campus to speak to students of color about HIV/AIDS. She brought along her friend and colleague, Craig Harris, who had organized the first Black AIDS conference. Craig, together with Suki and some others, also started the National Minority AIDS Council.

It truly altered my understanding of reality to meet this Asian American woman, who was older than my mother, bantering with a younger Black gay man and speaking so forcefully for HIV awareness while fighting against homophobia and discrimination. Suki began her presentation to a group of students and faculty by releasing a stream of expletives to shock the audience out of their stereotyped view of what an Asian woman was like. After being initially mortified, I felt as if a third eye had opened in the middle of my forehead.

Chinese Progressive Association

John J. Chin (Left) and Chinese Progressive Association members (ca.1980s)
Photo courtesy of John J. Chin

During college, I also had the opportunity to participate in a summer-long internship at the Chinese Progressive Association (CPA) in Manhattan's Chinatown. CPA was a small community organization, founded by Chinese American activists, operating out of the ground floor space of a Chinatown tenement. I was captivated by their stories of sometimes violent conflicts with other more conservative Chinatown organizations over real estate development and fair labor practices in the late 1960s and 1970s. They also seemed to know everyone who mattered in New York City politics—from City Hall to the labor unions.

As a Korean American who had gone straight from the white suburbs of Pittsburgh to Cornell University, my experience in Chinatown expanded my world. In addition to learning how to order a deli coffee like a real New Yorker and the Chinese word for steamed roast pork buns, I learned about the camaraderie of people who fought together for justice, and a voice, in the places where they lived and worked, and the importance of building community organizations to channel that energy.

Building APICHA

As with many others, New York City became my beacon after graduating from college. My move to the city in late 1989 was facilitated by landing my first "real" job, working as an investigator for the AIDS Discrimination Division of the New York City Commission on Human Rights during the Dinkins administration. At the time, the fear of HIV infection was still rampant, and there were many complaints of AIDS-related discrimination—people being fired from jobs, funeral directors who refused to handle bodies, dentists who refused to provide treatment. After I moved, Suki Ports helped pull me into the work of addressing HIV in Asian American communities—raising awareness, interrupting stigma, and breaking the isolation of Asian Americans living with HIV in New York City.

Few groups were more invisible than Asian Americans living with HIV, often closeted, isolated from or keeping secrets from spouses, families, and friends. Many of these individuals spoke little English, didn't have health insurance, were undocumented immigrants, and were afraid of being ostracized by their immigrant communities if their HIV status or sexual orientation were revealed. Knowledge among Asian Americans about how to prevent HIV infection was also dangerously low, a situation exacerbated by language barriers and a belief that Asians were not at risk. To address these issues, Suki got us started with building the Asian and Pacific Islander Coalition on HIV/AIDS (APICHA).

AIDS Walk 2013, APICHA Community Health Center
Photo Courtesy of APICHA

The power of autonomous organizing, building organizations and gathering data, was imprinted on me through my experience with founding APICHA. Starting out in late 1989 and into the early '90s, a small group of us sat around the huge conference table at the New York Foundation, planning out what this new organization would be. Like the mice and soldiers who came to life at night in *The Nutcracker*, we commandeered the offices of the NYC Commission on Human Rights after work hours, sitting at the computers and typing out our first grant proposals, banging on keyboards and shouting across the cubicle walls to share ideas.

One of the primary challenges in getting grant funds was a lack of data to support our case. In the 1980s, governmental HIV/AIDS statistics for Asians and Pacific Islanders and Native Americans were all lumped together as "Other," a practice that rendered these groups invisible. In 1989, at a national AIDS meeting in Washington, D.C., a group of Native Americans and Asians and Pacific Islanders, including Suki, managed to speak to Dr. James Mason, the U.S. Assistant Secretary of Health, and Dr. Gary Noble, the Assistant Surgeon General and Deputy Director for HIV at the Centers for Disease Control and Prevention (CDC). After the delegation explained to them the problem with the "Other" category, Dr. Mason committed to having the CDC issue their monthly reports using a separate column for Asians and Pacific Islanders, and another for American Indians, Alaskan and Hawaiian Natives.

Dr. Mason kept his word, and the "Other" category was eliminated for these groups. We could now finally track the course of the HIV/AIDS epidemic and demonstrate its impact on API communities in the U.S. This then helped contribute to the growth of APICHA from a small volunteer organization, to a paid staff of three, to its current staff size of 130. Today, APICHA is now known as Apicha Community Health Center, and recently achieved the status as a full-fledged federally qualified health center (FQHC).

Autonomous Organizing in Academia

After completing my Ph.D. at Columbia, and moving into research and academic environments, I was still guided by the lessons I learned about the power of data, organizations, and autonomous organizing. Without data, a whole subpopulation could be made to disappear; without organizational power, a marginalized group has no leverage for making demands for change; and the drive for building those organizations could come reliably only from within that marginalized group. My research aimed at generating the data that these organizations needed in order to shine a light on the populations and phenomena they cared about.[1,2,3,4,5,6]

In a way, I engaged in autonomous organizing as a researcher by working primarily with a very small group of scholars and researchers across the country who focused on HIV in Asian American communities —what many others might dismiss as just "jitneys in Manila." Research that would simply acknowledge the existence of HIV in Asian American communities felt groundbreaking enough to me—to show that it's there, it's a problem, and it's ignored. The urgency of simply making the problem visible, outweighed the need to answer grander scientific questions.

At some point however, HIV became more mainstream. In fact, there were complaints from other service sectors about HIV exceptionalism—the perception that a disproportionate share of research, healthcare and social service funding was going to HIV. And although HIV work in Asian American communities never became mainstream, the community organization that I helped to start became a stable, visible, and respected healthcare institution. In hindsight, these developments altered the way I understood my purpose as a researcher. Instead of generating data to make a case for a marginalized group, or to support the building of an organization, my work could be more reflective about what we built, and with maybe a more critical eye.

This critique took two paths. The first focused on how HIV and other human service organizations had succeeded or failed to honor their social movement origins as they became more established and formal—beholden to their government funders.[7,8] The second path focused on understanding the importance of community institutions within the Asian American community, such as churches and temples, which might support or detract from health promotion efforts within the community, particularly those concerning sensitive topics like HIV.[9,10,11,12,13,14,15]

One path looked outward beyond Asian American communities, and the other inward. But both paths aimed to answer larger questions about the power of community organizations in relation to vulnerable populations, and how well they served or failed to serve the populations they intended to support.

For research within the Asian American community, I focused on why our own communities were reluctant to discuss HIV, and whether key organizations, such as religious institutions, might contribute to that reluctance by supporting stigma and shame. It concerned me that institutions aiming to nurture our souls could also make some people feel ashamed, or stigmatized because of who they were, or what they've experienced. Stigma and shame are both associated with poor mental health and risky behavior that people may engage in to cope with negative feelings. Data also showed that young Asian American men who had sex with men were experiencing the highest increases in rates of HIV infection.

I wasn't interested in the individual or psychological level, but aimed for a community-level understanding. How do shame and stigma get transmitted through some of our most important and numerous community institutions—religious institutions? And if these institutions have the power to shape values and norms, could they help to shape values and norms that interrupt shame and stigma, leading to better physical and mental health outcomes for community members?

Maybe these questions had broader research and policy implications beyond my own personal history. Maybe I wasn't the stand-alone island of curiosity I had imagined. But I was studying things with personal relevance, and maybe there were ways of making them relevant to others.

Researchers and academics confront the same question that other creative professionals face: how do you take one's personal passions and interests and spark that interest in others? I used to think this was simply a transactional question—getting published, getting promoted, getting cited, getting grants. That transactional view was actually a barrier to communication. I see it now as an existential question, insofar as my research reflects who I am. We all struggle with wanting to be seen and valued, and wish that this could happen with minimal effort. But as we feel more confident in our value, and the solid foundation that we've built for ourselves, it doesn't feel as assaulting or diminishing to not be understood immediately. I've begun to see how efforts to bridge gaps in understanding, rather than being an unpleasant chore, are a contribution to strengthening our social fabric.

Asian Immigrant Women & Massage Parlors

With my more recent research on Asian immigrant women working in sexually oriented massage parlors, I've been confronted with an opposite problem—more immediate interest in my research.[16] The quicker interest has been gratifying, but it has also shown me that the fundamental problem of communication still remains. Sometimes the interest is not always what I had intended when starting my research, and so there's still a challenge in communicating what I think is important for people to understand.

Much of the interest with my recent project has come from key community organizations that provide essential services and advocacy for these women, an intended target audience. But some of their interest has seemed problematic, for example, resting on stereotypes of tragic trafficking victims who need to be saved (a real situation for some massage parlor workers, but probably more so for other sectors of the sex work industry). Others are interested because they want to know if their boyfriends or husbands are getting hand jobs during their periodic massage sessions. Another group has been annoyed by the proliferation of massage parlors in their neighborhoods, not understanding the complex underlying factors. I was once approached after a conference presentation by a government official who lauded my research as supporting his work to rid his town of massage parlors.

The above reasons for being interested in my research aren't necessarily wrong. However, I've found it rather surprising and enlightening to see that the interest itself hadn't removed the necessity of making the effort to communicate, explain, and bring the other person along.

Seeing Each Other

I used to think of my research as being immature because it was personally motivated. I strove for the clarity and abstractness of grand scientific questions and clean research design. I carried the notion that my problems with communicating would be solved by the right project, the right question. I see more clearly now that my research cannot just sit by idly and say, "Hey, look at me!" and leave it up to another person to make something of it. Research is just an opening to a conversation, an ongoing process of knowing, and greater engagement with others. Focusing on my own questions, and developing skills as a researcher, was a necessary step to arrive at a greater comfort with communicating my research to others. My research path paralleled the lessons I learned about autonomous organizing and building organizations. First, we re-group, look inward, and after feeling sufficiently centered and strong in our own thoughts, voices and positioning, we reach outward.

Looking back, I can see that I may have perhaps misunderstood my professor's admonition against studying "jitneys in Manila." There may have been layers of problematic intention behind that formulation, but I've become more appreciative that it encouraged us to reach out beyond our own thoughts. I may not have been an experienced enough scholar to understand that element of the idea at the time. Yet, even if I had understood it intellectually, I hadn't developed the confidence and the generosity to follow through on it. I had my own questions and I wanted my own answers, and that was that. But I can see now that there's a need for finding ways to communicate with those who might not care as much about what you're interested in, that there is value in fostering that understanding, in engaging in that ongoing conversation, and ultimately in seeing each other.

Notes

1 John J. Chin, Ezer Kang, Jennifer Haejin Kim, John Martinez, and Haftan Eckholdt, "Serving Asians and Pacific Islanders with HIV/AIDS: Challenges and Lessons Learned," *Journal of Health Care for the Poor and Underserved* 17:4 (2006): 910–927.

2 John J. Chin, ManChui Leung, Lina Sheth, and Therese R. Rodriguez, "Let's not ignore a growing HIV problem for Asians and Pacific Islanders in the U.S.," *Journal of Urban Health* 84:5 (2007): 642–647.

3 John J. Chin, Linda Weiss, Ezer Kang, et al., "Looking for a Place to Call Home: A Needs Assessment of Asians and Pacific Islanders Living with HIV/AIDS in the New York Eligible Metropolitan Area," *Journal of Urban Health* 84:5 (New York: The New York Academy of Medicine, 2007): 642-647.

4 Haftan Eckholdt and John J. Chin, "Pneumocystis carinii Pneumonia in Asians and Pacific Islanders," *Clinical Infectious Diseases* 24:6 (1997): 1265–1267.

5 Haftan Eckholdt, John J. Chin, and Dae-Duk Kim, "The needs of Asians and Pacific Islanders living with HIV in New York City," *AIDS Education & Prevention* 9:6 (1997): 493–504.

6   Hirokazu Yoshikawa, Patrick A. Wilson, JoAnn Hsueh, Elisa Altman Rosman, John J. Chin, and Jennifer H. Kim, "What front-line NGO staff can tell us about culturally anchored theories of change in HIV prevention for Asian/Pacific Islanders in the U.S.," *American Journal of Community Psychology* 32:1-2 (2003):143–158.

7   John J. Chin, "The Limits and Potential of Nonprofit Organizations in Participatory Planning: A Case Study of the New York HIV Planning Council," *Journal of Urban Affairs* 31:4 (2009): 431–460.

8   John J. Chin, "Service-Providing Nonprofits Working in Coalition to Advocate for Policy Change," *Nonprofit and Voluntary Sector Quarterly* (Online first publilshed July 24, 2017), http://journals.sagepub.com/doi/10.1177/0899764017721060

9   John J. Chin, Min Ying Li, Ezer Kang, Elana Behar, Po Chun Chen, "Civic/Sanctuary Orientation and HIV Involvement among Chinese Immigrant Religious Institutions in New York City," *Global Public Health* 6:S2 (2011): S210–S226.

10   John J. Chin, Joanne Mantell, Linda Weiss, Mamatha Bhagavan, and Xiaoting Luo, "Chinese and South Asian Religious Institutions and HIV Prevention in New York City," *AIDS Education & Prevention* 17:5 (2005): 484–502.

11   John J. Chin and Torsten B. Neilands, "Chinese Immigrant Religious Institutions' Variability in Views on Preventing Sexual Transmission of HIV," *American Journal of Public Health* 106:1 (2016): 110–118.

12   John J. Chin, Torsten B. Neilands, Linda Weiss, and Joanne E. Mantell, "Paradigm shifters, professionals, and community sentinels: immigrant community institutions' roles in shaping places and implications for stigmatized public health initiatives," *Health & Place* 14:4 (2008): 866–882.

13   Ezer Kang, John J. Chin, and Elana Behar, "Faith-based HIV care and prevention in Chinese immigrant communities: Rhetoric or reality?," *Journal of Psychology & Theology* 39:3 (2011): 268–279.

14   Ezer Kang, Darcie Delzell, John J. Chin, Elana Behar, and Ming Ying Li, "Influences of stigma and HIV transmission knowledge on member support for faith-placed HIV initiatives in Chinese immigrant Buddhist and Protestant religious institutions in New York City," *AIDS Education & Prevention* 25:5 (2013): 445–456.

15   ManChui R. Leung, John J. Chin, and Miruna Petrescu-Prahova, "Involving Immigrant Religious Organizations in HIV/AIDS Prevention: The Role of Bonding and Bridging Social Capital," *Social Science & Medicine* 2016:162 (2016): 201–209.

16   John J. Chin, Anna J. Kim, Lois Takahashi, and Douglas J. Wiebe, "Do Sexually Oriented Massage Parlors Cluster in Specific Neighborhoods? A Spatial Analysis of Indoor Sex Work in Los Angeles and Orange Counties, California," *Public Health Reports* 130:5 (2015): 533–542.

Author

John J. Chin is a Professor of Urban Policy & Planning at Hunter College/CUNY. Professor Chin's research focuses on urban health, immigrant communities and the role of community institutions in community planning and in the delivery of social and health services. He is also interested in how key community-based institutions in immigrant and minority communities shape community values and norms, particularly in relation to controversial or sensitive topics, like HIV.

Prior to coming to Hunter College, Prof. Chin was a Senior Research Associate at the New York Academy of Medicine, an Assistant Professor of Clinical Sociomedical Sciences at Columbia University (Mailman School of Public Health), and a Visiting Assistant Research Scientist at the University of California, San Francisco. He was a co-founder and Deputy Executive Director of the Asian & Pacific Islander Coalition on HIV/AIDS (APICHA). He has also worked for the NYC Commission on Human Rights and the NYC Comptroller's Office.

Gentrification and the Future of Work in New York City's "Chinatowns"

TARRY HUM & SAMUEL STEIN

Chinatown/Lower East Side Waterfront (May 6, 2017)
Photo by Antony Wong

NEW YORK CITY'S "CHINATOWN" neighborhoods continue to shape the socioeconomic experiences and trajectories of Chinese immigrants, however these local economies are undergoing transformative changes. The three neighborhoods with the largest concentrations of Chinese immigrants and Chinese Americans—Manhattan's Chinatown, Brooklyn's Sunset Park and Queens' Flushing—are experiencing many of the same processes as other working class spaces in hyper-invested cities like New York: rising rents; tenant displacement; luxury development; street life disciplining; and the replacement of family businesses and affordable services with boutiques and big chains.[1,2,3] Gentrification has challenged the dominant sociological conceptions of "bounded solidarity," with heightened class polarization clearly inscribed in the everyday social, political, and physical landscapes of so-called "ethnic enclave" neighborhoods.[4,5]

Though a long time in the making, these changes are nonetheless jarring for residents and observers alike. For roughly 150 years, Manhattan's Chinatown has been a center of working class Chinese life, labor, struggle and culture.[6] Most recently, Extell Development Group, the primary force behind "Billionaires' Row" in Midtown Manhattan, has initiated a luxury development cluster on the Chinatown/Lower East Side waterfront. Partially financed by Chinese transnational capital, the first of these developments is One Manhattan Square, an 815-unit, $1.4 billion "ultra-luxury, supertall residential skyscraper."[7] Soon it will be joined by several other similarly sized and priced towers in this historic, working class neighborhood where some of the city's oldest public housing is located.

For the past fifty years, Brooklyn's Sunset Park has been home to generations of Puerto Ricans and new immigrants from China and Latin America, as well as families from Manhattan's Chinatown, seeking affordable housing and homeownership.[8] In 2013, Jamestown Properties' acquisition of a majority ownership share of Industry City, a massive 16-building complex, has catalyzed a rebranding and redevelopment of the neighborhood's industrial waterfront, displacing numerous small garment-manufacturing shops. An infusion of development capital is also evident along Sunset Park's Chinese commercial corridor, 8th

Avenue, with new projects such as Winley Plaza introducing sleek, commercial condominiums to a neighborhood with high rates of Chinese and Latino poverty.

Flushing, Queens has also similarly developed as a multi-ethnic, working and middle class community of Chinese, Koreans, Latinos and African Americans.[9,10] Its downtown commercial center has evolved into an epicenter of Asian transnational real estate capital, with a large concentration of banks and mega-development projects. One of the most prolific Flushing developers is F&T Group, which is adding three million square feet of luxury residential, retail, and commercial space, including hotels in Flushing Commons and Tangram—just two of their numerous projects.

Taken together, New York City's "Chinatowns" are becoming increasingly inhospitable to both long-term residents and recent immigrants from working class backgrounds. Such immense changes in the landscape and intensive re-routings of both people and money can often be traced back to certain types of surpluses and crises.[11] In this particular case, the transition was punctuated and propelled by a political crisis—the attacks of September 11, 2001—and an economic crisis—the financial meltdown that peaked in Fall 2008. Though international in scope, the nexus of both events was Lower Manhattan (specifically the World Trade Center and Wall Street), just blocks away from Chinatown.[12] While 9/11 provided opportunities for new rounds of planning and spatial disciplining, the 2008 financial crisis ushered a dramatic and rapid influx of Chinese transnational capital in the form of real estate investment, acquisition, and new development.

These recent events and forces represent a significant shift in the overall function of multi-ethnic Chinese neighborhoods in New York City, and their relationship to both the broader U.S. and Chinese economies. Whereas historically U.S. Chinatowns were developed as strategies to absorb *Chinese surplus workers* and provide for their social reproduction in a manner that generally benefited *U.S. manufacturing capital*,[13] today these neighborhoods are being reshaped as strategies to absorb *Chinese surplus capital* and provide lucrative investment opportunities for transnational capitalists[14] in a manner that largely benefits *U.S. real estate capital*, including locally-based immigrant growth coalitions.

This shift represents an attack on Chinese workers—both those who have already immigrated, and those seeking to immigrate—who are forced to either find other, more disparate spaces to live and work, or pay an impossibly high proportion of their wages towards rent and living expenses. Though it is felt at the scales of the body, the home, the workplace, the neighborhood and the city, the gentrification of New York's multi-ethnic Chinese neighborhoods is a reflection of global changes, where people and money are shifting positions and remaking spaces to suit the fickle demands of "vagabond capitalism."[15] While New York City's "Chinatowns" are typically viewed as peripheral to urban processes because they are largely immigrant neighborhoods of color, these neighborhoods can, in fact, provide important insights on the interconnectedness between finance capitalism and post-2008 urbanization marked, in part, by the significant influx of Chinese foreign direct investment in the property markets of global cities.[16]

This essay utilizes employment data from the New York State Department of Labor (DOL) to document fundamental shifts in Chinatown, Flushing and Sunset Park's local economies, and examines the transition of New York City's "Chinatowns" from sites of surplus labor to sites of surplus capital.[17] The Quarterly Census of Employment and Wages (QCEW) provides an enumeration of private sector businesses, the number of employees, and total wages for employers covered by New York State Unemployment Insurance (UI) laws. QCEW is available by zip code, but the data may be subject to an undercount since it represents employers that pay contributions to fund the State's UI. Even so, QCEW provides a comprehensive profile of the types of private sector firms that make up a local economy by industry sectors, the size of the local labor force, and average wages. Using this data, we compared the neighborhood economies of New York City's "Chinatowns" during two periods, in 2000 (pre-9/11 crisis), and in 2015 (post-2008 "Great Recession").

Manhattan Chinatown/Lower East Side: Bifurcated Service Sectors

Parts of Manhattan's Chinatown fall within zip code 10013, which includes the highly affluent, non-Hispanic White neighborhoods of Tribeca and Soho; and zip code 10002, which encompasses the Lower East Side. Many advocates argue that Chinatown and the Lower East Side constitute a community of common interest based on the shared concerns of working poor Chinatown residents and the Latino, Black and low-income White NYCHA residents within 10002. An analysis of QCEW data for zip codes 10013 and 10002 underscores that while in the year 2000 garment shops in Soho remained part of Chinatown's neighborhood economy, by 2015 in zip code 10013 all manufacturing was eviscerated—a sharp contrast. Zip code 10002 is now the borough's sole working class enclave south of 96th Street.

Top Four Industry Sectors for Manhattan Chinatown by Zip Code

	2000				2015		
Zip Code 10002	Firms	Employees	Avg. Wages[1]	Zip Code 10002	Firms	Employees	Avg. Wages
ALL PRIVATE SECTOR	1,890	15,760	$30,066	ALL PRIVATE SECTOR	2,907	21,293	$33,837
TOP FOUR INDUSTRY SECTORS	567	7,891	----	TOP FOUR INDUSTRY SECTORS	975	10,896	----
% of Private Sector	30%	50%	----	% of Private Sector	34%	51%	----
SOCIAL ASSISTANCE	52	2,913	$26,681	FOOD SERVICES & DRINKING PLACES	433	5,048	$24,758
APPAREL MANUFACTURING	104	2,335	$12,453	SOCIAL ASSISTANCE	69	3,262	$28,828
RETAIL[2]	230	1,334	$21,088	RETAIL[2]	229	1,651	$26,752
FOOD SERVICES & DRINKING PLACES	181	1,309	$20,472	PROFESSIONAL SCIENTIFIC & TECH. SVCS	244	935	$58,989

	2000				2015		
Zip Code 10013	Firms	Employees	Avg. Wages[1]	Zip Code 10013	Firms	Employees	Avg. Wages
ALL PRIVATE SECTOR	4,525	54,726	$54,174	ALL PRIVATE SECTOR	5,730	80,044	$79,305
TOP FOUR INDUSTRY SECTORS	1,433	24,451	----	TOP FOUR INDUSTRY SECTORS	1,836	37,118	----
% of Private Sector	32%	45%	----	% of Private Sector	32%	46%	----
APPAREL MANUFACTURING	298	8,846	$15,342	PROFESSIONAL SCIENTIFIC & TECH. SVCS	1,045	14,309	$102,027
PROFESSIONAL SCIENTIFIC & TECH. SVCS	708	6,524	$77,699	FOOD SERVICES & DRINKING PLACES	445	9,325	$30,185
FOOD SERVICES & DRINKING PLACES	377	4,633	$29,126	AMBULATORY HEALTH CARE SERVICES	270	7,092	$32,688
SOCIAL ASSISTANCE	50	4,448	$26,486	SECURITIES & COMMODITIES CONTRACTS	76	6,392	$205,537

[1]Wages in 2015 Dollars
[2]Retail is Grocery and Clothing & Accessories

Prior to 9/11, QCEW data indicates that the composition of Chinatown's economy was fairly consistent in both zip codes 10002 and 10013, and included garment manufacturing as a primary employer. The top four sectors, which accounted for the employment of about half of each zip code's labor force in 2000, included apparel manufacturing, food services and drinking places, and social assistance. In fact, as late as 2000, apparel manufacturing was the largest employment cluster in Tribeca and Soho (zip code 10013), with 298 garment factories employing nearly 9,000 workers. While retail stores—groceries, clothing and accessories—were among the top four sectors in zip code 10002, in zip code 10013 it was professional, scientific and technical services firms, which rely on high levels of human capital and/or skills such as legal, accounting, architectural and design, advertising and public relations, and engineering.

By 2015, QCEW data indicates a heightened bifurcation, with the differences between firm and employment composition in zip codes 10013 and 10002 having sharpened dramatically. While employment in zip code 10002 remains labor intensive and service-based, zip code 10013 underwent a recomposition. Its top four employment sectors, comprising nearly half (46%) of the labor force (80,000+ workers), now include financial investments, securities, and commodities-related activities (with average earnings of $205,000); and professional, scientific and technical services (with average earnings of $102,000). The astronomical increase in the financial services sector in zip code 10013 indicates that the economies of Tribeca and Soho are now more tightly integrated with finance and Wall Street.

Social assistance, retail stores, and food and drinking places remain among zip code 10002's top four sectors in 2015. However, apparel manufacturing has been replaced by professional, scientific and technical services. By 2015, the economic composition of Chinatown/Lower East Side (zip code 10002) aligns with a bifurcated service economy defined by low-wage, low-paid service jobs in food and retail sectors (including social service assistance positions, administering public programs and services in working poor neighborhoods), the dominance of an immigrant professional class (serving a co-ethnic community), and advanced services defined as professional services for corporate clients. Moreover, relative to Sunset Park and Flushing, Chinatown's labor market is significantly less diverse, with one in two employees working in four industry sectors—food services, social assistance, retail or professional, scientific and technical services.

Sunset Park: Corporatized Health Care Services and the "Maker" Movement

Similar to Manhattan's Chinatown, at the start of the decade, apparel manufacturing remained the largest industry sector in Brooklyn's Sunset Park economy. Overall, more than 9,000 Sunset Park workers (26%) were employed in the manufacturing sector, with a majority (52%) in apparel production. Sunset Park's industrial economy also includes specialty trade contractors involved in various aspects of building construction, i.e., pouring concrete, plumbing and electrical work. By 2015, health care services replaced manufacturing as the neighborhood's largest employment niche, with approximately 10,000 workers comprising 26% of the neighborhood's labor force. The expansion of health care services is evident in the neighborhood's streetscape, which is dotted with numerous small medical outpatient offices, resulting both from health-related institutional expansion, and a community facility provision that grants developers a zoning bonus.

Top Ten Industry Sectors for Sunset Park in 2000 and 2015

Industry Sectors	2000			Industry Sectors	2015		
	Firms	Employed	Avg. Wages[1]		Firms	Employed	Avg. Wages
ALL PRIVATE SECTOR	2,341	34,841	$36,605	ALL PRIVATE SECTOR	3,784	39,505	$42,771
Top Ten Sectors	1,166	19,288	----	Top Ten Sectors	1,541	23,327	----
	50%	55%	----		41%	59%	----
APPAREL MANUFACTURING	272	4,677	$15,999	HOSPITALS	5	4,209	$65,464
SOCIAL ASSISTANCE	27	3,507	$24,446	AMBULATORY HEALTH CARE SERVICES	174	3,976	$48,301
SPECIALTY TRADE CONTRACTORS	162	1,832	$55,187	SPECIALTY TRADE CONTRACTORS	199	2,660	$56,536
NONDURABLE GOODS WHOLESALERS	177	1,725	$35,728	FOOD SERVICES & DRINKING PLACES	309	2,023	$17,901
ADMINISTRATIVE & SUPPORT SERVICES	46	1,688	$24,655	NONDURABLE GOODS WHOLESALERS	242	2,022	$35,249
DURABLE GOODS WHOLESALERS	117	1,601	$50,800	SOCIAL ASSISTANCE	85	1,975	$29,930
AMBULATORY HEALTH CARE SERVICES	64	1,550	$32,322	NURSING & RESIDENTIAL CARE	18	1,935	$28,684
FOOD MANUFACTURING	35	1,150	$39,638	GROCERY STORES	240	1,743	$17,987
FOOD SERVICES & DRINKING PLACES	136	806	$15,386	DURABLE GOODS WHOLESALERS	172	1,503	$57,046
GROCERY STORES	130	752	$21,799	ADMINISTRATIVE & SUPPORT SERVICES	97	1,281	$29,759

[1]Wages in 2015 Dollars
Data Source: 2Q 2000 and 2015 QCEW, NYS DOL

In 2000, Sunset Park was home to one major hospital—Lutheran Medical Center—that was instrumental in designating the neighborhood as a federal poverty area, in the late 1960s, to qualify for federal aid. Lutheran Medical Center continues to be a key stakeholder in community development, and its recent merger with the NYU Langone Medical Center establishes the presence of a major, corporatized health care institution.[18] This merger is an example of larger heath care trends in New York City, where community-oriented medical offices are closing and huge private medical institutions are consolidating.[19] The growth in Sunset Park's health services employment is especially marked for home health aides, increasing by 157% in the past fifteen years. In 2015, nearly 4,000 Sunset Park employees worked in ambulatory health care services (including home health aides), making this employment sector the neighborhood's second largest after hospitals.

Aside from health care consolidation, Sunset Park's neighborhood economy is notable for its anemic increase in the local labor force, which only grew by 13%, while the number of firms increased by 62%. The industry niches that did expand their workforce include grocery stores, and food services and drinking places. Since 2000, the numbers of these types of establishments has more than doubled (106%), with employment in grocery stores and restaurants increasing by 142%. Although these businesses are significant employers, with nearly 3,800 workers in 2015, wages not only stagnated, but also declined in real dollars. Well below the annual earnings of private sector employees, wages for grocery store and restaurant workers averaged $18,344 in 2000 and 2015. Average wages for top employment sectors fell about $400.

Brooklyn's reputation as the epicenter for artisanal manufacturing and the "maker movement" has been firmly established in the past few years. Food manufacturing has always been an important part of Sunset Park's industrial production, and in 2000 it was the second largest manufacturing subsector after apparel—although a much smaller sector numbering only 35 firms and 1,150 workers. With the dramatic decline in apparel production, food is now the neighborhood's largest manufacturing sector. The workforce, however, has not increased by much, numbering only 1,174 in 2015. In contrast, the number of firms has increased by 51%, connoting the trend of smaller food manufacturers. While average wages in food manufacturing have increased significantly from $39,344 to a little over $50,000, the average firm size (i.e., number of workers) has declined from 32 to 22 workers in 2015.[20]

Flushing: Transit Hub and Low-Wage Service Economy

As noted earlier, Downtown Flushing in Queens is undergoing transformative changes with the addition of millions of square feet of new luxury residential, retail, and commercial space. While these new developments represent billions of dollars of real estate investment and seek to attract affluent residents, the composition of Flushing's local economy underscores the prevalence of low-wage jobs in health care, retail, food, and personal services. In fact, Flushing compares poorly to Chinatown and Sunset Park, as average wages for private sector employees declined in 2015 for Flushing workers. While Chinatown and Sunset Park workers experienced modest wage gains (except those in the finance-related sectors with huge gains), the average annual wages for Flushing workers declined dramatically from $43,552 in 2000, to $38,944 in 2015.[21]

Flushing Neighborhood Economy - Top Ten Sectors in 2000 and 2015

Industry Sectors	2000			Industry Sectors	2015		
	Firms	Employed	Avg. Wages[1]		Firms	Employed	Avg. Wages
ALL PRIVATE SECTOR	2,903	29,543	$43,552	ALL PRIVATE SECTOR	5,293	46,071	$38,944
Top Ten Sectors	1,277	14,539	----	Top Ten Sectors	2,240	24,040	----
	44%	49%	----		42%	52%	----
AMBULATORY HEALTH CARE SERVICES	314	2,773	$68,801	AMBULATORY HEALTH CARE SERVICES	542	9,071	$39,703
NURSING & RESIDENTIAL CARE	19	2,603	$39,829	FOOD SERVICES & DRINKING PLACES	449	3,659	$17,377
FOOD SERVICES & DRINKING PLACES	241	1,975	$19,156	GROCERY STORES	146	2,135	$23,915
GROCERY STORES	115	1,776	$22,333	HOSPITALS	16	1,860	$41,461
SPECIALTY TRADE CONTRACTORS	104	1,154	$68,316	PROFESSIONAL SCIENTIFIC & TECHNICAL SVCS	383	1,510	$34,435
TRANSIT & GROUND PASSENGER TRANS	25	967	$69,192	TRANSIT & GROUND PASSENGER TRANSPORT	49	1,318	$74,230
REAL ESTATE	256	888	$35,496	GENERAL MERCHANDISE STORES	43	1,201	$22,190
DURABLE GOODS WHOLESALERS	111	812	$51,223	ADMINISTRATIVE & SUPPORT SERVICES	194	1,123	$32,265
SOCIAL ASSISTANCE	41	805	$23,392	PERSONAL & LAUNDRY SERVICES	365	1,100	$16,248
APPAREL MANUFACTURING	51	786	$9,861	NURSING & RESIDENTIAL CARE	53	1,063	$36,303

[1]Wages in 2015 Dollars
Data Source: 2Q 2000 and 2015 QCEW, NYS DOL

An astounding observation about Flushing's neighborhood economy is the dominance of ambulatory health care services, and the sharp contrast of average wages in 2000 and 2015. The number of workers in this sector quadrupled in 2015, while the average wage fell significantly, indicating sector growth in deskilled jobs such as home health aides. Health-related jobs in hospitals, as well as nursing and residential care facilities, also rank in the top ten employment sectors. With the steep decline in wages in the ambulatory health care services sector, it leaves transit and ground passenger transport as the highest paying employment sector among Flushing's top ten. This makes sense since Flushing is a heavily used transit hub where the Long Island Railroad, 7 subway line, and numerous bus routes converge near Main Street and Roosevelt Avenue.

In 2015, the number of firms and workers in professional and technical services ranked among Flushing's top ten industry sectors, but this was not the case in 2000. An important part of Flushing's neighborhood economy is based on professional services such as legal, finance, engineering, and architectural and design—essential services to support the development agenda of immigrant growth coalitions. A recent survey of small businesses in Flushing found a fairly extensive "second floor economy," comprised of a diverse array of professional service firms not apparent from the street level.[22] It is notable that the average wage for professionals employed in Flushing's immigrant neighborhood is significantly less than those in Chinatown/Lower East Side.

In addition to professional and health services, Flushing's local economy includes typical low-wage, immigrant niches in food services, grocery stores, and personal services such as nail and beauty salons. Similar to Sunset Park, the average annual wages for food service employees declined between 2000 and 2015. Moreover, Flushing's low-wage, immigrant economy is augmented by the increase of employees in personal services, with an average annual wage of $16,000. These sectors in serving and selling food products, and providing spa or salon services such as massages, manicures, and pedicures, exemplify the service sweatshop economy.[23] Flushing's sleek, new towers belie the working poverty of the local labor force that walk its streets.

Labor's Terrains of Struggle

Workers at Wing Kei Noodle, Manhattan Chinatown
Photo by Antony Wong

Our analysis of QCEW data finds that the local economies of Manhattan's Chinatown, Brooklyn's Sunset Park, and Queens' Flushing have fundamentally shifted from a downgraded manufacturing economy, to a bifurcated service economy with numerous low-wage niches. These changes are directly related to new patterns of international capital flows which are turning these three neighborhoods into real estate investment strategies, and undermine the social reproduction functions and capacity of working class, immigrant communities. Under these conditions, Chinese workers in New York have a limited set of options before them: remain in their neighborhoods to face a high risk of labor precarity (e.g., unemployment) while paying obscene rents; leave the city altogether to more distant locations and (temporarily) cheaper housing; or be constant, internal migrants finding work in low-wage service sectors across the Eastern Seaboard and beyond—stretching the space-time between home and work. The latter option has become increasingly common these days.

As New York's Chinese neighborhoods become sites of global capital accumulation, they have also become command and control centers for the flow of global labor to smaller cities, suburbs and exurbs throughout the East Coast, managed through a system of "employment centers" and transported through a network of "Chinatown buses" and van services.[24,25] Today, a major function of New York's Chinese neighborhoods is to absorb Chinese surplus capital into commercial real estate projects, house the low-wage migrant workforce needed to service them, and disperse enormous numbers of newly arriving Chinese workers through the rest of the country. Immigrant neighborhoods therefore become an increasingly important frontier for global capital, as well as a terrain of struggle for migrant labor seeking a spatial foothold.[26]

As the late Peter Kwong's work has demonstrated, there is a rich history of working class militancy in Manhattan's Chinatown, and it continues today. [27,28,29,30,31] As in many other places facing deindustrialization, the neighborhood's changing economic sectors, smaller workforces, and more flexible work regimes present challenges to labor organizers. Despite these challenges, groups such as the Chinese Staff and Workers' Association (CSWA), National Mobilization Against Sweatshops (NMASS), and Asian American Legal Defense and Education Fund (AALDEF) continue to organize low-wage immigrant workers—particularly in food, retail, personal services, and construction industries—and make militant demands of both employers and state regulators.[32]

As Chinatown becomes increasingly oriented towards real estate development, social movements are now turning towards other terrains of struggle. Over the past decade, CAAAV: Organizing Asian Communities has increased their organizing presence in rent stabilized and Single Room Occupancy buildings, and secured significant victories for both long-term tenants and recent migrants. CSWA and NMASS, though not traditionally housing-based organizations, have stepped up their organizing in Chinatown's public housing and run campaigns against slumlords and luxury developers.

Chinatown Working Group

Perhaps the most embattled struggles in New York City's "Chinatowns" are over land use planning and development. After being shut out of the 2008 East Village rezoning, which established protections against large scale developments for their more affluent neighbors, neighborhood organizations and representatives joined together to form the Chinatown Working Group (CWG).[33] This large, diverse and internally contradictory coalition—at its peak with over fifty members—spent seven years debating the neighborhood's future, with conflicts over affordability, height restrictions, and economic development.

With assistance from the Pratt Center for Community Development and The Collective for Community, Culture and the Environment, the CWG called for the social preservation of Chinatown's working class culture and built environment by laying out a land use plan that promoted tenants' rights, small business retention, and community control.[34] The New York City Department of City Planning (DCP), under liberal mayor Bill de Blasio, however, rejected the plan in Spring 2015, arguing that it did not create enough opportunities for new real estate development.[35] Several members of the CWG continue to push the city to adopt its plan as official policy, and have marched against the Mayor, the New York City Council, and developers building luxury condominiums along the waterfront.

Flushing West

Former Assi Plaza, off College Point Blvd, Flushing, Queens (April 2, 2017)
Photo by Antony Wong

Flushing's waterfront has long been viewed by elected officials and city planners as an underutilized area ripe for new growth. Rezoned in the late 1990s, the Flushing waterfront became an integral component of then Mayor Bloomberg's 2004 redevelopment vision for Northern Queens, including Willets Point (a 62 acre industrial site across Flushing Creek). In 2011, a local development corporation led by a former Borough President received one of the state's largest Brownfield Opportunity Area planning grants to conduct a baseline study of a 10 block area along the Flushing waterfront. Unable to complete the $1.5 million planning study, the remaining $800,000 was turned over to the DCP in 2015, which then proceeded to fold the research into a rezoning study.[36] The Flushing waterfront, now dubbed "Flushing West" by DCP, was selected by the de Blasio administration to undergo a rezoning as part of the Mayor's ambitious, but highly contested, *Housing New York* plan, centered on Mandatory Inclusionary Housing (MIH).[37] MIH requires residential developers in newly upzoned areas to provide 25-30% below market rate housing, either inside a new development or somewhere off site.

The Flushing Rezoning Community Alliance (FRCA)—a coalition of local community, social service, and faith-based organizations including the MinKwon Center for Community Action—formed to advocate for the neighborhood's racially diverse, working class population concentrated in the Downtown area, which also includes two NYCHA complexes. At a March 2016 community meeting, FRCA successfully secured a promise from New York City Council Member Peter Koo to only support the Flushing rezoning if it included housing for those earning 40% Area Median Income (AMI), or about $34,500 (which is significantly below the MIH's affordability categories of 60% and 80% AMI). While Koo's concession was considered a small victory in the community's struggle for equitable development, a few months later, he announced his opposition to DCP's Flushing West study and requested that it be halted. Stating concerns with strained infrastructure and outstanding environmental issues, Koo also stated that, "(D)evelopers also have told me that the numbers don't work." In the meantime, DCP's "pause" of the Flushing West rezoning has not translated into a slowdown in market rate development.[38] In fact, FRCA's fears that "a path of unchecked real estate profit for multi-national corporations on the backs of working class and immigrant New Yorkers," remains unabated.[39]

Illegal Conversions

Housing & jobs bulletin board in Sunset Park, Brooklyn
Photo courtesy of Tarry Hum

The high rate of Chinese working poverty in Brooklyn's Sunset Park is augmented by the prevalence of poor housing conditions, including overcrowding and illegal conversions. A common sight in New York City's "Chinatowns" are bulletin boards with numerous notices publicizing single rooms for rent. Many houses are subdivided into residential units (typically a single room) that exceed the property's certificate of occupancy. Sunset Park's hyper-speculative real estate market is the driving force behind such predatory landlord practices.[40] Investor-owners seek illegal conversion in order to maximize rental profits. Homeowners may similarly seek to capture untapped profits, or may need rental income to support ballooning mortgage debt. In either scenario, Sunset Park's modest two-family row houses have become "modern-day tenements" where working class immigrant families are struggling to afford a single, substandard room rather than an apartment.[41]

Brooklyn's Sunset Park anchors the fast growing Chinese immigrant population in neighboring South Brooklyn areas such as Dyker Heights, Bay Ridge, Bensonhurst, and Homecrest. Representing several of these neighborhoods, New York City Council Member Vincent Gentile's "Aggravated Illegal Conversions" bill was recently signed into law by Mayor de Blasio. This law increases the civil penalties to $15,000 per dwelling unit for illegally subdivided residential properties with three or more units beyond the number legally permitted.[42] Unpaid penalties constitute a property tax lien that the City can recoup through a forced sale. While the bill has tremendous appeal for Gentile's base of middle-class White homeowners, by empowering the state to police and vacate illegal conversions—and potentially dispossess offending property owners—it offers no protections for tenants in a housing market where the only source of "affordable" rental housing typically entails risk to personal safety and arbitrary eviction.

*   *   *

As long as real estate properties are viewed as investment vehicles with tremendous untapped value, predatory activities such as illegal conversions, harassment, eviction and speculative development will continue to shape the residential landscape of New York City's "Chinatown" neighborhoods. As real estate investment in these neighborhoods become central to their local-global economies, such pressure will only increase. In each neighborhood, labor strategies have had to evolve to encompass an existential fight over housing, land and planning, in addition to jobs, wages and hours. The transformations that Chinatown, Sunset Park and Flushing are undergoing not only are remaking the neighborhoods' built environments and economic sectors, but also the modes of struggle labor utilizes to reproduce itself and make political claims.

Notes

1   Samuel Stein, "Chinatown: Unprotected and Undone," in Tom Angotti and Sylvia Morse (eds.), *Zoned Out! Race, Displacement and City Planning in New York City* (New York: Urban Research, 2016).

2   Tarry Hum, *Making a Global Immigrant Neighborhood: Brooklyn's Sunset Park* (Philadelphia: Temple University Press, 2014).

3   Tarry Hum and Samuel Stein, "Flushing's Affordable Housing at Risk," *Gotham Gazette* (May 2, 2016).

4   Alejandro Portes and Julia Sensenbrenner, "Embeddedness and Immigration: Notes on the Social Determinants of Economic Action," *American Journal of Sociology* 98:6 (1993): 1320–1350.

5   Peter Kwong, *The New Chinatown* (New York: Hill and Wang, 1987).

6   Peter Kwong and Dusanka Miščević, *Chinese America: The Untold Story of America's Oldest New Community* (New York, The New Press, 2005).

7   Rey Mashayekhi, "Gary Barnett's Big Downtown Bet," *Commercial Observer* (March 15, 2017).

8   Hum, *Making a Global Immigrant Neighborhood*.

9   Christopher J. Smith and John R. Logan, "Flushing 2000: Geographic Explorations in Asian New York," *From Urban Enclave to Ethnic Suburb: New Asian Communities in Pacific Rim Countries* (Honolulu: University of Hawai'i Press, 2006): 41–73.

10 Christopher J. Smith, "Asian New York: The Geography and Politics of Diversity," *International Migration Review* 29:1 (1995): 59–84.

11 Ruth W. Gilmore, *Golden Gulag: Prisons, Surplus, Crisis, and Opposition in Globalizing California* (Berkeley: University of California Press, 2007).

12 Kevin F. Gotham and Miriam Greenberg, *Crisis Cities: Disaster and Redevelopment in New York and New Orleans* (Oxford University Press, 2014).

13 Kwong and Miščević, *Chinese America*.

14 William I. Robinson and Jerry Harris, "Towards a Global Ruling Class? Globalization and the Transnational Capitalist Class," *Science & Society* 64:1 (2000): 11–54.

15 Cindi Katz, "Vagabond Capitalism and the Necessity of Social Reproduction," *Antipode* 33:4 (2001): 709–728.

16 Kenneth Rosen, Arthur Margon, Randall Sakamoto, and John Taylor, *Breaking Ground: Chinese Investment in U.S. Real Estate* (Asia Society, 2016).

17 We define Manhattan Chinatown as zip codes 10002 and 10013, Sunset Park as 11220 and 11232, and Flushing as 11354 and 11355.

18 Jonathan LaMantia, "NYU Langone Moves Ahead with Lutheran Medical Center Merger," *Crain's New York Business* (July 21, 2015).

19 Ruth Ford, "Hospital Closures and Medicaid Shifts Took Toll on NYC's Health," *City Limits* (January 4, 2017).

20 Given possible seasonality in industry sectors, I calculated the average wage for Flushing's private sector employees in the 4Q 2015, and while the 2000-2015 difference was not as steep, the trend remains indisputably one of wage decline.

21 Hum, *Making a Global Immigrant Neighborhood*.

22 One Flushing, "Flushing's Economy: Challenges and Opportunities," *Community Profile May 2013* (Asian Ameicans for Equality, 2013).

23 Community Development Project at Urban Justice Center, Employment Law Unit at The Legal Aid Society, and National Center for Law and Economic Justice, *Empty Judgments: The Wage Collection Crisis in NY* (2015), https://cdp.urbanjustice.org/cdp-reports/emptyjudgements

24 Zai Liang and Bo Zhou, "The Rise of Market-based Job Search Institutions and Job Niches for Low-skilled Chinese Immigrants," *Journal of Social Science* (Russell Sage Foundation, 2017).

25 Kenneth J. Guest, "From Mott Street to East Broadway: Fuzhounese Immigrants and the Revitalization of New York's China-town," *Journal of Chinese Overseas* 7:1 (2011): 24–44.

26 Saskia Sassen, "When the Center No Longer Holds: Cities as Frontier Zones," *Cities* 34 (2013): 67–70.

27 Kwong, *The New Chinatown.*

28 Kwong and Miščević, *Chinese America.*

29 Peter Kwong, *Chinatown, NY: Labor and Politics, 1930–1950* (New York: Monthly Review Press, 1979).

30 Peter Kwong, *Forbidden Workers: Illegal Chinese Immigrants and American Labor* (New York: The New Press, 1997).

31 Peter Kwong and Samuel Stein, "Preserve and Protect Chinatown," *Issue Briefs* (Roosevelt House Public Policy Institute at Hunter College, 2015).

32 Community Development Project, *Empty Judgments.*

33 B.Y. Li, "Zoned Out: Chinatown and Lower East Side Residents and Business Owners Fight to Stay in New York City," *Asian American Policy Review* 19 (2009): 91–97.

34 Pratt Center for Community Development and The Collective for Community, Culture and the Environment, P*reserving Affordability & Authenticity: Recommendations to the Chinatown Working Group* (Chinatown Working Group, 2013), http://www.chinatownworkinggroup.org/2014-01-01%20Pratt%20Report%20to%20CWG.pdf

35 Abigail Savitch-Lew, "Chinatown Zoning Plan Meets Resistance in de Blasio Administration," *City Limits* (September 15, 2015).

36 Rebecca Baird-Remba, "City Unveils Details On Flushing West Rezoning: A Waterfront Promenade And A Possible Bus Terminal," *YIMBY* (October 9, 2015).

37 Bill de Blasio, "State of the City: Mayor de Blasio Puts Affordable Housing at Center of 2015 Agenda to Fight Inequality," *New York City Office of the Mayor* (February 3, 2015), http://www1.nyc.gov/office-of-the-mayor/news/088-15/state-the-city-mayor-de-blasio-puts-affordable-housing-center-2015-agenda-fight#/0

38 Abigail Savitch-Lew, "City Says Flushing Rezoning is 'Paused,' Not Dead; Some Investments Still on Track," *City Limits* (June 2, 2016).

39 Flushing Rezoning Community Alliance, *Flushing West: Recommendations for a Just Rezoning* (2016), http://minkwon.org/downloads/FRCA_Flushing_White_Paper_28apr16.pdf

40 Tarry Hum, "Illegal Conversions and South Brooklyn's Affordable Housing Crisis," *Gotham Gazette* (September 19, 2016).

41 Konrad Putzier and Cathaleen Chen, "NYC's multibillion-dollar enigma: A deep dive into the inner workings of the city's Chinese immigrant real estate market," *The Real Deal* (October 3, 2016).

42 Paula Katinas, "City Starts Crackdown on Illegal Home Conversions," *Brooklyn Daily Eagle* (June 6, 2017).

Authors

Tarry Hum is a Professor of Urban Studies at Queens College/CUNY and the CUNY Graduate Center. She is the author of *Making a Global Immigrant Neighborhood: Brooklyn's Sunset Park* which received a 2015 Honorable Mention for the Association of Collegiate Schools of Planning's Paul Davidoff Award. Hum is co-editing a forthcoming volume from Temple University Press, *Immigrant Crossroads: Globalization, Incorporation, and Placemaking in Queens, NY.*

Samuel Stein is a geography Ph.D. student at the CUNY Graduate Center and an Urban Studies instructor at Hunter College/CUNY. His work has been featured in various journals and magazines, including *Metropolitics*, *Progressive Planning*, *City Limits*, and *Jacobin*. His first book will be published by Verso in 2018.

A Guide to Responding to Microaggressions
Revisited

KEVIN L. NADAL

"Microaggressions are commonplace verbal, behavioral, or environmental actions that communicate hostility toward oppressed or targeted groups."

The New Landscape of Microaggressions

WHEN I FIRST WROTE THIS ESSAY on microaggressions for *CUNY FORUM* in 2014, the world was a different place. Barack Obama was President of the United States; state laws were changing slowly, but surely, to allow same-sex couples to marry; and people seemed to be more comfortable in recognizing the ways that racism, sexism, heterosexism, and other forms of discrimination were manifesting in our lives. Researchers argued that subtle forms of discrimination were becoming more common than overt forms of discrimination, and the term microaggressions began to gain traction. Hundreds of academic articles on microaggressions have been written, and thousands of articles and videos on microaggressions have been published in mainstream media sources, like *Time Magazine*, *The New York Times*, *Buzzfeed*, and more.[1,2] In 2017, the term microaggressions officially entered into the Merriam-Webster dictionary, indicating its emergence in the American vernacular.

Despite this, when Donald Trump announced his run for the presidency in 2015, he made comments that Mexicans were rapists and criminals, and that Muslims should be banned from the country. Weeks before the 2016 presidential election, recorded comments by Mr. Trump bragging about "grabbing women by the pussy" emerged, as well as women who alleged to being sexually assaulted or sexually harassed by him. When Mr. Trump won the electoral vote over Hillary Clinton (though she won the popular vote by almost three million), it became clear that some people were much more accepting of overt discrimination, or that they were at least willing to overlook it in Mr. Trump.

The day after the presidential election, hate crimes began to commence towards almost all minority groups. The Southern Law Poverty Center (2017) reported that in the month after the election, across the U.S., there were 315 hate crimes targeting immigrants; 221 hate crimes targeting Black people; 112 hate crimes targeting Muslims; and 109 hate crimes targeting LGBTQ people.[3] In February 2017, an Indian immigrant man named Srinivas Kuchibhotla (an engineer who had lived in the U.S. for over a decade) was gunned down in Kansas by a White American man who screamed, "Get out of our country!"[4]

While microaggressions are still a persistent part of people's lives, people of historically marginalized groups may now have to navigate both overt and more subtle discrimination in their everyday lives. As you read my original article on microaggressions, I challenge you, the reader, to reflect on how the notion that overt discrimination has always been present and persisted through the years, and also how some people from historically privileged groups may feel emboldened to act upon them. Perhaps it could be due to years of frustration of having to recognize liberal and progressive politics that emerged as the norm under the Obama administration. Or perhaps it could be due to a fear of losing their own power and privilege, as the minority becomes the majority. Regardless, in this world of uncertainty, it is important to strategize ways to combat microaggressions, while also fighting against overt oppression on all levels.

Microaggressions Guide

Racial	• *Assumptions of Criminality* (i.e., when people of color are assumed to be dangerous or deviant). For instance, if a clerk follows an African American around in a store, she or he is presuming that the person of color is going to steal.[5] • *Exoticization* (i.e., when people of color are objectified or treated as tokens). A common occurrence is when a non-Asian man tells an Asian American woman that she is so "exotic," or that "he has an Asian fetish." • *Assumptions of Intellectual Inferiority* (i.e., when people of color are assumed to be less intelligent or capable than whites). An example is someone overemphasizing to a Latina that she is "so articulate" (subtly communicating that they did not expect her to be). • *Pathologizing Cultural Values* (i.e., when people of color are criticized for their communication styles, behaviors, styles of dress). For instance, when an Asian American or Latina/o/x is told to "get rid of your accent," a subtle message is sent that one needs to assimilate.[6]
Gender	• *Sexual Objectification* (i.e., when a woman is treated as a sexual object). For instance, when a woman is catcalled on the street, or a man gazes at a woman's breasts, he is communicating that women's bodies are allowed to be sexualized. • *Assumptions of Traditional Gender Roles* (i.e., when an individual assumes that a woman needs to uphold traditional gender roles). For example, many women are told that they need to have a husband in order to be happy. • *Assumptions of Inferiority* (i.e., when a woman is assumed to be physically or intellectually incompetent, particularly in comparison to men). One illustration is when a woman is carrying a box and a man takes it away from her (without her permission), assuming she isn't physically strong.[7]
LGBTQ	• *Use of heterosexist or transphobic terminology* (i.e., when offensive language is used towards or about LGBTQ people). For instance, it is commonplace for young people to use the word "faggot" casually when describing someone as weak. • *Discomfort/ Disapproval of LGBTQ experience* (i.e., when LGBTQ individuals are treated with disrespect or condemnation because of their sexual orientation or gender presentation). One example includes a person staring at a same-sex couple holding hands, while another may be someone who makes prejudicial remarks about a transgender person. • *Assumption of Sexual Pathology and Abnormality* (i.e., when LGBTQ persons are presumed to be oversexualized or sexual deviants). One instance includes when someone presumes that all LGBTQ people may have HIV/AIDS, or stereotypes LGBTQ people as child molesters.
Religious	• *Endorsing religious stereotypes* (i.e., when people make presumptions about religious minority groups). An example is when someone makes a joke about Muslim people being terrorists or Jewish people being cheap.[8] • *Pathology of different religious groups* (i.e., when someone judges another religion as being inferior or substandard). For instance, when someone treats a non-Christian as a second-class citizen.[9]
Intersectional	• Occurs as a result of an individual's multiple groups and may influence the intensity or frequency of microaggressions. • Women of color may experience intersectional microaggressions as a result of their gender and race (e.g., a Latina who is denied service at a restaurant or store because of both her race and gender). • LGBTQ persons of color may experience intersectional microaggressions as a result of their sexual identity and race. For example, when a passersby ridicules a Black transgender woman, it can be due to her gender identity, her race, or both.

What Are Microaggressions?

In recent years, academic literature has increasingly focused on the subject of microaggressions. Microaggressions are brief and commonplace verbal, behavioral, or environmental actions (whether intentional or unintentional) that communicate hostile, derogatory, or negative racial slights and insults toward members of oppressed or targeted groups[10] including: people of color, women, Lesbian, Gay, Bisexual, Transgender and Queer (LGBTQ) persons, persons with disabilities, and religious minorities.[11] Some scholars today argue that racism, sexism, homophobia, and other forms of discrimination are no longer as blatant as they may have been in the past. Instead, people may demonstrate their biases and prejudices in more subtle ways, otherwise known as microaggressions.[12] The purpose of this article is twofold: (1) to discuss how different types of microaggressions affect people's lives, and (2) to provide a hands-on guide to strategies, approaches, and interventions to address microaggressions.

Types of Microaggressions

Derald Wing Sue and colleagues first described three forms of microaggressions:

> *Microassaults* are overt forms of discrimination in which actors deliberately behave in discriminatory ways, but do not intend to offend someone or may think that their actions are not noticed or harmful.[13] These types of experiences are similar to the "old-fashioned" discrimination that existed in earlier times, but different in that people may not openly proclaim their biases. For example, when someone says "That's so gay!" to connote that something is weird, the person is aware of the words that they choose; however, they may not realize that using such language is considered homophobic and can offend LGBTQ people. Similarly, when a comedian makes a racial joke or uses racial slurs, they intended to say the offensive comment, but would often end with "I was just joking" as a way of denying prejudice.
>
> *Microinsults* are statements or behaviors in which individuals unintentionally or unconsciously communicate discriminatory messages to members of target groups. For example, a person might tell an Asian American that they "speak good English" as a compliment. However, in reality, such a statement can be offensive to Asian Americans, implying that Asian persons do not speak English fluently. Instances like these can be especially upsetting to Asian Americans who do not speak any other language besides English, or whose families have been in the U.S. for three or more generations.
>
> *Microinvalidations* are verbal statements that deny, negate, or undermine the realities of members of various target groups. For example, when a white person tells a person of color that racism does not exist, they are invalidating and denying the person of color's racial reality. Similarly, when someone tells a woman that she is "being too sensitive," or that an LGBTQ person "should stop complaining," they invalidate the reality of discrimination in these people's lives.

How Do Microaggressions Affect People?

While some people may believe that microaggressions are brief and harmless, many studies have found that microaggressions have a significant negative impact on people's mental and physical health. For instance, a recent study has found that the more racial microaggressions that people of color experience, the more likely they are to also report depressive symptoms and a negative view of the world.[14] In another study, LGBTQ participants reported that when they experienced microaggressions, they felt depressed, anxious, and even traumatized.[15]

Other researchers have found many other harmful effects of microaggressions. One study found that when college students experience microaggressions, they also binge drink or develop other alcohol-related issues.[16] Two other studies found a relationship between microaggressions and intense psychological distress.[17]

How Can I Respond to Microaggressions?

What are you supposed to do when you are the victim of a microaggression? In an article on racial micro-aggressions, Sue and colleagues discussed the "Catch 22" that people experience when they witness or are recipients of microaggressions.[18] First, the individual may question if a microaggression has really occurred (i.e., "Did I hear him correctly when he made that comment?"). Next, the individual decides whether or not to take action. If the individual does respond, there is a likely outcome (e.g., arguments, defensiveness, denials, or additional microaggressions). If the individual does not respond, there is also an outcome (e.g., regret, resentment, sadness). Thus, the process of deciding how to respond to a microaggression can be stressful in itself.

In my research, I describe a three-step process that assists an individual with how to react to a micro-aggression by asking themselves the following:[19]

1. Did this microaggression really occur?

2. Should I respond to this microaggression?

3. How should I respond to this microaggression?

Did This Microaggression Really Occur?

Sometimes microaggressions may be so flagrantly obvious that a person can identify them effortlessly. For instance, when a man of color notices that a white woman clutches her purse as he enters an elevator, he may be able to identify this as a microaggression immediately. This has happened hundreds of times in his life and he is confident that she is assuming him to be a criminal. Similarly, when a person says "That's so gay!" in front of an LGBTQ person, the LGBTQ individual recognizes that the person is clearly using homophobic language.

With some encounters, an individual may question whether a microaggression has happened. For example, if a woman hears someone whistle as she walks down a street, she may think, "Did that really just happen or am I hearing things?" Similarly, if a coworker makes a seemingly transphobic comment in front of a transgender female colleague, the recipient might question whether she heard the statement correctly. When there are people around (particularly people who the individual trusts) to verify and validate the microaggression, it makes it easier for the individual to definitively label the event as a microaggression.

When there is no one around, it may be helpful to seek support from loved ones. For instance, with modern technology, people can easily call, text, email, or communicate with their social media networks about microaggressions. I myself have seen many people update their status on Facebook, describing micro-aggressions that happened to them on the subway or on the sidewalks. Most of the time, people respond in supportive ways.

Should I Respond to This Microaggression?

If an individual is certain (or moderately certain) that a microaggression did in fact occur, they have to ponder the potential risks or consequences of responding or not responding. Some questions include:

1. If I respond, could my physical safety be in danger?

2. If I respond, will the person become defensive and will this lead to an argument?

3. If I respond, how will this affect my relationship with this person (e.g., coworker, family member, etc.)

4. If I don't respond, will I regret not saying something?

5. If I don't respond, does that convey that I accept the behavior or statement?

How Should I Respond to This Microaggression?

If individuals do decide to take action, they must contemplate how to react. First, they can approach the situation in a passive-aggressive way. For instance, perhaps the victims make a joke or a sarcastic comment as a way of communicating that they are upset or annoyed. Perhaps the victims respond by rolling their eyes or sighing. Or, they do nothing in that moment and decide to talk to others about it first, in the hopes that it will get back to the perpetrator.

Second, victims can react in a proactive way. This might be effective when the victim simply does not have the energy to engage the perpetrator in a discussion. Sometimes individuals who experience microaggressions regularly may feel so agitated that they just want to yell back. For some individuals, an active response may be a therapeutic way of releasing years of accumulated anger and frustration.

Finally, an individual may act in an assertive way. This may include calmly addressing the perpetrator about how it made them feel. This may consist of educating the perpetrators, describing what was offensive about the microaggression. Oftentimes the perpetrator will become defensive, which may lead to further microaggressions (particularly microinvalidations). It may be important to use "I" statements (e.g., "I felt hurt when you said that."), instead of attacking statements (e.g., "You're a racist!"). It also may be important to address the behavior and not the perpetrator. What this means is that instead of calling the perpetrator "a racist," it might be best to say that the behavior they engaged in was racially charged and offensive. People don't like being called a racist, sexist or homophobe, so if you want to have an effective dialogue with a person without being defensive, it may be best to avoid using such language.

When the entire interaction is over, it is important for the victim of the microaggression to seek support. Seeking support can include practical support (e.g., if someone experiences microaggressions at a workplace, they can file a complaint with Human Resources). Individuals can also seek social support (e.g., talking to your loved ones or peers with similar identities who can validate your experiences). Processing one's emotions is also important because microaggressions have been known to lead to an array of mental health problems including depression, anxiety, and trauma.[20] Therefore, individuals who experience microaggressions may find it helpful and necessary to discuss their cognitive and emotional reactions with their loved ones or mental health professionals. In doing so, individuals may avoid accumulating negative and detrimental feelings, which may affect their mental health.

What If I Commit a Microaggression?

First of all, everyone commits microaggressions. We have all done or said something that we may not have intended to offend someone, but somehow still ended up doing so. Sometimes we are aware of our actions, and other times it takes another person to point them out to you. If we were completely unaware that something we said or did was hurtful or offensive, there really isn't anything we can do. However, when we are even slightly aware that we may have committed a microaggression or if we are confronted about it, there are several things that we can do.

When someone's behavior is noticeable, we might be able to detect that something we said or did may have caused it. If you are able to detect the potential cause, OWN UP TO IT! We need to admit when we commit microaggressions, learn from the wrongdoing, and apologize. We all make mistakes, consciously and not, and need to own up to them when we do.

For moments in which someone confronts you on your behavior, listen to what they are trying to tell you and try not to be defensive. The worst thing that we can do is to deny that someone is hurt or offended by something we said or did. In fact, invalidating their experience could be considered a microaggression in itself. So again, admit to the wrongdoing and genuinely apologize.

Furthermore, there are things that we can do to avoid microaggressions altogether. First, be aware of the language that you use. Common phrases like "That's so gay!" often go under the radar because people do not realize that the language is actually homophobic and insulting. If something is weird, say it is weird!

Why does it have to be called gay? Be aware of other subtle messages. For example, the color white is often used to convey that something is good (e.g., little white lie, white collar), while the color black is used to denote that something is bad (e.g., black sheep, blackmail, Black Friday).

Finally, education about microaggressions is important. The more people are aware of the term and concept, the less likely they will be defensive when confronted about their behaviors. If we teach kids about diversity and equality from a very early age, we have the power to transform them into open-minded adults. Let us teach our kids to not be afraid, but rather to respect each other.

AAARI Lecture Video (November 8, 2013): www.aaari.info/13-11-08Nadal.htm

Notes

1   John Eligon, Alan Blinder, and Nida Najar, "Hate Crime Is Feared as 2 Indian Engineers Are Shot in Kansas," *The New York Times* (February 24, 2017), https://www.nytimes.com/2017/02/24/world/asia/kansas-attack-possible-hate-crime-srinivas-kuchibhotla.html

2   Kevin L. Nadal, Chassitty N. Whitman, Lindsey S. Davis, Tanya Erazo, and Kristin C. Davidoff, "Microaggressions Toward Lesbian, Gay, Bisexual, Transgender, Queer and Genderqueer People: A Review of the Literature," *The Journal of Sex Research* 53 (2016): 488-508.

3   Hatewatch Staff, "Update: 1,094 Bias-Related Incidents in the Month Following the Election," *Southern Poverty Law Center* (December 16, 2016), https://www.splcenter.org/hatewatch/2016/12/16/update-1094-bias-related-incidents-month-following-election

4   Gloria Wong, Annie O. Derthick, E. J. R. David, Anne Saw, and Sumie Okazaki, "The What, the Why, and the How: A Review of Racial Microaggressions Research in Psychology," *Race and Social Problems* 6 (2014):181-200.

5   Derald Wing Sue, Kevin Leo Nadal, Christina M. Capodilupo, Annie I. Lin, Gina C. Torino, and David P. Rivera, "Racial Microaggressions Against Black Americans: Implications for Counseling," *Journal of Counseling and Development*, 86:3 (2008): 330-338.

6   David P. Rivera, Erin E. Forquer, and Rebecca Rangel, "Microaggressions and the Life Experience of Latina/o Americans," D. W. Sue ed., *Microaggressions and Marginality: Manifestation, Dynamics, and Impact* (New York: Wiley & Sons, 2010): 59-84.

7   Christina M. Capodilupo, Kevin Leo Nadal, Lindsay Corman, Sahran Hamit, Oliver B. Lyons, and Alexa Weinberg, "The Manifestation of Gender Microaggressions," Derald Wing Sue, ed., *Microaggressions and Marginality: Manifestation, Dynamics, and Impact* (New York: Wiley & Sons, 2010): 193-216; Kevin Leo Nadal, Marie-Anne Issa, Jayleen Leon, Vanessa Meterko, Michelle Wideman, and Yinglee Wong, "Sexual Orientation Microaggressions: Psychological Impacts on Lesbian, Gay, and Bisexual Youth," *Journal of LGBT Youth*, 8:3 (2011).

8   Kevin Leo Nadal, Katie E. Griffin, Sahran Hamit, Jayleen Leon, Michael Tobio, and David P. Rivera, "Subtle and Overt Forms of Islamophobia: Microaggressions toward Muslim Americans," *Journal of Muslim Mental Health* 6:2 (2012): 16-37.

9   Kevin Leo Nadal, *That's So Gay! Microaggressions and the Lesbian, Gay, Bisexual, and Transgender Community* (Washington, DC: American Psychological Association, 2013).

10   Kevin Leo Nadal, "Preventing Racial, Ethnic, Gender, Sexual Minority, Disability, and Religious Microaggressions: Recommendations for Promoting Positive Mental Health," *Prevention in Counseling Psychology: Theory, Research, Practice and Training* 2:1 (2008): 22-27.

11   Daniel Solorzano, Miguel Ceja, and Tara Yosso, "Critical Race Theory, Racial Microaggressions, and Campus Racial Climate: The Experiences of African American College Students," *Journal of Negro Education* 69 (2000): 60–73.

12   C. Pierce, J. Carew, D. Pierce-Gonzalez, and D. Willis, "An Experiment in Racism: TV Commercial," C. Pierce, ed., *Television And Education* (Beverly Hills: Sage, 1978): 62–88.

13   Derald Wing Sue, Jennifer M. Bucceri, Annie I. Lin, Kevin Leo Nadal, and Gina C. Torino, "Racial Microaggressions and the Asian American Experience," *Cultural Diversity and Ethnic Minority Psychology*, 13:1 (2007): 72–81; Derald Wing Sue, Christina M. Capodilupo, Gina C. Torino, Jennifer M. Bucceri, Aisha M. Holder, Kevin Leo Nadal, and Marta Esquilin, "Racial Microaggressions In Everyday Life: Implications For Counseling," *The American Psychologist* 62:4 (2007): 271–286.

14   Kevin Leo Nadal, Katie E. Griffin, Yinglee Wong, Sahran Hamit, and Morgan Rasmus, "Racial Microaggressions and Mental Health: Counseling Clients of Color," *Journal of Counseling and Development* 92:1 (2014): 57–66.

15   Kevin Leo Nadal, Yinglee Wong, Marie-Anne Issa, Vanessa Meterko, Jayleen Leon, and Michelle Wideman, "Sexual Orientation Microaggressions: Processes and Coping Mechanisms For Lesbian, Gay, and Bisexual Individuals," *Journal of LGBT Issues in Counseling* 5:1 (2011): 21–46.

16 Arthur W. Blume, Laura V. Lovato, Bryan N. Thyken, and Natasha Denny, "The Relationship of Microaggressions With Alcohol Use and Anxiety Among Ethnic Minority College Students in a Historically White Institution," *Cultural Diversity and Ethnic Minority Psychology* 18:1 (2012): 45–54.

17 William A. Smith, Man Hung, and Jeremy D. Franklin, "Racial Battle Fatigue and the 'Mis'Education of Black Men: Racial Microaggressions, Societal Problems, and Environmental Stress," *Journal of Negro Education*, 80:1 (2011): 63–82; Jennifer Wang, Janxin Leu, and Yuichi Shoda, "When the Seemingly Innocuous 'Stings': Racial Microaggressions and Their Emotional Consequences," *Personality and Social Psychology Bulletin* 37:12 (2011): 1666–1678.

18 Derald Wing Sue, Christina M. Capodilupo, Gina C. Torino, Jennifer M. Bucceri, Aisha M. Holder, Kevin Leo Nadal, and Marta Esquilin, "Racial Microaggressions In Everyday Life: Implications For Counseling," *The American Psychologist* 62:4 (2007): 271–286.

19 Kevin Leo Nadal, "Responding To Racial, Gender, and Sexual Orientation Microaggressions in The Workplace," Michele A. Paludi, Eros R. DeSouza & Carmen A. Paludi Jr., eds., *The Praeger Handbook on Understanding and Preventing Workplace Discrimination: Legal, Management, and Social Science Perspectives* (Santa Barbara, CA: Praeger, 2011).

20 Kevin Leo Nadal, *That's So Gay! Microaggressions and the Lesbian, Gay, Bisexual, and Transgender Community* (Washington, DC: American Psychological Association, 2013).

Author

Kevin L. Nadal is a Professor of Psychology at John Jay College of Criminal Justice/CUNY and the CUNY Graduate Center. Prof. Nadal studies the harmful impacts of microaggressions, or subtle forms of discrimination, on the mental and physical health of people of color, lesbian, gay, bisexual, and transgender (LGBTQ) people, and other marginalized groups. He was the first person of color to serve as Executive Director of the Center for LGBTQ Studies (from 2014 to 2017), and the first openly gay president of the Asian American Psychological Association (from 2015-2017).

Prof. Nadal has published seven books and over a hundred works on multicultural issues in the fields of psychology and education, including *Filipino American Psychology: A Handbook of Theory, Research, and Clinical Practice* (John Wiley and Sons, 2011), *That's So Gay!: Microaggressions and the Lesbian, Gay, Bisexual, and Transgender Community* (APA Books, 2013), and *Sage Encyclopedia of Psychology and Gender* (Sage, 2017). He also contributes to *HuffPost* and *Buzzfeed*, and was the recipient of the highly-coveted 2017 American Psychological Association Award for Contributions to Psychology in the Public Interest.

Digital Archives on Asian America for Research and Teaching

RAYMOND PUN & MOLLY HIGGINS

Following an earlier publication on digital collections and archives on Asian and Asian American Studies for CUNY FORUM, Volume 1:1, this updated article provides a selection of new digital resources relating to Asian American Studies. This list is a compilation of visual resources in Asian American Studies and cultures, with an emphasis on how teachers, librarians, and educators can access and utilize them for instructional purposes.

Introduction

TODAY, LIBRARIES AND ARCHIVES are scrambling for funds to digitize their hidden collections for researchers and educators to discover and use in their projects or programs. These collections of varying sizes, digitized and undigitized, exist across government organizations, academic special collections, and community organizations. The first systematic attempt to map these collections was the Asian/Pacific American Archives Survey Project, established in 2008 by New York University.[1]

While this project made significant progress in illuminating hidden archival collections, especially undigitized collections, the project was last updated in 2015 and is far from comprehensive. It is critical to continue to highlight different Asian American groups, particularly in today's politicized landscape across immigration rights, diversity, and civil liberties. There are many well known digital collections such as the Digital Collections of the New York Public Library (NYPL) and the Library of Congress that have been highlighted in a previous article.[2] In this essay, we highlight several new resources relevant to Asian American Studies (including one on Asian Canadian experiences) that have been digitized and how educators can consider using these collections as teaching aids.

Southeast Asian American Archive (SEAAdoc)

University of California, Irvine (UC Irvine) Libraries created the Southeast Asian American Archive. According to their website, this educational resource focuses on post-1975-refugees and immigrants from Cambodia, Laos, and Vietnam and the communities they have developed in the U.S.[3] With over 1,500 photographs, visual images and 4,000 digitized sites, documents, and texts from UC Irvine Libraries, the collection can be used to explore the experiences and lives of Southeast Asian Americans in a historical study. From their experiences as refugees in camps to resettlement in the U.S., these powerful materials may serve as important teaching tools for educators to consider: teaching the history of immigrants and refugee experiences in the U.S. in today's politicized rhetoric on the immigration issue.

SEAAdoc
http://seaadoc.lib.uci.edu/

Pioneering Punjabis Digital Archive
http://pioneeringpunjabis.ucdavis.edu/

One undeveloped feature to note is that the "Teach" tab has not been updated recently. However, this repository can still be used in classrooms for students to search for specific Asian groups in the U.S. and write about topics such as newsletters by Cambodian Americans, or performance images from Laotian women. The site also has a reproduction tab in case researchers would like to incorporate these images in their own publications.

Japanese American Relocation Digital Archives (JARDA)

2017 marked the 75th anniversary of President Franklin D. Roosevelt signing Executive Order 9066 on February 19, 1942, designating military zones as internment camps for Japanese Americans in the U.S. during World War II.

The University of Southern California (USC) digitized a series of photographs from the Hearst Collection of the *Los Angeles Herald Examiner*. There are over 200 photos that capture the lives of Japanese immigrants and Japanese Americans living in California from 1921 to 1958, depicting their lives before and after their relocation during the war. According to the Achives' website, photos include internment camp experiences in selected areas such as Manzanar, Santa Anita, Tanforan, and Tule Lake.[4] In addition, it also covers the post-war repatriation to Japan.

Educators will find this photo repository useful for teaching about this tragic moment in American history, and how Japanese Americans lived and survived internment. Their experiences in these black and white photos are an excellent primary source for documenting the clothes and material goods of the period. Through their facial expressions, much is revealed about the untold stories and lived experiences of these American citizens. For those interested in teaching students about Executive Order 9066, this digital archive would be the best place to start for classroom discussions. These photos are freely available for anyone to browse online and the site contains "cultural references that reflect 1940s terminology."

Pioneering Punjabis in America Digital Archive

From the University of California, Davis (UC Davis), the Pioneering Punjabis Digital Archive is a new digital archive focusing on the South Asian American experience. According to the site, the archive offers a glimpse of South Asians as they immigrated from the Punjab region of northern India to California during the 20th century.[5] There are over 700 multimedia resources such as videos, interviews, speeches, diaries, images, photographs, texts, letters, and documents from Punjabi Americans and their stories and experiences in California's history for the past 120 years.

Although the site is limited with basic tab features, it still contains a wealth of information on different Punjabi communities in California. From farming to religion to cultural festivals, the digital archive brings together resources and stories of the contributions made by Punjabi Americans in America. Educators may find the "Classroom Toolkit" and "Sample Teaching Plan" helpful in teaching about the South Asian diaspora in American history. There is a lot of potential with this site, and also the possibility of expanding into different directions covering other South Asian Americans as well. This resource would also complement the South Asian American Digital Archive (SAADA) site and offer an array of resources in primary sources on the lives of South Asian Americans.[6]

Densho
http://www.densho.org/

Calisphere
https://calisphere.org/cal-cultures/

Densho: The Japanese American Legacy Project

The Densho digital archive focuses broadly on the Japanese American experience from early immigration in the early 1900s through the movement for redress in the 1980s, with a special focus on the mass incarceration of Japanese Americans during World War II.[7] This digital collection includes a wealth of oral histories, photos, documents, and newspapers. The video interviews are fully transcribed and segmented for ease of viewing. The interviews and images are indexed by topic, location and chronology, and can be searched using keywords.

The archive is part of a larger nonprofit, dedicated not only to preserving the history of Japanese Americans, but also educating people about the history of Japanese internment and linking it to the state of civil liberties today. To this end, Densho provides context for the materials, including an encyclopedia, curricula for students in Grades 5-12, and an historical narrative that they call the "core story."

Calisphere: California Cultures

Calisphere is part of the California Digital Library, which works across all of the University of California Libraries to improve the way print and digital resources are published and accessed across UC campuses.[8] As a result, the California Cultures Asian Americans collections include many resources from collections held by individual UC campuses, conveniently brought together in one place. Users can search the collection, or browse by specific collections like Chinese Opera and Theater, Koreatown Newspapers, or the Ethnic Tobacco Education Networks.

Several teaching aids are available as part of the California Cultures Collections. Three of them are curricula about the Japanese internment, aimed at Grades 4-5, 6-8, and 9-12. There are also three related essays that place Asian American communities within the context of California's multicultural history.

Library and Archives Canada – Chinese

The Chinese section of the Library and Archives Canada focuses largely on the Canadian government's immigration records, for those people interested in genealogical research.[9] This archive provides a good parallel to the narrative of Chinese in the United States. Chinese began immigrating to Canada in the 19th century and were heavily involved in the construction of the Canadian Pacific Railway. In 1885, the Canadian government passed a head tax on Chinese immigrants in an effort to reduce their numbers. This was followed by a stricter Chinese Exclusion Act, which was not repealed until 1947.

To find pictures of Asian Americans in Canada, users can search more widely using the Archive Image Search. It accepts searches in both English and French.

Conclusion

These are but a few selections of many growing digital archives and collections on Asian America. Libraries and archives still have much work to do to make their collections digitized, accessible, and discoverable. We find that these collections can enhance research value and also one's interest in exploring the past and how Asian American groups have lived and adapted to life in America.

Beyond research, these resources can be used as teaching aids for all classes from K-12 to higher education. We urge readers to explore them and to creatively engage with their students, researchers or community members. These collections are not only meant to inform, but also to educate others on what it means to be Asian American in the past and today. By exploring Asian American lives through images, we are no longer just invisible or hidden figures, but rather important members who make up American society and history.

Notes

1   Asian/Pacific American Archives Survey Project, http://apa.nyu.edu/survey/

2   R. Pun, "Public Digital Archives in Asian and Asian American Studies," *CUNY FORUM* 2:1 (AAARI-CUNY, 2014).

3   Southeast Asian American Doc (SEAAdoc), http://seaadoc.lib.uci.edu/

4   Calisphere: Japanese American Relocation Archive (JARDA), https://calisphere.org/exhibitions/t11/jarda/ (As of this publication, JARDA is now part of Calisphere.)

5   Pioneering Punjabis Digital Archive, http://pioneeringpunjabis.ucdavis.edu/

6   South Asian American Digital Archive (SAADA), https://www.saada.org/

7   Densho: The Japanese American Legacy Project, http://www.densho.org/

8   Calisphere: California Cultures, https://calisphere.org/cal-cultures/

9   "Chinese," *Libraries and Archives Canada*, http://www.bac-lac.gc.ca/eng/discover/immigration/history-ethnic-cultural/Pages/chinese.aspx.

Authors

Raymond Pun is the First Year Student Success Librarian at California State University, Fresno. Previously, Raymond was a Reference Librarian at New York University Shanghai and the New York Public Library. He holds an M.A. in East Asian Studies from St. John's University, M.L.S. from Queens College/CUNY, and B.A. in History from St. John's University.

Molly Higgins is a Reference and Digital Services Librarian at the Library of Congress. Previously, Ms. Higgins was a Health Sciences Librarian at Stony Brook University – SUNY. She holds a B.A. in Asian American Studies from the University of California, Berkeley, and a M.L.I.S. from the University of Washington, Seattle.

On-Line Tools for Education & Open-Source Learning

ANTONY WONG

"As a web technologist for many years, I can see that your open-source approach to information is way ahead of the curve. Other institutions will become marginalized or extinct, while your brand will become more trusted and valuable."

—Phil Tajitsu Nash

SINCE JANUARY 20, 2017, in a post-U.S. presidential election period of *fake news*, *alternative facts*, *border walls*, *Muslim bans*, and late-night (and deleted) Tweets, now more than ever, Asian American Studies must make sure that it seeks out, documents, communicates, and archives its own authentic stories in order to create materials for liberatory education. Both editor Russell C. Leong in his introduction to *Asian American Matters: A New York Anthology*, together with contributor Phil Tajitsu Nash, point to the pressing need to create intellectual and activist platforms for transmitting the lessons of 50 years of Asian American Studies—its activism, art, scholarship, and commitment to social justice.

Here, I present current examples of open-access websites that educate and extend virtually the life and work of those whom have fought and continue to fight for Asian American Studies and Asian Americans in higher education and the community.

Asian American Studies Online
www.asianamericanstudiesonline.com

At its annual conference in May 2016, the Asian American and Asian Research Institute (AAARI) debuted Asian American Studies Online (AAS Online)—a new website created with WordPress, a free open-source content management system (CMS). AAAS Online features select essays from *CUNY FORUM*, news articles on recent happenings in Asian American Studies, an Asian American history time-line, and links to national Asian American and Pacific Islander data and resources. Conference attendees received a limited edition USB flash drive that contained a portable version of the website that is accessible both online or offline when an Internet connection is not available.

Features of AAS Online:

Articles

First published by AAARI in Fall 2013, *CUNY FORUM* serves as a New York-based print commons for scholars, writers, artists, practitioners and activists to develop research, to create dialogue, and to promote change around Asian American and Asian topics within the context of the Americas. In its past four volumes, *CUNY FORUM* has featured essays on the history and state of Asian American Studies at institutions such as The City University of New York, UMASS Boston, UPENN, the

Asian American Studies Online USB

AAARI YouTube Channel
www.youtube.com/aaaricuny

University of Illinois at Urbana-Champaign, and the University of Maryland. A majority of these essays, over fifty in total, on topics such as community research and transcultural voices, are available on AAS Online to view, download and print.

Videos

Since Fall 2002, AAARI has amassed an expansive online media library, now with over 890 videos covering a wide-variety of topics including youth & identity, health, religion, media, arts, literature, and history. AAARI's Friday Evening Lecture Series alone accounts for over 310 videos, which is equivalent to over 465 hours of Asian American and Asian-related content. AAS Online features twenty videos from Fall 2011 to Spring 2016 to showcase the diversity of this content.

Timeline

AAS Online contains an Asian Pacific American timeline with over 170 national and local New York City events from 1758 to 2016. The timeline was created with TimelineJS, an open-source tool that enables anyone to build visually rich, interactive timelines with nothing more than a Google spreadsheet.

Data Links

With the assistance of the UCLA Asian American Studies Center, AAS Online contains links to various Asian American and Pacific Islander data, including on civil and human rights, immigration, education, health, housing and economic justice; and policy and fact sheets on the East Asian, South Asian, and Southeast Asian communities.

Through AAAS Online's website and its offline USB counterpart, AAARI hopes that educators will utilize the comprehensive materials and resources that have been assembled together, in their future classroom lesson plans, research and projects.

Thomas Tam Way
www.thomastamway.wordpress.com

Featured in my 2013 essay, "AAARI Education Online: Open Access Media," for *CUNY FORUM, Volume 1:1*, Thomas Tam Way serves as a digital memento to the late Dr. Thomas Tam, the founding Executive Director of AAARI, first Asian member of the CUNY Board of Trustees, and co-founder of organizations such as the Chinatown Health Clinic (now known as the Charles B. Wang Community Health Center) and Asian CineVision (organizer of the long-running Asian American International Film Festival). For the occasion of the fifth anniversary of Dr. Tam's passing in 2013, I created this personal WordPress website where Dr. Tam's visual memories, teachings and legacy could be archived and accessed digitally online by those who knew him and those who haven't yet.

Thomas Tam

Thomas Tam Way features films shot, directed and edited by Dr. Tam throughout his life, including *Sunrise on Mulberry Street*, a feature length project conceived in response to the real life suicide of two Chinese-American sisters in Manhattan's Chinatown. The site also features two AAARI lectures by Dr. Tam on the Agama Sutra and Yogacara Buddhism—a layman's introduction into the teachings and philosophies of the Buddha.

With the recent passing of Peter Kwong, Distinguished Professor of Urban Policy & Planning at Hunter College/CUNY, earlier this year, a similar website could be developed to curate Prof. Kwong's large scholarly work in the area of Chinese-American labor and activism.

Digital Tools for the Classroom

The following are some examples of how scholars are currently using digital tools to teach Asian American Studies in the classroom, and to preserve the cultures and histories of Asian American communities.

Video

Shirley Tang, Associate Professor in the Asian American Studies Program and the School for Global Inclusion and Social Development at UMASS Boston, teaches a digital storytelling course, "Asian American Media Literacy." Students use video to develop a critical eye toward popular media representations and to create alternative media products based on their own real life stories, highlighting themes of family migration, war, violence, disability access, poverty and health disparities that Asian Americans currently face. These digital stories are exhibited in an annual Digital Storytelling Festival hosted by the UMASS Boston Asian American Studies Program, and are utilized as educational resources for classes, training workshops, conference presentations, and local and national research archives.

Audio

Manan Desai, Assistant Professor of American Culture at the University of Michigan, is involved with the First Days Project, an online audio archive of 266 immigrants and refugees sharing their first experiences in the United States. In 2013, the South Asian American Digital Archive (SAADA) realized that the stories of immigrants' first experiences in the United States weren't being systematically collected, preserved, and shared, and thus the First Days Project was born.

SAADA itself is an online digital archive for South Asian American materials, and is one of many online resources cited in the essay, "Public Digital Archives and Visual Resources for Asian and Asian American Studies," featured in *CUNY FORUM, Volume 2:1.*

Maps and Timelines

Minju Bae, a doctoral student of History at Temple University, studying multi-racial coalition politics in New York City, volunteered at CAAAV: Organizing Asian Communities, a community-based organization in Manhattan's Chinatown that brings multi-racial peoples together in anti-racism campaigns, from police reform to tenants' rights. Bae assisted CAAAV with organizing their digital newsletter archive through the use of Neatline, an online tool that allows scholars, students, and curators to tell stories with maps and timelines. Using metadata from CAAAV's newsletters from the 1980s through the 2000s, she mapped out when and where significant events took place throughout New York City, illustrating CAAAV's work beyond just the borders of Chinatown.

First Days Project
www.firstdaysproject.org

AAARI Asian American Timeline
www.aaari.info/aatimeline

Conclusion

Online resources and digital tools to supplement and enhance the teaching of Asian American Studies in and outside the classroom are all readily available for everyone to use, reference, and share, as illustrated by the aforementioned examples. Today, there no longer exists a digital divide, only a physical one that hinders the dissemination of Asian American Studies.

Cost no longer is an inhibiting factor in the creation of websites or content. Free resources such as WordPress allow anyone within a few minutes of signing up to begin posting online. Sites such as YouTube allow for live streaming of events and unlimited videos to be stored online for sharing with audiences. Today, anyone with a computer, or even just a smartphone, with access to the Internet can develop their own lesson plans and become liberatory educators.

By providing *CUNY FORUM* and other media content to be freely available for online consumption by educators, students, and the general public, AAARI is breaking down the physical divide that limits the reach affecting print publication of this particular genre, by utilizing digital connections and methods to reach those beyond New York City and the East Coast.

AAARI Conference Video (May 13, 2016): www.aaari.info/2016resurgent.htm

Author

Antony Wong is Program Coordinator at the Asian American and Asian Research Institute, of The City University of New York, and Assistant Publisher of CUNY FORUM. He received his B.A. from Hunter College/CUNY, and M.B.A. from the Zicklin School of Business at Baruch College/CUNY.

PETER KWONG
鄺治中

Ellora Caves, Maharashtra, India
Photo by Dušanka Miščevic

May these pages, collectively, serve to honor and advance the activist scholarship and generous spirit of Peter Kwong, Distinguished Professor of Urban Policy & Planning, and Professor of Asian American Studies, at Hunter College, of The City University of New York.

—Russell C. Leong

Behind-the-scenes of *China's Unnatural Disaster: The Tears of Sichuan Province* (2008)
Photo by Ming Xia

Why We Do This Work

VIVIAN LOUIE

I WAS BORN IN MANHATTAN'S CHINATOWN, but by the time I was age 14, I had lived in three vastly different worlds in the United States. Those three initial worlds became central to my identity and life's work, namely, to how I understand the world to be, how I think the world should be—and to my friendship with the late scholar/activist Peter Kwong. Peter understood those transitions in my life and how they had shaped me. Throughout the years, I've learned from him, and his work, about the complex social and economic transformations that made those individual transitions possible. His writings about immigration, labor, and urban communities told the contours of my life story, and that of so many people.

From Chinatown to Jamaica

My immigrant parents had moved my older brothers and me from Chinatown to Jamaica, Queens. We were part of the exodus that Peter wrote about, when post-World War II America finally opened up, residentially, to previously segregated Americans, with the notable exception of African Americans. Back then, our Queens neighborhood was mostly native-born whites, although in the pocket where we lived some were Holocaust survivors, raising their second families after losing their first in the concentration camps. Our family went from seemingly knowing everyone in Chinatown (back then, there was only one Chinatown in New York City), to being one of the few Chinese families in the neighborhood.

Film still from *Day at Textile Factory* (2017 CUNY Asian American Film Festival) www.aaari.info/2017aaff.htm

My mom commuted an hour each way, first to the Chinese-owned garment factory in Chinatown and then later, to its new location in the Garment District. We went from living in an old tenement building where the lobby seemed to always smell of cat urine, to a brand new attached multi-family home with our very own tiny yard. But of course, we hadn't really left Chinatown. My grandparents and step great-grandma were still there, along with other kinfolk and dear friends. Until I was 14, we would go down to Chinatown every weekend to visit. My mom got her hair done at John's Beauty Parlor on Elizabeth Street, loaded up on vegetables, fruit and meat (haggling all the way in Chinese), and played mahjong on her one day off.

After moving, I realized I lived in two entirely different worlds, with two different sets of friends—my Jewish, Latino, Italian, black and Asian friends in Queens; and my Asian friends back in Chinatown. Young as I was, I often wondered why my friends in Chinatown had so little, and lived in such crappy housing, amid the unsafe streets of the 1970s—where youth gang wars had come to the neighborhood. I also wondered why my mom, who spoke little English, and couldn't read or write in it, but literate in Chinese, had to work in the garment factory.

The Garment Factory

I used to accompany my mom to work before I started school—my daycare setting. I was struck by how hot it was in the factory; how hard it was to hear because of the roar of the sewing machines and the whoosh of the towering floor fans; and how the lady workers drank tea stored in their little glass jars. And I wondered why they had to work so hard for so little—my mom would sit spent on the long subway rides back home, tallying up what she made on the piecework. As I grew older, I realized the clothes she and her friends made were marketed towards middle-class professional women, like the one I eventually became, and who made a lot more than my mom did. It didn't seem right. It also didn't seem right that the factory bosses, also Chinese, made enough to live in the wealthy suburbs.

At the same time, I knew my mom relished the friendships she made, the chatter, and the gossip—the social identities of work that gave her independence. The information shared about their children's schooling, and ways to grow their earnings. Theirs was a powerful network of comfort, knowledge-sharing, and care. Truth to say, my mom even liked her bosses. Even as I write this, I can hear Peter saying, "Vivian, what are you talking about?" But it was true. She recognized and experienced the inequality, which benefited the bosses way more than it did her, but she found a way to appreciate their humanity as well. She does this even today, as she continues to cope with the physical remnants of performing such punishing and repetitive work, with few breaks for decades, resulting in chronic hip and shoulder issues.

Alone in Andover

Through one of her garment factory friendships, my mom learned of an elite New England boarding school, to which I applied and was awarded a scholarship. I had the benefit of a high quality public school education, and so I was prepared for the opportunity at Andover, where I wanted to go intellectually.

In my 11th grade American history class I got to pick the topic for my own research paper to investigate through primary sources, and picked the Chinese Exclusion Act. I had never read about it in school, but my family made sure that I knew all about it. I read Jean Paul Sartre's *No Exit* in French; and Dostoyevsky's *The Brothers Karamazov* and Toni Morrison's *The Bluest Eye* in English. Students were encouraged to find the connections between different time periods, writings and issues.

This transition however was the hardest that I had ever made. The expectation of my peers to downplay my heritage was not exactly subtle. Like any teenager, I wanted to fit in, but I quickly learned that there were certain things that I would not do to gain acceptance. There was only one hall phone for the entire dormitory, and my mom made her weekly phone calls to me, asking whoever happened to pick up the phone, in her high-pitched English, "May I please speak Vivian?" And of course, by necessity, we spoke entirely in Chinese, with everyone around me able to listen in. I didn't have the choice to hide who I was, and in truth, I didn't want to.

Even back then, I intuited that success was not worth it if one had to deny who you were to get it. My dormmates had taken me aside one day to educate me in some words that I should use to describe my black, Latino, Jewish, Catholic and Asian friends back home. Some of their words were new to me, but others I recognized—and recognized them all as being intentionally offensive, demeaning, and just plain wrong. I told them as much, and that it didn't matter that they had learned to say such things from their parents. No harsh words were exchanged between us, but during that first year, I grew used to eating alone and being by myself.

From Journalism to Dissertation

By the time I met Peter, these experiences had crystallized into an inchoate set of interests that later became more defined and informed my career: to describe inequalities and to understand why they exist; why we have such trouble talking about them; and also, what we can do to change them. We became acquainted while I was a young freelance journalist. I would pitch stories on the complexities of Asian American communities and issues, and Peter, who had just launched the Asian American Studies Program at Hunter College/CUNY, was one of my sources. We kept in touch long after I left journalism and started my doctoral studies in another state. He was immensely helpful when I moved back to New York City to conduct and write up my dissertation research on the transition to college among Chinese Americans at Hunter College and Columbia College.

When I moved again, this time for a job in Boston, we continued to stay in touch. Peter was a big supporter of my work on family, school, and the community contexts in the academic success of children of immigrants, and the identities of both immigrants and their children. Because of this, he understood why I later joined the William T. Grant Foundation's new initiative to support research on reducing inequality in youth outcomes, and why it was a good fit for me.

Change the World

It wasn't until my tenure as the CUNY Thomas Tam Visiting Professor at Hunter College in 2013-2014, that I began to more fully grasp the scope of *Peter's* work—and in truth, not until he passed away, that my understanding deepened. This was because whenever Peter and I would chat, it was mostly about me. How was I doing? What did I think of this piece of work? And always, he asked how my mom was doing. A woman he'd never even met, but somehow, through all those decades he spent studying and writing about workers in Chinatown— advocating for workers, organizing with the workers, and joining the workers—he knew who she was. Now that he's gone, and myself much older, I realize what a gift that was. Because, of course, he could have instead talked about his own numerous accomplishments.

Dušanka Miščevic & Peter Kwong, New York City
Photo by Russell C. Leong

Certainly, Peter was never shy about speaking his mind. The only difference—Peter spoke his mind about things that mattered, and what we could do to change the world. When we talked about the 1992 Los Angeles riots, he never mentioned his *Village Voice* article on its multiracial and multicultural aspects, which earned him the prestigious George Polk Award and a Pulitzer nomination. Nor did he mention his earlier 1990 *Village Voice* article, which he and Dušanka Miščevic, his wife, frequent collaborator and recognized scholar in her own right, co-wrote on the Chinese drug trade, which was also nominated for a Pulitzer. I don't mention these accomplishments here to tout them, but instead, to highlight Peter's work in advancing the goals of social justice. If doing that work led to recognition, then that was great, but also incidental. Personal recognition was not the point of doing the work that he did.

Uptown Scholar, Downtown Activist

At a memorial service held on April 9, 2017 at Downtown Community Television Center (co-founded by Peter), there were several film outtakes shown of Peter, including one from the 1970s with him on a truck pulling out fresh produce, sold at a discount, to Chinatown residents. Another clip, now of a much older Peter in the 1990s, filmed in China, was from a documentary on what drove Fujianese immigrants to leave their home and pay human smugglers exorbitant sums of money to come to America. I left the memorial thinking, "How could one person have done so much in so many realms?"

There is a tendency by many to think that Peter only studied and wrote about Chinese Americans and Chinese immigrants, which of course he mostly did. But that misses the larger insight into Peter's true work—the forces that drive inequality. He explored them in the case of Chinese Americans and in China too, and that's a critical difference. In the case of Chinese Americans, he coined the terms "Uptown Chinese" and "Downtown Chinese," to capture the social class differentiation amongst Chinese immigrants, what this meant for their children, and showed how this distinction was the result of much larger social forces. This distinction however does not only apply just to the Chinese. When I did research on Colombian immigration to the United States, I found similar differences between the Uptown Colombians and the Downtown Colombians.

Film stills of Peter Kwong from *Chinatown Food Co-op* (1971)
https://youtu.be/QDc_7dBmSGo

Through his research and advocacy, Peter was always committed to what we could all do to create greater *equality* in our society. He did this both in the classroom and on the streets. The point is, to never stop trying, and to always remember why we do this work.

Author

Vivian Louie is Program Officer at the William T. Grant Foundation. She received her Ph.D. and M.A. from the Yale University Department of Sociology, M.A. from the Stanford University Department of Communication, and A.B. from Harvard University. Louie has previously worked as a newspaper journalist, journalism teacher and youth magazine editor, and an associate professor in education and lecturer in sociology at Harvard. She previously served as the 2013-2014 CUNY Thomas Tam Visiting Professor at Hunter College/CUNY.

Dr. Louie has written two books, *Compelled to Excel: Immigration, Education, and Opportunity Among Chinese Americans* (Stanford University Press, 2004) and *Keeping the Immigrant Bargain: The Costs and Rewards of Success in America* (Russell Sage Foundation, 2012), co-edited a third book, *Writing Immigration: Scholars and Journalists in Dialogue* (University of California Press, 2011), and written numerous scholarly articles.

My Journey to Spirituality

PETER KWONG

> "People have asked me what is a leftist scholar engaged
> with civil rights and labor issues doing with a religious leader
> like the Dalai Lama. My answer is—it came naturally."

DURING THE PAST THREE YEARS, I have met His Holiness the 14th Dalai Lama three times: twice as his host at Hunter College in New York and once as his guest in Dharamsala, on the Indian side of the Himalayas, the site of Tibetan government-in-exile. People have asked me what is a leftist scholar engaged with civil rights and labor issues doing with a religious leader like the Dalai Lama. My answer is—it came naturally.

In the winter of 2010, a representative from the Office of Tibet in New York approached me to help organize a forum at Hunter College, where His Holiness could meet with American academics of Chinese descent. I accepted the request without hesitation, because I consider the question of Tibet a critical national minority issue that needs to be resolved by China. Two years earlier, I had written a commentary in *The Globe and Mail* and *Metro News* entitled "Direct Talks Will Benefit Both China and the Dalai Lama." In it, I urged the Chinese leaders to resume direct negotiations with the Dalai Lama, in the aftermath of a major riot by Tibetans in Lhasa in March 2008, to agree on the repeatedly postponed attempts to

Peter Kwong & His Holiness Tenzin Gyatso the 14th Dalai Lama
Hunter College Ceremony (Oct 19, 2012)
Photo by Antony Wong

establish an autonomous rule for Tibet. China could use the occasion, just before her "coming-out party" —the Olympic Games, to show the rest of the world her good will and determination to build a harmonious society, which she claimed to want to do.

Unfortunately, the Chinese government chose to pass up the opportunity and continued its repressive measures. A number of Chinese dissidents risked persecution and spoke out against the government's Tibetan policy. But by and large, Chinese people were not, and are not, informed about the situation in Tibet. From an early age in school, they have been taught that Tibet has always been a part of China and that the Dalai Lama is a "splittist" bent on Tibetan independence. Never mind that China's own historical records show that Tibet through the centuries has been an ally, an opponent, a tributary state, and occasionally a region within Chinese control. Moreover, the Dalai Lama has again and again publicly renounced the struggle for independence, stressing that his aim is negotiated autonomy for Tibet under Chinese rule. But in China, factual information that deviates from the official position is simply censured.

The people are told that any moderate position on Tibet plays right into the hands of colonial Western and Japanese powers determined to divide China.

Prolonged inaction on the part of the Chinese government has only encouraged extremist positions on both sides, resulting in some of the Dalai Lama's followers pushing for independence and continuing violent suppression on the part of the Chinese local government in Tibet. As the official Chinese propaganda continued, the Dalai Lama thought of engaging in dialogue with members of the overseas Chinese communities as a way of presenting his side of the story. He hoped that whatever insights and understanding he could provide would hopefully filter back to China through Chinese language media, the blogosphere, and overseas scholars.

For His Holiness' forum at Hunter College in 2010, we invited leading academics, artists, and professionals of Chinese descent from all over the East Coast. A few refused to come because of their mistrust of the Dalai Lama. Others feared being reported to Chinese authorities, and that this might harm their chances of returning to China. Most, however, were curious to meet this international celebrity at an exclusive invitation-only event.

The Dalai Lama arrived in an ebullient mood, and after exchanging courtesies with Hunter officials dived right into the history between China and Tibet. He recalled his 1954 visit to Beijing at the age of nineteen and meeting with top Chinese leaders, and spoke of witnessing the dramatic transformation of the country in a short period of time soon after the Communist Revolution. These achievements made the Chinese Communist Party very popular, no less because its members were honest and dedicated to the service of the people. They inspired people to join in the rebuilding of a new China.

The party's Marxist ideology, with its emphasis on equal distribution, rather than profit as in a capitalist society, especially impressed the young Dalai Lama. "Tibet at that time was very, very backward," he explained. "The ruling class did not seem to care, and there was much inequality. Marxism talked about an equal and just distribution of wealth. I was very much in favor of this." So much so, in fact, that he expressed his wish to Mao Zedong to become a Communist Party member. But Mao rejected this, saying that he could be more useful in other ways.

Mao was initially a caring figure who treated the Dalai Lama like a son and was sympathetic to the Tibetan people. He led the central government into setting up a "Preparatory Committee for the Establishment of the Tibet Autonomous Region," and at the First National People's Congress in 1954 appointed the Dalai Lama a Vice Chairman of its Standing Committee. Unfortunately, hopes for an autonomous Tibet were dashed when the party became radicalized during the Great Leap Forward campaign to establish people's communes. Leftists in the party were unwilling to grant special status to Tibet, where they thought the people were shackled under "serfdom." Meanwhile, Tibetan resentment against Chinese policies increased and led to open resistance.

Under these circumstances, His Holiness had to escape China in 1959. While frustrated, he held out hope that one day he would be able to return. He has been patient because he appreciates the challenges that the Chinese leaders have to go through to achieve progress on the Tibetan issue, considering all the other daunting problems they face. He even has positive things to say about them. Many of the leaders who have realized the importance of resolving Tibetan conflict have engaged him periodically in private negotiations over the past fifty some years. Deng Xiaoping told him in 1979 that "except independence, all other issues can be resolved through negotiations." To Deng, the bottom line was that Tibet must remain within China, which the Dalai Lama fully agreed to as long as there would be a guarantee for the preservation of Tibetan cultural and spiritual identity. In the 1980s, under Chinese Communist Party General Secretary Hu Yaobang, the Chinese government initiated a number of liberal policies, including orders to promote local Tibetans to leadership positions, to require the Han Chinese officials to learn Tibetan, and to relax Beijing's controls over religious worship. Hu also ordered the slowing down of Han migration into Tibet as a way to ease frictions between the Han Chinese and Tibetans, and apologized to the Tibetan people for China's misrule of their region. The Dalai Lama did not even have anything negative to say about Hu Jintao, who was the party secretary of Tibet when he declared martial law in late 1997, and led the suppression of non-violent protests by Tibetans. Hu continued his iron-fist rule during his tenure as Party Chairman from 2002 to 2012, yet the Dalai Lama still credited him for seeing the need for China to ease its internal conflicts by promoting the building of a "harmonious society"—a feat His Holiness believes would eventually lead to the resolution of conflict with Tibet as well.

Chinese leaders' repressive policies come from fear. They fear what might happen if Tibetans were allowed to live freely and others under Chinese rule started to demand the same. But fear only brings on more fear and continues the cycle of violence. To the Dalai Lama the only way to conquer fear is by reaching out to one's enemies, to understand their suffering within a spirit of compassion. The more we care for others, the easier it is to solve the problems and to grow our own sense of well-being.

In this way, the Dalai Lama turned a political discussion inward, leading us to reflect on our own ethical values. He wants us to change the way we look at the world, so as to find the peace within ourselves. From that inner peace, spring love and compassion. We are then able to remove any fears and draw strength to confront our problems.

The audience at Hunter College was spellbound by these insights and walked away enriched with a better understanding of the nature of the China/Tibet conflict, as well as lessons about compassion and the possibility of elevating one's self to become a better human being. On his way out, the Dalai Lama too expressed satisfaction with the gathering, having noticed the impact he had on the audience. He told me that it was important to continue to organize these types of events in the future.

The forum had stirred up my long dormant inner spiritual exploration as well. I grew up in a westernized Chinese family. My father dismissed all religion as superstition. However, during my teens, my mother persuaded me to join her Methodist church in Taipei. I attended her church for many years because I loved singing in the choir; otherwise, I would have become disenchanted with church very early on. I found the church elders to be people with all the human failings hiding behind religious piety and an air of self-righteousness. I found church rituals hollow and was particularly disturbed by the practice of praying for particular objectives, such as winning a basketball game. It was puzzling to me why God would not respond to the prayers of the opponents as well. Worse, when the country goes to war, churches never question the state's moral justifications, but bless the soldiers and pray for victory before they go off into the battlefield. When churchgoers witness poverty they give charity, yet refrain from advocating for political or economic changes. As an activist, I fault their passivity in perpetuating the status quo. These failings turned me against the church and religion in general.

As I listened to the Dalai Lama that day, I realized that his teachings were different. What intrigued me the most was his secular wisdom, accumulated from centuries of human experience. I wished I had acquired insights into this worldview much earlier to save myself much pain and suffering. This awakening led me to want to learn more about his teachings from a secular perspective.

In the winter of 2011, my wife and I joined with three others to travel to Dharamsala in India at the invitation of the Tibetan government-in-exile. I was overwhelmed by India's distinctive sense of humanity. Poverty and social stratification aside, it is amazing that a country of that size could accommodate so many diverse cultures and religions. It is the birthplace of two of the world's major religions, Hinduism and Buddhism, as well as Jainism and Sikhism. It is home to the third largest Muslim population in the world, and also a significant number of Christians, Zoroastrians, Baha'is, and many others. The country's democratic system is far from perfect, but it allows for a vibrant environment for a civil society to prosper. This is so different from China, where one party tries to control all aspects of the lives of all the citizens, including their speech, religion, education, artistic expression, and civic association.

We had a private audience with His Holiness for an hour-and-a-half in his unpretentious residence. The topics ranged from his reaction to the latest Chinese attacks against him, to Indo-Tibetan relations, reincarnation, and Buddhism in China. He was intensely focused and made sure each sentence was said in clear and simple language. In responding to a question raised by the youngest member of our delegation on the subject of peace, he said that peace comes through compassion. But peace does not mean sitting quietly and doing nothing so as to avoid conflicts. It means convincing the other side to join in the common search for productive resolutions. For him, peace is an activist vision of making positive changes.

This led me to reflect on myself, an activist, who tends to be confrontational and refuses to compromise whenever I think I am right. But the fact is, in any conflict, truth does not reside exclusively on one side.

Shutting down communication with one's opponents deprives one of the possibilities to find common ground on which the two sides could agree to reach a resolution. That's why activist scholars like myself have created fields of contention littered with antagonistic trenches.

After the meeting, the Dalai Lama presented each one of us with a white silk scarf, *katag*—the traditional Tibetan offering, placing it around our necks, blessed the strings of rosewood and sandalwood prayer beads that we had brought along, and then insisted on taking individual photos with us, although our meeting had ran well over the scheduled time. As someone who has met every major figure in the world, he still insists on attending to all these details, showing his determination to touch each and every person he meets with full attention and respect.

This Indian experience convinced me that I should organize another group of Chinese Americans to meet with him in New York. Before parting, I raised the possibility and he readily agreed. Another forum was held in October 2012 with six hundred Chinese scholars, artists and professionals in attendance. Again, his messages were met with enthusiastic response.

Most memorable was his answer to the question of nationalism. How does one explain that nationalism can be a positive force in liberating people from oppression, yet can also be a cause of destructive conflicts? His answer was that loving one's country was fine, but that love has to be rational and not blind. Attachments to things that are too strong can cause one to lose objectivity. For instance: religions are good, but can become bad when, institutionalized, they lose their spiritual essence. He even criticized lamas in his own monasteries, because he knew that many of them were taking advantage of peoples' attachment to the religious order to extort money and even sex from them. In a show of detachment, he said that he would even abandon certain Buddhist scriptures if disproved by modern science. It is liberating to hear a leader of an established order be bold enough to make these kinds of statements, like a rebel.

His willingness to forsake attachments and make changes marks him as an innovative thinker, unique in our time. His Holiness is at once a philosopher, a religious teacher, a god-like figure to the Tibetan people, and an embodiment of ideal Tibetan values. Yet, so much of his waking life is unseen by the outside world, consisting of prayers, meditation, prostrations, recitation of special mantras, reading, and studying Buddhist philosophy. He consults Tibetan state oracles, and interprets ancient Buddhist metaphysical tenets. The wisdom we receive from him is the crystallization of this extensive practice and knowledge.

On a temporal level, he has made a singular contribution in revitalizing the potential and influence of eastern civilization. People like myself, who grew up in China in the middle of the last century, were inculcated with the urgent task of modernization through science and technology in order to build a strong and prosperous China, and to avenge the humiliation suffered at the hands of western powers. We were encouraged to reject Chinese culture and philosophy as outdated and superstitious.

Now many of us, including Westerners, have come to realize the limits of western science based on empirical evidence alone. We are effective in solving specific problems but lack the ability to explain root causes. A western doctor can often cure symptoms, but is less inclined to address environmental, psychological, and dietary factors of a sickness. Moreover, each area of natural and social sciences is compartmentalized, making interconnected analyses difficult. These shortcomings are increasingly leading people to try out more holistic Eastern approaches. It is also making many of us reevaluate Eastern traditions that we once rejected. The problem is that western concepts and language still hold global sway, and Eastern thinking lacks an effective narrative to convince.

Because of his deeply-grounded knowledge of Eastern traditions, the Dalai Lama has become one of the most effective spokespersons and interpreters of Eastern religion and philosophy in the West. Yet at the same time, in his explorations of metaphysics and reality, he also reaches for answers from the other side. Due to his intense personal interest in the sciences, he is engaged in dialogue with western scientists, most notably through the encouragement of scientific research into Buddhist meditative practices. He is trying to integrate western scientific knowledge in the context of the eastern holistic outlook, aiming to achieve inter-connectedness of all sciences, philosophies, and religions.

One of the more powerful signs of his openness to changes from the Western perspective was his willingness to accept democratic ideas. Appreciating the injustices of the past Tibetan society, the Dalai Lama called for the elimination of feudal practices. He endorsed an open election to select officers in his government-in-exile. The new Tibetan constitution includes a clause for his impeachment. He even offered that the next Dalai Lama be chosen by popular vote. More than any other world leader, he is not just building a bridge between East and West, but pushing for an integrated platform of global knowledge. That alone makes him a foremost global citizen of the twenty-first century.

When I first encountered His Holiness, I thought my attraction to him was because I had grown older and more philosophical, thus more receptive to his teachings. But I have since come to see my interest in him as a reflection of my desire to rediscover my Eastern origins buried under Western education. Moreover, I desire to integrate my two backgrounds into an effective balance. My exposure to His Holiness' wisdom has so far been limited to his secular teachings. I have not become religious and am certainly not interested in joining any form of organized religion. But as there are no boundaries between scientific, philosophical, spiritual, and religious understanding, at this point, while not religiously inclined, I am ready for a journey of spiritual discovery.

Author

Peter Kwong (1941-2017) was Distinguished Professor of Urban Policy & Planning at Hunter College/ CUNY, and Professor of Sociology at the CUNY Graduate Center. He was a pioneer in Asian American Studies, a leading scholar of immigration, and an award-winning journalist and filmmaker, widely recognized for his passionate commitment to human rights and social justice. As a scholar, he was best known for his work on Chinese Americans and on modern Chinese politics. As a journalist, his exposés of Chinese drug syndicates and Los Angeles racial riots had been nominated for the Pulitzer Prize. As a documentary filmmaker, he was a recipient of a CINE Golden Eagle Award, and a co-producer of *China's Unnatural Disaster: The Tears of Sichuan Province* for HBO, which was nominated for an Academy Award in 2010.

AAARI Videos Featuring Peter Kwong

https://goo.gl/9fMz9b

CUNY Conference on Building Coalitions & Coalescing a Pan-Asian/Pacific/American Identity
CUNY Graduate Center (May 23, 2017)

12/10/04
The New Profile of Chinese Americans

2/10/06
Chinese America: The Untold Story of
America's Oldest Community

2/13/08
Hunter College/CUNY -
Asian American Studies Program Open House

5/15/09
China's Unnatural Disaster:
The Tears of Sichuan Province

5/6/11
How Do Asian American Voters Stack Up Against
New York City's Longer Established Voting Groups

6/2/11
Into East River(s): Chinese / American Artists
and Asian American Poets

4/27/12
Future of Ethnic Neighborhoods

5/2/13
Tenure and Promotion at CUNY

11/4/13
Emboldening and Supporting a
Forum for Thought & Change

5/5/14
Mapping Asian American Research

10/10/14
CUNY Mapping Seminar Book Panel

11/19/14
Major Demographic Issues Concerning
Asian American Communities in New York

12/15/14
Tales From the Field: Research Methods
and Approaches in the Community

3/11/15
Current Challenges to Ethnic Media in New York:
With Joe Wei and Angelo Falcon

5/1/15
MothSutra: For Bicycle Delivery Men, NY -
a Reading, Graphic Poem, and Visual Book

4/12/16
Why Asian Americans Need Diversity Too:
The Critical Importance of Racial Diversity
in Higher Education

5/13/16
Political Strategies for Advancing
Asian American Studies on the East Coast

10/4/16
Racial Profiling and a Rush to Judgment
Against Asian Americans in the Name of
National Security

5/23/17
Peter Kwong in Memoriam:
Friend, Scholar, Mentor and Community Leader

2018-2019 Article and Essay Submissions

The purpose of CUNY FORUM is to provide an open space and a public commons for dialogue, debate and divergence from the status quo.

The FORUM seeks to create a fresh approach to Asian American scholarship: inclusive of new constituencies, comparative theories and ideas, while inviting writing that seeks to transform a society still polarized by its class, gender, race, and belief-based systems.

For 2018-2019 we are accepting submissions in the following categories:

- Original social science and historical research
- Research summaries / practitioners' essays
- Original essays
- Literary works
- Reviews of literature and media
- Graphic artworks

All submissions are reviewed by a combination of the FORUM's editors and editorial advisors. Original research is subject to additional outside blind review.

Articles for publication consideration should be sent to:

CUNY FORUM EDITOR
c/o Asian American and Asian Research Institute
The City University of New York
25 West 43rd St., Suite 1000
New York, NY 10036

Two print copies should be mailed to the address above, and one electronic copy should be sent to: cunyforum@aaari.info

ISSN 2329–1125

AAARI Board (2017-2018)

Chair   Ron Woo (The City University of New York)
Vice Chair   Vinit Parmar (Brooklyn College)
Treasurer   TBD
Secretary   Carol Huang (City College of New York)

Members
Young Cheong (Brooklyn College)
Ravi Kalia (City College of New York)
Rose Kim (Borough of Manhattan Community College)
Kiyoka Koizumi (Brooklyn College)
Sambhavi Lakshminarayanan (Medgar Evers College)
Catherine Ma (Kingsborough Community College)
Ann Matsuuchi (LaGuardia Community College)
Diana Pan (Brooklyn College)
Ryoya Terao (NYC College of Technology)

Honorary Members
Betty Lee Sung (Professor Emerita, City College of New York)

Community Resource
Edward Ma

Executive Director
Joyce O. Moy

Program Coordinator
Antony Wong

College Assistants
William Tam
Zhu-Hui Wu

Research Interns
Claire Chun
Ming Xue Sun

Asian American and Asian Research Institute
The City University of New York
Phone: 212-869-0182 / 0187   E-mail: info@aaari.info
Fax: 212-869-0181   URL: www.aaari.info

Facebook: aaaricuny   iTunes: aaari
Twitter: aaaricuny   YouTube: aaaricuny

NOTES

NOTES